Southern Liberal Journalists and the Issue of Race, 1920–1944

Fred W. Morrison Series in Southern Studies

John T. Kneebone

Southern Liberal Journalists

and the Issue of Race, 1920–1944

The University of North Carolina Press
Chapel Hill & London

© 1985 The University of North Carolina Press

All rights reserved

Manufactured in the United States of America

Library of Congress Cataloging in Publication Data

Kneebone, John T.

   Southern liberal journalists and the issue of race, 1920–1944.

   (Fred W. Morrison series in Southern studies)

   Bibliography: p.

   Includes index.

   1. Race relations and the press—Southern States—
History—20th century.   2. Southern States—Race
relations.   3. Liberalism—Southern States—History—
20th century.   I. Title.   II. Series.

PN4893.K58   1985   302.2′322′0975   85-1104

ISBN 0-8078-1660-4

For my parents

Contents

Acknowledgments   xi

Introduction   xiii

1   Coming of Age in the Progressive South   3

2   Illuminating the Benighted South   21

3   Al Smith, Thomas Jefferson, and the Solid South   37

4   About Face or Forward March?   56

5   Tilting the Color Line   74

6   Dead Laws and Live Demagogues   97

7   Roosevelt and Rational Democracy   115

8   Southern Policy for the Southern Regions   133

9   The New Deal Is Dealt   153

10   Adolf Hitler and the American Way   175

11   The Conservative Course in Race Relations   196

Epilogue: Because Injustice Is Here   215

Notes   233

Bibliography   279

Index   299

Acknowledgments

The writing of history depends upon assistance from a community of scholars, librarians, and institutions, offered in a spirit of cooperation that makes acknowledgment always necessary and always inadequate. My greatest debt is to those southern liberals and scholars of southern history whose published works blazed the trail I have traveled here. Many other persons aided in this study, and it is impossible to express my gratitude to all of them here. Friends listened patiently while I talked through my ideas, colleagues offered observations that gave me food for further thought, and those who knew the journalists, southern liberalism, and the South generously contributed their special perspectives and judgments. I am especially grateful to Virginius Dabney for permission to examine his papers at the University of Virginia and for enduring a formal interview.

My research required me to press request after request upon the Interlibrary Loan librarians at the University of Virginia and Princeton University. Their unfailing cheerfulness and efficiency eased my conscience and speeded the work along. Archivists at the University of Virginia, the Library of Congress, the Alabama State Archives, Princeton University, and the Southern Historical Collection at the University of North Carolina recommended relevant manuscript collections and created a stimulating environment for scholarship. I was able to travel to North Carolina with the help of Douglas Greenberg and a grant from the Princeton University Committee on Research in the Humanities and Social Sciences. Without the time for writing provided by a Mellon Faculty Fellowship in the Humanities at Harvard University and a Bankhead Fellowship at the University of Alabama, completion of this work would have been much more difficult, if not impossible.

I first learned of the tormented historiography on the Civil War and Reconstruction from John V. Mering at the University of Arizona, whose rigorous standards for scholarship I am still trying to meet. At the University of Virginia, Paul M. Gaston introduced me to southern history and then directed my dissertation with wise suggestions, searching criticism, and the inspiration of his example. Edward L. Ayers's skillful reading contributed importantly to the final revisions of that dissertation. Barry Rutizer, Daniel H. Borus, and William A. Link criticized early drafts, and Armstead Robinson and Kenneth W. Thompson did the same for the final version. As I revised the dissertation, several friends and colleagues read all or parts of the manuscript. I am especially grateful for the comments and the encouragement of Michael Bernstein, Richard Challener, Jeff Norrell, Nancy J. Weiss, and George Wright. I am also grateful to the anonymous readers for the University of North Carolina Press for their valuable criticisms and suggestions for improvements. Above all, with her intelligence, hard work, and love, Suzanne Hill Freeman made me a better person and this a better book. I am indebted to all but remain solely responsible for any inadequacies in this work.

Introduction

In 1952, two years before the Supreme Court ruled racial segregation in public schools unconstitutional, Will W. Alexander recounted for interviewers from Columbia University's Oral History Project his career as a southern liberal reformer. Between the two world wars, Alexander had served as executive director of the Commission on Interracial Cooperation, the most influential southern liberal organization for the improvement of race relations. Early in his work with the CIC, Alexander explained, he discovered that almost all southern newspapers were sensitive to the dangers of racial conflict and welcomed the CIC's efforts to publicize improvements and decrease public tensions. A much smaller number of southern journalists proved especially aware of the necessity for reform, becoming themselves active participants in the CIC and other southern liberal organizations. Through their writings, they gained reputations within and without the South as articulate spokesmen for southern liberalism. "I should say," Alexander declared, "that the best newspapermen in the South have for the last thirty years been the most constructive single influence in changing racial patterns."[1]

By the time of Alexander's interview, southern liberal journalists realized that black Americans intended to dismantle the South's system of racial segregation—but ironically, these spokesmen for a better South responded with caution and equivocation. Rather than coming as a fulfillment of their work, the assault on segregation seemed to expose the ambiguities of their commitment to racial justice and to make their doctrines seem increasingly anachronistic.

This book is about those journalists and the changing patterns of their thinking on race, reform, and history through the decades preceding the Civil Rights protest movement. As Alexander's comments suggest, newspapermen, rather than newspapers, should be the focus of attention. The urban press in the South recognized the danger that sensationalized reporting on race relations could lead to public violence or rioting. In 1925, the Southern Newspaper Publishers Association included in its formal code of ethics the newspaper's obligation to show "respect and tolerance for those of different religions, races, and circumstances of life." Responsible journalism, however, meant that southern blacks—and race relations—tended to become even more invisible in the white press. To find regular discussions of racial issues in southern newspapers, one had to turn to the editorial pages and to the commentary of individual journalists.[2]

The journalists studied here publicized southern liberalism to the South and the nation. Rather than merely serving as conduits for the CIC's press service, they joined southern liberal organizations and took an active part in policy debates. They thus helped to define the southern liberalism that they publicized. Indeed, because of their strategic position as journalists—between reformers and the public, between southern intellectuals and a mass audience—they also served as censors of southern liberalism, declaring by their editorial judgments which ideas and programs for social change deserved commendation and which deserved condemnation. The public course of southern liberalism before the Civil Rights movement may be traced through their editorials and essays.

Most important for the historian, these journalists, by the nature of their profession, produced an extensive public record of analysis and commentary. Daily journalism required them to respond immediately, and in print, to current events and issues, exposing the interconnection between ideas and experience in their thinking on race, reform, and history. Because they often discussed the same topics, moreover, it has been possible to treat them as a group, seeking the common ground upon which they stood as southern liberals.

Contemporary sources identify a fair number of newspapermen at various times as southern liberals, but certain names—Julian LaRose Harris, Grover C. Hall, Louis I. Jaffé, W. J. Cash, Mark Ethridge, John Temple Graves, Jonathan Daniels, Gerald W. Johnson, George Fort Milton, Virginius Dabney, Hodding Carter, and Ralph McGill—appear most often. The requirements of historical analysis narrowed this field further: to determine what southern liberals said to the South—and to measure the limits of permissible public discussion of race and reform—required concentration on journalists who expressed regular editorial opinion on these subjects. To ascertain whether southern liberalism's message to the South differed from that presented to nonsouthern audiences, I selected those local commentators who also wrote for national journals of opinion. Finally, I chose those among these journalists who supplemented their journalism with the study of history. Interpretations of the region's past provide justifications for southern liberal reform programs and serve as a sensitive test of changing racial attitudes.

This book, therefore, is based primarily on the writings of five leading southern liberal journalists. The oldest of them, Gerald W. Johnson (1890–1980), helped Howard W. Odum make the University of North Carolina a center for southern liberal scholarship before becoming a columnist for the *Baltimore Evening Sun*. He stood out in the 1920s as a leading southern liberal critic and continued to address southern issues through his long career. George Fort Milton (1894–1955), of the *Chattanooga News*, chaired the Southern Commission on the Study of Lynching, played a leading role in the Southern Policy Committee, and, like Johnson, won a national reputation as a historian and biographer. Virginius Dabney (1901–   ), of the *Richmond Times-Dispatch*, became the historian of *Liberalism in the South*, joined Milton on the Southern Policy Committee, and helped to found the Southern Regional Council in 1944. The final two subjects of this study—Ralph McGill (1899–1969), of the *Atlanta Constitution*, and Hodding Carter (1907–1972), of the *Greenville* (Miss.) *Delta Democrat-Times*—became best known after World War II as southern spokesmen for racial justice. Thus, comparison of their thinking with that of the others affords a further test of the development of southern liberalism in the 1930s and its relationship to the Negro protest against the Jim Crow system in the 1950s and 1960s.

That relationship has proven a troublesome issue for scholars of southern liberalism. Writing in the early 1960s, as Negro protest spread across the South, Wilma Dykeman and James Stokely found the *Seeds of Southern Change* in the career of Will W. Alexander: although Alexander's prescription of always doing "the next things" avoided a clear declaration of goals, they inferred that he, and those southern liberals associated with the Commission on Interracial Cooperation, had looked ahead to the elimination of Jim Crow and worked for reform within the framework of racial segregation as a strategic ploy necessary to escape destructive white racist resistance.[3] This thesis may fit the case of Alexander, but since 1962, scholars have rejected its extension to southern liberalism in general. Instead, they tend to follow Gunnar Myrdal's critical assessment of 1944. Myrdal contended that southern liberals, overly fearful of southern reaction and entangled in regional mythology, lacked the courage and power to free the South from racial injustice. This judgment, of course, questions the chosen means of southern liberals, but not their ends. Although men of good will, they simply did not realize that the task would require militant protest and federal intervention.[4]

Recent histories of southern liberals have restated these themes. Charles Eagles's study of *Jonathan Daniels and Race Relations* seems to follow Dykeman and Stokely by describing southern liberals as those persons who "looked down the road that the South eventually did follow and tried to lead their region in that direction." Yet, when he turns to Daniels, Eagles perceives an evolutionary progression in his attitudes, which changed gradually from insistence upon permanent segregation to a grudging acceptance of racial equality. Daniels's evolution not only raises the issue of how far down "the road" southern liberals did look—an issue that Eagles addresses—but also leaves open the question of whether they thought that road would lead to the Civil Rights movement.[5] Moreover, the metaphor of evolution downplays the mediation between events and existing explanatory frameworks. In fact, like the other journalists, Daniels made sense of new events and issues through his interpretations of earlier ideas and experiences.

Rather than evolving, southern liberalism actually came apart during World War II, when Negro protest and southern liberal criticism of that protest made racial segregation no longer compatible with liberalism. Because southern liberalism had become a coherent ideology for reform in the South, based upon the lessons of history, the challenges of the 1940s presented the journalists and other southern liberals with an intellectual crisis. An evolutionary narrative framework cannot account adequately for the discontinuity between the southern liberalism of the 1930s and the Civil Rights movement.

In his broad survey of southern liberals and their organizations, Morton Sosna acknowledges the differences between the outlook of the 1930s and the Civil Rights movement. He points out ambivalence over racial change, alarmed reactions to independent black protest, and charges that "the reluctance of so many white Southern liberals to abandon separate-but-equal during this period [after World War II] was Southern liberalism's most conspicuous failure." To explain why some southern liberals, like Virginius Dabney, opposed the Civil Rights movement, while others, like Ralph McGill, came to support it,

Sosna then introduces a new factor: evangelical religious faith.[6] This distinction—between southern liberal religious skeptics and southern liberal believers—only makes more curious the general agreement between the Dabneys and the McGills in the earlier period. What did southern liberals advocate for southern race relations before the Civil Rights movement? Why did that advocacy not flow more smoothly into recognition of the protest movement's promise for southern liberalism?

These problems in interpretation arise in large part from the definition of southern liberalism solely in terms of racial reform. Throughout my research, I treated "southern liberal" as a label and sought out various journalists and others because their contemporaries had so identified them. At the same time, the topic of southern liberalism gains its significance from the fact of the Civil Rights protest movement and the consequent transformation of southern race relations. Thus, some attempt to clarify the meaning of southern liberalism is necessary, even though any definition risks freighting the term with a more precise meaning than the words ever actually carried.

Sosna identifies southern liberals as those white southerners who saw that the South's racial system worked injustices on blacks and who supported efforts to eliminate those injustices. This definition is very broad, as he acknowledges, although it does indicate that southern liberals tended to perceive race, rather than class relations or capitalist development, as the primary source of social inequality, thus distinguishing them from the southern radicals of the same period about whom Anthony P. Dunbar has written.[7]

Sosna's definition also implies that liberal doctrines by their nature set those persons who held them in opposition to existing southern racial practices. Certainly, segregation and disfranchisement—both as arbitrary authority over the politically powerless and as group distinctions restrictive to individuals—violated traditional liberal convictions. It is significant, therefore, that the journalists gained their liberal reputations in the 1920s not as racial reformers but rather as defenders of the intellectual and cultural liberties of white southerners such as themselves against indigenous forces of intolerance. Upholding these general liberal doctrines did create tensions in their thinking when they turned to the discussion of race relations.

To leave the definition there, though, is impossible. The contradictions between liberalism and racism existed, but that only makes the long devotion of southern liberals to cautious programs of reform and their reluctance to challenge the Jim Crow system more difficult to explain. Sosna, of course, turns in the end from liberalism to religious faith as the likely source of anti-segregationist convictions. To be sure, when the journalists lifted moral principle to an honored place in the liberal pantheon as they campaigned for American entry into World War II, they undermined their own arguments for gradualism and compromise in racial reform. Nonetheless, they still held to those arguments.

In the end, definition of southern liberalism must emphasize the adjective. Downplaying the southernness of these people tends to identify them with a national racial liberalism that takes its tradition from a history emphasizing the ideals of Jefferson's Declaration, the abolitionist movement, the Radical Republicans during Reconstruction, and Negro protest in the twentieth century. Southern liberals, however, shared a different interpretation of that American history. No doubt, as Sosna proposes, few of them would have agreed with Ulrich B. Phillips's thesis that absolute devotion to white supremacy constituted the "central theme" of southern history, but even fewer would have claimed the abolitionists or the Radical Republicans as part of their tradition.[8] Understanding southern liberalism necessarily requires analysis of interpretations of the past and the methods of reform that these justified.

Despite differences in historical experience, the South assuredly was and remains American. Not even the proslavery argument could banish the "submerged faith" of American liberalism, to use Louis Hartz's phrase, from southern social and political discourse.[9] As in the rest of the United States, public devotion to a liberal faith easily coexisted with white supremacy, especially as pseudoscientific racism gave legitimacy to racial inequality. Thus, to treat "southern liberalism" as a contradiction in terms, or to set southern liberals in opposition to regional traditions, and to seek the sources of southern liberalism outside the South, only tends to mystify the phenomenon while setting a standard that few southern liberals actually met.

The Richmond editor who counseled southerners to follow the leadership of "progressive men, with large and liberal views, who draw their inspirations from the present and the future, and not the past," could have been Virginius Dabney, or any of the other journalists, writing in the 1920s or 1930s—but in fact he was writing in

1869, endorsing a "New South" built upon industrial development and full participation in the nation. It is out of this tradition—the quest for southern progress—that the journalists came. Unlike the earlier publicists who, as Paul M. Gaston explains, first created the "New South Creed," then proclaimed their visions realities, and thus bequeathed a blinding myth of innocence and triumph to subsequent generations of southerners, the journalists first took up the burdens of southern liberalism as critics of a South they considered backward and benighted. To use Gaston's analogy of the New South myth to the fable of the emperor's new clothes, the journalists perhaps failed to announce the emperor's nakedness but they did proclaim that his clothes were shabby and ill fitting and ought to be exchanged for more up-to-date fashions. No southerner could completely escape the seductive attractions of the New South myth, but, from the beginning of their careers, the journalists sought southern progress rather than defensively insisting upon its existence.[10]

In recent years, scholars have explored southern intellectual history between the two world wars, demonstrating through different interpretative frameworks the vitality of this "cultural awakening." By concentrating on individuals, and often on literary manifestations of cultural transition, these scholars have inevitably neglected the effects of contemporary—and temporary—public issues and events on changing ideas. The experience of the journalists, who publicized and participated in the southern intellectual debates while also commenting on current affairs, provides a complement to these studies, grounded on day-to-day experience.[11]

More important, these scholars have tended to assert the fact of southern social change rather than exploring its relationship to the cultural tensions they discern. Indeed, Daniel Joseph Singal contends that insufficient social change occurred in the South to explain the intellectual awakening and thus he presents his work as a local case study in the western world's transition from Victorianism to Modernism, distinctive primarily for the swiftness of the transition.[12] One area of social change in the interwar period, however, did carry obvious intellectual implications: race relations. The Great Migration of blacks from the rural South during World War I and afterwards made race a national, not just a southern, issue. Outside the Jim Crow South, blacks organized and began to exert pressure for reform, setting their own independent agenda for progress. During this period also, racism fell from intellectual respectability, and alert white southerners recognized that the Jim Crow system stood without easy ideological justification. The recovery of southern intellectual history no doubt required scholars to avoid reductive emphasis on the centrality of racism in southern history, but changes in race relations and in the idea of race during the 1920s and 1930s did create tensions for that generation of southern intellectuals.

The intellectuals and the journalists had been born within the Jim Crow system of segregation and disfranchisement. The publicists of the New South insisted that regional progress depended upon the preservation of white supremacy; their followers, the reformers of the Progressive Era, endorsed the systematic legal subordination and separation of black southerners as the fundamental precondition to further progress: only if race relations remained forever frozen in that pattern could the South have social order and social reform. The generation then coming of age learned these lessons, emotionally as well as intellectually.

By the end of the 1920s, though, the journalists recognized that changes in race relations had occurred and that changes would continue. With other southern liberals, they strove to devise programs of reform that would contribute to southern progress without provoking the chaos of racial conflict. Their desire for better race relations flowed from their desire for southern progress, therefore, not from devotion to abstract liberal principles. Nonetheless, they recognized and struggled with the most difficult issue—both as intellectual problem and as public policy—before the South in the 1930s. That they reacted to Negro protest and the early stages of the Civil Rights movement with trepidation evidences, ironically, their success at devising a coherent and satisfying ideology and program for southern liberalism. Examination of that southern liberalism shows that the journalists neither intended nor expected the Civil Rights movement.

Southern Liberal Journalists and the Issue of Race, 1920–1944

1 Coming of Age in the Progressive South

The South's leading liberal journalists came from various backgrounds and lived in different regions of the South. All had one common characteristic: as public advocates of southern liberalism, each of them spoke as a southerner. Each of them had learned of his region's past in childhood and built his ideas on this foundation.

They could—and did—trace their ancestry back through southern history. John Temple Graves II, for instance, proudly acknowledged his blood connection to William Calhoun, the brother of John C. Calhoun. George Fort Milton's great-grandfather, Dr. Tomlinson Fort, helped bring the Western and Atlantic Railroad to the settlement at Moccasin Bend on the Tennessee River that became Milton's home of Chattanooga. In the ancestry-conscious Old Dominion, Virginius Dabney could claim the finest of family trees: among others, he counted as one of his forebears that powerful and protean symbol of the South and the nation, Thomas Jefferson. Not long after Jefferson had concluded its purchase from France, Hodding Carter's great-great-grandfather came to Louisiana from Kentucky and soon became a wealthy New Orleanian. In order to have a retreat from recurrent outbreaks of yellow fever, he bought vast tracts of land north of the Crescent City in Tangipahoa Parish. Although the family holdings had diminished to some three hundred acres by the time of Carter's birth in 1907, his father was still one of the parish's most substantial landholders. These men, then, grew up with what Carter once called "the assurance of belonging to a past that had antedated the community's."[1]

Such assurance did not require ancestors of prominence. Harry S. Ashmore, who received the Pulitzer Prize in 1958 as editor of the *Little Rock Arkansas Gazette*, explained this best in describing his own South Carolina childhood. After recounting the Confederate service of his grandfathers and the ties of kinship he shared throughout the state, Ashmore concluded: "I grew up, then, in a place my own people, for better or worse, had helped create; if we actually owned very little of it (there were Ashmores of varying kind and condition, but I never met a rich one) it was nevertheless in a larger sense mine."[2] Family heritage bound these men to the South's past and, as southern liberals, they would seek precedent and justification in the region's history.

William Faulkner once declared that "for every Southern boy fourteen years old, not once but whenever he wants it, there is the instant when it's not yet two o'clock on that July afternoon in 1863 . . . and Pickett himself . . . waiting for Longstreet to give the word and it's all in the balance." Although he described this adolescent's daydream in 1948, it perhaps had its greatest appeal for his own generation of white southerners, those born in the decades on either side of 1900. Jonathan Daniels, born in 1902, declared, "Mine, I suppose, was the last Southern generation reared in a combination of indignation and despair."[3] Yet Daniels described his generation's rearing in terms too narrow, for he and his fellows came of age during a rare period in their region's history when young white southerners could remain loyal to the peculiar acts and heritage of their ancestors without considering themselves any the less American as a result.

This was the era of Progressivism, when southern reformers addressed social and economic problems with language and methods similar to their nonsouthern counterparts, an era climaxed by the election of Woodrow Wilson, a southern-born Democrat, to the presidency.[4] This was also the era when southern whites disfranchised black voters and elaborated the legal system of racial segregation. Northern opinion acquiesced in the racial settlement. To the future southern liberals who grew to adulthood during these years, the Progressive Era gave a powerful legacy in race relations. In the years to come, even as they gradually abandoned the racist doctrines that justified segregation, they would still strive to reform the Jim Crow system, not to overthrow it.

Children born in the South at the turn of the century first learned their history from those who witnessed it: their grandparents. For example, while George Fort Milton's father concentrated his attention on Tennessee's contemporary political battles, Milton's grandmother related to him his family history. She told him of her childhood in Milledgeville, Georgia's antebellum capital, and of visits that leaders such as Alexander H. Stephens, Howell Cobb, and Robert Toombs made there. She had watched from the gallery as the state's secession convention voted to leave the Union, and she described to the boy the scene that night when former governor Herschel V. Johnson, a friend of her father, came to their home and wept as he spoke of the state's decision. In 1865 Sarah Fort married Dr. Harvey Oliver Milton, returned from his war service as a surgeon with Alabama troops. Their son, Milton's father, was born in 1869, as the family struggled in the difficult years after the war. Milton long remembered his grandmother's tales of life "in a cabin in a corn patch in Reconstruction."[5]

In 1877, the Miltons abandoned farm life and moved to Chattanooga where Sarah's brother, Tomlinson Fort, lived. This man perhaps did even more than his sister to make the Civil War a vivid memory for young Milton. In 1907, he took his thirteen-year-old great-nephew to Richmond for that year's Confederate Reunion. From there they headed north, through the battlefields of Fort's military service. Tracing the path of the Confederate army, they ended their northward journey at Gettysburg, where Milton's great-uncle had been severely wounded.[6]

Although Virginius Dabney's paternal grandfather had died in 1895, six years before his birth, there was a special bond between them: his name, too, had been Virginius Dabney. The first Virginius Dabney served the Confederacy on the staff of General John B. Gordon, but left the South after the war and made his career as master of the New York Latin School and as an author. In 1886, he published a popular novel of life in the Old Dominion before the war, *The Story of Don Miff.* Writing with wit and sentiment, he told the story of the happy days of aristocratic Virginia that the Civil War had swept "into the abyss of the past." Dabney intended his book to stand as a monument to his father's memory but willingly conceded the clearer picture and finer eulogy to his sister's *Memorials of a Southern Planter,* first published in 1887. Susan Dabney Smedes wrote her father's history for the enlightenment of his descendants. "They will hear much of the wickedness of slavery and of slaveowners," she feared. "I wish them to know of a good master."[7]

Young Virginius Dabney thus could read two compelling accounts of his family and the South in which they lived. His great-grandfather, Thomas Smith Gregory Dabney, had embodied the highest ideals of the planter class, earning the respect of neighbors, the loyalty of his slaves, and the love of his children. When the war came it devastated his land and changed his life; he moved to Baltimore after the war, far from the old plantation and the antebellum South. As did George Fort Milton, Virginius Dabney inherited a family history broken by war.[8]

Indeed, the war's omnipresence in the lives of grandparents made it, through family stories, the central event in southern history for their grandchildren. Hodding Carter, born more than four decades after Appomattox, listened to his grandmother's tales of the Reconstruction years when she sewed her husband's Ku Klux Klan robes and he went out with his fellows and, Carter affectionately recalled, "saved a large section of the South through some well-timed night riding and an unerring aim." Perhaps his grandmother exaggerated, but she also showed him evidence in the pardon that President Andrew Johnson had granted to her mother after the war: this pardon, necessary in order to retain the family holdings, had required the woman, a widow since the fighting at Shiloh, to travel to Washington and swear her allegiance to the South's conquerors. Aunt Rachel, who lived with the Carters, told the boy of life in Union-occupied New Orleans under General Ben Butler, whose memory "she hated." And, outside the home, there were the aging veterans of whom young Carter and his playmates "were so proud and not a little afraid," telling stories that made the Civil War and Reconstruction "a personal, bitter, and sacred reality." To question the veracity of this history seemed not only a heresy, but also an act of disloyalty to one's family. As Carter said, "Did we not have our grandfathers and grandmothers as proofs?"[9]

One could repeat the outlines of Carter's experience from the boyhood recollections of any of these men. They learned of the past from family members—John Temple Graves declared that his grandmother's narratives of life in Yankee-occupied Georgia were "the first dramas" that he knew—and they learned simply by virtue of their existence in the turn-of-the-century South. Even Ralph McGill, whose East Tennessee heritage provided him with grandfathers who had fought on each side during the war, thrilled to the romance of the Lost Cause and fought "bloody-nosed fist fights" in defense of the Confederacy. The South's many memorial rituals to the veterans of the conflict added an almost religious quality to the child's discovery of his tradition. When McGill served as a guide to veterans in Chattanooga for the fiftieth anniversary of the Battle of Chattanooga, in

1913, it seemed no less appropriate than a Catholic boy's service as an acolyte.[10]

Although the daydream of a different Gettysburg must have occupied the occasional thoughts of these boys, almost all learned at an early age that they could honor the heroes of the Confederacy without feeling bound to defend the South's secession from the Union. A remarkable number of the South's liberal journalists identified themselves with the tradition of antebellum Unionism, which some had learned of in the stories of their ancestors. Milton's great-grandfather, Tomlinson Fort, represented Georgia in Congress from 1827 to 1831. These were the years of national battles over tariff policy that led in 1832 to South Carolina's effort to nullify the impost within its borders, an act that historians have described as the "prelude to civil war." Although he had voted against the offending tariff, Fort did not condone nullification. In the summer of 1831 he wrote to his friend John C. Calhoun, unaware of the South Carolinian's central role in the state's action, and petitioned him to speak out against the proposed policy. Fort retired from Congress that year and delivered a farewell address to his constituents expressing his "great regret" that many Georgians supported South Carolina's rebellious course. Although Fort died in 1859, Sarah Milton's story of Herschel Johnson's visit to her father's home for commiseration after Georgia left the Union suggests that had he lived, Fort would have also opposed secession.[11]

Thomas Smith Gregory Dabney admired Henry Clay and voted with Clay's Whig party. As civil war loomed, Dabney stood by his "Old-Line Whig" principles, "and that," Susan Dabney Smedes wrote, "is as much as to say he was a Union man." For Dabney, the first lost cause was the unsuccessful fight he and other Mississippi Unionists waged to prevent their state from leaving the Union.[12]

Others learned, if not ancestral Unionism, at least a view that—with hindsight—described the decision at Gettysburg and Appomattox as for the best. Jonathan Daniels wrote that his paternal grandfather "had been a protesting non-combatant in the divided Union"; his death from wounds received when irregulars fired upon a passenger ship, leaving a widow and three sons to struggle in poverty, seemed to Daniels to symbolize the tragedy of the Civil War for the South. Gerald W. Johnson recalled an uncle, a Confederate veteran, who insisted to his nephew: "Yes, they had more men, and more artillery, and more rations, and everything else, but, boy, don't you ever believe that that was what whipped us. We lost that war because God Almighty had decreed that slavery had to go." Johnson heeded these words. A novel he published in 1930 tells the story of a Scottish family in North Carolina before 1865. The novel's heroine, family matriarch Catherine Campbell Whyte, counseled her legislator son-in-law to vote against secession, and even in the midst of the war-wrought devastation of her family she damned the war as "the Devil's work" for which both North and South deserved blame. Ralph McGill could easily reach a similar conclusion, for he grew up in East Tennessee, a stronghold of Unionism. [13]

This Unionist aspect to their understanding of the South's past carried important implications for their thinking as writers and editors. Knowing their ancestors as good and honorable people, they could never accept any sweeping condemnation of the South and its past. Nor could they see secession as anything other than a decision reached in political controversy, never as the inevitable expression of southern destiny. Combining this with their knowledge from family experience that the war had brought reversals in the South's fortunes, they saw the surrender at Appomattox as the beginning of a new era in southern history.

Out of the Unionist tradition, then, they put their historical focus on the war's aftermath, Reconstruction, as the main determinant of the South's history since the war. In this view external factors, specifically the actions of the victorious North, were the shaping forces in the region's new age. In the early twentieth century, however, the nation was nearing its destination on the road to reunion between North and South, as nationalism overwhelmed sectionalism. With their Unionist sympathies, these young men found it easy to accept the contemporary national popular and scholarly interpretations of the Civil War and its aftermath without questioning the teachings of their forebears.

The most powerful statement of this nationalist interpretation was D. W. Griffith's magnificent film "Birth of a Nation," which appeared in 1915. Griffith presented the Civil War as a battle between honorable, heroic men, who fought on both sides for valid reasons. The North's victory marked a triumph for the nation, a triumph that the South accepted so long as it remained expressed in the nobility and mercy of Abraham Lincoln, a truly national figure. But the Emancipator fell to an assassin, and vengeful northern partisans grasped the reins of the government, perverting the national victory into triumph of a single section. These bitter men, the Radical Republicans, imposed on the defeated white South the horrors of Negro rule, which Griffith exemplified in scenes of comically inept black legislators and in the attempted rape of an innocent white girl by a dissolute black brute. Desperation inspired the film's southern protagonist to conceive a patriotic white organization, the Ku Klux Klan, which raced across the countryside to redeem the black-besieged South. Austin Stoneman, the film's leading Radical Republican, happened to be present when the Klansmen saved his daughter from the foul embrace of a lust-maddened Negro politician. Finally seeing the error of his ways, Stoneman repented his Reconstruction policies. The film ended with North and South now standing together as a single great nation.

"Birth of a Nation" cost more to make than had any previous film, and ticket prices reflected this. Robert Sklar suggests that Griffith made the high cost of admission a virtue and purposely sought to attract an audience of "community leaders and opinion makers" to his cinematic epic. Indeed, President Woodrow Wilson—no ordinary community leader and opinion maker—saw the film at a special White House performance and, according to legend, endorsed it as "like writing history with lightning." The film more accurately deserved the description of history written with license, but the phrase well characterized its impact on American audiences.[14]

A young southerner in those days could hardly avoid the movie. Ralph McGill recalled posters on display at Chattanooga's Lyric Theatre depicting "a rearing, pawing, hooded sheet-covered horse, bearing on its back a man similarly garbed. The film Birth of a Nation was coming to town. It played night after night to a packed house." W. J. Cash saw the film in 1916 and remembered "alternately bawling hysterically and shouting my fool head off." Hodding Carter never forgot the night he saw the movie. He was on a family visit to New Orleans in 1916, and his parents took him to the theater. As it turned out, this was the night that the residents of the Confederate Veterans Home at Beauvoir attended as special guests of the management. Rebel yells filled the auditorium with noise from the opening scene and, Carter remembered, set him "to trembling." Caught up in emotion, his father yelled, too, and as the Klan galloped to the rescue, he threw his hat in the air, never to see it again.[15]

The movie treated the South's opposition to the Reconstruction policies that granted political equality to blacks as heroic action in the national interest. According to the film, the North squandered whatever virtue it had acquired through the war for the Union in its misguided Reconstruction policies. The white South, through the Ku Klux Klan, had won the final battle and gained reunion on its own terms, terms that brought the national unity of white Americans acting "in common defense of their Aryan birthright," as one screen title had it.[16]

The lasting message of "Birth of a Nation" for these future southern liberals was its historical sanction for the conviction that the white South, not the federal government, should determine the status of blacks in the South. With its melodrama and visual impact the film made a powerful statement of this thesis, but D. W. Griffith had hardly climbed out on a historiographical limb in making his movie: professional historians, who wrote sober monographs on the Reconstruction period, had already reached similar conclusions. Led by William Archibald Dunning and his talented students, scholars developed a nationalist interpretation of the then recent past of Civil War and Reconstruction in accord with their assumption of the natural dominance of the "Teutonic" or "Anglo-Saxon" people. Their nationalism, however, was that of blood and attitudes rather than that of governmental policy. Indeed, the political moral of Reconstruction was the virtue of local self-government. Through this interpretation of history, which depended on race consciousness, a young white southerner could feel fully part of the nation without sacrificing to the federal government control over the region's affairs.[17]

The racist interpretation of the nation's recent history coincided with the reformist activity of the Progressive Era, a national phenomenon in which many southerners joined with enthusiasm. As in the rest of the country, Progressivism in the South reflected perceptions of disorder in an urbanizing and industrializing society, and a variety of reformers set out to regulate business activity, expand public education, make government more responsive to public opinion, and otherwise employ governmental power for what they perceived as social benefit. In the South, disfranchisement of black voters and enactment of a formal system of racial segregation were fundamental to the reform movement.[18]

In Virginia, for example, Progressive Era reform looked for political leadership to Andrew J. Montague and Carter Glass. Both these men advocated a convention to revise the state's constitution, the main purpose of which, said Glass, was to disfranchise black voters. The reformers believed—wrongly, as it turned out—that the elimination of black voters and of the fear of black domination, which the conservative Democratic organization cited to justify its high-handed and fraudulent political methods, would enable them to obtain office and put their reforms into effect. The convention met in 1901–1902, and delegates wrote into the new constitution measures typical of the southern Progressive Era: direct election of state officials, state regulation of railroads and other corporations, and disfranchisement of all those who could not meet new voting requirements designed to eliminate black voters.[19]

Richard Heath Dabney, professor of history at the University of Virginia and father of Virginius Dabney, agreed that black voting had no place in Virginia politics. In a lengthy letter to the *Richmond Times* while the convention was in session, he argued that prejudice was natural and that when blacks and whites competed, only hatred and violence could result. He proposed not only disfranchisement but an end to Negro education as well. Education merely prepared blacks to vote and to compete with whites, leading to increased conflict.[20]

The elder Dabney's advocacy of the exclusion of blacks and his fears of race war represented a conservative position in the Progressive Era's debate over the place of blacks in southern society. In fact, his letter expressed most of all concern for maintenance of the social order that race hatred and violence threatened. Subordination of blacks was a means to this end, not an end in itself.

An essay by George Fort Milton, Sr., much more the Progressive-style reformer than Dabney, illustrates a different contemporary justification for racial segregation. In 1894, the year of his son's birth, Milton published an essay on the Negro and the South in the *Sewanee Review*. He said that the common existence in the South of blacks, who were "the lowest order of mankind," and "the Southern people," who were "a branch of the highest development of the Aryan Family," constituted the "negro problem." In contrast to Dabney's call for exclusion, Milton contended that the "great task" before the South was "the elevation, mental, moral, and industrial, of this antithesis of human development, and its final assimilation into the body politic without injury to that organism." Quickly, he assured his readers that the word "assimilation" did not mean "amalgamation," which was "horrible and repugnant in its contemplation."[21] Obviously, though, to avoid biological amalgamation, some controls over human behavior must exist. These might range from inculcated inhibitions to public pressure, from the terror-tactics of lynching to the legally enforced separation of the races, but Milton's insistence on racial purity required that society control individual behavior.

To understand the power that racial segregation came to hold over the minds of southern liberals, it is necessary to recognize that, as John W. Cell points out, "segregation was by no means the harshest, most draconian solution to the Negro Question of which white Americans were capable." Set against a background of lynchings and race riots, the Jim Crow system takes on the aspect of moderation. Indeed, Howard N. Rabinowitz observes that some southern blacks, too, put forward the doctrine of separate-but-equal as a preferable alternative to exclusion. The arguments of Dabney and Milton help to explain why white southerners quickly came to view segregation as an absolute social necessity: with race war and amalgamation set as the opposing nightmarish potential outcomes to the natural, undirected development of race relations, the Jim Crow system ascended between them as the protector of social order and the white South.[22]

The Progressive Era bequeathed to the following generation of southern liberals a potent intellectual legacy on the subject of race relations. The definition of "good" race relations was order; its measure, an absence of conflict and violence. This helps to explain the liberals' wholehearted participation in campaigns against such manifestations of brutality as lynching. It also suggests a reason why they worked for their reforms for so long within the system of segregation. The alternative to racial separation, their Progressive predecessors had taught them, was conflict and chaos—a situation in which both blacks and the South as a whole would suffer. These lessons, acquired in childhood, bore a potent and hidden emotional content, difficult to overcome with reason alone.

Childhood lessons in race relations also influenced the interpretation that Milton, Dabney, and other liberal journalists would give to post–Civil War southern history. As Jack Temple Kirby points out, the historical interpretations of the Reconstruction era that came from Dunning and his students, and that of the film "Birth of a Nation," were "both a cause and an effect" of the enactment of the Jim Crow system.[23] While these historians studied the Reconstruction period, they reached conclusions that justified the racial "reforms" of their own time and encouraged a foreshortened and distorted view of the region's history. The Dunning school and "Birth of a Nation" implied that the triumph of the southern whites that overthrew Radical Reconstruction led directly to the Jim Crow laws. For southern reformers, this interpretation had a positive appeal. At last, the historians seemed to say, the South had settled the issues of the Civil War, and it now could get on with more important matters of regional reform and improvement. Segregation, however, did not come in systematic form until twenty years after the end of Reconstruction, years that the historians did not discuss. The period between the end of Reconstruction and the early twentieth century tended to disappear from southern history because of this focus on the ordering of race relations.

Their heritage as southerners was but part of the education that the liberal journalists obtained during the Progressive Era. For their time and place, in fact, they were highly educated, and all brought to southern journalism a breadth of interests and knowledge. Over the years, the South has produced a remarkable number of talented newspapermen. Pat Watters, a modern southern journalist, suggests in explanation that a limited range of professional opportunities combined with "the Southern penchant for action" to make newspaper work attractive to young southerners of an intellectual bent. This seems to have been the case with the liberal journalists.[24]

After George Fort Milton's mother died in 1897, father and son drew closer together. The senior George Fort Milton, then editor of the *Knoxville Sentinel,* attracted a circle of intellectually inclined persons who gathered at his home for conversation on the topics of the day. In a letter to one of his father's friends, Milton recalled those days when, he said, "I would sit admiringly by and listen to your conversation and hope that someday I would be able to talk that way or understand your words."[25]

Milton attended the Baker-Himel School in Knoxville and showed his intention of following his father into journalism by founding and editing the school's monthly newspaper. From there he went to the University of Tennessee and then to the University of Virginia, where he took his degree in 1916. As an undergraduate, he continued his training in journalism by working as a local "stringer" for the *Washington Times* and even tried his hand, unsuccessfully, at light fiction for the popular magazines. But he believed that his education at home had made the difference in his life.[26]

Virginius Dabney, too, credited his family, and especially his father, with the formative influence on his educational development. He received his early education at home under his father's direction and quickly advanced far beyond the level of knowledge expected of boys his age. Dabney graduated from Episcopal High School in Alexandria, one of Virginia's leading private schools, at the age of sixteen, and then attended the University of Virginia where he again studied under his father, "with a combination of awe, apprehension, and affection," in three of the elder Dabney's courses in history. He later said that his interest in history was "inherited."[27]

While at Virginia, Dabney showed no special interest in journalism, although, like Milton, he served on the staff of the college annual. After his graduation in 1920, uncertain of his future career, he remained another year for his Master's degree in French. The following year was spent teaching algebra at his high school alma mater. Then his father suggested newspaper work. Dabney later recalled that the idea had appealed to him immediately; through his father's agency, he came to Richmond as a cub reporter with the afternoon *News-Leader.*[28]

Hodding Carter also began his education early, entering school as a seven-year-old advanced to the fourth grade. This he modestly ascribed to his mother's "perseverance and thoroughness" as a teacher rather than to his own precocity. He built well on her foundation, though, and graduated as valedictorian of his class. Later, during his studies at Maine's Bowdoin College, he made his talents more obvious as editor of the annual *Bugle* and winner of the Forbes-Rickard Prize in Poetry.[29]

These fortunate educational experiences were more the rule than the exception for the South's liberal journalists. Parents and home atmosphere had much to do with their deciding on careers in writing and journalism. Mark Ethridge, who gained a liberal reputation with the *Macon Telegraph* and the *Louisville Courier-Journal*, described his parents as "voracious readers" and gave them credit for his intellectual interests. On the other hand, Ralph McGill's parents had little formal learning. For this reason, however, they gladly sacrificed to give their son the education they had not enjoyed. He enthusiastically seized the opportunity and, he recalled, at an early age "was drunk with books." Of course, sons of journalists, such as Jonathan Daniels and John Temple Graves, found their proud fathers happy to encourage their preparation for newspaper careers of their own.[30]

Several of these men gained practical experience in journalism while attending college. Daniels edited the student newspaper at the University of North Carolina, and Louis I. Jaffé, later of the *Norfolk Virginian-Pilot*, held a similar post on the Trinity College weekly. Students at Wake Forest College knew W. J. Cash's brash and iconoclastic editorial style long before he gained a national audience with his book, *The Mind of the South*. Gerald W. Johnson, whose father and uncle published North Carolina's two major Baptist journals, gained invaluable experience after his graduation from Wake Forest College when he became the twenty-year-old operator of a paper in Thomasville, North Carolina. He abandoned proprietorship after a year, and two years later, in 1913, joined the staff of the *Greensboro Daily News*, where his talented writing soon gained wider recognition.[31]

Even those men who did not earn a college degree showed their respect for academia and their desire for knowledge. Ralph McGill attended Vanderbilt University after World War I, but official displeasure with a college prank forced him to depart before graduation. He moved to a reporting job with the *Nashville Banner*. For the next few years he covered everything from state politics to the sensationalized death of Floyd Collins trapped in a Kentucky cave before he established a reputation as a sports writer, the position that brought him to the *Atlanta Constitution* in 1929. Throughout his life, though, McGill delighted in reciting lines of poetry first memorized in Professor Edwin Mims's English class at Vanderbilt. Mark Ethridge had to abandon higher education after a year at the University of Mississippi for the greater security of paying employment as a reporter with the *Columbus* (Ga.) *Enquirer-Sun*. Two years later, in 1916, he moved to the *Macon Telegraph* and returned to formal education in his spare time at the local Mercer University.[32]

Of course, advanced education was no prerequisite for skilled journalism, as the story of the *Montgomery Advertiser's* Grover C. Hall indicates. Hall grew up in an isolated part of rural Alabama, an isolation he enjoyed exaggerating in his declaration that "there was never a Roman Catholic, a Harvard graduate, or a football in Henry County" during his youth there. In 1905, at the age of seventeen, Hall left the local country school and continued his education as a printer's devil on his brother's newspaper, the *Dothan Eagle*. After several years of practical experience on small journals, he came to Montgomery as the *Advertiser's* associate editor in 1910. During his years with the *Advertiser*, Hall demonstrated through his erudite and cogent editorials that the lack of a college education did not necessarily prevent one from becoming an editor of distinction.[33]

By the second decade of the twentieth century, when the older of these journalists were beginning to write for newspapers, the campaign for disfranchisement and segregation had triumphed. As a result, Dewey W. Grantham says, "the 'race problem' began to assume a somewhat less somber prospect in the minds of many white southerners." One of the factors behind this change, and certainly the climax to the Progressive Era in the South, was Woodrow Wilson's election to the presidency in 1912. The national victory of this southern-born Democrat symbolized what C. Vann Woodward describes as "the return of the South."[34]

Virginius Dabney had good reason avidly to follow Wilson's career because his father was a close friend of the educator-politician. When Wilson determined to run for president, Richard Heath Dabney helped organize Virginian sentiment for Wilson before the Democratic party's convention. Despite his distaste for reform, the elder Dabney's activity brought him into the company of Virginia's political Progressives and against the conservative Democratic organization, which opposed the New Jersey leader.[35] Wilson's victory, then, was a very personal triumph for Dabney and his son. For Virginius Dabney, this return of the Democratic party to national power, with a southerner and a friend at the helm, undoubtedly also emphasized the South's potential for self-respecting participation in national affairs.

Dabney was not the only young southerner to thrill to Wilson's success. Ralph McGill recalled, "Woodrow Wilson won me completely

and I became an almost fanatical follower of the Princeton leader."
Because his father was a Republican, McGill supported Wilson "se-
cretly" in 1912, but he campaigned openly for him in 1916 even
though he was not yet old enough to vote himself. Years later, he suggested the appeal Wilson had for educated young southerners: "He
was the first Democrat to take the oath since Grover Cleveland in
1893. He was the first native Virginian to repeat the solemn obligations since Zachary Taylor; the first Southerner since Andrew
Johnson. He was the first scholar, student of government and intellectual since Thomas Jefferson."[36] A Democrat, a southerner, and a
scholar. Wilson not only symbolized regional self-respect for these
young men, but also evidenced that they, too, could aspire to great
things.

Much more so than Virginius Dabney, whose father followed his
personal convictions into occasional coalition with reformers, it was
George Fort Milton who identified himself through his father with the
Progressive Era's reforms. As owner and editor of the *Knoxville Sentinel* and, after 1909, of the *Chattanooga News*, the senior Milton became a weighty figure in the state's Democratic party by virtue of his
journalistic prominence. In 1908, his by-line appeared in *The North
American Review* over an essay endorsing Edward Ward Carmack's
candidacy for governor of Tennessee. Carmack was the candidate of
the state's Progressives and favored a "long list of reforms," the most
controversial of which was a state-wide ban on the sale of alcoholic
beverages. In Virginia, on the other hand, the Prohibitionists had
formed an effective coalition with the state's conservative Democratic
organization. Richard Heath Dabney excoriated them for their efforts
to expand government at the expense of personal liberties, and again
stood with the state's political reformers.[37]

George Fort Milton, Sr., however, was a Prohibitionist and had
nothing but praise for Carmack, whom he described as an exponent
of "the fundamental principles of Democratic faith." By 1908, Prohibition had become the "chief bone of contention" in Tennessee politics.
The warfare, however, took place largely within a single party, the
dominant Democrats, as that year's bitter gubernatorial primary indicated. Despite Milton's efforts on his behalf, Edward Carmack lost to
the incumbent, Malcolm Patterson, whose continued opposition to a

Prohibition law produced a split in Democratic party ranks. Anti-Patterson Democrats organized under the name of Independents and gave their support in the 1910 governor's race to Ben W. Hooper, the dry candidate of the Republican party, who was victorious.[38]

The elder Milton was in the thick of the intraparty battle. He helped organize the Independent Democrats, and his newspapers endorsed Hooper in 1910. He also gave early and enthusiastic support to Woodrow Wilson's 1912 presidential candidacy—in fact, he was one of the two Wilson delegates in the state's divided delegation to the party's national convention in Baltimore. The younger Milton grew to adulthood during these turbulent years, and his visit with his father to the Baltimore convention gave him his first taste of national politics and made him a fervent Wilson man.[39]

The younger Milton's own political activities in the 1920s reflected his earlier experiences. His father's views, he claimed, laid "the foundation" for his own independent course in 1928 when he supported Republican Herbert Hoover for the presidency.[40] His support for Prohibition, too, isolated him from the other journalists. Rather than a measure identified with social progress, after World War I Prohibition came to symbolize in the minds of southern liberals the intolerance and backwardness of the South.

The First World War was a watershed in southern history. Gerald W. Johnson wrote a decade later that while the "call to arms" had naturally aroused the South's "martial spirit," it also "strengthened the self-confidence of the section and put it in the mood to attempt great things." Whether the South was ready for it or not, the war did bring changes to the region. In fact, historian George B. Tindall argues that the war's greatest effect was simply the creation of "situations of dynamic change in an essentially static society."[41]

Several of the journalists traveled from the South to serve in Europe with the American Expeditionary Force. However inconvenient soldiering made it, they now had the opportunity to experience at first hand something of that western civilization which had hitherto been a matter of books and classrooms. Although too young for service in the war, Virginius Dabney had already visited France with his father in 1912; it was, Dabney declared, "a liberal education for an eleven-year-old boy." Despite the lack of such a knowledgeable guide as Richard Heath Dabney, George Fort Milton did take advantage of a short leave to wander the streets of Paris. Before returning to the *Greensboro News*, Gerald W. Johnson spent several months studying at the University of Toulouse. Louis I. Jaffé mustered out of the military in March 1919, and then spent four months in the Balkans with the Red Cross before serving in Paris as director of the health agency's news service; in November he returned to Virginia to become the editor of the *Norfolk Virginian-Pilot*. While in Europe these newsmen encountered new sets of values and behaviors that they inevitably compared with those of their South. At the beginning of their careers, then, they had gained an awareness of alternatives to the southern way of life.[42]

The primary response to serving in the Great War, however, was the discovery that wars involve waste and suffering. Milton declared that the war "was a drab, unpleasant, tiresome business, with little of panoply, glory or song," and worst of all, in his opinion, was the too-frequent sight of "blood-spattered, water-soaked human bodies." Even though Johnson's behind-the-lines duties meant that he saw only "the lighter side of war," he insisted that he had seen enough to know that the true victims of war were the noncombatants who found their homes transformed into battlefields. When the military figures had "almost faded" from memory, Johnson still recalled the luckless refugees.[43]

After the Armistice, these young men joined the majority of Americans in swearing eternal opposition to future wars. Johnson said that he now understood why the Confederate veterans he knew in North Carolina had remained "snorting pacifists" in 1917, and he announced that in the event of another war it would require at least "a corporal and seven strong men" to force him into a uniform. More sedately, Milton expressed his belief that the "real 'pacifists' of the world today are the soldiers who know what it all means and who do not see how it can aid the world to have such slaughter again."[44] This antiwar stance would contribute importantly to their conclusion that the Civil War was a needless war, the conviction that guided their thinking as southern liberals.

For many American intellectuals, the war's unexpectedly bitter fruits—violations of civil liberties at home and a vindictive peace in Paris—contributed to a deep disillusionment with human nature and with the prospects for social reform.[45] Dabney, Johnson, and the others shared these attitudes, but they expressed them more in response to developments in the South, especially the pressure politics of the Anti-Saloon League and the Ku Klux Klan, than out of disgust over the war. They gained their initial reputations as southern liberals through criticism of a South that seemed blindly devoted to the past and resistant to change; they sought to illuminate the "benighted South."

2 Illuminating the Benighted South

In 1930, the University of North Carolina Press commissioned Virginius Dabney to write a history of liberalism in the South. This assignment testified to the twenty-nine-year-old Dabney's quick rise to prominence among southern liberals and writers. The project also reflected a major southern intellectual development in the decade just ended. Throughout the region, young authors found success, both critical and professional, by writing on southern themes. Most of these writers were convinced that, as Gerald W. Johnson put it, "the dead hand of the past, a fixation of ideas arising from the notion that the Golden Age is behind, and not ahead," caused southerners to cling to romantic visions rather than to face reality; these young writers examined their region with a critical eye, questioned traditional verities, and challenged southerners to study the present honestly.[1]

The most vocal of these southern liberal critics were, like Dabney and Johnson, newspapermen. Indeed, by the time that Dabney began his study of the South's liberal tradition, these journalists had formed a loose but spirited fellowship. They studied one another's opinions, cheered colleagues under fire, and provided professional opportunities for talented young newspapermen of a liberal persuasion. Dabney, who benefited from such support himself, summed up in *Liberalism in the South* the confidence that liberal newspapermen had acquired during the 1920s: "It is to the more forthright and intelligent newspapers," he wrote, "that Southern liberalism must look in the future for much of its aggressive leadership."[2]

During the 1920s, the South and its ways came under sharp critical attack both from without and from within. Historian George B. Tindall contends that the decade's critics created a lasting image of the "benighted South" with their denunciations of the region's purported intellectual and cultural poverty. "Fundamentalism, Ku Kluxery, revivals, lynchings, hog-wallow politics—these are the things that always occur to a northerner when he thinks of the South," wrote one of these critics at mid-decade.[3]

Not only the South suffered intellectual assaults in the 1920s—so also did democratic theory, confidence in the common man, and American culture in general. In the disillusioned aftermath to World War I, Edward A. Purcell, Jr., contends, the concepts and methodologies of the social sciences converged into a sweeping challenge to democratic theory. For example, social psychologists' emphasis on man's irrational tendencies, especially men conceived in the mass, made a democrat's faith in the people's capabilities seem either naiveté or else the false piety of a cynical demagogue. At the same time, ethical justifications for either democratic government or social reform disappeared from intellectual discourse as social scientists, legal realists, and philosophers contended that a priori logical systems had no absolute validity.[4]

Holding these views, social scientists naturally insisted on an experimental, empirical method. Study of American politics in action, rather than in theory, indicated to them that democracy worked imperfectly at best.[5] A low estimate of the average citizen and an insistence on practical measures of governmental effectiveness convinced many intellectuals during the 1920s that the rule of a qualified elite would better serve the cause of efficient and fair government.

Such was the conclusion of Walter Lippmann, for example, in his influential *Public Opinion* of 1922. Lippmann argued that because humans cannot directly experience every event, our ideas and actions depend on "mental images" of reality outside personal experience. In new situations, people often acted wrongly and dangerously because of the promptings of these inaccurate "stereotypes."[6] Lippmann proposed "interposing some form of expertness between the private citizen and the vast environment in which he is entangled" and called for a redefinition of good government according to measurable criteria such as housing and health. His highest hopes rested on the social scientists, who tested reality with scientific methods rather than according to the codes of stereotypes, but he also praised any who strove to see reality uncovered and all who punctured the "buncombe" of stereotypes with criticism. In particular, responsible journalists must go beyond reporting the news to explanations of the "truth" behind events. The newspaper could either reinforce the stereotypes or destroy them with honest and expert reporting.[7]

More important than Lippmann as a popularizer of these ideas, and of the attitudes that they seemed to sanction, was the Baltimore critic and essayist H. L. Mencken. Indeed, in 1926 Lippmann himself described Mencken as "the most powerful personal influence on this whole generation of educated people." Certainly he was the most influential figure of the decade for southern journalists. Appropriately, his famous essay of 1917 in which he characterized the South as a cultural desert, the "Sahara of the Bozart," sounded the charge for the southern critical attack.[8]

For Mencken, though, the South appeared as an extreme example of tendencies evident everywhere in the United States. In 1920 he and his editorial partner, George Jean Nathan, presented *The American Credo*, a collection of what they claimed to be "some of the fundamental beliefs" of the nation. These were, in fact, common superstitions and ethnic or class stereotypes, nearly five hundred of them, that the collectors said formed the intellectual foundations for American political and social practices.[9]

In America, Mencken and Nathan said in their inimitable way, there existed "the nearest approach to genuine democracy, the most direct and accurate response to mob emotions." President Woodrow Wilson, in particular, received their sarcastic praise for "his magnificent skill at playing upon every prejudice and weakness of the plain people," but American politics in general exhibited the spectacle of "the practical politician" manipulating the stereotyped "ideas and prejudices of the inferior majority" for his own benefit. The nation suffered from mob rule. The South, then, appeared to Mencken and Nathan as entirely American. At the bottom of lynchings, for example, was simply "the mob man's chronic and ineradicable poltroonery." They concluded that "the southern poor white, taking him by and large, is probably no worse and no better than the anthropoid proletarian of the North."[10]

This outlook helps to explain why many intellectual young southerners regarded Mencken so highly, despite his slashing attacks on the region's backwardness. The problem with the South, he seemed to say, was that it was quintessentially American. Moreover, no worshipper at the shrines of the Lost Cause exceeded Mencken's admiration for the antebellum southern aristocrat, the flower of a civilization destroyed in war and now supplanted by the poor whites and their demogogic leaders. He called on the South's "civilized minority" to save the region. Unlike northern critics who insisted that the South become more like the rest of the nation, Mencken almost seemed to hope that the South might become less American.[11]

At the same time, no more inviting target for Menckenian strictures against American public thought and behavior existed than the South of the 1920s. Here, it seemed, the worst elements of democracy held sway. Behind the preachers, who self-righteously enforced Prohibition laws, and the religious fundamentalists, who prohibited the teaching of evolutionary theory in the public schools, stood the white-robed ranks of the Ku Klux Klan, an organization founded on ideas Lippmann considered stereotypes and devoted to the defense of the American Credo that Mencken had held up to ridicule.

Even without the inspiration of burning crosses, the violent postwar "Red Summer" of 1919 warned of the potential for horrifying racial conflicts in the charged atmosphere of a changing South. In a period of labor unrest and fears of radicalism, race riots broke out across the nation. Blacks fought back against white attackers and demonstrated a militant refusal to suffer white brutality. In the South, meanwhile, lynchings and vigilante attacks evidenced white determination to maintain black subordination.[12]

The Commission on Interracial Cooperation was organized in the South, as one of the founders explained, in response to that year's "acute racial situation." The commission's leaders took the Jim Crow system for granted and abandoned the fearful language of the Progressive Era with its warnings against black competition or domination. Instead, the CIC sought to bring local white and black leaders together in order to defuse with communication the misunderstandings and fears that could explode into racial violence. The organization soon expanded its program of interracial communication to include a continuing effort to educate all southerners away from the attitudes that made lynchings and violence acceptable.[13]

As its focus on the local cooperation of racial leaders suggests, the CIC concerned itself especially with the urban South. The cities presented new problems in race relations. While terror and violence might serve to enforce racial subordination in rural areas, in the cities such tactics could produce race riots and throw the entire city into chaos. As urban residential segregation gave Jim Crow a physical reality, it also made possible the rise of a small black elite from business, the professions, and the church, less dependent on whites than were blacks in the impoverished countryside. The CIC proposed to work with this black leadership class to avoid the potential dangers of racial conflict in an urban setting. The white members of the CIC also represented the cities; primarily of middle-class background, they usually came from the clergy, the schools, and journalism.[14]

Southern liberal journalists took an active role in publicizing the CIC's work. This press support for interracial cooperation seems a natural outgrowth of the newspaper's position as an urban institution. Journalists concerned with the racial tensions of urban life found the CIC a useful guide to better race relations in the South's cities.[15]

Journalists also knew that sensationalized reporting and irresponsible editorializing could provide the sparks to set off race rioting and violence. Atlanta had suffered a fearsome riot in 1906 when rampaging white mobs controlled the city for several days. Two years later, Ray Stannard Baker, a northern journalist, investigated race relations in the South and emphasized newspaper sensationalism as a main cause of the riot. In particular, he blamed the *Atlanta Evening News* for publishing extras with lurid headlines proclaiming a wave of Negro rapes as tensions grew before the riot.[16]

The role of newspapers in bringing on the Atlanta riot troubled many southern journalists. Virginius Dabney followed Baker's account when he wrote *Liberalism in the South*, but he held John Temple Graves, the paper's editor, personally responsible for the riot and charged him with "cold brutality" toward the Negro. John Donald Wade had made the charge first in his sketch of Graves's life for the *Dictionary of American Biography*, and W. J. Cash repeated Dabney's attack in *The Mind of the South*.[17]

Graves's son never forgot the Atlanta riot. He lived in Washington during the Red Summer of 1919 and again experienced the terrors of a city suffering a race riot. (Seventeen-year-old Jonathan Daniels lived through it too, and he comprehended its meaning when he saw the "fear on the faces" of the family servants as they left for home after work.) Graves wrote a novel of life in Washington after World War I, published in 1923, and he included a short-lived race riot in the action. One character, a newspaper reporter, had been absent from the city during the violence but had to file a story nonetheless. Graves wrote that the reporter created his eyewitness account by "remembering another race riot—in Atlanta—years ago when he was a boy. . . . A few facts from the afternoon papers and all the rest, all the color and atmosphere, from Atlanta!"[18]

Finally, in 1943, John Temple Graves II published *The Fighting South* and availed himself of the opportunity to defend his father. He said nothing of the *Atlanta Evening News*'s bold headlines. Instead, he reported that at the height of the rioting, local blacks, "led by their Baptist preacher," came to the Graves home and told the editor that "they considered him the best friend the colored people had in the country and . . . put themselves in his hands for advice and protection." Yes, Graves admitted, in later years distinguished men had held his father responsible for the riots, "but the colored people of Darktown didn't think so."[19]

Graves's vindication of his father reveals a crucial aspect of both his thinking and that of many other white southerners: close personal relationships with blacks based on the obligations of noblesse oblige exculpated one from charges of "cold brutality" toward the Negro, despite the subordination and impotence that paternalism entailed for blacks. Such a defense, however, veiled the systematic degradations that southern institutions perpetrated on blacks while heaping personal responsibility for any acknowledged evils on those who committed direct acts of anti-Negro violence.

Considered together with his long and vivid memory of the Atlanta riot, Graves's assertion of his father's innocence also suggests deeper tensions born of the contrast between visceral reactions to contemporary violence and the southerner's conception of a noble regional past. Hodding Carter's memories of childhood events exemplify this contrast. Wandering in the woods near his home one day, young Carter suddenly confronted, hanging before him, the burned black body of a lynch mob's victim. The eleven-year-old boy vomited at the sight, and after thirty-five years he declared that he still sometimes saw the body in his sleep. Carter also described a game of Ku Klux Klan he and his friends played, draping themselves in sheets and chasing black children through the woods. No doubt he imagined himself acting as his heroic grandfather had done during Reconstruction. In the boy's mind, the game had no connection with the horrible lynching.[20]

The Ku Klux Klan of the 1920s challenged this comforting disconnection between obvious southern evils in the present and the grandeur of a heroic past by claiming the sanction of southern history. Tension between past and present certainly already existed, but the

Klan's claim to embody the southern tradition gave interpretations of the past added significance for southern liberals. The Ku Kluxers of the 1920s not only caused their southern critics to put forward a countertradition but also set them in a position to begin judging the southern past by the same standards that they applied to the present. Criticism of the modern Klan, for example, inevitably raised questions about the Reconstruction Klan. Hodding Carter told a revealing story of a visit home to Louisiana from college in 1924: at a family gathering he was forthrightly declaring his dislike for the Klan, when he noted the anger on his grandmother's face; quickly he assured her that he referred only to the modern Klan, not at all to her husband's Klan.[21]

Class biases aided southern liberals in distinguishing between these Ku Klux Klans. Despite the supposed solidarity of racism, class and cultural antagonism between southern whites had long existed. The conflicts of the 1920s were squarely in this tradition. Carter, for example, explained that he opposed the Klan "mainly because [he] didn't like the hometown people who led it."[22] The difference between the Klans was the difference between his grandfather and those hometown people.

Many southern liberals, especially in the 1920s, employed a sense of class differences to sidestep the problem of reconciling a sacred, yet often indefensible, past with contemporary liberal attitudes. John Temple Graves's defense of his father's part in the Atlanta riot, an example of this problem in miniature, shows this clearly. In *Liberalism in the South*, Dabney singled the elder Graves out for criticism primarily because he was "an upper class Southerner" whose attitude toward blacks seemed more akin to those of "the underprivileged whites."[23] The younger Graves's defense, in which he ignored the newspaper sensationalism and emphasized the dependence of terrified local blacks, seems obviously unsatisfactory unless one recognizes that his deeper purpose was to demonstrate that, regardless of his role in precipitating the race riot, the elder Graves had fully met the obligations of his class.

Conditions in the 1920s encouraged such class-conscious arguments. The southern evils that liberals opposed seemed to them uniquely lower-class phenomena born of ignorance. The South's civilized minority—the decent, educated southerners—had a patriotic duty to fight back. Yet they employed the ideas of modern liberalism in this battle, and advocacy of liberal tenets in the present produced tensions when southern liberals analyzed their region's illiberal past.

During the 1920s, though, these tensions remained well hidden. The intellectuals' abhorrence of moralizing and their preference for empirical observation allowed southern liberals to examine the South and its past without testing their deepest loyalties. Whereas anti-liberal southerners justified their actions as expressions of God's will, southern intellectuals found it effective strategy to reject analyses grounded on absolute morality. In addition, religious fundamentalists and the Klansmen insisted that the political process and public officers respond to the demands of local majorities.[24] The liberals, on the other hand, turned to assertions of individual rights and found use for the arguments that Mencken and Lippmann had employed to criticize democratic government in general.

One student of southern thought during the 1920s wrote that, like regional local color in the 1880s, "southern self-criticism became virtually a literary sub-genre." Many of its leading practitioners came from journalism. During the decade, Pulitzer Prizes went regularly to southern newspapers and editors who took on the Ku Klux Klan, lynchings, and political apathy. Early leaders of this vigorous regional press included Julian LaRose Harris, whose *Columbus* (Ga.) *Enquirer-Sun* received its Pulitzer award in 1926, and Grover C. Hall of the *Montgomery Advertiser* and Louis I. Jaffé of the *Norfolk Virginian-Pilot*, whose laurels came in 1928 and 1929, respectively.[25]

But the "loudest and clearest voice" belonged to Gerald W. Johnson, whose talented pen and prodigious output soon made him the South's "leading native interpreter." Although Virginius Dabney praised him highly in the text of *Liberalism in the South*, a more striking indication of Johnson's domination of southern self-criticism appears in Dabney's bibliography, to which he contributed more works than all but one of the other 297 authors listed there.[26]

H. L. Mencken discovered Johnson's outspoken editorials for the *Greensboro Daily News* in the early 1920s and recommended him to editor friends. Johnson jumped at the opportunities that Mencken's praise opened and proved himself skilled as an essayist also. In 1924 he moved to the University of North Carolina's journalism department. There he strengthened his friendship with Howard W. Odum, whose Institute for Research in Social Science was inspiring vigorous sociological analysis of southern problems. Johnson contributed essays and editorials to early issues of Odum's *Journal of Social Forces* and then, in 1926, joined Mencken at the *Baltimore Evening Sun* where he wrote a weekly column, often on southern affairs, for the next seventeen years.[27]

The ideas behind Johnson's observations and analyses of the South resembled those of Mencken and Lippmann. Always he maintained a skeptical attitude toward the virtues of democratic government. Democracies were "intellectually inert" because the masses feared new ideas. The average man had little capacity for dealing adequately with complex ideas and simply responded happily to politicians' clever manipulations. When the unthinking majority acted in firm, but ignorant, conviction of its own moral righteousness, nonconformity took on the appearance of sin. Sanctified censorship, always a potential product of democracy, prevented rational investigation of social problems and posed a threat to any dissenting minority. Intellectual integrity and the courage to declare the truth, rarities under majority rule, represented the single most effective medicine for the ills of democracy.[28]

In 1928, Johnson wrote that Prohibition, fundamentalism, and the Ku Klux Klan represented the three issues that had "really agitated the great mass of the people" since 1922. All three he found comprehensible in terms of his general arguments. The Klan, for example, was "a perfect expression of the American idea that the voice of the people is the voice of God." Both fundamentalists and Prohibitionists embodied a "moral certainty that rises so near to the sublime" that they could justify employing the police "to sustain the faith."[29]

When Johnson moved from southern specifics to generalizations, however, he usually did so in defense of Dixie, declaring that the South's problems were, potentially if not actually, those of the nation as a whole. In fact, Johnson's essays always expressed optimism for the South's future. He even considered the Ku Klux Klan an agent of good because "it has revealed to the South that its lack of keen and relentless self-criticism, the only effective social prophylaxis, has laid it open to invasion by any sort of disease." Similarly, even as he predicted the spread of southern religious fanaticism to the rest of the nation, Johnson noted that "the South is rapidly beginning to educate her children, and it is rare indeed that moral certainty can stand long against education."[30]

The main ingredient in Johnson's conception of this healthy future was its southern foundation. Effective criticism could come only from southerners. He gave two reasons for this: "in the first place because they have the Southern viewpoint, and can therefore be understood, and in the second place because they have the most and most reliable information, and therefore can most frequently spot the joints in the Southern armor." What he meant by "the Southern viewpoint" appears clearly in his use of race and history to explain and defend the South before the nation. In explaining the Klansman, for example, he pointed out that "the South actually was under Negro domination once, and after half-a-century the memory of that experience still keeps its racial sensibilities abnormally acute."[31]

Reconstruction, for Johnson, proved the South's racial attitudes reasonable, explained modern political phenomena, and showed the fatuity of self-righteous but ignorant critics of the South. During that period, the North supposedly gave political control in the South to the freedmen. Naturally, in such a situation the democratic traditions and institutions were "corrupted and tainted for the South." Indeed, so low did democracy fall in the estimation of the white South, and so imperative was an end to Negro rule, that otherwise law-abiding southerners countenanced political frauds and extralegal violence to regain control of government. Unfortunately, the corruption of political practices then permitted corrupt men to enter southern politics. Since that time, though, the region's best men, "the spiritual heirs of Jefferson and Marshall," had not only struggled to rebuild from the war's destruction but had also "been fully occupied in recapturing the leadership of the South itself, trying to sweep back the tide of demagogy, ignorance, stupidity, and prejudice that the dynamiting of civilized government loosed upon the luckless country."[32]

Threatening their success, however, was the continuing crazy notion of some northerners "that the Negro is only a sun-burnt white man" requiring protection from brutal southern whites. Wise efforts of southerners to deal with the presence of free blacks, beginning with the Reconstruction-era Black Codes, had appeared to northerners as cruel attempts to return blacks to slavery. Northern suspicions meant that intelligent southerners had to undertake a positive program for improving race relations. "In short," Johnson declared, "every unnecessary hardship inflicted on the black South postpones the day when the white South can resume its full membership, political, moral and intellectual, in this union."[33]

Such a program for improved race relations required that southern liberals hold off threats from two directions. Pressure on the South from unthinking outsiders could provoke unthinking white southerners to mistreat blacks, thereby reinforcing northern suspicions and increasing pressure on the South. The southern liberal had to convince northern reformers that their methods were counterproductive while at the same time he restrained the white masses who voted for demagogues, joined the Klan, and worshipped religious intolerance. The predilection for mistreatment of blacks could produce northern intervention in southern affairs, as Congressman L. C. Dyer's proposed federal antilynching law threatened.[34] Such intervention, though, could cause a repetition of Reconstruction's chaos and destroy the foundation for a future South that the region's finest men had struggled to construct.

This program differed from southern reform thinking in the Progressive Era. In the earlier period campaigns for disfranchisement and segregation were waged under the banner of white supremacy. In the 1920s, southern liberals, while they accepted the Jim Crow system, stressed the need to improve the condition of blacks. Moreover, they qualified the white supremacy doctrine; they now questioned the capabilities of the white masses, no matter how pure their Anglo-Saxon heritage. This conclusion eliminated from southern liberalism the tendency toward "Herrenvolk democracy"—a society based on democratic equality for whites only—that, as Dewey W. Grantham says, was pervasive in the Progressive South. As a result of their experiences in the 1920s, in fact, the southern liberal journalists viewed the idea of democratic equality itself with skepticism.[35]

Johnson concluded that the newspaper and its editor had a crucial role in southern reform. Journalists occupied a strategic position; they could not only work to educate the southern public but could also help to explain the South to northern audiences. As early as 1923, Johnson insisted that only through the newspapers could southern reformers convince the public of the necessity for change. "It is," he wrote, "a publicity job, propaganda, if you please, which requires neat and delicate handling." In his essays on southern journalism, he devoted most of his attention to the identification and praise of that special breed of newspaperman who rejected regional apologetics and strove to awaken the South from complacency.[36]

The best-known of these journalists at that time, Julian LaRose Harris, the son of Joel Chandler Harris, edited the *Columbus* (Ga.) *Enquirer-Sun* and fought against the Ku Klux Klan's influence in state politics. Because of the newspaper's small staff, Harris relied primarily on editorials. These editorials, which Louis I. Jaffé said employed "the frontal-attack-stink-bomb method," directed harsh comment also at those who failed to speak out against organizations and laws that they disliked. Harris especially hoped to hearten Georgia's small-town editors "to think straight and write fearlessly."[37]

Harris's biographers turn to psychological factors to explain his dissenting stance. One declares that his travel in Europe and in the North caused Harris to feel "a deep alienation from southern life, its politics and religion." Another argues that he desired "to emerge from the shadow of his more famous father." At the same time, they agree that he chose worthy targets for his nonconformity. As Harris himself once exclaimed, "what a legacy for one's conscience to know that one had been instrumental in mowing down the old prejudices that rattle in the wind like weeds."[38]

Personality traits might also explain Grover C. Hall's independent and iconoclastic editorializing. He was simply a maverick. In 1910, he began his career at the *Montgomery Advertiser* with editorial endorsement of Alice Roosevelt Longworth's right to smoke cigarettes. Years later, he still held to this libertarian creed, declaring "surely it is none of my business what another person thinks so long as he does not ask the legislature to turn his opinions into law, under which I *must* live."[39]

Quirks of personality alone, however, do not explain the appearance of outspoken journalists, critical of southern complacency and bigotry, throughout the region in the 1920s. Moreover, their arguments displayed a general similarity that makes a broader explanation necessary. Contemporaries assumed that anyone with intelligence, a modicum of courage, and an editorial forum would criticize the Klan, fundamentalists, and Prohibitionists. At mid-decade, for example, H. L. Mencken announced the existence of a rebellious minority in the benighted South and explained that "the very heat of the fundamentalist and Ku Klux fury is hurrying them out of the egg."[40]

Extending his metaphor, then, one must say that Mencken played the role of mother hen to this brood of southern writers. According to Fred C. Hobson, he insisted that the South's "civilized minority . . . would save the South from itself." To hasten this event, Mencken offered private encouragement and public exposure in his magazine, *The American Mercury*, to numerous southern critics.[41]

Virginius Dabney, for example, published an essay on "Virginia" in *The American Mercury* in 1926. Mencken not only suggested the topic but also aided in the writing, at one point demanding that Dabney "let some irony and some humor into it." Even before the essay appeared, Mencken included Dabney in a list of the South's outstanding journalists. Dabney recalled that he "was walking on air for days after the note of acceptance arrived," and in his memoirs declares that Mencken influenced his thinking more than any other person except his father.[42]

Simply reading *The American Mercury*, dominated by Mencken's slashing assaults on imbecilities he had discovered in the South and elsewhere, nourished a critical spirit among many young southerners. Mencken pointed out the targets and, through the example of his uninhibited style, provided aspiring writers with powerful weapons. Ralph McGill, then a reporter for the *Nashville Banner*, read *The American Mercury* avidly. He said later that he had considered Mencken "our knight in shining armor who each month slew the dragons of dullness in the pulpits in Washington, the governor's office, the legislature and in the seats of the mighty generally."[43] Thus, while enabling established southern essayists to address a national audience, Mencken and his magazine—entertaining as well as educating—helped spread the rebellious spirit through the South.

For southern liberal journalists, though, the *Baltimore Evening Sun*, Mencken's newspaper home throughout his career, did as much to bind them together. Engaged in continual crusades against Prohibition, religious fundamentalism, and the Klan, the paper gave much space to the discussion of southern controversies. Southern editors could find support in the *Evening Sun* for their own positions and a number of them also contributed essays to the paper's editorial page. Many years later, Virginius Dabney wrote to Hamilton Owens, the *Evening Sun*'s long-time editor, repeating his gratitude for "the opportunity to break into the *Evening Sun* editorial page back in 1925." In his recent autobiography, Dabney writes that his association with the paper was a turning point in his career. After 1926, Gerald W. Johnson's presence on the paper assured that southern liberal journalists would continue to give attention to the *Evening Sun's* editorial page and, as Owens wrote, "gave it ground for speaking authoritatively on matters affecting the South."[44]

Before long, however, southern writers did not have to send their work north of the Potomac for publication. By the mid-twenties the intellectual ferment of the decade had spawned several magazines with a regional focus. One of the first of these, *The Reviewer*, published its initial issue in Richmond in 1921. Mencken, as usual, offered publicity and advice to *The Reviewer* and to its editor, Emily Clark. He directed her to make the magazine a forum "for realistic discussion of Southern Problems by Southerners." However, although it did publish essays by Johnson and others, *The Reviewer* always faced North rather than South, and its literary emphasis prevented it from becoming the sort of regional forum that Mencken desired.[45]

Howard W. Odum's *Journal of Social Forces*, which began publication in 1923, also won Mencken's approval and advice. The early issues, with essays and editorials by Gerald W. Johnson, mixed the work of social scientists with candid and critical discussions of southern problems. In 1925, though, religious fundamentalists raised a storm of protest against heretical articles in the *Journal*. Daniel Joseph Singal explains that Odum responded to these critics by shifting the *Journal's* focus completely to social science and away from the controversy that Mencken sought.[46]

A closer approximation to the Menckenian ideal, and a longer-lasting liberal influence in the South, was *The Virginia Quarterly Review*. Under the editorial guidance of James Southall Wilson, the *VQR* began publication in 1925. The initial issue announced its intention to be "an organ of liberal opinion" and expressed its desire to publish discussions of the South. From the beginning Wilson sent copies of the quarterly to a selected list of southern newspaper editors. Assistant editor Stringfellow Barr asked a college friend, George Fort Milton of the *Chattanooga News*, to draw up the original list of names, and Wilson subsequently wrote to these men soliciting manuscripts and authors. In a typical letter, he told Grover C. Hall that he sought "at least one article provocative of intelligent interest in Southern problems on the title page of each issue" and informed him that despite low rates for contributors, the quarterly boasted "one of the most intelligent groups of readers to be found in the South." While Hall offered no manuscripts of his own, he did suggest several worthy young southern journalists, including John Temple Graves and Mark Ethridge. Through the following decades, the *VQR* regularly published the work of southern liberal journalists and became the arena for many southern intellectual controversies.[47]

H. L. Mencken, the *Evening Sun*, and the magazines offered ambitious southern journalists the opportunity to communicate with like-minded persons, and they provided a constant intellectual stimulation for individual editors advocating liberal policies. From his post at the *Norfolk Virginian-Pilot*, Louis I. Jaffé discussed editorial writing with Harris, obtained Gerald W. Johnson's occasional editorial assistance, and engaged in a discussion of the effects of unpopular editorials on newspaper circulation with Hall. Later in the decade, Jaffé offered advice and guidance in liberalism to a young reporter at the *Richmond Times-Dispatch*, Virginius Dabney.[48]

In addition, established editors informed one another of talented newcomers to the profession and welcomed these young journalists to their circle. An excellent example of this is Jaffé's search for an associate editor for the *Virginian-Pilot* in 1929, after John Newton Aiken had moved to the *Baltimore Evening Sun*. As he told Grover C. Hall, Jaffé hoped to replace Aiken with "a budding Gerald Johnson–Grover Hall–Julian Harris—a well-educated, level-headed liberal who can write intelligently, vigorously and attractively about the things that the editorial page holds out to discuss and illumine, and can do it without alienating the customers. That, as you know, is no mean trick." Hall suggested both W. J. Cash, whom he considered "a bit sour in his outlook on the Southern scene," and Lenoir Chambers, of the *Greensboro Daily News*. When Gerald W. Johnson also recommended Chambers, Jaffé offered him the position, adding that Johnson had suggested his name. Chambers accepted and eventually succeeded Jaffé as editor of the *Virginian-Pilot* in 1950.[49]

In the 1920s, the threatening zealotry of traditionalists, the lusty inspiration of Mencken, and a growing network of liberal journalists promised opportunity and action for young southern newspapermen. Hodding Carter left his Louisiana home in 1923, at the age of sixteen, to attend Maine's Bowdoin College. There, he said, his mind received "its first healthy jolts" because "never before had folklore, mores, inherited certainties been really challenged." Had he remained in the South, he might well have met similar challenges, from Mencken and others. Although he devoted himself primarily to writing poetry while in college, after graduation in 1927 Carter entered Columbia University's School of Journalism. He would return to the South to make his career in newspaper work.[50]

In October 1928, the year that Carter came home to Louisiana, Gerald W. Johnson again examined the condition of southern journalism. He saw increasing success in the liberal editors' efforts to inject "candor" into discussions of southern affairs.[51] By that time, an identifiable southern liberal journalism did exist. Opposition to the Ku Klux Klan, fundamentalism, and Prohibition, combined with opportunities to write on southern subjects for publications with a wide distribution, enabled liberal journalists across the South to discover colleagues who held similar views. Professional fellowship not only steeled individual newspapermen to stand fast against pressures for conformity, but also gave a general coherence to the group's outlook.

Had Johnson published his essay later in 1928, he very likely would have reached a more pessimistic conclusion. The presidential campaign of that year climaxed the early development of southern liberal journalism. As the Solid South broke apart over the candidacy of Alfred E. Smith, the journalists saw the South's white masses apparently voting according to the dictates of prejudice. In their view, the campaign against Smith constituted a war against liberalism in the South.

3 Al Smith, Thomas Jefferson, and the Solid South

By May 1931, Virginius Dabney could "see daylight" on his research for *Liberalism in the South*. In order to make his discussion as current as possible, he wrote to various southern figures asking for nominations of contemporary liberals worthy of inclusion in the book. For the chapter on journalism, Grover C. Hall and Gerald W. Johnson provided him with generous lists of deserving editors and newspapers. Both men, however, specifically banned George Fort Milton, editor of the *Chattanooga News*, from the liberal fellowship.[1]

Milton himself considered his views and those expressed in the *News* legitimately liberal. Unlike Dabney, though, he played down the Ku Klux Klan, expressed little fear for intellectual freedom in the South, and defended Prohibition. These views squared with his political loyalties during the 1920s. Hall's complaint that Milton "yet accepts [William Gibbs] McAdoo as a prophet and will commit any indecency for the sake of prohibition," indicates the major points of conflict between Milton and the journalists Dabney honored.[2] While Hall and his fellows saw Alfred E. Smith's candidacy in the 1928 presidential election as a crusade for liberty in the South, Milton left the Democratic party and supported Herbert Hoover.

This bitter election climaxed the development of southern liberal journalism in the 1920s. For the first time, Dabney and others argued that the modern southern liberals, not the Ku Klux Klan, carried on the true southern tradition. In defense of an Irish-Catholic presidential candidate from New York, they linked themselves with Thomas Jefferson and a southern liberalism bottomed on individual liberty. The hatreds exploited so openly in the campaign against Alfred E. Smith taught them a lesson in the dangerous falsehood of prejudice while reinforcing their distaste for the introduction of moral issues into politics. Moreover, they joined Grover C. Hall in interpreting the attacks on Smith as "a war to end the war for liberalism in the South," and his overwhelming defeat—with five states from the "Solid South" in the Republican column—left them in shock. The election of 1928 convinced the journalists that the southern electorate, ever susceptible to exploitation of ignorance and prejudice, constituted a major obstacle for liberalism in the South.[3]

In August 1920, Ralph McGill, then a student at Vanderbilt University, spent his days at the state capitol watching the Tennessee legislature debate ratification of the Nineteenth Amendment. "This is historical," McGill told himself. "I will always remember this." Tennessee became the thirty-sixth state to ratify the amendment and thereby made woman suffrage part of the Constitution. Perhaps McGill noticed in the capitol a heavyset young man imploring hesitant legislators to vote for ratification. George Fort Milton and his new bride spent "the hot months" of that year in Nashville lobbying for the amendment.[4]

Milton's work for woman suffrage demonstrated his devotion to the causes his parents had advocated before the First World War. In adolescence, he had watched proudly as his father steadfastly editorialized for a state prohibition law while the paper's advertising revenues and circulation declined in "wet" Chattanooga. The younger Milton's efforts for woman suffrage helped culminate another family crusade: his stepmother, Abby Crawford Milton, became a well-known speaker for the right to vote and, after the amendment's ratification, served as the first president of the Tennessee League of Women Voters.[5] The addition of the Eighteenth and Nineteenth Amendments to the Constitution began the 1920s on a celebratory note for the Milton family.

With the vote assured to women, the Miltons turned to politics and the presidential candidacy of William Gibbs McAdoo. As Woodrow Wilson's Secretary of the Treasury and son-in-law, McAdoo naturally presented himself as heir to the former president's following, and clearly pinned his hopes for 1924 on a repetition of Wilson's 1916 winning combination of electoral votes from the West and the South. The Milton family wholeheartedly labored on McAdoo's behalf: Milton, Sr., and his wife in Tennessee, and the younger Milton on McAdoo's national staff as publicity director. In articles published during this period, the younger Milton never missed an opportunity to boost McAdoo's candidacy. In the process, he put forward an analysis of conditions in the South very different from the critical view of liberal journalists such as Gerald W. Johnson.[6]

McAdoo enjoyed strong southern support, and finding fault with southern thinking or behavior would do his campaign no service. Therefore, Milton addressed southern intolerance and backwardness–the usual subject matter of Johnson's essays–cautiously if at all. He preferred to speak of "that fundamental idealism and leaning toward liberalism which is inherent in the mass." Johnson, who described the Klan as a perfect expression of popular attitudes, reached much more pessimistic conclusions.[7]

Their opinions of the Eighteenth Amendment differed, too. Johnson believed Prohibition a disturbing example of the intolerant spirit that he feared threatened individual freedom in the South. Milton, on the other hand, considered Prohibition a salutary reform. Instead of dry fanaticism in the South, he saw an understandable "exasperation at the efforts of other sections to nullify the Constitution."[8]

Through 1923, Milton's essays brimmed with confidence; McAdoo's future looked bright. Early in 1924, though, probers into the fraudulent leasing of oil reserves at Teapot Dome in Wyoming exposed the candidate's association as a well-paid lawyer to one of the unsavory oilmen. McAdoo explained his innocence of wrongdoing, but the brush of scandal tarred his image. Campaign contributions slowed to a trickle, and Milton began paying his own expenses as publicity director. Despite victories in several state primaries that spring, the McAdoo campaign limped toward New York City and the party's convention in July.[9]

Waiting at home in New York City was McAdoo's strongest rival, Governor Alfred E. Smith. An Irish-Catholic who had risen through the ranks of Tammany Hall to become a popular and effective governor, Smith both led and symbolized the Democratic opposition to McAdoo. Through the 1920s, a gulf of misunderstanding separated the Democratic party in the Northeast from the more rural party of the South and West. To many of those Democrats urban machines represented corruption and malign opposition to beneficent reforms such as Prohibition. Urban Democrats of immigrant stock, for their part, considered the Eighteenth Amendment a punitive measure and an abridgment of their freedom. The problems of farmers seemed as distant to them as did tenement houses and labor unions to rural members of the party. In 1924 Smith and McAdoo, each a symbol—almost a caricature—of these two wings, carried these antagonisms into an irreconcilable conflict at the party's convention.[10]

The battle began immediately as the delegates took up the question of the party's position on the Ku Klux Klan. William Gibbs McAdoo, alone among the party's major candidates, had avoided condemnation of the Klan. His effort to maintain support in the South no doubt had dictated a cautious approach to the secret organization, but his slip into the muck of Teapot Dome had weakened his campaign to the extent that he now feared to alienate any supporters. With a Catholic looming as his strongest opponent in the party, McAdoo's silence sufficed to cast him as the Klan's candidate.[11]

George Fort Milton was no Klansman but as a McAdoo loyalist he tacitly accepted the label. Angry, scornful opposition to the Klan marked the southern liberal of the 1920s, but Milton never joined the chorus of criticism. Rather than confronting the Klan issue, he acted as though it did not exist. Opponents of the secret order, and of McAdoo, refused to accept this willful blindness. Milton's experience at the 1924 convention, however, embittered rather than enlightened him.

The divided convention balloted to choose a nominee 102 times without success. Neither McAdoo nor Smith could corral sufficient votes for victory, and neither would give way to the other. At last, long after the nomination had lost its usefulness to anyone, both men retired from the battle, and exhausted delegates quickly settled on John W. Davis.[12]

Smith forces deemed the result a partial victory and looked forward to 1928, but McAdoo had suffered a complete and bitter defeat. He considered Smith merely a figurehead under the direction of his real enemies, the corrupt urban political bosses and the liquor interests. George Fort Milton agreed with his "Chief." In an essay published shortly after the election, he claimed that McAdoo's enemies had employed "the Klan shibboleth and the oil subterfuges" to deny him the nomination. Milton continued to believe that had McAdoo been the party's nominee, he would have been elected president.[13]

All Milton's efforts had gone for naught, and he returned to Chattanooga, now as editor of the *News*. George Fort Milton, Sr., had died the previous April. Although the younger Milton returned to politics after the funeral, before leaving he had published a signed editorial in the *News* declaring his intention to continue his father's policies. Describing the *News* as "a liberal newspaper" and "a public institution," he swore "to keep the faith of the heritage," including his father's advocacy of Prohibition.[14]

Editorial comment on current affairs apparently did not fully satisfy Milton's intellect and, as an avocation, he turned to the study of the past. By the summer of 1925 he had embarked on a biography of Tennessee's last president, Andrew Johnson. Undoubtedly he found rehabilitating the reputation of a man cast into political oblivion and held up to public ridicule a pleasant task after the previous year's defeats.[15]

Milton had hardly begun his study of Johnson's tempestuous presidency before he had to give his attention to a controversy closer to hand: the trial of John Thomas Scopes for teaching the theory of evolution at Dayton's high school, less than forty miles north of Chattanooga. The Tennessee legislature had passed a law prohibiting the public schools from teaching evolutionary theory, which religious fundamentalists believed contradictory to the explanation of Creation in the Book of Genesis. The nation fastened its attention on the small town after Scopes's arrest brought him the assistance of famed attorneys Dudley Field Malone and Clarence Darrow, and the prosecution, in turn, added reinforcement in the person of William Jennings Bryan. To southern liberals, who believed that the Protestant clergy exerted dangerously excessive authority over the region, Scopes became a martyr to academic freedom and his case, a symbolic showdown between religious obscurantism and scientific knowledge.[16]

Milton did not see the conflict in such clear-cut terms. He did consider the law "foolish, and an attempt to throttle the freedom of thought," and he desired its repeal. On the other hand, he contended that the bill originated in the valid premise that state agencies should be subject to the state legislature. Although he did not directly confront the question of whether majority opinion should determine the teachings of the schools, Milton granted a greater power to popular rule than did southern liberal observers. He expected the trial to make a determination of the conflict between the state's right to direct "official actions" of its employees and individual rights of thought and religion. "The constitutional debate is sure to be a mighty one," a *News* editorial predicted, "and whatever way the case turns out, beneficial results are highly probable."[17]

That prospect vanished quickly. Hundreds of reporters intent on a colorful story descended on Dayton and sent home millions of words describing the trial's stormy progress toward its climax in Darrow's famous cross-examination of the Great Commoner. To antifundamentalists, Bryan collapsed so utterly before Darrow's inquisition that Scopes's conviction seemed almost irrelevant. Yet, the law remained on the books. Milton complained afterward that "the real issues were forgotten in the fury of the fight."[18]

Milton's plaint hardly typified southern response to the trial. George B. Tindall argues that it awoke southerners to the benighted image their region cast in the rest of the nation. The journalists, already raising loud complaint against southern intolerance and intellectual cowardice, reasserted their contention that militant fundamentalism menaced liberty in the South. Although fundamentalism flourished in all of Dixie, the southern journalists did emphasize that Tennessee, not the South, bore responsibility for the trial—but reporters for national journals at the trial saw no reason to make such a distinction and treated the most fantastic religious sects and spectators as specimens of southern culture.[19]

Intellectual Tennesseans took offense. Edwin Mims of Vanderbilt University sought to refute this image by assuring the nation that the South boasted numbers of liberals, progressives, and intellectuals—terms he used interchangeably—who were waging "a veritable war of liberation" against such backwardness as that manifested at Dayton. His book's title, *The Advancing South*, expressed his argument. Mims asked his colleagues at Vanderbilt, poets John Crowe Ransom and Donald Davidson, to join his defense, but they refused. The trial's "jeering accompaniment of large-scale mockery directed against Tennessee and the South," as Davidson described it, infuriated them, but they could not follow Mims's example. In their view, his book consisted of little more than a plea for admission to the enemy camp. Through the rest of the decade, Ransom, Davidson, and like-minded friends gradually constructed their own vindication of the South, one that would challenge rather than congratulate the southern liberals.[20]

George Fort Milton shared neither the journalists' outrage nor Mims's embarrassment. At the trial's beginning the *News* did observe that the entire South was "on trial" at Dayton, but subsequent editorials made little of the issue. In fact, Milton arranged to publish H. L. Mencken's dispatches to the *Baltimore Evening Sun* on the *News*'s editorial page. Although Mencken's caustic reports on the "anthropoid rabble" at Dayton flooded the paper with angry letters, Milton found Mencken himself likeable and corresponded with him for some time after the trial.[21]

Milton's anger and bitterness resulted primarily from the harsh treatment that liberals gave to William Jennings Bryan. The Great Commoner's campaign against religious modernism in the 1920s hardly dampened Milton's admiration for his glorious past, and Bryan's sudden death, immediately following Scopes's conviction, saddened the editor. When scornful eulogies prolonged the ridicule Bryan had suffered during the trial, Milton reacted with anger. "Both Mr. Wilson and Mr. Bryan," he told Bryan's wife, "are suffering the fate of all the great Democratic characters from Jefferson down, of being belittled, besmirched, traduced, and tarnished by implacable enemies and false friends."[22]

Milton's reaction reveals the differences between his views and those of the other journalists. He endorsed the reforms of the Progressive Era, including Prohibition, and believed that only through perpetuation of the political alliances forged during that period could progressive liberalism survive. Thus, he maintained that southerners, on the whole, remained progressive in their political attitudes. His loyalty to McAdoo reinforced this tendency to downplay the activities of the Ku Klux Klan or of single-issue pressure groups, such as the Anti-Saloon League. Rather, McAdoo's defeat and Bryan's humiliation convinced him that the old Progressive forces were under attack and put him on the defensive.

Meanwhile, for Johnson and his fellow journalists the Progressive Era's legacy had turned sour. Woodrow Wilson's prestige, while still high in the South, had come under a cloud as Americans decided that clever propaganda had tricked the nation into entering World War I. The harsh criticism, from Mencken and others, of Wilson's disrespect for civil liberties during the war, at least silenced the journalists if it did not change their opinions of the president. Another legacy of the reform era, Prohibition, seemed to them an unnecessary restriction on liberty, enacted and enforced by narrow-minded fanatics. More important, the rise of the Ku Klux Klan and agitation for antievolution laws seemed proof that majority opinion in the South favored bigotry and willful ignorance. They saw themselves as a minority under attack; political action was the tactic of their enemies. Thus, the Scopes trial reinforced their defensive fears, too.

Despite the differences between Milton and the other journalists, their discussion of southern politics in the years preceding the 1928 election focused on a common topic: the phenomenon of the Solid South. All dismissed the Republican party as irredeemably tied to wealth and privilege; they concluded that the Democratic party alone provided a vehicle for liberal policies, and that the South, solidly Democratic, would have a major role to play in such a party. Yet the region's one-party system kept "reactionary" politicians, Republican in all but party label, within the Democratic fold.[23]

The journalists' explanation for the Solid South justified this situation and prevented them from acting to change it. They believed that Reconstruction, when the newly enfranchised freedmen voted for the Republican party, and the defeated white South fought back to dominance through the Democratic party, had bound the region to a single party. That experience remained oppressively powerful in the collective memory of the South; fear of the Negro voter remained close to the surface in southern thinking.[24]

In an essay written in 1925, before a Smith candidacy seemed likely, Johnson expressed this interpretation of the Solid South at its most pessimistic. Within the Democratic party, the West and the North—he made reference to the McAdoo-Smith battle of 1924—fought to nominate a candidate. Then the South handed its votes to the winner. The region's vote "is always counted and never counts," he complained. "It is dead." Johnson could conceive of no solution to this problem. The South voted Democratic because of a "social question," the only answer to which was the maintenance of white supremacy.[25]

In contrast to Johnson's pessimism, Louis I. Jaffé presented the southern liberal viewpoint at its most optimistic in an essay on "The Democracy and Al Smith" for *The Virginia Quarterly Review* in 1927. The essay made him one of the first southern editors to endorse Smith's candidacy, but allies joined him quickly. Julian Harris reprinted the entire article, in three installments, on the *Enquirer-Sun's* editorial page. Virginius Dabney expressed his agreement with

Jaffé's conclusions immediately after reading the essay. Two years later, he recalled it to Jaffé, saying that it "gave me a bigger kick than any magazine article I have ever read."[26]

In America, Jaffé argued, "the basic political competition must be . . . between those whose hard lot in life impels them to seek new formulas for the management of Government, Wealth, and Justice, and those whose easier lot in life impels them to defend and expand the status quo." Yet the Democratic party sought the allegiance of the latter group and thus differed little from the Republican party. Party competition continued only "because political life, like animal life, must have two sexes." The South bore especial blame for this situation. The party there was "essentially Bourbon" and its leaders purposely discouraged political participation so as to keep "the electorate . . . ringed and ruled."[27]

The nomination of Smith might change this. In the first place, the Democratic party as a whole required "the healing ventilation of its religious and moral fixations that must precede national rehabilitation." In the South, moreover, the excitement of an election campaign with Smith as the candidate would bring out the voters in great numbers. An expanded electorate promised to break up the Bourbon "political monopoly" and bring about "an alignment of the South's voters on the basis of living principles instead of the basis of inherited fears." With Prohibition and anti-Catholicism put to rest, the Democratic party could return to the living principles of individual liberty, separation of church and state, and state rights.[28]

Milton, too, foresaw a "political shakeup" in the South in the event of a Smith candidacy. In September 1927, after Milton addressed an open letter to him, calling for a declaration of his intentions, McAdoo withdrew from the race, opening the way for Al Smith to become the party's nominee. Now the South no longer looked Solid. In fact, Milton declared that "compared to the rock-ribbed Republican North, the Solid South is a quivering mass of political jelly, a quite insubstantial foundation upon which to build Tammany's White House hopes." Smith could not carry the South with "his dripping wet views, his Tammany background and environment, and his general Manhattan point of view." Milton foresaw this split in the South bringing benefits to the region: it might lead to a two-party system and certainly would demonstrate that the national Democratic party could not take the South's votes for granted.[29]

Thus, Milton and Jaffé arrived at the same point of view on the Solid South. Unable to rise above the racial orthodoxy that justified Democratic supremacy below the Potomac, they had to hope for a political cataclysm, in the form of Al Smith, to challenge the political status quo of the South. Indeed, Jaffé preceded his bright expectations for a realignment of the South's voters with the assurance that "the Caucasian instinct" would prevent such a split from having "racial complications."[30] Rather than marking a new day for southern politics, however, the election of 1928 proved a disaster for southern liberalism.

The presidential campaign of 1928 has become famous in American political lore. The Democratic party chose Alfred E. Smith as its nominee and set off a furious campaign of anti-Catholicism. Although Smith's religion undoubtedly hurt his candidacy, historians also point out the similarity of the two parties on economic policy and argue that Republican claims of responsibility for "Prosperity" made success for any Democratic candidate, Catholic or not, unlikely. At the time, however, a Hoover victory hardly seemed so inevitable. In April 1927, for example, Grover C. Hall offered a sporting proposal to Jaffé: "I am," he wrote, "now offering to bet $1 even that Al will be nominated and $1.25 against $1 that if nominated he will be elected."[31]

Milton, too, took Smith's prospects seriously. Long before the campaign opened, the *Chattanooga News* began an editorial barrage against Smith's candidacy. Almost daily throughout 1928, editorials developed anti-Smith arguments of several interlocking parts, first citing the sanctity of the Eighteenth Amendment, next damning the evils of Tammany Hall, then questioning Smith's qualifications for the presidency, and finally appealing to antiurban and antiimmigrant prejudices. In fact, the *News*'s obsession with Smith became so obvious that Milton even ran an editorial satirizing the paper's tendency to transform a discussion of a rainy day into an attack on Smith's wet views.[32]

The most important theme of Milton's editorial campaign was Prohibition, "that great social, economic, political and moral issue." The Democratic convention that year did endorse a platform plank promising strict enforcement of Prohibition, but the candidate rebelled. Smith sent a telegram to the convention declaring his intention to continue his criticism of the law. The *News* believed he had tossed down the gauntlet. If Smith chose "to make the demolition of prohibition the issue of this campaign," against the party's platform, then party members owed him no loyalty. Above all, the *News* considered Prohibition a question of principle. With Smith and his followers in control, it lamented, "the Democratic party shall go wrong on a great moral issue."[33]

Around this central theme of Prohibition's virtues swirled the dark currents of prejudice. One of Milton's editorials labeled Smith "the favorite candidate of the mongrel hordes of the east" and another claimed that "he and his policies are repugnant to [the nation's] best sentiments and traditions." Such statements undoubtedly conveyed a veiled anti-Catholicism to many of his readers, but throughout the campaign Milton and the *News* denounced attacks based on Smith's religion. The issue was "Rum, not Rome." Editorials protested— perhaps overmuch—that religious hatred should not be a factor in politics. At any rate, manipulation of xenophobia and prejudice remained secondary to the Prohibition issue in the *News*'s anti-Smith crusade.[34]

The other journalists sought to counter these arguments by convincing voters that Smith, despite his religion and background, stood squarely in the tradition of the Democratic party and the South. The 1928 presidential campaign encouraged a major step toward development of a useable southern liberal interpretation of history. Defending a presidential candidate from New York, an Irish-American and a Catholic, the journalists discovered in their regional past a tradition that they could assert against Smith's southern opponents. Jaffé made the conflict explicit on the eve of the election: "Are the voters of Virginia going into partnership with the Ku Klux Klan to repudiate the state's past and jeopardize its future? . . . Are we going to betray George Mason, James Madison and Thomas Jefferson and take to our hearts the teachings of the cyclops and the kleagles?"[35]

The tradition that the journalists enlisted for battle bore devotion to individual liberty as its shield and wielded the principle of state rights as its sword. This aged southern political concept proved most effective in protests against the Eighteenth Amendment. Smith's public dissatisfaction with Prohibition angered southern drys such as Milton, but state-rights orthodoxy enabled liberals to place Smith's views within southern tradition. Jaffé, for example, argued that when the Democratic party accepted federal Prohibition, the principle of state rights "was definitely 'sold down the river.'"[36]

Northern opponents of Prohibition used the state rights arguments to mock the southern drys for insisting on strict enforcement of the Eighteenth Amendment while approving nullification of the Fourteenth and Fifteenth Amendments guaranteeing citizenship rights to blacks. In 1927, Milton attempted to answer these charges. He put forth the customary southern arguments: a veiled assertion of black inferiority, references to the horrors of Reconstruction, and the crushing fact that southern suffrage laws, with their restrictive provisions applying equally to blacks and whites, had met the Supreme Court's standards of constitutionality. Thus, he concluded triumphantly, northerners could not use "the spectre of Negro domination" to force southerners into a "corrupt bargain" permitting nullification of the Eighteenth Amendment.[37]

In this essay, Milton predicted increased black voting in "the next generation." He counted himself among those southerners who believed that the Negro "would be a greater asset if he were trained for political, legal, and economic equality with the Whites." Unfortunately, in the cities, North and South, blacks tended to cast "their ballots in bloc at the bidding of a local political machine." The black vote, Milton claimed, "has hitherto served merely as a tool for debauching elections, and maintaining corrupt and unfit men in power." With that, Milton had clearly, if unconsciously, equated black voters with the "dense masses of newly naturalized immigrant voters" who maintained political machines such as Al Smith's Tammany Hall.[38]

Smith's southern liberal defenders ignored his background in urban politics. Through their identification of Smith with the Jeffersonian tradition, the journalists abstracted the candidate into an embodiment of southern liberal principles. Moreover, unlike Milton, they stood for state rights and condemned the Eighteenth and the Fourteenth and Fifteenth Amendments with equal vigor. Jaffé equated southern clergymen who organized against Smith with a hypothetical group of New England ecclesiastics, "members of a society against racial discrimination," organizing to lead northern Democrats out of a party that nullified the Fourteenth and Fifteenth Amendments. Similarly, Johnson compared "the dry fanatics" in the South with the abolitionists. Their numbers were few, he warned, "yet they produced a war that all but wrecked the nation."[39]

Although these journalists never appealed to prejudice as palpably as did Milton with his references to the "mongrel hordes" of the eastern cities, some welcomed southern racism as an aid to Smith. In July, Johnson predicted that "the mental picture of raids conducted by Negro prohibition enforcement agents" would hold the Klan in Smith's camp. Grover C. Hall argued that Smith would win in the South because of weak Republican organization and because of the "social necessity" of solid Democratic voting.[40] Their crusade for Smith caused these journalists to hope for a Solid South in 1928.

Smith lost the election, and five southern states—Florida, North Carolina, Virginia, Tennessee, and Texas—cast their votes for Hoover. Historians argue that "the strength of the Democratic presidential vote varied directly with the ratio of Negro to white." Hoover's votes came from predominantly white counties, in particular "the industrial and 'native-white' regions of the Appalachian mountains" and the Piedmont, while the conservative black belts, rural, agricultural counties with large, nonvoting black populations, remained loyal to the Democratic party and to Smith. The journalists perceived none of the irony in this result. Indeed, Grover C. Hall found solace in the observation that Smith's 7,000-vote majority in Alabama "came out of the counties in which The Advertiser has the bulk of its circulation."[41]

The defeat hurt most of all because they had seen Smith's candidacy as a symbol of the cause of liberalism in the South. Thus, they concluded afterward that the votes for Hoover were, as Jaffé put it, votes "for political clericalism, Kluxery, and reaction." The journalists agreed with W. J. Cash's contention that the election of 1928 showed "not that the mind of the South had changed, but that it was unchanged." The election results reconfirmed their low opinion of the southern electorate and convinced them that a liberalizing political movement in the South was but a hopeless dream. "Obscurantism is in the saddle and is riding hard," wrote Johnson after the election.[42]

Meanwhile, George Fort Milton had acted on principle and moved the *Chattanooga News* to open endorsement of Herbert Hoover. The *News* observed Hoover's progress toward the nomination with pleasure but remained carefully noncommittal until early October. The

Republican candidate visited Tennessee and made an address at the new factory town of Elizabethton on the 6th, and Milton attended. Hoover spoke in general terms on several topics, including the need for development of the nation's waterways. In Norfolk, Jaffé dismissed the oration as "Platitudinarianism at its Best." For Milton, though, Hoover's speech was sufficient to bring the *News* into open opposition to Smith's candidacy. Without quite endorsing the Republican, the editorial praised his stand on three issues: Prohibition, international peace, and water power.[43]

Three weeks later, when the *News* finally declared for Hoover, editorials emphasized Prohibition and principle. On 26 October, an editorial presaged the endorsement with the assertion that "there are occasions when principle must be put paramount to partisan regularity." On election eve, the *News* declared that voters faced "a choice of men—and of moralities." The *News* chose Hoover, "a better Democrat, an abler administrator, and a better man."[44]

After the election, Milton turned to hard work on the Andrew Johnson biography, which he published on 19 November 1930, his thirty-sixth birthday. In the book, *The Age of Hate: Andrew Johnson and the Radicals*, Milton argued that Johnson was "one of the neglected great of our political history." For Milton, the source of this greatness lay in Johnson's uncompromising refusal "to surrender what seemed to him essential public principles."[45]

Gerald W. Johnson also tried his hand at biography in the late 1920s. Unlike Milton, who mined manuscript collections and hoped for serious attention from scholars as well as from laymen, Johnson wrote with a breezy, flippant style and without extensive research. Differences in method aside, a comparison of his works with Milton's reveals again the gulf between their attitudes. In his biographies of Andrew Jackson and John Randolph of Roanoke, Johnson emphasized actions and their results rather than morality and principle. For example, he wrote that Jackson's appeal to mass sentiments during his war with the Bank of the United States was "far from altogether admirable, but it had one advantage which no amount of moralistic opposition could counter-balance—it worked."[46]

The necessities of Milton's plea for Andrew Johnson's greatness prevented him from following Gerald W. Johnson's example. The Tennessean's presidency was a tale of political defeat, congressional impeachment, and near conviction, not a series of actions justifiable by their success. Instead, as his title, *The Age of Hate,* suggested, Milton argued that the triumph of the Radicals over Johnson opened the way for the evils of the Reconstruction of the South. Johnson's principled opposition to the Radicals, regardless of his failure, won him glory. Ironically, in Milton's portrayal, the principle that Johnson clung to most rigidly was state rights, the very doctrine that opponents of Prohibition brandished against the Eighteenth Amendment. Gerald W. Johnson, whose scathing references to moralists had obvious contemporary application, observed in his biography of John Randolph that "the cycle of history has swung the doctrine of States' Rights into prominence again."[47] Although Milton failed to see the irony, his biography of a state rights advocate who opposed the Prohibitionists of his day marked a beginning for his own gradual retreat from his principled stand of 1928. The turning point came in 1933 with the repeal of the Eighteenth Amendment as Milton worked on his second book, a biography of Stephen A. Douglas; with that, Milton joined Johnson and the other journalists in the conviction that moralism and liberalism had nothing in common.

Although he cited Milton's biography of Andrew Johnson in his chapter on literature, Virginius Dabney excluded Milton's newspaper from *Liberalism in the South.* He penciled a note to himself that "Milton is as hysterical in defense of prohibition as Wayne Wheeler [general counsel and chief lobbyist for the American Anti-Saloon League] himself." Backed by the similar opinions of Gerald W. Johnson and Grover C. Hall, Dabney ignored the *News* in his chapter on liberal journalism. Instead, he praised Chattanooga's morning paper, the *Times*—the "Tammany Times" in *News* editorials from 1928—for its devotion to "the rights of the states" and its support for Al Smith.[48]

The political strife of 1928 powerfully influenced Dabney's exposition of *Liberalism in the South.* For example, he devoted three chapters to the separation of church and state, and the rest of the book abounded with uncomplimentary references to reactionary clergymen. Throughout southern history, he indicated, courageous liberals had resisted the efforts of ecclesiastics to dominate and to constrict intellectual inquiry.[49]

Appropriately, then, Dabney identified the origins of southern liberalism with Thomas Jefferson, whose shade had hovered protectively over candidate Smith in Dabney's editorial-page columns. According to Dabney, liberalism, arising with the American Revolution, represented a third force in American history that stood opposed to both "the theocracy of the North and the aristocracy of the South." Under the leadership of "the tawny-haired planter from Albemarle," liberalism had inspired the forging of the new nation.[50]

He then turned to the Old South and divided its history into two periods, the first of which was "The Era of Jefferson." A period of liberal decline, "The Era of Calhoun," followed. The defense of slavery against abolitionist attacks brought restrictions on free speech and intellectual freedom. Irritated by abolitionist goads, even southerners "who disapproved of slavery" turned on their attackers and "became apologists for the system."[51]

While he acknowledged that without slavery the Civil War would not have occurred, Dabney insisted that "the thesis that the South went to war to perpetuate the chattel system is scarcely tenable." Rather, southerners believed that "the integrity of state rights was threatened" from outside the region and "the only alternative, they felt, was secession and war." In light of the prominence that he gave to state rights as a guiding principle for southern liberals, this contention almost transformed the war into a struggle for liberalism. Nonetheless, Dabney showed that liberalism, which he identified with the southern antislavery movement, had suffered defeat in the Old South. Slavery had endured.[52]

A thesis of liberal failure had crucial implications. In the first place, as Dabney's treatment of secession exhibited, it raised uncomfortble questions about the Confederacy and the Lost Cause. More important, though, the idea of failure led to the conclusion that it had required the intervention of northerners to solve the antebellum "Negro problem," to abolish slavery. Failure in the past also implied that contemporary southern liberals alone could not solve the Negro problem, and northerners might be justified in applying force to the South again.[53]

In his biography of Andrew Johnson, George Fort Milton offered a historiographical way out. When secession came in 1861, Johnson cast his lot with the Union, not with the North or the South. Through the example of Johnson, Milton intimated that during the 1850s an alternative, Unionism, had existed for southerners unable to agree with abolitionist strictures on the South nor with the extremity of secession. In this book, however, the argument remained undeveloped.

Johnson not only made no criticism of slavery, but he also argued against secession on the grounds that "our Southern institutions depend on the continuance of the Union." Milton passed over these utterances without comment. Andrew Johnson's style of Unionism could not solve the problem of slavery.[54]

During Reconstruction again Johnson occupied middle ground between sectional extremes. Where Unionism had separated him from the antebellum southern fire-eaters, devotion to state rights now separated him from the postbellum Radical Republicans. In his treatment of Johnson's presidency, Milton focused on the issue of suffrage for the freedmen. The Radicals passed laws to ensure black rights, and Johnson vetoed them. Milton argued that Andrew Johnson had no objections to enfranchising Negroes—he simply believed in the principle that the states, not the federal government, should determine suffrage qualifications.

This contention that Andrew Johnson, first as Unionist and then as state rights advocate, offered an alternative to northern and southern extremes on the issues of secession and black rights expressed an early version of what would become the shared historical interpretation of the journalists. While they could still blame the North for Reconstruction, they could not defend the Old South's proslavery stand nor the doomed attempt at secession. The surrender at Appomattox had proved those positions untenable. Therefore, the journalists sought a southern liberal alternative to the events of that period, rejecting the idea of historical inevitability and conjuring up visions of what might have happened. Milton set the precedent with his argument that had Johnson's desire for extension of the ballot only to qualified blacks become acceptable to both the white South and the Radicals, the horrors of Reconstruction need not have occurred.[55]

Because they wholeheartedly accepted southern orthodoxy on the evils of Reconstruction, the journalists rarely wrote on that period except in vague generalizations about corruption and chaos. At bottom, though, they assumed that voting and participation in government by the freedmen constituted the main source of disorder. History seemed to prove the validity of southern resistance to Negro suffrage in the present.

Interestingly, events of the 1920s, in particular the 1928 election, made the journalists more willing to endorse the right to vote for some blacks. In *Liberalism in the South,* Dabney argued that demagogues, "who usually capitalized on the race issue and looked to the lower class whites for their support," represented "the most striking feature of the political scene in the South since the turn of the century." Because racist appeals to white solidarity benefited the demagogues whom they loathed, the journalists began to downplay the significance of race and emphasized education and responsibility as the most important qualifications for voting. For example, when Dabney proposed that blacks who could meet educational and poll tax requirements be allowed to vote, he based his argument on the assertion that "an educated and respectable Negro is a greater asset to the community and more deserving of the franchise than an unlettered swineherd from the pine barrens."[56]

Although the fight against anti-Catholicism in 1928 taught the journalists the falsehood of prejudice, anger and despair at the "antics" of the demagogues and their lower-class followers, not conversion to racial egalitarianism, carried Dabney to his declaration that "the contention that a white man, no matter how degraded, is innately superior to a black man, no matter how intelligent and respectable . . . is absurd on its face."[57] The 1928 election seemed to show that the impoverished and uneducated white southern lower class, not the Negro, represented the gravest danger to efforts to liberalize the South. At the same time, however, southern liberals who disapproved of the political choices of poor, uneducated white southerners were hardly likely to feel much enthusiasm for increasing the political participation of poor, uneducated black southerners.

On 22 October 1932, after reading his new copy of *Liberalism in the South*, Louis I. Jaffé sent a congratulatory letter to Dabney. At the letter's close, Jaffé expressed the opinion that "the most dangerous ogres of academic, political and religious obscurantism are dead in the South, albeit a few are still breathing and troublesome." These could be managed, he thought. Now southern liberals must confront "unfinished business," including "the intolerance of entrenched economic Bourbonism in the face of new and determined social forces demanding more protection and a larger share of the usufructs of industry for the worker" and "the South's tragically perplexing race problem." Here, he declared, were "the battlegrounds that beckon to those who are to have an honored place in the sequel to 'Liberalism in the South.'"[58]

Indeed, by 1932 the primary issues facing southern liberals had changed from those of the 1920s. The Ku Klux Klan had lost its political puissance through scandal and incompetent leadership. Fundamentalist militance had dissipated after the Scopes trial, while Smith's defeat in 1928 had defused the issue of Catholicism in the South. Although Prohibition still existed, even in the South sentiment for repeal seemed ever stronger. The journalists could conclude with Dabney that the tide had turned against ecclesiastic political domination.[59]

The change began soon after the 1928 election. In the summer and fall of 1929, violent conflicts between labor and management in the southern textile mills raised new issues that challenged the journalists to reconsider their primary emphasis on individual and cultural liberty. Moreover, the stock market crash that year led to severe economic depression, and hard times occupied the attention of all. Southern liberals awoke to problems of poverty and suffering that the smoke from the battles of the previous decade had obscured.

The transition in southern liberal thought, however, began with the response to an intellectual challenge from within the South. In 1930 a group of "Twelve Southerners," headed by John Crowe Ransom and Donald Davidson, who had spurned Edwin Mims's proposals for a liberal defense of the South after the Scopes trial, published *I'll Take My Stand: The South and the Agrarian Tradition.* Dabney, Milton, and their colleagues rejected the argument of the book. The ensuing debates with the Nashville Agrarians, as the Twelve Southerners became known, enabled them to discover the South of rural poverty.

4 About Face or Forward March?

In the aftermath of the Scopes trial, as the journalists turned their attention to the candidacy of Alfred E. Smith, three poets associated with Vanderbilt University, who previously had been concerned only with their art, determined to defend their southern loyalties. The character of their defense quickly revealed itself. "Our cause is, we have all sensed this at the same moment, the Old South," John Crowe Ransom told Allen Tate. He continued: "Our fight is for survival, and it's got to be waged, not so much against the Yankees, as against the exponents of the New South." Likewise, Tate announced to Donald Davidson that he had "attacked the South for the last time, except in so far as it may be necessary to point out that the chief defect the Old South had was that in it which produced, through whatever cause, the New South." Davidson responded enthusiastically, "You know that I'm with you on the anti–New South stuff."[1]

Through essays, books, poems, and discussions, the trio developed their defense and drew like-minded colleagues to their enterprise. They soon determined to spread their views to a larger audience. In 1930, Ransom, Tate, Davidson, and nine collaborators—the Twelve Southerners—published their manifesto, *I'll Take My Stand: The South and the Agrarian Tradition.* Tate had proposed that the group go on to form "an academy of Southern positive reactionaries," an institution that would maintain the battle lines drawn in the book; "in short," he wrote, "this program would *create an intellectual situation interior to the South.* I underscore it because, to me, it contains the heart of the matter."[2]

I'll Take My Stand did create just such a situation. Liberal journalists accepted the Agrarians' challenge and responded with essays and reviews objecting to nearly every count in the book's indictment of modern society. Although their criticisms originated with the arguments that they had made in the 1920s against southern intolerance, the debates with the Agrarians changed the journalists' outlook. Well before the inauguration of the New Deal, they began to turn away from their liberalism of the 1920s, with its emphasis on the liberty of the individual, and committed themselves, as southern liberals, to the solution of the South's economic problems in the public interest.

Differing interpretations of southern and human history lay at the heart of the debates. The journalists put forward an anti-Agrarian interpretation that assumed continuity and progress, even in the South. Where the Agrarians insisted that the situation required radical action to halt the spread of industrialism and recreate the humane agrarian community of the past, their opponents conceived their own role to be that of public-spirited guides for the South as it progressed toward an inevitable urban and industrial future.

The Twelve Southerners became known as the Nashville or Vanderbilt Agrarians because of the city and university where the group's leaders lived and worked. Their enterprise—at least that of the leading figures—had begun with poetry. In order to have an outlet for their writing they decided to publish a magazine, the first issue of which appeared in 1922; its title, *Fugitive*, gave the group its name. The reception of the publications of the Fugitives helps to explain the angry reaction of these future Agrarians to the Scopes trial in 1925. They thought of themselves as artists, concerned with poetry as an art form, but observers enlisted them into the southern liberal uprising against the benighted South. Their Vanderbilt colleague Edwin Mims, for example, included them in his *The Advancing South* as proof of southern intellectual progress. From the poets' viewpoint, these writers valued their poetry only insofar as it could be considered progressive, not on its merits as art. Tate complained to Davidson that Mims "doesn't see that, although a body of liberal opinion is necessary, the first duty of a society is to produce first class minds, liberal or illiberal."[3] They soon concluded that southern liberals, narrow-minded and complacent, were ashamed of the virtues of the South and indifferent to the dangers of the progress that they celebrated.

Their response, the book *I'll Take My Stand*, began with a statement of principles to which all twelve authors subscribed. The enemy, they declared, was "industrialism," an economy that taught men to despise honest labor and that increased the production of material commodities beyond any actual human needs. In industrial society, with nature "transformed into cities and artificial habitations" and with men holding "the illusion of having power over nature," neither religion nor the arts could survive. Moreover, in place of the concrete, industrialism substituted the spurious abstractions of social science. With that, the authors insisted, the individual disappeared and the collective organization of society triumphed. "The trouble with the life-pattern," the statement concluded, "is to be located at its economic base." In the place of industrialism, then, people should turn to an agrarian economy, which "does not stand in particular need of definition." Agrarianism proposed an "economic preference" for agriculture and a rejection of "superfluous industries."[4]

One must depend heavily on this statement of principles to summarize the argument of *I'll Take My Stand* because the individual essays differ and even contradict one another. For all the differences, though, one theme reappeared in every essay: even in 1930, the South represented the nearest approach to the desired community of Agrarianism. Each of the Twelve carried his argument into the smoky heart of industrialism, enumerated the failings of that economy, and then returned to a South free from its evils. The initial paragraph of the statement of principles foreshadowed this approach. All Twelve first declared their allegiance to "a Southern way of life against what may be called the American or prevailing way" and only then stated that the terms "Agrarian versus Industrial" best represented this distinction.[5]

The Twelve Southerners' view of the South, not their critique of industrialism, became the focus of critical response to the book, especially below the Potomac. Southern critics interpreted the book, as Ralph McGill put it, as "a symposium in defense of the south and the agrarian tradition."[6] Perhaps the Twelve welcomed that. Certainly, they charged their southern critics with treason to the regional heritage. As a result, the debate between the Agrarians and southern liberals centered on the nature of the South in the present and in the past.

When the Agrarians began planning their "symposium on Southern matters" in early 1929, they apparently hoped to lead a united South against the industrial North. Ransom and Davidson drew up a list of potential contributors that included liberal journalists such as Julian Harris, Grover C. Hall, Louis I. Jaffé, Gerald W. Johnson, and Stringfellow Barr of *The Virginia Quarterly Review*. Davidson later said that the list showed "how catholic our intention, or how great our innocence of mind, was in those days." Quickly they learned that their southern orthodoxy seemed to others the rankest heresy. Only Johnson and Barr actually received invitations to join, and the former spurned the offer "with a curt jocular quip." Barr responded more seriously with an outline of his thoughts on the southern economy, but the group found his ideas unacceptable and banished him from their enterprise. The Agrarians contacted none of the others on their list. The first battle, they now realized, would take place below the Potomac. Their book's statement of principles observed that some southerners seemed willing to embrace industrialism and declared, "it is against that tendency that this book is written."[7]

On 5 September 1930, with the book still more than two months away from publication, Davidson informed Tate that there was "some excitement already in the air." George Fort Milton had learned of the forthcoming Agrarian manifesto and devoted a lead editorial in the *Chattanooga News* to its argument. As would other southern liberal critics, Milton contended that whereas the book raised crucial questions, it offered no practical answers. Agreeing that "industrialization"—a revealing change of words from the Agrarians' "industrialism"—was "probably the South's most formidable present problem," the editorial complained that the Twelve proposed only "the impossible medicant of turning back the clock." For that reason, Milton gave them the derisive title "The Young Confederates."[8]

Milton's concluding note of ridicule was echoed in the initial reactions of other journalists to the Agrarian thesis. The Agrarians were identified not only with the late Confederacy but also, and more often, with the Ku Klux Klan, fundamentalists, and Prohibitionists. That is, the journalists responded to *I'll Take My Stand* from the perspective they had developed in the battles of the 1920s. Agrarianism represented another example of that dangerous southern tendency to allow emotional loyalties to divide the world between good and evil, and then to act according to moral imperatives. Gerald W. Johnson exploded in wrath at the Twelve Southerners' declaration that agrarian society "does not stand in particular need of definition." Here, he thought, was another example of the South's distaste for thinking. "Facts are the inconvenient things," he gibed. "Let us stick, rather, to emotions."[9]

Harsh words alone, however, could not silence the Agrarians. In fact, Ransom, Tate, and Davidson carried the battle to their critics. After his excommunication from Agrarianism, Stringfellow Barr expanded his outline into an essay that he published in the *Virginia Quarterly Review* a month before *I'll Take My Stand* appeared. He argued that, since industry had already come to the South, southerners must exercise their traditional "social responsibility" to ensure that the region did not suffer the sordid conditions that early industrialization had brought to England and New England. The Agrarian triumvirate, in an open letter to the quarterly and to several southern newspapers, provocatively attacked Barr's essay as a repudiation of the true southern heritage.[10]

Shortly after their letter appeared, George Fort Milton visited the *Virginia Quarterly Review*'s office and "suggested in a jocular way that a debate ought to be arranged." Lambert Davis, the quarterly's managing editor, thought it a fine idea and sent a challenge off to Nashville. After the *Richmond Times-Dispatch* offered to sponsor a confrontation in the Virginia capital, Ransom agreed to meet Barr there on 14 November 1930. Apparently unaware of these developments, Milton proposed in the *News* a debate between the "Young Confederates" and the "Young Virginians," whom he identified with the quarterly. "In any event," he declared, "the question has been stated, the agenda for the South's intellectual debate for the next few years has been prepared."[11]

Once he learned of the Richmond confrontation, Milton began planning to stage another debate in Chattanooga. He also did his part to make the Richmond debate a success. He hired Donald Davidson as a special correspondent for the *News*, so that the latter could afford the expense of accompanying Ransom to Virginia. At the same time, he offered assistance to Barr in his preparations. Declaring his conviction that Ransom was "utterly devoid of humor," he suggested that "a few shafts of biting irony" would have good effect.[12]

Although he later claimed that he had entered the debate primarily to publicize the quarterly, Barr took the clash more seriously than did Milton. He and Ransom would speak to a large and prestigious audience. The *Times-Dispatch* drummed up attention with a week of front-page stories, and on the fourteenth, the City Auditorium's 3,500 seats were filled. Novelist Sherwood Anderson moderated, and the notables in attendance included the governor of Virginia and H. L. Mencken. Virginius Dabney was in Charlottesville and unable to attend, but Louis I. Jaffé of the *Norfolk Virginian-Pilot* motored up for the show.[13]

Four days earlier, Jaffé had recommended the debate—"the Southern kulturkampf"—to readers of the *Virginian-Pilot*. His editorial said that three schools of thought about industrialism existed in the South: one uncritically welcomed manufacturing to the region and enthused over "Science and the celebrated Higher Standard of Living"; the Agrarians voiced the second point of view; and the third school of thought, exemplified by Stringfellow Barr, Jaffé designated the "pragmatists." This last group of southerners recognized that industrialization of the South was irrevocable and that regulation was necessary to ensure its social responsibility. The editorial clearly placed the *Virginian-Pilot* in the pragmatist camp with its judgment that the Agrarians were "weeping for the moon."[14]

As Jaffé predicted, Barr contended at Richmond that simple considerations of practicality rendered Agrarianism impossible. For nearly an hour, Ransom exhorted the South to take up Agrarianism on the grounds that industrialism produced "a kind of life of which the human values are sorry and inferior." Barr then rose in rebuttal: since the South had already adopted the machine, he declared, the only reasonable question for debate was "how will it adopt it." To laughter and applause, he concluded his short statement with the recommendation that the Agrarians abandon "I'll Take My Stand" for "a motto more appropriate to their problem: 'Sit Down and Think!'" The debate ended, and supporters of both speakers flocked to the stage with congratulations.[15]

The large local audience and the press attention that followed inspired other public debates across the South. Ransom agreed to meet W. S. Knickerbocker, editor of the *Sewanee Review*, in New Orleans on 15 December, and, entering into the southern spirit of Agrarianism, he invited Tate to join him on his foray against "General Knickerbocker and his Yankee sympathizers." He met "Col. Barr, the Virginia renegade," again in Chattanooga on 9 February 1931, and afterward gathered with friends and enemies at the home of "the Republican General Milton" to continue the discussion into the night. A month later, he debated with William D. Anderson, president of the Bibb Manufacturing Company, in Atlanta. Following the debate, Anderson brought workers from his mills onto the stage. Ransom watched— one hopes with wry amusement—as "they entertained with songs and recitations." Davidson, too, entered the lists against Knicker-bocker in May at Columbia, Tennessee, and closed the public debates in 1936 at the annual meeting of the Southern Historical Association where he took on W. T. Couch, editor of the University of North Carolina Press, in "the feature session of the meeting." In addition to these public encounters, southern liberals and Agrarians continued the debate in scholarly journals, newspaper columns, and with pointed asides in works on other subjects.[16]

As the war of words continued through the 1930s, southern liberal critics of Agrarianism followed Barr's lead. Industry was already established in the region, Dabney wrote; the Nashville group had struck out on a "quixotic quest." They argued an "academic question," said Gerald W. Johnson. "The condition, not the theory, is that industrialism has arrived."[17]

Despite their enthusiasm for urban and industrial growth, however, the journalists refused to defend unqualified industrialism. During the negotiations leading to the Richmond debate, Barr proposed "Regulated Industrialism versus Agrarianism" as the topic for debate. Davidson quickly responded that his group preferred simply "Industrialism vs. Agrarianism" in order to provide "a fair field for contrasting arguments." Barr agreed to Davidson's title but did not change his argument. In fact, he admitted at the outset of his address that industrialization had wrought great evils in the past. That conceded, however, he went on to argue that should southerners delude themselves with the Agrarian "digression," very likely "all the agony and bloodshed which accompanied the coming of industrialism in other countries" would recur in the South. Unlike the Agrarians, who considered such miseries inherent to industrialism, Barr asserted that they resulted solely from men's "gross misuse of the machine." The liberal journalists, too, regularly prefaced their discussions with acknowledgment that the spread of industry posed difficult problems for the South. As Milton granted, there was "much of sound common sense to the pleas of these Nashville writers."[18]

Nonetheless, industry's potential benefits to the South outweighed its dangers. "It is largely by virtue of the South's industrial advance," Dabney said, "that the region is now sufficiently prosperous to begin . . . obliterating the evidences of backwardness which formerly cursed it." Therefore, southerners must guide industry with the civilizing restraints of legislation and regulation. "Industrialization can be an infinite blessing to the South," Milton wrote, "but it must be controlled in the public interest." Jaffé agreed: southerners must "impart into Southern industrialism a humaneness and social responsibility that will curb its rapacity and put it to decent uses."[19]

Behind this faith that southern social responsibility could tame industrialism stood the scholarly authority of Broadus Mitchell, a Virginia-born economist at Johns Hopkins University and the author in 1921 of *The Rise of Cotton Mills in the South*. Mitchell's history supplied the background for the journalists' thinking on industrialization in the South, and even after violent strikes in 1929 alerted them to labor exploitation in the mills, their prescriptions for reform reflected the continuing influence of his works. He identified 1880 as the date marking the beginning of the South's modern economic development. Freed from the economic stagnation of plantation slavery, the region turned to reunion and regeneration through industrial development, development "conceived and brought into existence by Southerners" themselves.[20]

Above all, Mitchell claimed, these mill builders desired to aid "the necessitous masses of the poor whites, for the sake of the people themselves." For him, "observation of Southern character," rather than "facts"—for he cited none—sufficed to prove the philanthropic motive. The key to his interpretation, however, was his conviction that the men responsible for the rise of the mills were "ex-Confederates," schooled on the antebellum plantation in the duties of noblesse oblige. This plantation heritage explained "the readiness of Southern men to realize and assume responsibility in public matters, and the spirit of social service which characterized the awakening" of industry in the New South.[21]

The contention that the old aristocracy's values guided the new economy provided Mitchell with a critical perspective on conditions in the present that, at least for his contemporaries, made the book more than merely a paean to the mill owners. Through the 1920s, he wrote numerous essays attacking the modern-day mill owners for their indifference to the "economic evolution" that made unionism necessary and beneficial. These articles earned him a reputation as "a leading Southern liberal," as Virginius Dabney dubbed him in *Liberalism in the South*. Ironically, his liberal credentials made his earlier interpretation of the rise of the cotton mills seem even more credible.[22]

In 1929, as the Agrarians organized their symposium, a wave of strikes rolled through the textile mills of the South. "It is enough to say that hell has pretty well broken loose, and the old story of labor fights is being repeated," Davidson told Tate. "It all means more ammunition for us."[23] In fact, the labor conflict alerted southern liberal journalists to the issues raised by *I'll Take My Stand* and prepared them to reply to the Agrarians. Their response to the labor strife suggests their familiarity with Mitchell's work.

The journalists condemned the mill owners' repressive tactics as violations of civil liberties and rejected the contention that alien agitators were responsible for the walk-outs of otherwise contented workers. Milton complained that state troops "served as a partisan arm of the management" during strikes at Elizabethton, Tennessee. Johnson told North Carolinians not to believe wild claims that the Communists caused all the turmoil; conditions in the textile industry there were a native product. "Innocent men were shot down in cold blood, and one innocent woman suffered the same fate because these employers refused then, and apparently refuse still, to read the times aright, and to recognize the right of labor to organize," Dabney asserted afterward.[24]

Rather than endorsing the strikes, however, the liberals called for cooperation to replace conflict and encouraged employers to recognize their social responsibilities. In the long run, such a policy would benefit all. Mass production required increased levels of consumption, and southern manufacturers who chose to depend on cheap labor for profits were not only digging their own graves but also holding back the entire South. As Milton contended, "from an economic standpoint, the future depends as largely on justice for workers as on any other thing."[25]

Such arguments exhibited much greater animosity toward reactionary owners than they did approval of the unions. Mark Ethridge observed that even southern liberal journalists sympathetic to labor "would much prefer to see the manufacturers do what manifestly must be done to meet the standards of economic and social justice without having to be forced into it." Thus, he said, they had given enthusiastic support to "the more enlightened manufacturers who are endeavoring to set in motion reforms to clean up shoddy economic conditions and to make possible better social conditions." Indeed, even Dabney, who argued in *Liberalism in the South* that "paternalism is now an outmoded approach to the problem of industrial adjustment," praised those manufacturers who were trying to reform their industry. Significantly, he said next to nothing about unions in his catalog of southern liberalism.[26]

The ghosts of Mitchell's heroic cadre of ex-Confederate mill promoters yet haunted the liberal journalists' thinking. Their discussions of industrial conflicts emphasized the need for cooperation between the owners and the workers. The South did not need unions so much as it needed socially responsible employers and public officials. Mitchell's history demonstrated that industrial progress and social responsibility had once gone hand in hand; under the guidance of southern liberalism they might do so once again.

For this reason, Ransom's charge in the Richmond debate that Stringfellow Barr treated the southern tradition "not at all as a prescription to live by, but as a gardenia to stick in his buttonhole when he goes travelling in New York" struck the journalists as a mere rhetorical flourish. The best traditions of the Old South not only survived the Civil War but, in the 1880s, tamed industrial development and turned it to the benefit of society. Southerners who upheld their tradition in the present ought to do as much. "The industrial system is simply too complicated for each man to act on his own," Barr said. Efforts to make this economy responsible must be put "on a community, not an individualistic, basis." Milton told the Agrarians that "intelligent social planning, rather than literary lectures, is demanded by the modern world."[27]

These convictions squared with the lessons liberals had learned during the 1920s, a period when they espoused individual liberty. They criticized their intolerant foes for lack of realism. The Prohibitionists, for example, celebrated the virtues of the dry laws while drunkenness and crime increased around them. Similarly, the Agrarians would protect the South from industrialism, even though industry had already come South to stay. "It will not be abolished, nor will its hands be set back out of respect to any theory whatever," Johnson said.[28]

The journalists preferred the empirical methods of the social scientist. The South must take a realistic, practical approach to its problems, they argued, and that required respect for facts, not devotion to a set of absolute principles. To solve the problem of industrialization, Johnson told the Agrarians, the South "must labor with facts. She must struggle drearily through tons of statistics, through endless miles of dull reports and dry analyses. She must eschew guessing and *know*."[29]

These arguments implied two related assumptions. Human reason, once unshackled from the restraints of prejudice and ignorance, could discern social problems and devise effective solutions to them. "Surely," Milton declared, "it would seem that a rational solution of any social problem could be reached after all the relevant facts have been studied."[30] Necessarily, then, no totally irreconcilable interests existed in society. After study of the facts, all reasonable men should be able to agree on the proper course of action. Useful social reform depended on reason and cooperation, not on ideology and conflict. Thus, as they entered the years of New Deal reforms and labor organizing in the South, the journalists espoused a program for economic development that had little room for labor initiative and less for conflict.

The contention that the South no longer could choose between industrialization and retention of an agrarian economy proved an effective tactic in the debates with the Agrarians. Rather than pitting "Industrialism vs. Agrarianism," as Davidson insisted the Richmond debate be titled, the journalists chose to discuss current conditions in the South. The Twelve Southerners had left themselves open to this tactic. The South of *I'll Take My Stand* appeared primarily as an image defined against industrialism, a "metaphor" in Louis D. Rubin's analysis, rather than an actual region in the United States of 1930. At the same time, though, the Twelve implied that this "South" corresponded closely to the South itself. Their critics denied the correspondence and, charging that the Agrarians ignored southern realities, forced them onto the defensive.[31]

In comparison to the recitals of the industrial economy's evils, the book did ignore the depressed state of agriculture and the sordid increase of farm tenancy in the contemporary South. Even Herman Clarence Nixon, "a populist fallen among conservatives" as George B. Tindall describes him, in his heavily factual essay on the southern economy said simply that "the tenant system" was but "a modified reproduction of the ante-bellum plantation with a new agrarian gentry in the making." Ransom himself suggested that such rural poverty as existed resulted from farmers giving themselves over too much to the leisure of agrarian life and thus performing "insufficient labor."[32]

Liberal critics struck hard at this vulnerable point. Agrarians made much of industrial overproduction, Barr charged at Richmond, but they said nothing of agricultural overproduction. How could Ransom urge the city-bound farmer to return to the land "where he cannot make a living?" After describing tenant farmers living "in the utmost squalor" and landowners barely able to hold their property, Dabney asked the same question. In a column for the *Times-Dispatch*, he detailed suffering among tenants in Arkansas and Mississippi. "What do the Nashville Agrarians think of this?" he asked. Johnson reviewed *I'll Take My Stand* for the *Virginia Quarterly Review* and angrily asked of the authors: "Have they never been told that the obscenities and depravities of the most degenerate hole of a cottonmill town are but pale reflections of the lurid obscenities and depravities of Southern backwoods communities?"[33]

The Nashville Agrarians did begin to think about the condition of the tenant farmer in the South, and in the following years Agrarianism narrowed to an emphasis on the independent small-property-owner as the foundation of liberty and democracy. In part, this development reflected the retirement from active Agrarianism of those among the Twelve Southerners who preferred the grandeur of the plantation and the grace of the aristocrat. Obviously, though, the critics had struck deeply with gibes that these ivory-tower agriculturalists knew nothing of the degraded conditions of southern farm life.

Even as they condemned Agrarianism's unreality, the journalists were also shifting their own views. During the 1920s they had tended to see southern problems as the product of rural ignorance, inflamed by clever demagogues and bigoted preachers. They now looked at the southern economy and saw a system of agriculture that perpetuated poverty and its consequences. The rural whites who joined the Klan or pushed the monkey bills were victims, they concluded, not villains. Both the southern liberals and the Agrarians came to view a bankrupt agriculture as the primary source of southern poverty.

Nonetheless, the war of words continued. For every Agrarian argument, the liberal journalists had a ready response. In 1935 Donald

Davidson, himself an ardent Agrarian polemicist, complained that the debates were leading nowhere because "the contending parties have too often argued in different terms."[34]

In retrospect, the Agrarians concluded that their critics had misunderstood the argument of *I'll Take My Stand*. As Frank Lawrence Owsley said, "by the use of the word 'Agrarian' we got tagged and everybody thought we ought to go out and plow. And this was a philosophy, not an economy." Critics, the group suggested, had wrongly restricted debate to narrow, programmatic grounds.[35]

The Twelve Southerners themselves, though, had established the terms of debate. Their philosophy and their economics arose from their interpretation of the South and its history. "With all its imperfections," Davidson said, "our native South was the best existing available model of the traditional society" that the group championed. Even Allen Tate, whom scholars judge the least southern of the Twelve, declared privately that the group "should have stood flatly on the immediately possible in the South." The Agrarians' identification of their cause with the South, as myth and as reality, inevitably turned debate to specific questions about Dixie, rather than to philosophy.[36]

At bottom, incompatible interpretations of southern history separated the liberal journalists from the Agrarians. The latter set forth the Old South as an exemplar of the Agrarian way of life. Historically, they argued, an unavoidable conflict with the industrial North resulted in war and the destruction of the Old South's civilization. The journalists responded that the Old South's agricultural economy, unsound as were all agrarian economies, had begun to collapse well before the Civil War. Evidence of industries emergent during this period revealed to them a process of economic evolution in the Old South. The Civil War delayed and distorted southern development, but hardly destroyed a unique civilization. Rather than an alien importation, as the Twelve Southerners claimed, industrial growth in the modern South actually represented a return to the healthy economic development that defeat in the Civil War had slowed.

For the Agrarians, southern history changed course with the Civil War. The antebellum South had established a rooted life grounded on land and agriculture. The North, however, developed fundamentally differently because, as Frank Lawrence Owsley said, it "was commercial and industrial." Thus, within the Union, "two divergent economic and social systems, two civilizations, in fact," struggled for dominance. "Southerners saw that what was good for the North was fatal to the South." The "irrepressible conflict" finally exploded into war, and the Old South, "the seat of an agrarian civilization which had strength and promise for future greatness second to none," fell before the triumphant industrial North. Since 1865, the South had struggled in poverty under oppression from her alien conqueror. The Agrarians called southerners to forswear industrialism and return to their true heritage.[37]

Portrayal of the Old South as a static community, finished with "pioneering" and established on the land, flowed from the Agrarians' conviction that the conception of time as linear and progressive was an artificial construct of industrialism. "Life is a timeless cycle, not a line," Davidson wrote, "and the agrarian life establishes man within that natural cycle, where he belongs." At the same time, depiction of a static Old South served their crusade in the present. As Davidson recalled, they believed that "some true and commanding image of [the South's] past must be restored." Thus, rather than deriving lessons for the present from history, the Agrarians presented the past itself, in the form of an image, as an ideal toward which to aim. With human slavery—"a feature monstrous enough in theory, but, more often than not, humane in practice"—dismissed as "no essential part of the agrarian civilization of the South," the Agrarians held forth the Old South for the modern South to admire and emulate.[38]

The journalists rejected the Agrarians' image of the Old South. They denied that the antebellum agrarian economy ever achieved stability or success. Dabney contended that the South "was economically decadent in 1860," and Johnson insisted that it "was swiftly crumbling into ruin long before the blast of war struck it."[39]

From the journalists' perspective, the Old South's economic decay appeared as irrepressible as the war between industrialism and agrarianism seemed to the authors of *I'll Take My Stand*. "No purely agrarian civilization can endure," Dabney stated. Johnson wrote that the Old South "was falling into ruin because no purely agrarian polity can maintain a fine civilization for any great length of time." In his 1929 biography of John Randolph of Roanoke, he explained the Virginian's extreme conservatism as the result of bad advice he had received from his mother. "The future was to belong," Johnson declared, "not to those Americans who clung stubbornly to their lands, but to those with the foresight and the energy to break new paths, to clear new fields in commerce and industry."[40]

As Johnson's declaration indicates, the journalists did believe in progress. Sometimes they revealed the belief unconsciously, as when Dabney, discussing southern education, employed "upward march" as a synonym for liberalism. Similarly, Milton entitled his proposal for a debate between the Agrarians and the liberals with the question: "About Face or Forward March?" Often this faith appeared implicitly, especially in references to the "frontier." Rather than an environment stimulating natural virtue, the frontier symbolized primitive, anti-social conditions. Milton, for example, explained lynch law in the Old South as a reflection of "the frontier mind." Indices of urban and industrial growth measured the distance from the frontier, and heralded the advance of progress.[41]

The Agrarians considered faith in progress the most typical, and most fallacious, of industrial doctrines. In fact, Lyle H. Lanier devoted his essay in *I'll Take My Stand* to "A Critique of the Philosophy of Progress." Progress, "perhaps the most widely advertised commodity offered for general consumption in our high-powered century," served to justify industrialism. Lanier claimed that "the conviction that our noisy social ferment portends progressive development toward some highly desired, but always undesignated, goal is perhaps the central psychological factor in the maintenance of our top-heavy industrial superstructure." Indeed, for the Agrarians, the concepts of progress and industrialism coincided. Neither defined its objective; each proposed instead "the infinite series." "Our progressivists," Ransom said, "are the latest version of those pioneers who conquered the wilderness, except that they are pioneering on principle, or from force of habit, and without any recollection of what pioneering was for."[42]

The conviction that an understanding of ends must precede a discussion of means enabled the Agrarians to make their ultimate criticism of the journalists. After Gerald W. Johnson scorned Agrarianism for its manifest impracticality, an infuriated Donald Davidson challenged him to "stop laughing for a minute and try to define his own liberalism. . . . Can he be a little more explicit about the 'glittering civilization' that he sees in his dreams?" Similarly, Allen Tate asked, "what kind of society do these men of the New South want?" So far as he could determine, he wrote, "our 'realistic' friends, the Liberals, get history to tell them what it is possible to do; it is invariably what they themselves want done. And what they want done is precisely what the drift of events will bring them."[43]

The journalists made no answer to these criticisms. Instead, they considered the Agrarian crusade merely an exercise in self-indulgent nostalgia. Johnson explained that "the Agrarians exhibit conspicuously the tendency of most romantics to imagine that the Golden Age belongs to the past; and so they drift toward sterility." Thus, when Davidson complained that southern liberals "never discuss general assumptions, but only specific remedies for specific ills," the journalists took it as praise. Their experiences in the 1920s had taught them the dangers of obeying absolute principles. Combining those lessons with their faith in the progressive direction of history, they stood on practicality and quickly dismissed Agrarianism. Only five years after the publication of *I'll Take My Stand*, Johnson spurned a suggestion that he write on the Agrarians for the *Virginia Quarterly Review*. "What credit is to be gained from beating up a blind man?" he asked.[44]

Nonetheless, the debates with the Agrarians did influence the thinking of the liberal journalists. In 1940, Virginius Dabney looked back on what he said had been "a decade of rediscovery" in the South and credited *I'll Take My Stand* with inspiring it: "The vigorous discussion of the past, present and future of the South which opened with the twelve agrarian theses, continued right on through the decade." By admonishing the Agrarians to view the South as it was, the liberal journalists obliged themselves to do the same and instead of the "benighted" or "advancing" South of the 1920s they discovered a complex and varied region. Renouncing doctrines, they argued that factual knowledge best enabled one to understand the South, and to prescribe for its ills.[45]

Undoubtedly, the uncompromising defense of the South in *I'll Take My Stand* appealed to feelings of regional patriotism that the battles of the 1920s had stifled. John Temple Graves, who called himself a liberal, said that *I'll Take My Stand* was one of his favorite books—yet he remained committed to "sound and permanent industrial development" as the best means to southern progress. The Twelve Southerners' "championship of a southern way of life" was what most appealed to Graves; for him, the Agrarians' "economics were not as important as their taste in living." Beyond stirring pride, *I'll Take My Stand* also had a liberating effect on southern liberalism. The Agrarian manifesto demonstrated that the South could be discussed without giving either apologies to northern opinion or obeisance to the Ku Klux Klan.[46]

W. J. Cash later contended that despite idealization of the Old South, the Agrarians had "from the first a good deal more realism in them" than had "any of the earlier apologists and idealizers." Especially he credited them with recognition of the significance of "the small landholding farmers—the yeomen."[47] That Cash himself held a high opinion of the yeoman's role in southern history no doubt influenced his judgment, but the Agrarians clearly did force the journalists to jettison stereotyped views of the South. They initially reacted to the arguments of *I'll Take My Stand* with almost reflexive references to the Klan and Prohibition. The debates with the Agrarians turned them to fresh study of conditions in the South.

Above all, the Agrarian debates brought economic problems to the center of the liberals' attention. During the six months before the Richmond debate, for example, Virginius Dabney in his weekly column wrote most often on the topic of Prohibition.[48] *I'll Take My Stand* ignored such issues as irrelevant in the face of the crucial question of the proper economy for the South.

When the journalists argued that Agrarianism could not solve the South's economic problems, they implied that liberalism could do so. Although not yet offering specific programs, in the course of the debates they did commit themselves to guiding the economic improvement of the region. The economic issues of the 1930s—rehabilitation of southern agriculture, labor organization, and regulation of industry—made their first appearance on the liberal journalists' agendas for reform during the Agrarian debates.

Moreover, the journalists made this commitment in response more to the Agrarians than to hard times. In their opinion, the most prominent political issue was still Prohibition, not action to restore prosperity. "About the depression [the Democrats] know that they can't do much," Johnson wrote. "No political party can do much about that." When Milton insisted that the issue in 1932 should be "Bread, Not Booze," it reflected more his fear that the Democrats would oppose Prohibition than the conviction that the depression required governmental action.[49] While labor struggles and hard times certainly sharpened the journalists' new focus on the southern economy, the Agrarian debates represented the passageway from the issues of the 1920s—individual liberty and cultural liberalism—to those of the reformist 1930s.

As the Depression deepened, the journalists continued to develop the economic proposals that they had first expressed in the debates with the Agrarians. From the Agrarians, who insisted that "the trouble with the life-pattern is to be located at its economic base," they gained the conviction that the South's problems originated in economic ills. They devoted their attention in particular to the rural South as the cotton tenancy system collapsed under the weight of drought and depression. A healthy agriculture would strengthen the essential urban and industrial growth that they foresaw in the southern future. Their expectation of social progress reinforced their insistence on practicality, with its consequent indifference to the discussion of ends. These convictions also bottomed their approach to problems of race relations.

5 Tilting the Color Line

Roland Hayes, whose parents were slaves and whose magnificent singing voice earned him international fame, returned to his native state in 1925 to perform in Atlanta. The Commission on Interracial Cooperation sponsored his performance at the city auditorium. City law required racial segregation, and blacks usually took poorer seats in the balcony. The CIC experimented: the auditorium was segregated vertically—half the seats from top to bottom were reserved for blacks, the other half for whites. No incidents marred the concert, and Hayes sang to an enthusiastic audience of 5,000. The CIC's executive director, Will Alexander, judged the concert a huge success. "While we had not broken the segregation taboo we had dented it," he recalled. "That was the first time I ever saw segregation that did not seem to discriminate." The CIC's seating arrangement symbolized the southern liberal program for race relations—a segregation that did not discriminate.[1]

The racial views of southern liberal journalists during the 1930s fit no simple pattern. By the close of the 1920s, scholars had challenged those verities—innate black inferiority and the biological origins of race prejudice—that had justified the Jim Crow system in the Progressive Era. The journalists followed their liberal colleagues and gradually incorporated the new, more flexible racial ideas into their own thinking on race relations. With their thoughts on this emotional issue in flux, however, they avoided specific statements of their racial views. The journalists supported the Commission on Interracial Cooperation, though, and they attempted, with other southern liberals, to tilt the color line toward the perpendicular.

The subject of race was not a part of the debates with the Nashville Agrarians. The authors of *I'll Take My Stand* viewed a racially segregated South as a given, and some of them expressed crude anti-Negro sentiments. The journalists raised no objections, for they also accepted racial segregation. The main reason that the journalists did not discuss the topic of race relations separately, however, was that they had incorporated it into their general conception of southern development. They contended that industrial and urban growth and economic progress were the dominant trends in the modern South, and that, as blacks moved to the cities and entered the industrial economy, race relations would change for the better.

The journalists' experiences in the 1920s convinced them that southern liberals could improve race relations without weakening segregation. The Commission on Interracial Cooperation set an influential example by working for more equitable treatment of blacks within the Jim Crow system. M. Ashby Jones, a prominent Baptist minister in Atlanta and one of the founders of the CIC, called on the white South to grant the Negro "his rights in the simple terms of humanity," but went on to assert that "the races should be separated by such social barriers as are necessary to preserve the purity of the blood of the two peoples." Similarly, Howard W. Odum's program for the North Carolina Interracial Conference proposed efforts to improve "the welfare of all the people," but insisted on "recognition by both races . . . of the permanence of separate race relationships." Rather than undermining segregation, wise reform could protect it.[2]

The issue of lynching dominated discussions of race relations in the 1920s and seemed to verify these expectations. Incidents of mob violence steadily decreased after 1900; between 1917 and 1919, however, as the Negro migration and a growing militant spirit frightened whites into repressive acts of murder, the number of lynchings doubled. By 1919, moreover, lynching victims were almost exclusively blacks. The National Association for the Advancement of Colored People had long fought the practice, and after World War I, with a massive lobbying effort, the NAACP managed to get Congressman Leonidas Carstarphen Dyer's antilynching bill to the floor of Congress before a southern filibuster in the Senate killed the measure.[3]

The campaign for a federal antilynching bill disturbed the journalists. The NAACP's effort to force the federal government to prosecute southern lynchers reminded the *Chattanooga News* of the abolitionists' crusade against slavery. The campaign, it charged, was in the "New England" tradition of interference in southern affairs. Present-day reformers had no more right than the abolitionists to tell the South how to treat the Negro, Johnson asserted. More calmly, he advised northerners to stop their attacks, which only provoked hostile reactions and made problems intractable. They should instead, he thought, encourage the South to develop a habit of self-criticism, for only southerners themselves could halt indigenous evils such as lynching.[4]

Mob violence declined sharply after 1922, however, and the threat of a federal antilynching bill soon dissipated. The *Chattanooga News* proudly announced at the end of 1924, a year in which only sixteen lynchings occurred compared to fifty-seven in 1922, that "the lynching evil is less in evidence now than at any time within the past generation." The decline seemed proof of great progress in race relations. In contrast to "the South's conscious program of race relations," Johnson claimed, lynchings were merely "convulsive reactions to local stimuli."[5]

After 1925, it appeared that the NAACP had succeeded only in convincing white Americans that lynching was the single important issue of race relations. Outside pressure for reform of southern race relations decreased with the lynching rate. The journalists turned their attention to the more pressing problems of the Ku Klux Klan, fundamentalism, and Prohibition. In fact, their commitment to southern liberalism emerged in battles over issues that touched on race relations only indirectly.

Nonetheless, the journalists continued to denounce lynchings. Mob violence not only shamed the South but also might revive agitation for a federal antilynching law. Having claimed the decline in lynchings as proof of the South's ability to reform itself, they and other southern liberals now had a definite interest in halting the practice.

Louis I. Jaffé, who received the Pulitzer Prize in 1929 for his editorials against lynching, successfully lobbied for legislation making "the punishment of lynchers . . . a primary obligation of the State." He did not expect the law alone to end lynchings, though. These acts of "savagery" had their source in irrational emotions. In the editorial cited by the Pulitzer Committee, Jaffé said, "It must be recognized that the rise and fall of the lynching curve is governed by racial passions that remain still to be brought under civilized control."[6]

The journalists shared Jaffé's opinion of the irrational motivations behind lynching; their analysis therefore differed from that posed by the NAACP. Negro leaders agreed with southern defenders of the practice in that they considered mob violence primarily a method for maintaining the subordination of blacks through terrorization. The journalists, on the other hand, emphasized the irrationality of the mob, viewed lynchings as products of blind emotions, and denied a direct connection between lynching and the structure of southern race relations. Behind his irony, Julian Harris betrayed these assumptions in his complaint that "we first explain to the world that the Negro is a child, and then, when he commits a heinous crime, we lynch him as if he were a Harvard professor."[7]

Indeed, it began to appear that those white southerners who mistreated blacks or exploited racial prejudices posed the gravest threat to segregation. In this atmosphere, southern liberals could make increasingly outspoken criticisms of injustices and advocate without qualms a more equitable treatment of blacks. The elimination of lynching, for example, would improve race relations in the South, would gain the confidence and cooperation of Negro leaders, and would reduce the possibility of federal supervision of southern racial practices.

In 1929 Oswald Garrison Villard, editor of the liberal *Nation* and a founder of the NAACP, looked South and saw many evidences of progress. He credited forthright liberal journalists with making it acceptable for southerners to criticize their region and praised the CIC as "a magnificent beginning in bridging the gulf which has heretofore separated the races." Nonetheless, Villard emphasized that many problems remained and especially pointed at lynching, "the greatest disgrace to America." In that year, however, only ten mob murders took place. The *Chattanooga News* looked to the new decade with optimism: "Someday, we hope, Tuskegee Institute [which collected lynching data] will be able to announce that the South has gone through a year without a single lynching."[8]

Suddenly, in 1930, the number of lynchings doubled, and southern liberals confronted a situation that required action. The year's initial lynching at Ocilla, Georgia, set the pattern: at gunpoint, a mob took from the sheriff's custody a man charged with the rape and murder of a young white woman; after cutting off the man's fingers and toes for souvenirs, the mob burned him to death. Georgia had suffered no lynchings since 1926, and the *Macon Telegraph* reacted with shock and rage to the mob's "ferocity." Mark Ethridge of the *Telegraph* then traveled to Ocilla in order to investigate the lynching himself. By that time, however, public opinion had grown venomous, and Ethridge was warned out of town. The experience made him an outspoken foe of lynching and, as the violence continued through 1930, he advocated close investigation of the conditions that produced mob murders.[9]

Months passed after the Ocilla lynching without another mob incident in the South. Then, in late April, three lynchings occurred in three states in less than a week. Two weeks later, in Sherman, Texas, a mob hungry for a man accused of rape burned down the courthouse in which authorities had hidden him and, after hanging the prisoner's lifeless body, proceeded to destroy all nearby Negro-owned property.[10]

Will Alexander of the Commission on Interracial Cooperation was then in Texas for a meeting, and he hurried to Sherman. After touring the shattered town, Alexander prepared a report for CIC members that particularly criticized local leaders for failing to accept any responsibility. Two more lynchings occurred in May, another pair in June, another on the 4th of July—and the South had matched the lynching total of 1929. Alexander decided that the CIC could not remain inactive. After discussions with Howard W. Odum and with associates at the CIC office in Atlanta, he proposed that the CIC sponsor an investigation of each lynching that year in order to determine the causes of mob violence and develop means to end it.[11]

On 26 July, Alexander asked George Fort Milton to become chairman of the Southern Commission on the Study of Lynching. Joining him were Odum; Julian Harris, then news editor of the *Atlanta Constitution*; Alex W. Spence, a Dallas attorney; W. P. King, book editor for the Methodist Episcopal Church, South; and W. J. McGlothlin, president of Furman University. Black members included John Hope, president of Atlanta University; B. F. Hubert, president of Georgia State College; sociologist Charles S. Johnson of Fisk University; R. R. Moton, president of Tuskegee Institute; and Monroe N. Work, also of Tuskegee. Two young sociologists, Arthur F. Raper and Walter R. Chivers, shouldered the responsibility of doing the field work. Raper, a member of the CIC staff who earned his Ph.D. under Odum, investigated the white community while Chivers, a professor at Morehouse College, did the same on the other side of the color line.[12]

Although he had always been desirous of better race relations, Milton's decision to lead the SCSL identified him publicly with racial liberalism. In September 1930, for example, he responded to a correspondent critical of the SCSL: "As a Southern man, of Confederate stock, one who has lived his life in the South and loves the South, I deem it an imperative duty of Southern people to plan for a better adjustment of race relations in the South, so that a greater measure of human well being and content will result. It is because of this feeling that I took pleasure in becoming chairman of this Committee." Milton's editorials reflected his new position, containing increasingly harsh criticisms of the South. As lynchings continued, the *News* sarcastically pointed out "the convenient temporary attack of amnesia so prevalent among Southern sheriffs following lynchings." After a Mississippi lynching, some residents admitted that they believed the mob had made a mistake. "It would not do for these citizens to give their names, of course," the *News* sneered. "They do not want to be considered pro-negro." [13]

On the other hand, Milton was resolved that southerners must reform the South, and that outsiders should not interfere with the region. The SCSL showed him that the South could reform itself, and his faith in the potential of southern liberalism increased. A *News* editorial contended that the interest of northern intellectuals in labor struggles in Harlan County, Kentucky, reflected the failure of southerners to acknowledge these conditions and to work toward correcting them. "A start in the right direction has been made by the Commission on the Study of Lynching, which was composed of Southerners. Southern people should correct abuses in the South." However, optimism, mixed with the desire to forestall northern intervention in the South, meant that slight evidence of change grew large in discussions of the South directed at northern audiences. Nearly a decade after the SCSL's formation, in *The Yale Review*, Milton cited its work as evidence of "distinct betterment in race relations" below the Potomac. [14]

Milton reveals some of the virtues and some of the limitations of the CIC's approach to the improvement of race relations. Ann Wells Ellis explains that the commission emphasized efforts directed "toward liberalizing whites' racial views" as the necessary prerequisite for reform. Thus, interracial cooperation brought the "best people" of both races together in situations where work for common goals would enable the whites to recognize blacks "as human beings worthy of respect and dignity." Just as it remained silent on segregation, the CIC never directly fought conflicting attitudes, such as paternalism, that its white members might hold. Its policy was that blacks could speak for themselves and whites, through participation in CIC programs and contact with blacks, would gradually change their attitudes. [15]

Certainly, his work with the educated, cultured men of the SCSL demonstrated to Milton that Negro life in the South was too complex for simple generalizations. Moreover, as he learned something of the indignities and frustrations that sophisticated and highly intelligent blacks—persons with intellectual interests and cultural tastes similar to his own—endured in the South, the injustices and petty cruelties of Jim Crow struck home. The carefully discreet arrangements made by Milton in order that the Negro members of the SCSL could meet with their white colleagues at the whites-only Signal Mountain Hotel in Chattanooga evidence his emerging sensitivity to their situation. These arrangements, of course, still represented accommodation to segregation, not protest against it. [16]

Events soon conspired to test Milton's southern liberalism. On 26 April 1931, nine Negro youths accused of raping two white women went on trial at Scottsboro, Alabama. With a crowd waiting outside the courthouse for the verdict, they were quickly tried and sentenced to death. The circumstances of the trial and disturbing questions about the veracity of witnesses convinced many outside the state that the Scottsboro boys, as they became known, had not received justice. The American Communist party decided that the case symbolized the evil rule of the South's master class; they publicized the case and transformed the fate of the Scottsboro boys into a cause célèbre of the 1930s. In addition, after considerable maneuvering, the International Labor Defense, an arm of the party, took over their defense. The case dragged on through years of retrials and appeals, all clouded by prejudice, falsehood, and anger, while the nine defendants grew to adulthood in prison. [17]

In nearby Chattanooga, the *News* expressed horror at the crime—although without reference to the race of those involved—and called for "speedy indictments." Even in May, following the trials, the *News* complained that northerners had falsely described the people outside the courthouse as a mob. Photographs, it claimed, showed "merely a curious, interested populace." One of these northern critics, Edmund Wilson, in his report on the case for the *New Republic*, quoted from early *News* editorials to prove his charge that mob hysteria had been whipped up before the trial. Milton naturally denied Wilson's charge, but the criticism must have hurt because well before the essay appeared he had begun to question the jury's verdict. At the SCSL's meeting on 20 July, he declared that the Scottsboro case fell within the commission's scope and that in light of the national interest, the SCSL and the CIC should conduct an investigation to aid in the defendants' appeals. [18]

The only result that Milton could foresee from the Communist involvement, he told Alexander, was harm "to the attempt we are making to cause the South to look with reason and justice upon the general negro problem." Milton's charge that the Communists were "anxious these boys die, not live" was unfair. The ILD, through attorney Samuel S. Leibowitz, presented a defense at the second trial that assuredly should have acquitted the defendants. In fact, Leibowitz's defense convinced Milton of their innocence. "We cannot conceive of a civilized community taking human lives on the strength of the miserable affair," the *News* declared. Milton and the other journalists regularly argued for clemency through the subsequent years of legal battles and criticized the prosecutors and Alabama officials for allowing the case to drag on. [19]

The Communist party's increased activity in the South made southern liberal reform even more urgent to Milton. Communist organizers among blacks resembled demagogic politicians preying on whites. The *News* complained that Negroes were "being used as pawns and dupes by the hybrid Communist agitators," and that nervous whites foolishly overreacted to the agitation, which only provided the Communists with more ammunition for propaganda. Instead, the South should initiate reforms to preempt the radicals. "It will be only by a real cleaning-up of our own mess," Milton told a friend, "that we can hope to keep such outrageous radical groups as the ILD from continually disturbing our serenity and impelling mob reactions which will make things worse and worse." [20]

The SCSL did mark an important step in the development of southern liberal reform. Here were southerners undertaking investigation of a southern evil, rather than defensively denying that the problem existed. Southern liberals had long insisted that if only southerners would acquire factual knowledge of conditions, they could improve them. Thus, Milton and the other commission members decided to issue a pamphlet reporting their findings in the fall of 1931. Arthur Raper did the writing and gracefully endured Milton's rigorous editing and gibes at his "Ph.D. education with its consequent stylistic fog." Milton also labored to ensure public attention to the report. His planning paid off, and when *Lynchings and What They Mean* appeared at the end of October, it received national attention.[21]

The report emphasized that few victims of the mob were even accused of rape, and it argued that lynching actually endangered white women by "undermining the power of police and courts, [their] legitimate protectors." The NAACP had made this point years before, but it bore repeating. Many southerners, even if they condemned the mob, connected lynchings with sexual assaults; Stringfellow Barr's observation to Milton that Raper was a humorously inappropriate name for an investigator of lynchings betrayed this association. Such a conclusion from a commission of southerners carried more weight than the same argument coming from the NAACP. In *Liberalism in the South,* Dabney relied on Walter White's study of lynching for his discussion of mob violence, but to establish that rape had little to do with lynching, he turned to the SCSL's report, even though the NAACP's lynching investigator also made that point.[22]

The SCSL found that lynchings typically occurred in sparsely populated, impoverished counties, and that both victims and murderers shared limited education and economic insecurity. The Negro's political, social, and economic impotence left him unprotected before the mob, while racial prejudices gave a sanction to the mob's acts. Lynchings occurred more often in areas with a relatively small Negro population than in the black-belt plantation regions. The report traced the situation back to "antebellum days when the slave system excluded the poorer whites from the richest portions of the South." The descendants of these underprivileged whites "inherited a prejudice against the Negro"; moreover, they now considered the Negro an economic competitor and resented "the attitude of the more prosperous citizens toward 'their Negroes.'" Lynching was a way for lower-class whites to show "the dominant group that they themselves are not without power." The SCSL discovered that two of 1930's mob victims were innocent and reported "grave doubts" about the guilt of eleven others. *Lynchings and What They Mean* depicted without blinking a pathological state in the rural South.[23]

Milton's newspaper heralded the report as "a diagnosis and a cure." "Here we have, in definite scientific data," the *News* said, "all the necessary facts concerning the malady which has made the South a synonym for barbarity in other countries. We need but study these illuminating disclosures, and to apply remedy." The journalists did study the report, but reached differing conclusions about the nature of the disease. In the *News*, Milton emphasized the SCSL's determination that "illiteracy and lynching go hand in hand." The discovery that mob violence tended to occur in the poorest rural counties seemed most important to others. Obvious reasons existed for stressing the economic causes of lynchings: through the prosperous 1920s lynchings had declined precipitously, only to more than double in 1930, a year of economic depression.[24]

Lynchings and What They Mean did not, however, propose any specific economic measures in its suggestions for eliminating lynchings. Rather, the SCSL declared that it expected "lynchings ultimately to be eradicated by the growth of a healthy public opinion that will no longer tolerate them" and called for efforts "to stimulate this growth."[25] Several factors explain this conclusion.

The SCSL's discovery that lynching flourished in an environment of rural poverty supported the arguments that the journalists had made against the Nashville Agrarians. "In no case did a lynching occur in a thriving city, or in a country community of thrifty and prosperous farmers," Johnson pointed out. "Lynching is a phenomenon characteristic of stagnated societies whose populations are cursed with half-starving bodies and rotting minds." This conclusion reflected a shift in the journalists' perception of the sources of southern ills. In the 1920s they had blamed the common man, ignorant and prejudiced, for the Klan and similar benighted phenomena; now, under the pressure of hard times, and through the intellectual agency of the debates with the Agrarians, they began to see more impersonal forces behind the South's problems. Jaffé, for example, declared that lynchings would continue "so long as the South is unable or unwilling to raise the economic and educational level" of its people.[26] The poor whites, living in poverty without education or hope for the future, were the victims of their degraded environment.

On the other hand, the poor whites made up the mobs, and the SCSL hardly expected them to join a campaign against lynching. In fact, should the lower-class whites gain more power, conditions would likely become worse. Already, the report said, the potential votes of the mob members and of their sympathizers—even though most of them did not actually vote—frightened public officials into silent acquiescence. Democracy in the South protected the lynching tradition.[27]

Thus, the SCSL concluded that "the primary responsibility for the lessening of crime and the eradication of lynching rests upon that portion of the white population which controls political, social and economic conditions." The journalists directed their campaigns to liberalize public opinion at this group. Already these responsible southerners disliked mob violence; now southern liberals must encourage them to withstand the "pressure for conformity" and fight against the mob.[28]

Will Alexander, who was planning to invite Gerald W. Johnson to write a book-length study of the SCSL's findings, picked up the March 1932 issue of *The North American Review* with a great deal of interest. The magazine carried an essay by Johnson on lynching, based on the SCSL's report. But as Alexander read, his consternation mounted. Johnson would not do: he had argued that the SCSL's report provided evidence "proving the need of revivifying and strengthening the race prejudice of [the South]."[29]

Johnson said that bad economic conditions resulted in lynchings; "Southerners with money in the bank do not lynch." The typical mob members—"those inexpressibly forlorn outcasts known in the South as the poor white trash"—suffered even more now with the Depression and, lacking income and security, they were becoming uncertain of their superiority to blacks. Because they always acted "on emotion, not reason," these insecure whites grew hysterical and became "a deadly menace to the Negro." Johnson concluded that with "money in his pocket," the poor white would regain his race prejudice. A confident sense of his superiority would calm his emotions and end lynchings.[30] At bottom, Johnson was calling for the improvement of economic conditions in the rural South, just as other southern liberals had done, but his conspicuous justification of race prejudice as a protection against lynching made his essay unacceptable.

The SCSL had condemned race prejudice in its report, stating that upon the assumption of innate black inferiority "ultimately rests the justification of lynching." Although never specifically refuting this assumption, the report did treat prejudice as the product of social conflicts, originating in the nonslaveholding white southerners' resentment of the great planters. Moreover, it assumed that prejudice was a problem to be solved rather than a natural emotional response to biological differences between whites and blacks.[31]

Race prejudice's incompatibility with liberal doctrines of the individual's dignity and liberty also contributed to the disreputable tone of Johnson's essay. The concept of race divided human beings into groups, the characteristics of each biologically determined, whereas liberalism valued the individual and desired social conditions open enough for all persons to develop their capabilities to the fullest. The conflict was hardly novel. Southern liberals of the Progressive Era had faced the same problem, but the assumption of black inferiority had made qualification of liberalism necessary and acceptable. By the end of the 1920s, this assumption no longer satisfactorily justified Jim Crow.[32]

During that decade, social scientists began to undermine the validity of the racial dogma that white southerners had learned in childhood. Led by Franz Boas, cultural anthropologists developed a relativistic explanation of human society that assumed cultural rather than biological causes for human social diversity. Employing similar assumptions, Robert Ezra Park and other sociologists argued that prejudice resulted from group conflicts over status. "Children do not have it," Park said; prejudice was "an acquired trait, quite as much as the taste for olives or the mania for collecting stamps."[33]

These ideas began to appear in the writings of the journalists. With race relations freed from the rigid permanence of biology, reforms could be advocated more easily. Indeed, prejudice itself became an attitude susceptible to reform. After their experience in the presidential campaign of 1928, moreover, the journalists knew well the danger and unreality of prejudices. Even Johnson preceded his argument for "more and better race prejudice" with the following admission: "All the pundits are agreed that race prejudice is terrible; and even Southerners, who are stuffed with it, and know that they are full of it, mouth hypocritical agreement when it is denounced."[34]

Naturally, the journalists did not proceed to divest themselves of racism, for that had roots too deep and complex for easy extirpation.

They also feared that too advanced a public stand on race issues would provoke a sharp reaction from less tolerant southerners. Milton told Arthur Raper to write *Lynchings and What They Mean* with a southern audience in mind. "The report," he said, "if it is to be really useful, must appeal more to Southern people with inherited prejudices somewhat glossed over by education than to people who accept unreservedly the more modern racial documents." As Milton's warning indicates, southern liberals—their own attitudes in flux, too—navigated very carefully through the minefield of southern race relations. [35]

For guidance, they turned to sociology. Such reliance was not new. During the Progressive Era, southern intellectuals had cited concepts of this vigorous discipline to justify the emerging Jim Crow system. For example, Franklin Henry Giddings's concept of "consciousness of kind" appeared to southerners as an explanation of racial prejudice that gave segregation laws the authority of nature. Similarly, William Graham Sumner's dictum that laws, or "stateways," cannot change the "folkways," or mores, justified southern defiance to the Fourteenth and Fifteenth Amendments. Sociologists gave to Jim Crow the sanction of eternal social laws, and their authority helped encourage northern acquiescence in the southern racial settlement. [36]

By the 1920s, as Fred H. Matthews points out, sociological thought had come to rival literature, religion, and political theory as a source of facts and values. Moreover, as social amelioration became increasingly the task of government agencies that relied on expert advice, sociology attracted persons interested in reform who in the past might have chosen careers in the ministry or politics. [37] Not surprisingly, sociologists were prominent in southern liberalism. The SCSL, for example, not only sent out sociologists to discern the causes of lynchings, but also included among its members the two most influential of southern sociologists—Howard W. Odum and Charles S. Johnson.

Odum, a Georgian who had studied with Giddings at Columbia University, headed the University of North Carolina's Institute for Research in Social Science. A man of vast energy, in the 1920s he founded and edited the *Journal of Social Forces*, taught classes, and published several books on Negro folklore and on the South. Typically, when the SCSL's report appeared, he was in Chicago waging an unsuccessful battle to obtain a Hall of Social Science for the 1933

World's Fair. Milton arranged with *The Nation* for the sociologist to publish an essay on the SCSL's findings and Odum agreed, although he warned that he could devote only an evening to the writing. Perhaps as a result, his essay primarily discussed lynching reform in relation to sociological doctrine.[38]

Odum explained that lynchings were "a product of the folkways," those community customs and attitudes with such power that all members must conform to them. Passing an antilynching law promised no improvement. The folkways associated with lynching, Odum wrote, were "so strong that the enforcement of law by local or State forces would mean literally civil war in the community." Thus, he and other southern liberals faced a hard problem. Lynchings solved nothing and only exacerbated the very factors that caused them. Moreover, mob murder was illegal, even in the deepest South. Odum said that lynchings set "the folkways over against the stateways in lawless revolt." How could southern liberals, aware of the folkways' power, hope to eradicate lynching?[39]

Odum's emphasis on the difficulty of changing folkways displayed the powerfully pessimistic, antireform element in American sociological analysis of race relations. The concept of folkways itself comes from the work of an archlibertarian, William Graham Sumner. In 1906 Sumner defined folkways as customs that arose "from efforts to satisfy needs," won "authority," and then over time became "regulative," taking on the "character of a social force." They arose "no one knows whence or how," he proclaimed, and men could modify them "but only to a limited extent." Sumner particularly insisted that traditional American methods of reform—"legislation and preaching"—would have no effect on the folkways of southern race relations.[40]

Odum placed the SCSL's recommendations into a framework that accepted Sumner's ideas while abandoning his laissez-faire outlook: "education, publicity, civic appeal, and courageous leadership" could gradually transform the folkways. Odum cited the increasing number of prevented lynchings to support his optimism. With its emphasis on the gradual modification of public opinion, Odum implied, the SCSL showed comprehension of social laws and, as the general decline in lynchings proved, such methods had good effect.[41]

Behind Odum's adaptation of Sumner's ideas was a sharp awareness of changes in the South. The same consciousness of social change that underlay the debates with the Agrarians bottomed southern liberal thought on race relations. Over the years, in fact, Odum revised Sumner's static sociology in light of the rapid change he perceived going on about him. He associated the folkways with the rural and isolated "folk society" that modern urban and industrial society, the "state civilization," was replacing. In order to adapt to the new conditions, people developed "technicways," originating in the demands of technological innovation, which superseded the folkways. The technicways had little of the rigidity that Sumner gave to the folkways. Indeed, technological society changed too swiftly for slowly maturing folkways to arise. Thus, as the southern people moved from the conditions of the folk society into the new world of state civilization, they would shed their folkways. The fact of southern social change promised results for southern liberal efforts to improve racial attitudes.[42]

Odum's essay helps to explain the reasoning behind the chosen means of southern liberal reform, but in order to understand more of what the liberals foresaw for the future of race relations it is necessary to turn to the other sociologist on the SCSL, Charles S. Johnson, and through him to his teacher, Robert Ezra Park of the University of Chicago. Park and his talented students dominated sociological research on race relations between the two world wars. Although northern-born and -educated, Park went South in 1907 for what became a seven-year stay at Tuskegee Institute as an assistant to Booker T. Washington. Park developed his interest in race relations during these years as he studied conditions in the South and absorbed Washington's accommodationist philosophy. Park's biographer contends that he incorporated Washington's tactics, devised for a specific time and place, into his theory and teachings. Certainly Park, like Washington, assumed that changes in race relations occurred by social evolution rather than revolution. Both men also assumed that race relations tended, however slowly, always toward assimilation rather than separation.[43]

In 1914 Park became a professor of sociology at the University of Chicago. His growing scholarly reputation, especially as a student of race relations, attracted many young southerners to study with him. Park's theories of race relations filtered into southern liberalism not only through his own prolific writing, but also through his students who worked in the South. One of these, Charles S. Johnson, who considered Park an influence on his life second only to his father, took command of Fisk University's department of social science and made it an outpost of Park's doctrines in the South.[44]

Park assisted in the demystification of race prejudice and went on to place race relations into a sweeping conception of processes of worldwide social change. The mingling of diverse peoples was the essence of civilization, in his view, and the city, with opportunities abounding for contacts between people, was the arena in which the new world civilization would develop. "America and, perhaps, the rest of the world," Park wrote, "can be divided between two classes: those who have reached the city and those who have not yet arrived."[45]

American race relations exemplified the process of change. The migration of blacks away from the rural South to "the vivid, restless, individualistic life of cities" had changed race relations. In the United States, "where, humanly speaking, there are no class distinctions," no official barriers to advancement existed and blacks naturally sought to improve their status. Group consciousness intensified among the whites, accustomed to the Negro's remaining in his place, and race prejudices and antagonisms resulted. In fact, prejudice proved that blacks actually were improving their status. "There is more conflict because there is more change, more progress," he wrote. "The Negro is rising in America and the measure of the antagonism he encounters is, in some very real sense, the measure of his progress."[46]

Park's sanguine outlook reflected his conception of a "progressive and irreversible" course in race relations from groups' first contacts to their ultimate assimilation. He explained "the race relations cycle" as a progression "of contacts, competition, accommodation and eventual assimilation." At bottom, Park's theories of race relations retained something of a utopian liberalism. Group distinctions, characteristic of the early stages of the cycle, conflicted with individualistic democracy, which recognized no caste or classes. In the later stages of the cycle, however, accommodation eased group hostility and enabled individuals to discover common interests and friendships that transcended the boundaries of group identity. Ultimately, assimilation would restore, or create, a society of individuals free from narrow group consciousness. Thus, the democratic United States, "where changes in underlying conditions proceed more rapidly than they do elsewhere," presaged the potential shape of the entire world as its societies progressed at varying speeds along the race relations cycle.[47]

In 1928, Park published an essay in which he noted evidence from the South that the next stage of the cycle loomed. Whereas race relations in the region had once placed whites over blacks in a caste relationship, the development in the cities of a Negro social structure comparable to that of the whites was transforming race relations. He used diagrams to explain the change:

The situation *was* this

All white
All colored

It is now this

White	*Colored*
Professional occupation	Professional occupation
Business occupation	Business occupation
Labor	Labor

With this development, "biracial organizations" arose in which "race distinction"—the vertical line—remained, but attitudes changed as individuals discovered common interests across the color line. Such organizations were "a unique product of the racial struggle in this country," Park concluded; "they do not exist outside of the United States."[48]

Park's diagram of vertical segregation helps explain the reasoning behind southern liberal reform programs. Some even described their goal in terms similar to Park's. "The 'color line' should be perpendicular," Charlton Wright, late of the *Columbia* (S.C.) *Record*, declared in 1933. Mark Ethridge echoed him in 1937: "[the Negro] wants a tilting of the color line from the horizontal to the vertical, so that he may have on his side the rights and privileges to which he is entitled, just as the white man on his side enjoys the rights and privileges of American civilization." In 1934, Charles S. Johnson discussed "the cultural development of the Negro" and quoted Park's diagrams of the shift from horizontal to vertical segregation. Significantly, Johnson, a black man, labeled this the direction of change without suggesting that it represented a solution in itself to race problems. Wright and

Ethridge, both white, insisted that barriers to intermarriage, "social equality," must remain.[49]

Despite the sticking point of social equality, the concept of vertical segregation made possible the cooperation of white and black southern liberals for reform. Moreover, Jim Crow seemed to even the most optimistic of them certain to persist well into the future. "I think the first thing for us to do, as sensible people," Mark Ethridge said, "is to adjust our thinking to terms of generations, rather than of years." Negro liberals agreed. For the time being, at least, they would have to accept segregation.[50]

Thus, rather than engaging in seemingly fruitless debate over distant ends, southern liberals sought practical measures of reform. The campaign against lynching, for example, promised great benefits for southern blacks without challenging Jim Crow. Similarly, eliminating inequities in the courts and in education would certainly improve conditions for blacks, yet racial purity need not become an issue.

For white liberals, vertical segregation allowed them to advocate reform without suggesting revolutionary changes. As Ethridge pointed out, southern segregation laws "provided that there shall be 'separate but equal' accommodations." White liberals would simply have the South live up to its professions. As long as the color line remained, the disconcerting question of social equality need not arise. As Virginius Dabney confidently declared in 1933, "it is entirely possible for a southern white man to be uncompromisingly in favor of justice to the Negro and uncompromisingly against intermarriage."[51]

At the same time, black liberals participated in interracial cooperation without swallowing their pride or abandoning their faith in the future. In Park's race relations cycle, the vertical segregation that maintained the color line for white liberals appeared as a stage in an irreversible process. Thoroughly practical as a condition of their survival in the South, black liberals could support CIC programs to eliminate the most indefensible injustices with the conviction that each small improvement, valuable in itself, marked progress toward an end to humiliation and subordination.

The CIC programs offered to both black and white liberals a practical means to reform without raising white opposition in the South. Vertical segregation also served as a flexible and vague goal that gave to those white southern liberals with (in Milton's phrase) "inherited prejudices somewhat glossed over by education" sufficient space for continuing the changes in their attitudes away from the rigidities of earlier racial doctrines. The consensus on vertical segregation made interracial cooperation possible.

The journalists' view of race relations flowed from their interpretation of Negro slavery. They contended that under the slave regime, close human contacts between masters and slaves mitigated the evils of bondage in the abstract. Moreover, slavery, as a labor system, neared an end even before the Civil War. Just as the War had distorted the natural economic development of the South, so, too, had it set back the natural evolution of race relations. History demonstrated to the journalists the wisdom of the southern liberal approach to racial reforms.

George Fort Milton's service as chairman of the SCSL won him an invitation to lecture to the Institute of Race Relations at Swarthmore College on the historical background of American racial problems. In these lectures, delivered in July 1933, he claimed that two different slaveries had existed. The abolitionists attacked "commercial slavery," the system of quick profits and harsh treatment that arose as cotton agriculture boomed across the frontier regions of the Old Southwest. They ignored the existence of "feudal slavery," found usually on the large, established plantations, where slaves received kind treatment and reciprocated with loyalty.[52]

Robert E. Park also emphasized slavery in his discussions of the historical background to contemporary race relations. Masters and slaves on the isolated plantations of the Old South lived in close proximity and established "intimate and friendly relations" with one another, which made the slave system's theoretical rigor much milder in practice. Park cited increasing numbers of individual manumissions as evidence that slave loyalty awoke the masters' consciences and overrode the imperatives of the system. Indeed, his interpretation of slavery made the abolitionist movement irrelevant: "the intimate association of master and slave may be said steadily to have corrupted the institution of slavery, and in so doing, hastened it on its course to its predestined extinction."[53]

The journalists agreed with Park that slavery, no matter how amiable its actuality, was doomed. Rather than the kindness of masters, though, they contended that economic factors predicted the institution's fate. Behind their conviction was the authority of a professional historian, Charles W. Ramsdell. In 1929, Ramsdell argued that slavery, which he identified primarily with cotton agriculture, had "natural limits" to its expansion. Climatic conditions to the west and north prevented the slave system from spreading much beyond its boundaries in the 1850s. Ramsdell concluded his essay with a speculative prediction that the vast expansion of cotton production after 1830 would soon have led to "a sharp decline in cotton prices." Assuming slaveholders to be economically rational, Ramsdell predicted that losses would have quickly changed the planters' opinion of emancipation. Within "perhaps a generation, probably less," slavery would have died of natural causes.[54]

The natural-limits thesis neutralized the major objection that history might pose to the southern liberal program for reforming race relations. Unfriendly critics could point out that slavery, the "Negro problem" of the antebellum period, had required militant abolitionist protest and four years of war to eliminate. Even William Graham Sumner conceded slavery to be a deviation from the laws of folkways. "Outside forces" emancipated the slaves "against the mores of the whites" of the South and now opinion agreed on slavery's evil. "It is the only case in the history of the mores where the so-called moral motive has been made controlling," he said with wonder.[55] The example of slavery called into question the southern liberals' certainty that only gradualism and evolutionary change produced lasting reform.

In his lectures at Swarthmore, Milton contended that neither the abolitionists nor the defenders of slavery perceived that slavery had expanded as far as geography and climate would permit. Americans fought a terrible Civil War over the future of a foredoomed institution. Milton offered his own "rough guess" that slavery's "final decline and fall would have come about 1880" as industrial expansion forced the South to accept "freedom as a necessary technique in the economic struggle to maintain herself." Responsibility for the war therefore fell primarily on the abolitionists, and secondarily on the southern fire-eaters who led the nation into a needless conflict.[56]

This interpretation of the war flowed smoothly into the journalists' already strong conviction that Reconstruction had determined political and racial conditions in the modern South. Milton declared that, rather than improving race relations, the war and its aftermath had set back their progress. The hatred and conflicts aroused during Reconstruction poisoned the good will between the races that had sur-vied Emancipation and the luckless freedmen suffered most of all. In Milton's opinion, without the war, "probably the relations between white and Negro races today would have been substantially better than they were in the 'Eighties and 'Nineties, and perhaps today." He concluded his lectures with the claim that the South had returned to a progressive path in race relations. "The changes are slow, at times almost maddeningly so," he admitted, "but still there are these changes, the social climate is gradually becoming more temperate, the real meaning of peace and good will is growing every day."[57]

The journalists' interpretation of the history of race relations coincided with that of the South's economic history put forward in the Agrarian debates. Again they described an evolution in the South toward progress that had been set back and distorted by the Civil War. Southerners who defended slavery were as blind to economic reality as were those who defended the agrarian economy. As the SCSL's report on lynchings seemed to confirm, city growth and the economic opportunities brought by industrial expansion improved race relations. Race prejudices and injustices flourished primarily in the rural, agricultural areas of the South.

Perhaps most importantly, the journalists managed to sidestep the moral condemnation of slavery. Indeed, they believed that such an absolute judgment had irreparably flawed the abolitionist attack on slavery. As Milton put it, "slavery in America was worse than a crime, it was a blunder, and worse than a blunder, it was an anachronism, an about-face from the great march of time."[58] Not only did history validate southern liberal reform, its apparent progressive direction gave them confidence that, barring another emotional debauch, they would achieve success as reformers.

Faith in progress both inspired and inhibited southern liberals. Confidence might spur "a long-ranged optimist," as Will Alexander once described himself, to apply the lubrication of reform to the heavy wheels of history, but it also could justify caution. The southern past warned that unrealistic attempts to hurry progress along could backfire into reaction and regression. Southern liberals had given the concept of folkways a flexibility absent from William Graham Sumner's formulation, yet the sociologist's antireform convictions, although muted, survived. The liberals feared the consequences of reforms made before the times were ripe for them.[59]

Practical efforts to ease injustice and improve attitudes not only avoided the pitfalls of protest and radicalism but also assuredly laid the groundwork for a better future. Southern liberals did not believe it necessary to examine the nature of that future too closely. As one of the CIC's founders said, "It is a safe principle to do the duty of the hour, trust one's principle, and leave the results to God."[60]

Hard times during the 1930s overshadowed problems of race relations and seemed to reinforce the assumptions behind vertical segregation. The Great Depression, especially severe in its impact on blacks, forced Negro leaders and organizations to concentrate on economic rather than strictly racial issues. Naturally, emphasis on the economy also appeared in southern liberal thought. For many, racial problems seemed the symptoms of the larger economic illnesses of the region. Only cure the economy's ills, and racial injustices would ease.[61]

Such arguments assumed, however, that white southerners would always control the direction and rate of change in race relations. In part, the southern liberals made this a conscious policy. Those whites who had power in the South bore the responsibility for reform. The conviction that whites would determine the character of race relations appeared more insidiously in discussions of slavery. The peculiar institution, albeit a discredited labor system, seemed to many almost a model of good race relations. The slaves accepted their relationship with their masters and, except in isolated instances, never resented their subordination. As the industrial revolution transformed the American economy, the masters would have modified the slave system toward freedom. The bondsmen remained the passive beneficiaries of their masters' decisions, not actors in their own history.[62] This view did give to black liberals a veto of sorts over white-led reform. Just as in slavery, satisfactory race relations in the present required the acquiescence of blacks as well as whites. White southern liberals listened carefully to the complaints of Negro leaders; nonetheless, this view of slavery, which never mentioned revolts and runaways, reveals the bias in their reform programs. Southern liberalism had no place for black pressure groups or protest.

The consensus on interracial cooperation held together only as long as goals remained far ahead in a misty future. By the early 1940s, segregation itself had replaced vertical segregation as the issue defining racial liberalism, and southern liberalism began to come apart at the seams. Through most of the 1930s, however, the methods of interracial cooperation seemed effective in practical terms and very much in the mainstream of national liberalism.

No significant challenges to the liberals' thinking came from outside the South. Indeed, President Franklin D. Roosevelt carefully avoided racial issues in politics. Numerous southern liberals served in his administration, and they influenced the New Deal's approach to race relations. As John B. Kirby observes, the New Deal faith that programs of economic reconstruction would benefit blacks and improve race relations also rationalized excessive caution when specifically racial issues arose.[63]

The New Deal showed to the journalists that action to improve the economy was possible, and they supported Franklin D. Roosevelt with enthusiasm. During these years they became more appreciative of democracy and the common man. Ironically, majoritarianism reinforced their disinclination to challenge southern racial practices.

6 Dead Laws and Live Demagogues

Jonathan Daniels, the editor of the *Raleigh News and Observer*, set out by automobile in 1937 to explore and report on the region below the Potomac. The following year, he published an account of his experiences, *A Southerner Discovers the South.* The book revealed a region self-consciously caught up in actual and potential social change, partly the product of the Depression's dislocations and partly the vigorous response to opportunities that New Deal programs had created. An essential theme that unified Daniels's lively anecdotes and observations was, as he put it, "the newly exciting question of democracy."[1]

Indeed, as campaigns against the poll tax and other restrictions on the ballot suggest, southern liberals now perceived lower-class southerners as a constituency desirous of reform and willing to follow liberal political leaders. Historians explain this new faith in the people as a product of President Franklin D. Roosevelt's popularity and the potential of his New Deal reforms. They also observe that, despite their democratic sentiments, southern liberals never actually managed to obtain mass support in the South. Southern liberals, courageous yet impotent, could not carry their faith to the people.[2]

The journalists, too, revised their skeptical opinion of majority rule. Both the repeal of the Eighteenth Amendment and the political career of Huey P. Long contributed importantly to the development of the journalists' majoritarianism and influenced their response to the New Deal. Prohibition repeal—which they interpreted as an uprising of the people against a foolish law—seemed to show that, given time, the people could control their emotions and examine issues intelligently. Similarly, Long's political success through programs to aid the poor, rather than merely through appeals to prejudices, seemed to the journalists a demonstration that the people sought leaders who represented their interests. Demagogues arose only when responsible leaders refused to act; liberal reform in the South was both possible and necessary.

Examination of these sources of the journalists' new majoritarianism also sheds light on the failure of southern liberalism to seek and earn mass support. Although the masses might be much more willing to follow responsible leaders than had seemed to be the case in the 1920s, the journalists never trusted them completely—they still feared the people's tendency to obey their emotional impulses in political matters. Moreover, Prohibition repeal seemed to them proof that no legislated reform could withstand opposition from local majorities. Thus, rather than inspiring them to stronger efforts to free the South from discriminatory racial practices, majoritarianism actually undermined their commitment to the rights of the black minority.

The unprecedented economic collapse after 1929 produced confusion among the journalists. At first, the Depression seemed but a sharp slump in the business cycle that would eventually regain its equilibrium, and hope inspired regular predictions of an imminent upturn. In fact, Prohibition seemed to them likely to be the primary issue of the coming presidential campaign.[3]

While other southern liberals looked forward to the Democratic party nominating a wet candidate, George Fort Milton strove to keep the party and the nation dry. Rather than a "noble experiment," the *News* declared, Prohibition should be considered a "noble accomplishment." His editorials insisted that "bread, not booze," should be the issue in 1932, but, to Milton, booze seemed more crucial; in his correspondence, he judged the potential Democratic presidential candidates according to their views on Prohibition.[4]

Despite the *News's* best efforts, the anti-Prohibition tide swelled through 1932. No King Canute, Milton began moving to higher ground. In April, an editorial endorsed a national referendum on the Eighteenth Amendment, which it predicted would return a majority for Prohibition. Rather than a referendum, though, the Democratic party's platform in 1932 called for repeal. Despite his dissatisfaction with Hoover, Milton complained, that repeal plank had "just about prevented my supporting Roosevelt." Finally, in September, he admitted to a friend that "it might be necessary for us to have a return to the old conditions, so that our current generation can know how greatly they were worse than even the bad state of things today."[5]

Meanwhile, Virginius Dabney and Gerald W. Johnson watched happily as the nation turned against the Eighteenth Amendment. As long-time critics of Prohibition and the Prohibitionists, they considered its demise a liberal victory. "Certainly few more significant things have happened in the South during the present century," Dabney exulted in 1933.[6]

In the 1920s, when majority opinion in the South seemed behind the dry laws, the journalists who opposed Prohibition based their arguments on the defense of minority rights, emphasizing individual liberty and state rights. They considered Prohibition a misguided reform, brought on by "moralists" who manipulated the emotions of the people, and their criticisms bore antidemocratic undertones. Now, the people had risen against Prohibition and pulled down the power of the "political parsons." Johnson wrote that repeal evidenced that "the country never was convinced" of Prohibition's value "but was whipped into line by a group of shrewd and ruthless fanatics." Over the past decade, the nation had seen "a practical demonstration" of Prohibition and learned from it. "We are voting today in the light of knowledge, not of theory," he said, "and this is what has made it unanimous."[7] The demise of the Eighteenth Amendment demonstrated that although impassioned reformers might succeed in forcing their beliefs into law, the people would sooner or later refuse to obey unrealistic laws and would overthrow them. This interpretation of repeal depended on the journalists' conception of the Eighteenth Amendment as a legal aberration, enacted in a sudden burst of moral fervor. They ignored the long history of the antiliquor crusade, as well as any conditions that might have justified it.

Virginius Dabney's biography of Methodist Bishop James Cannon, the Prohibitionist "czar" of Virginia and eventually of the nation, exhibited the typical characteristics of this interpretation. The Virginia "dry movement," he said, arose in a "decidedly psychopathic atmosphere." The wets, who relied on "reason and argument," made little headway against the Prohibitionists, who "appealed primarily to the emotions." The dry victory, however, came too swiftly. The Prohibitionists "rushed national prohibition through before the country was ready for it," and this mistake contributed mightily to "the subsequent collapse of enforcement." In addition, Cannon's own hypocritical self-righteousness—and Dabney described the Bishop's peccadillos in detail—contributed to the general disgust with the Anti-Saloon League and Prohibition. On 5 December 1933, "a milestone in the social history of the United States," the Eighteenth Amendment became null and void. Significantly, Dabney oriented Cannon in his times with but a single paragraph claiming the Bishop's "marked affinity" for the doctrines of the censorious vice-crusader, Anthony Comstock.[8] On such narrow historical grounds, Dabney and the other journalists expanded the supposed lesson of Prohibition into a general law of social reform, particularly relevant to southern race relations.

George Fort Milton, an ardent dry until after repeal, exhibits in his change of opinion how the journalists applied the lesson of Prohibition to southern race relations. Opponents of Prohibition often contended that the dry laws could not change customary behavior, that no government could legislate against the folkways. In 1930, the *News* dismissed this argument as a "bit of cheap cynicism, masquerading as natural philosophy." Five years later, however, Milton explained that he opposed a federal antilynching law because public opinion in the South did not support it, and no reform could succeed against the wishes of the people. As southern liberals had done many times before, he cited the failures of Reconstruction-era racial reforms in order to back his argument. "The more recent failure of our federal prohibition statutes," he went on, "gives a modern point to the indispensable necessity of local support."[9]

At the beginning of the election year of 1932, Milton told a friend: "The present age reminds me a good deal of that of the 'Fifties, with its emotional disturbance and its general shift in the economic equilibrium." During the period when Prohibition collapsed he was writing his Douglas biography, published in 1934 as *The Eve of Conflict: Stephen A. Douglas and the Needless War*. He argued in the book that the Industrial Revolution had created "a new economic world of *laissez faire*" and "loosened the leash upon emotions." Yoking together the antebellum "anti-liquor, anti-foreign, anti-slavery" movements, Milton contended that the wild flood of change and emotion converged in these "three great ferments of the Fifties." His Stephen A. Douglas— "a realist in an emotional age"—struggled heroically to keep the agitated nation on a statesmanlike course as it passed through these storms.[10] By then, Milton had changed his opinion of dry laws.

Well into 1933, however, he insisted on distinguishing between the antebellum reform crusades and the modern-day Prohibition movement. To a correspondent who noted similarities between the slavery controversy and the contemporary liquor battle, Milton pointed out that the Constitution backed Prohibition's defenders whereas it had stood against the abolitionists. Yet he went on to employ Douglas's view of slavery to criticize the modern Prohibitionists. The Little Giant knew "that slavery would have died of its own weight, because of its economic insufficiency, had agitation quieted down"; similarly, Milton claimed, the Prohibitionists had moved too quickly and imposed a national law "before the public mind had come up to the point of accepting it." Just as slavery would have eventually died had Americans followed Douglas's lead, Milton felt that "had the prohibitionists delayed for ten years or more, they would have had a much better chance for general public acceptance of their doctrines." Any reform, even if obviously required by the times, must wait until the public was prepared to accept it.[11]

Modern conditions did require Prohibition, *News* editorials contended. The complex society of the present must have public controls over the individual for the benefit of the "social organism" as a whole. "Thus it is contrary to the main development of human society for control of liquor to be abolished," the *News* concluded. Before final ratification of the Twenty-first Amendment, Congress modified the Volstead Act to permit again the sale of beer and wine. The *News* noted darkly that "beer is back," but declared that "the pendulum must inevitably swing back to control of intoxicants in a few years."[12]

On the other hand, in *The Eve of Conflict* Milton presented the antebellum Prohibition movement as unrealistic reform at its emotional worst. To demonstrate this point, he described an 1853 referendum on liquor in Vermont: the state's towns returned majorities for Prohibition that overwhelmed the negative vote of the more rural areas, and Vermont went dry. Milton concluded from this evidence that "the Prohibitionists had successfully aroused the group emotions of the city crowds but the people of the country, not subjected to these appeals, did not want this extension of group control of individual life."[13]

News editorials had made the same argument in regard to Prohibition repeal but with a twist—contemporary *opponents* of Prohibition aroused the group emotions. "The psychological set-up of these present years reminds us of the national psychology in the 1850's," one editorial declared. "Then there was such an upstirring of passion and emotions, such a searching after will-of-the-wisps, that those who sought to work out intelligent means of social adjustment and control were brushed aside without any heed at all." Even though "the relaxation of control over beer and liquor runs counter to the general tendency of the age," Americans appeared ready to abandon Prohibition. "That this tendency is the result of the emotionalism of this uncertain age we have no doubt." On 7 August 1933 the *News* explained "Why Prohibition Lost": "The longer one lives the more one is impressed with the danger in the world of emotionalism run mad, and the supreme need for intelligence as the arbiter of human affairs. It is a much longer task to secure people's assent by reasoning and education than it is by the flaunting of some great emotional shibboleth."[14]

In *The Eve of Conflict*, Milton contended that Douglas, too, sought "to make intelligence the arbiter of American affairs." The Little Giant, however, had seemed to earlier historians much more the political opportunist than the wise statesman. Indeed, Gerald W. Johnson, in his 1933 study of *The Secession of the Southern States*, described Douglas as the man "to whom it was given to precipitate the war through the method of attending strictly to his own business." That "business was politics" and his ambition was the presidency, Johnson continued. First Douglas "played to the slavery gallery . . . , and then to the anti-slavery gallery," in the hope of gaining the votes of both. His strategy created only enemies and distrust. Moreover, although he could not win the Democratic party's nomination in 1860, his ambition would not permit him to step aside— the statesmanlike course, according to Johnson—and the party split apart. Lincoln and the Republicans won the presidency, and secession followed.[15] Johnson's animus toward Douglas reflected his conviction—which Milton shared—that the Civil War was a horrible mistake. After the tense struggle to exclude the divisive issue of slavery from politics through the Compromise of 1850, Douglas, the political opportunist, reintroduced it in order to further his own ambition. Milton, who intended to demonstrate the Little Giant's greatness, had a difficult task ahead of him.

In Douglas's defense, he declared that the Senator had introduced his divisive Kansas-Nebraska Bill in 1854 not to gain backing from the slave states for his presidential aspirations, but rather because he envisioned a national economic program to develop and unite the country in the enjoyment of the fruits of the Industrial Revolution. Douglas believed that regardless of acts of Congress, climate and geography would determine where the slave system would exist. He stood by the doctrine of Popular Sovereignty, which removed the issue from Congress's jurisdiction entirely, by contending that the people of the territory itself should control their own internal affairs, including the regulation of slavery. The right of local control, according to Milton, "was the underlying philosophy of Douglas's Popular Sovereignty."[16]

In 1857, however, the Supreme Court ruled in the Dred Scott case that neither Congress nor territorial legislatures had the power to prevent masters from taking their human property into any territory. Douglas faced a campaign for reelection in 1858, with a victory necessary to keep his presidential hopes alive, and the Court had not only ruled against the Republican party's commitment to congressional action against slavery in the territories, but also seemed to have invalidated Douglas's own Popular Sovereignty. The Republican candidate, Abraham Lincoln, agreed to a series of debates across the state of Illinois, and at their second appearance in Freeport he directed at Douglas a set of hypothetical questions, all related to the validity of Popular Sovereignty in light of the Supreme Court's ruling that slaves were constitutionally protected property. How could the people of a territory keep Negro slaves out, now that the Court had spoken?

Douglas answered with what became known as his Freeport Doctrine. He claimed that Popular Sovereignty yet existed, regardless of the Court's decision: "It matters not what way the Supreme Court may hereafter decide as to the abstract question whether slavery may or may not go into a Territory under the Constitution, the people have the lawful means to introduce it or exclude it as they please, for the reason that slavery cannot exist a day or an hour anywhere, unless it is supported by local police regulations." Lincoln made no response, and Milton continued his narrative without discussing the Freeport Doctrine further.[17] Nonetheless, Douglas's apparent recommendation that the people of a territory ignore unpopular national laws and court rulings seemed further evidence in support of those who considered the Little Giant an unprincipled politician, more concerned with office than with statesmanship. Was not the Freeport Doctrine, countenancing local defiance of the Supreme Court, but an expedient bit of campaign sophistry?

On 30 November 1933 Milton sent a draft of an address on Douglas's historical reputation to Roy F. Nichols. "You will find here the reason why I think that Douglas' Popular Sovereignty position was the correct one, in line with the real actualities of the American method of government," he told Nichols. "I think the prohibition instance proves the case quite completely."[18]

Five days later, Milton spoke to the Illinois State Historical Society on "Douglas' Place in American History." He noted that contemporaries "promptly branded [the Freeport Doctrine] as a clever but demagogic evasion of the truth." Actually, Milton claimed, the Little Giant "shrewdly read the realities of American public action." He gave two examples to back this claim. First, the Radicals during Reconstruction placed the Fifteenth Amendment into the Constitution in order to ensure suffrage for blacks, but "local opinion stood forth sternly against it"; as a result, "in some areas it remains to this day a nullity in practical effect." Prohibition was his second example: "In some states public opinion did not sustain it," Milton said, and so "the Eighteenth Amendment and the Volstead Act of Congress became worse than nullities." Thus, rather than being an expedient evasion, Milton concluded, the Freeport Doctrine "showed Douglas a supreme realist" who understood "the actualities of the American plan of self-government."[19]

Earlier in 1933, *News* editorials had associated the emotionalism of the 1850s with modern opponents of Prohibition, but now Milton's linkage of Douglas's antebellum realism with the demise of the Eighteenth Amendment produced a consistent analogy between the 1850s and the present. The great ferments, the "emotional" reforms of "anti-liquor, anti-foreign, anti-slavery," had their analogues in the antiliberal movements of the 1920s. Prohibition, of course, fit exactly. Milton described the nativist Know-Nothing party of the 1850s as "in essence a percursal [sic] of our recent Ku Klux Klan."[20] Clearly the antislavery movement was no more intelligent nor successful than the Anti-Saloon League had been. From this perspective, it, too, deserved condemnation.

Gerald W. Johnson also found in the Civil War period analogues to the modern Prohibition laws. In 1930 he wrote that "the war was regarded on both sides as 'a great social experiment, noble in motive and far-reaching in purpose.'" In a discussion of the Fugitive Slave Act, he reached a conclusion similar to that which Milton had developed in regard to the Freeport Doctrine. "Legally, it did no more than the Volstead Law did with respect to the Eighteenth Amendment, that is, put into effect a plain mandate of the organic law; but its effects were even more disastrous," Johnson wrote. "The North simply refused to obey the law."[21]

The Civil War period should teach lessons to modern liberals, Johnson believed. Nearly two decades later, in 1950, he declared that "in general the prohibitionists were pious, sincere, and rigidly moral. Their aim, like that of the abolitionists, was to do good," but both produced "national disasters."[22] Anyone who criticized the modern Ku Klux Klan and the drys, his argument implied, must judge the abolitionists harshly.

The lesson of Prohibition seemed especially relevant to the reform of race relations through government action. After the mid-1930s, proponents of a federal law against lynching reopened the debates of the early 1920s. The journalists had then objected to the law on the grounds that it would inspire hostility in the South without eradicating mob violence. They made similar arguments against the Wagner-Costigan bill of the 1930s; now, however, they also criticized the bill for violating a general social law, proved by Prohibition. "I suspect that our experience with Federal prohibition should afford conviction that it is very difficult to impose a Federal rule on any section which is determinedly resistant to it," Milton told a friend in 1934. In 1937, Virginius Dabney declared that he now favored a federal antilynching law. Significantly, he emphasized that public opinion polls showed a southern majority sympathetic to such a law. "That fact," he wrote, "should assure the public support which in the last analysis must determine the effectiveness of any law." John Temple Graves, however, opposed the same bill as unnecessary—"the lynch spirit of the South is dying out"—and unworkable "because no law, federal or local, works unless local sentiment supports it."[23]

After 1933, every time that federal action against southern racial practices loomed, the purported lesson of Prohibition—that successful reform required majority support—reappeared in the minds and editorials of the journalists. For example, in 1949 Ralph McGill explained southern distaste for a Federal Fair Employment Practices Commission to combat discrimination in hiring: "It seems to us more of an effort to legislate in the field of morals and social doctrine," he wrote in *The Atlantic Monthly*. "We keep thinking of prohibition enforcement." Five years later, the Supreme Court had ruled racial segregation in the public schools unconstitutional. As the beginning of the school term approached, Hodding Carter, editor of the *Greenville Delta Democrat-Times*, published a signed editorial in which he forthrightly declared his conviction that "the Court could not have made a different decision in the light of democratic and Christian principles and against the world background of today," but he cautioned against any effort "this fall or in the immediate future to enroll Negro children in hitherto all-white schools." This was no "threat or warning, but . . . basic fact," Carter continued. "The farce of national and state prohibition should be proof enough that if a federal law or policy is not acceptable to a majority or to a dominant and organized minority [blacks outnumbered whites in the Mississippi Delta] it is not obeyed." [24]

The repeal of the Eighteenth Amendment, of course, only confirmed convictions that the journalists already shared. Two years before repeal, the Southern Commission on the Study of Lynching had concluded that educating public opinion was the most effective means to eliminating mob violence. For the journalists, white resistance to Reconstruction-era civil rights legislation provided ample historical backing for this southern liberal contention; the example of the Eighteenth Amendment, however, greatly strengthened it. Prohibition, which had no intrinsic relation to race issues, gave to their arguments the apparent weight of a general social law. Moreover, repeal seemed to them a definitely liberal advance. Thus, through Prohibition's association with the nineteenth-century campaigns to end slavery and to give citizenship rights to blacks, the journalists could conclude that abolitionism and Radical Reconstruction had little in common with genuine liberalism.

Through that turbulent year of 1933, the journalists underwent a sharp, yet subtle, transformation in their thinking. Almost as though they had passed imperceptibly through a mirror, after repeal they addressed the issue of Prohibition as majoritarians. In the 1920s, when dry laws had seemed the will of a tyrannous majority, at least in the South, the journalists had defended minority rights. Now they interpreted repeal as an uprising of the people. If the enactment of Prohibition proved the people still susceptible to emotional appeals, its repeal indicated their ultimate common sense. Here seemed evidence of growing tolerance, even liberalism, in the South.

In the 1930s the journalists grew increasingly appreciative of ma-

joritarian democracy, but their attitudes became shaped into a peculiar form. The demise of Prohibition led them to insist, as a law of
history, that local minorities—southern Negroes, for example—remained at the mercy of local majorities. Although they insisted that
gradual education of the majority would eventually build the support
necessary to reform, they never gave themselves any credit for help-
ing to shift southern opinion on Prohibition. Rather than serving as a
case study in the elimination of unjust laws and the changing of public
opinion, the noble experiment became nothing more than a negative
warning for would-be reformers. By the mid-1930s, the impassioned
editorials that the journalists had written on the Eighteenth Amendment in previous years seemed forgotten.

The journalists revised their view of rule by the majority during
Prohibition repeal without realizing that any change had occurred,
primarily because, with the exception of Milton, they had always opposed the dry laws. During these years, also, they joined a general
trend among southern liberals toward greater appreciation of popular
democracy. Nonetheless, the lessons of Prohibition, smoothly flow-
ing into the general majoritarianism of the New Deal era, helped to
prevent the journalists from following the democratic logic to a racially egalitarian conclusion.

Although the sudden demise of Prohibition convinced the journalists that reformers must proceed cautiously, they did not conclude
that reformers should abandon their efforts entirely. Their changing
estimates of Huey Pierce Long, the most powerful political leader in
the South until his murder in 1935, reveal their discovery of the crucial necessity, and the possibility, of liberal social reform in the South.
Thanks to Long, the journalists also revised their view of the common
man and his political choices. In the 1920s, demagogues had seemed
the inevitable products of democracy as ignorant and prejudice-ridden
voters succumbed to the blandishments of clever leaders. After Long,
however, the journalists concluded that the people simply sought
leaders who would represent their interests. Demagogues flourished
when social and economic conditions had deteriorated and when responsible liberals, the preferred leaders for the masses, had failed to
address themselves to the people's problems.

Whether declaiming the glories of "potlikker," personally controlling
Louisiana's state government while serving in the U.S. Senate, or

threatening to run for president at the head of a poor people's party, Huey P. Long compelled attention. He brought Louisiana's poor people into state politics, while avoiding rather than exploiting racial prejudices, and gave them return for their votes in the form of expanded state services and the satisfaction of knowing that one of their own ran the state. The higher taxes that his programs required infuriated the state's wealthier and more powerful citizens, and Long stoked the fire by skillfully using the wealthy as targets for resentments. Their enmity grew to a burning hatred that made state politics the scene of bitter struggles for power. Long lusted after power himself— whether for the people or for its own sake remains moot—and his passion justified violent and unscrupulous political methods. A dictator, a showman, a tribune of the people—the Kingfish defies easy analysis.[25]

Hodding Carter lived in Long's Louisiana, and his interpretation of Long differed sharply from those of the other journalists. Carter made his first newspaper, the *Hammond Daily Courier*, an indefatigable antagonist of the Kingfish—or "Crawfish," as Carter called him. "We hit at Long in every way we knew how or could discover, above the belt, below the belt, with the belt off, any way at all," he recalled.[26] In time, Carter came to hate Huey Long and all that he represented. Quick-tempered, passionate, and young, he commonly used vilification, rather than reasoned arguments, to make his editorial points.

Carter regularly referred to Reconstruction in his editorials, and his understanding of that period in southern history informed his discussions of "the most arrant thiever of votes since the carpet-bag Reconstructionists." The Kingfish and his henchmen had "brought about a chaotic condition unparalleled in the history of Louisiana since the days of the carpet-bagger." They were "fomenting class hatred reminiscent of carpet-bagger days," Carter claimed.[27]

Carter's articles on Long for national magazines emphasized Louisiana's high illiteracy rate and the Kingfish's appeal "to arrogant ignorance." Long set "the poor whites, who constitute the majority of Louisiana's electorate," against "the taxpaying and articulate opposition." Although in the *Courier* Carter avoided such explicit contentions, through the Reconstruction analogy he implied as much. Long's constituency had proved as unsuited for participation in government as the former slaves had in the 1870s.[28]

In the summer of 1934 Long seized almost complete control of the government in Louisiana, and the *Courier* came nearer and nearer to advocating violent overthrow of Long's regime. The precedent of Reconstruction, "when the manhood of the South rose in defense of the honor of their mothers, wives, and sisters, and in defense of the sacred principles of Democracy," gave a sanction to Carter's reckless editorials. Fortunately, no such uprising occurred and the *Courier* dropped its flirtation with violence soon after.[29]

During this period, Carter gained some liberal recognition outside Louisiana for his independent, uncowed newspaper opposition to Long. The Kingfish had split with FDR, and Carter could set the New Deal against Longism. The *Courier* charged that Long had "deliberately attempted to disrupt and pull apart the national administration when President Roosevelt enjoys the greatest union of popularity, support and progress that has ever been accorded a president of our mighty land." As Long embarked on his national campaign to "Share our Wealth," in the spring of 1934, the *Courier* seemed to realize a relationship between Long's political success and real grievances of Louisiana's populace. "Opponents of the Crawfish have no quarrel with the people," one editorial said. "It is acknowledged fact and a blight upon the pages of the history of our great nation and the world that national wealth, power, and labor have been ill-distributed. The cornerstone in the great work of recovery has been laid by our president and his advisers and supported by all citizens irrespective of party affiliations. Save for the yelping of a few liver-colored curs, this great work improves day by day." The *Courier* continued to point out that compared to the results of the New Deal, Long offered only promises, but by the end of that summer anger and bitter dreams of revolution had overwhelmed other editorial themes.[30]

On 8 September 1935, Huey Long was murdered. The killing seemed to shock Carter, and he made no comment until the thirteenth. The state now had laws designed for a dictator but with no leader of Long's ability to replace him, the *Courier* said, and it called on Louisianans to "work toward the goal of democracy" in order that "the tragedy of political assassination as a means of political freedom may never be re-enacted."[31]

Ten days later, Carter announced his candidacy for the state house of representatives. He stood for "Home Rule and Honesty" and enjoyed the use of federal work-relief orders to gain support, but on election day, 23 January 1936, the *Courier*'s headline read: "Machine Carrying Everything." The people had spoken, and the next day's editorial announced that "the Courier will not continue to be a voice shrieking in the wilderness."[32]

In the spring of the previous year, at a Long-sponsored southern writers' conference, David Cohn, a businessman, writer, and friend to the Carters, had told Hodding Carter that he was butting his head against a wall in Louisiana. A group of prominent citizens in Greenville, Mississippi—Cohn's hometown—desired a more active newspaper, and Cohn suggested that the Carters consider moving to the Mississippi Delta. In December 1935, while running for the legislature, Carter visited Greenville and met with William Alexander Percy, a plantation owner, gentleman, poet, and leader of the group seeking a better newspaper. Percy very much impressed Carter, but it was the electoral defeat that made up his mind. In the spring of 1936 the Carters sold the *Courier* and moved to Greenville.[33]

During this same period, the other journalists also observed Huey Long's career. They had the advantage of relative detachment—unlike Carter, whose newspaper suffered from punitive taxation and political intimidation—which no doubt allowed them to reflect on Long's significance rather than devote their energies to denouncing him. By the time Long died, they had revised their view of southern demagoguery.

Although extremely literal, Carter's analogy to Reconstruction bore resemblances to arguments that the journalists had made in the past. Overthrow of the Radicals had required fraud and violence, which then became tradition in southern one-party politics and opened the way for unscrupulous demagogues to seize power. That hectic period, the journalists believed, saw the poor whites begin their rise to dominance in southern politics. They did not, however, explain Huey Long with references to Reconstruction.

At first, "Hooey" Long (as Dabney called him) seemed but one more ridiculous southern demagogue—yet behind the Kingfish's bucolic buffoonery, the journalists soon realized, lay intelligence and political skill. Long spoke on national radio in February 1934 and, announcing formation of the Share Our Wealth Society, called for a redistribution of wealth in America. The journalists began to analyze

Long's political successes. "The demagogues," the *News* argued, "are symbols as well as empty windbags"; people did vote them into office, and that fact indicated "that the people sense something wrong in government and that they demand change." Those most responsible for demagogues were "the men of true statesmanlike mind" who failed "to offer themselves as the people's representatives" and to enact necessary reforms.[34]

In March 1935 the editor of the *Virginia Quarterly Review* requested that Gerald W. Johnson write an essay on the Nashville Agrarians. He declined but declared, "if we run away, taking refuge in phantasies, such as agrarianism," southerners would lose the opportunity "to set up a modern economy" without enslaving themselves to the machine. "But who is doing such fighting for humanity against the machine as is being done in the South?" he asked. "The gentry? Far from it; the battle is being waged by sons of bitches." Johnson complained that "the Southern gentleman simply doesn't fight; his gonads are atrophied; he is either a cynic or an agrarian." The quarterly could do a public service by "trying to put some spirit in him."[35]

Taking his own advice, Johnson proceeded to write a provocative essay for the quarterly on the failures of southern politics. The editor suggested that he revise the essay to acknowledge the bad effects of Reconstruction on the South, but Johnson refused. That was an excuse that the region had used for too long. "No," he continued, "the basic trouble with the South is the social illiteracy of the so-called better element."[36]

Johnson's essay opened the January 1936 issue, and Huey Long was the obvious inspiration for his argument. "I have no admiration for his ideas," Johnson said. "I cherish profound suspicion of his integrity, public and private. I regard his methods as detestable. Nonetheless, the late Huey Pierce Long has the distinction of having injected more realism into Southern politics than any other man of his generation. Huey made millions of Southerners think of the political problems of 1935 as something quite different from those of 1865. Huey really counted." Too many southerners still believed that Long's "ruffianly" behavior explained why "the wool-hat boys" supported him. They were wrong, Johnson said—look at Long's record of road building and expanding public services. He "evinced a sense of responsibility to the poor white trash," and they voted for him. But, Long's enemies charged, these reforms had come at tremendous expense to Louisiana. "That is part of the cost of leaving social improvement to demagogues," responded Johnson.[37]

The "Southern gentry" claimed that the demagogues gained power through appeals "to passions and prejudices of the poor white trash." Johnson rejected that as nonsense. Every successful demagogue actually delivered "some part of the goods promised," and they promised "not anything radical, but just those things which any government with a keen sense of social responsibility would have provided long ago." The southern gentry must wake up to this fact or face continued rule by demagogues.[38]

Before Huey Long, the liberal journalists viewed southern politics with disgust. The only leaders that the region seemed to produce were either conservative or disreputable. The latter type—the demagogue appealing to the prejudices of the white masses—aroused their ire most often, but the stolid, respectable conservatives hardly won their enthusiasm. Milton examined the southern political scene for W. T. Couch's *Culture in the South* and discerned only "a drabness most distasteful." Since the glorious days of Jefferson and other southern statesmen who had provided leadership for the entire nation, politics below the Potomac had degenerated terribly.[39]

According to the journalists, the explanation lay in the South's history since the Civil War. The degeneration began during Reconstruction, when the social necessity of overthrowing Radical rule forced the white South into the Democratic party. "Initially the means for the redemption of a prostrate people, this one-party government has become a curse upon the nation as well as upon the South," Milton wrote. The exigencies of redeeming the South from the carpetbaggers, scalawags, and their Negro allies also opened the way for demagoguery. In the 1890s, new leaders such as Benjamin Tillman in South Carolina directed their appeals to the masses and rode into office on a wave of resentment against the upper classes and the Negro. The leaders who overthrew Reconstruction—aristocratic heroes such as Wade Hampton in South Carolina—found themselves pushed from the political scene. There seemed a direct line from the insurgency of the 1890s to the barbaric politics of the modern South.[40]

As the journalists debated with the Nashville Agrarians and studied the causes of lynching, however, they discovered terrible poverty and insecurity in the rural South. Without abandoning their detestation of demagoguery, they began to understand that poor southerners did have reason for resentment. In *Liberalism in the South*, in fact, Virginius Dabney described the Populist uprising of the 1890s as, on the whole, "a liberalizing force in the South." Contemporary historical scholarship influenced Dabney's conclusion. He acknowledged a "sense of obligation" to John D. Hicks's *The Populist Revolt*, which he said had been indispensable in the preparation of his chapter on "The Rise of the Common Man." Hicks pointed out that "much of the Populist program has found favor in the eyes of later generations," and his interpretation linked Populism to a general liberal reform tradition.[41]

More important, Hicks's history tended to support the journalists' conviction that the Populists bore primary responsibility for the introduction of anti-Negro demagoguery to southern politics. Both the Populists and the Democrats sought black votes, which revived "the bugaboo of negro domination," and all whites closed ranks "until the menace of the negro voter could be removed." Legislation to disfranchise black southerners followed, and only then could "the rural whites" return to their struggle against the conservative Democrats. "Populism may have had something to do with the withdrawal of political power from the southern negro," Hicks concluded, "but it also paved the way for the political emancipation of the lower class of southern whites."[42]

As a southern liberal fighting the apparent consequences of this political emancipation, Dabney could not view the results of the Populist revolt with Hicks's equanimity. Although he concluded that "a pronounced improvement in the status of the average man was one consequence of the movement," Dabney contended that "this social and political cataclysm" produced "deplorable" results. The common man's ascendancy "was the signal for the emergence of a whole school of rabble rousers who usually capitalized upon the race issue and looked to the lower class whites for their support." Disfranchisement, he agreed, was intended "to remove the blacks from the political picture," but afterward the poor whites, viewing the Negro "as an economic rival," refused "to permit any soft-pedaling of the race issue." Thus, despite its positive achievements, the Populist revolt in the South created the modern racial demagoguery that southern liberals abhorred.[43]

This interpretation of Populism and political demagoguery provides the context in which the journalists viewed Huey Long. History demonstrated that the southern masses considered the maintenance of white supremacy more crucial than the enactment of liberal economic reform. Although none of the journalists joined Hodding Carter in equating Long with the Radical Republicans, neither did they reject the traditional interpretation of Reconstruction as a disaster for good government in the South. Both periods in southern history seemed to demonstrate the danger of irresponsible leadership. Thus, as the journalists concluded that liberal programs addressing the conditions and interests of the lower class could win mass support, they called for responsible liberal leadership, not popular democracy.

Huey Long awoke the journalists neither to the virtues of demagoguery nor to complete faith in the people. Indeed, his ability to arouse resentments and emotions confirmed the journalists' fear of passion in politics. Southern liberal reformers would have to walk a tightrope. The example of Prohibition showed the perils of reform fueled by emotion rather than by reason. In particular, the journalists eyed warily the potential for disruption that racial issues posed; their increased concern for the welfare of the poorer whites only reinforced their disinclination to advocate early reform of southern race relations.

The journalists' interpretations of Prohibition repeal and of Huey Long coincided with their response to the New Deal. President Franklin D. Roosevelt provided them with a model for responsible leadership and his expansion of the government's role in society seemed a properly rational approach to reform. At the same time, though, they did not simply turn to the federal government against illiberal governments in the South. Prohibition warned against reforms that lacked adequate local support. Moreover, despite their enthusiasm for the New Deal, the journalists never wholeheartedly endorsed a democratic liberalism based on mass support. They were majoritarians, not egalitarians.

7 Roosevelt and Rational Democracy

At the close of *Liberalism in the South,* Virginius Dabney turned to the critical situation of the present. Writing as the 1932 presidential campaign got underway, he declared that "the dearth of leadership since the great crash in 1929 has been appalling." Neither President Hoover nor Congress had faced up to the realities of drought and depression. "As for Southern liberalism," Dabney went on, "it has had little to contribute to the solution of the problems which so perplex the world in the present crisis."

The time had come for southern liberals to aspire again to greatness, Dabney believed. The economy's collapse and the failure of leadership had revealed "the fact that there is a serious lack of clarity and coherence in our political and social concepts" and made imperative "a reexamination of many hypotheses which we had previously regarded as axiomatic." He concluded with a powerful exhortation to his colleagues: "Herein lies an almost unexampled opportunity for Southern liberalism to reassert itself as a vital force in our national life. By furnishing an adequate answer to some of the principal questions raised by the existing economic distress, Southern statesmanship can establish itself once more as a controlling factor in the national councils. At the same time it should thereby be able to give to the dignity and worth of human beings everywhere a greater measure of reality."[1]

During the 1930s, southern liberals accepted Dabney's challenge. These years began inauspiciously for the journalists, however. Continued hard times following the debates with the Agrarians made their predictions of southern progress through regulated industrialism sound naively optimistic. Themselves confused and concerned by events, the journalists bemoaned the lack of ideas and able leaders in this time of crisis. To their happy surprise, Franklin D. Roosevelt proved to be the leader they desired. His New Deal programs to combat the Depression restored and revised their confidence in the future.

FDR's first term also provided them with a positive model of proper leadership in a liberal democracy, which George Fort Milton summed up in his concept of "Rational Democracy." Although Roosevelt inspired the model, by the beginning of his second term the journalists judged him against it. Rather than uncritically endorsing the New Deal, therefore, in their writings the journalists molded FDR's presidency to fit their own approach to liberal government.

As the Depression deepened, the journalists generally agreed with the thesis that the economic distress originated in a maldistribution of goods rather than in excessive production. Before 1933, though, they offered only cautious suggestions for combatting the hard times. Gerald W. Johnson emphasized that the nation's undiminished productive capacity showed that the collapse was man-made rather than an act of God, and thus that men could right the economy, but his only definite proposal was for an abolition of the useless (in his opinion) government aid to agriculture. Milton took a more positive position, advocating in the *News* a controlled inflation to increase consumer purchasing power and "some sort of social legislation to prevent the disastrous unemployment which comes whenever business feels timid." Rather than pushing particular economic remedies, however, they searched for a leader who could bring the nation out of depression.[2]

President Herbert Hoover's efforts to use the federal government to revive the economy certainly received no applause from the journalists. Dabney complained that grants of federal aid to the states threatened to establish a too-powerful central government at the expense of local self-government. Thomas Jefferson "must be revolving in his grave," he wrote, to see the Democratic party making no objection to the states' looking "to Washington every time they need money for anything." Milton and Johnson called for a balanced budget. Johnson also charged that Hoover's attempt to restore prosperity through aid to businesses would lead to state capitalism. "It may be that we are destined to go into Bolshevism," he grumbled, "but, if so, we should head in, not back in."[3]

None of the Democrats offering themselves as alternatives to Hoover aroused their enthusiasm, either. Although the governor of New York, Franklin D. Roosevelt, seemed most likely to head the party's ticket in 1932, the journalists hesitated to jump on his bandwagon. Milton, of course, feared that the party would call for repeal of the Eighteenth Amendment if Roosevelt, a wet, were the candidate, but Dabney and Johnson also remained unexcited by his candidacy.[4]

Dabney did consider Roosevelt a fairly attractive candidate, especially for his views on Prohibition, and certainly much more electable than Alfred E. Smith. He worried, though, that the governor lacked "forthrightness and courage"; the "times call for another Grover Cleveland," he said, and Roosevelt must exhibit these qualities to convince the country to follow him. Although he argued that Roosevelt was "distinctly in the liberal tradition," Dabney gave him no ringing endorsement. On the Sunday before the election, he wrote that "this writer will vote for Roosevelt, but he confesses that in some respects he prefers [the Socialist party's candidate, Norman] Thomas to any of the presidential candidates." Only Thomas had been "completely honest with the voters."[5]

After the Democratic convention called for the repeal of Prohibition, Milton, too, spoke of casting his vote for Norman Thomas. Neither Hoover nor Roosevelt pleased him, although the *News* expressed its admiration for the enemies—Alfred E. Smith and Tammany Hall, in particular—that the latter had made. Then, in early October, Roosevelt invited Milton to meet with him at Hyde Park. The candidate absolutely charmed the editor. They discussed governmental development of the Tennessee River and a realignment of the political parties along conservative and liberal lines, but Milton's report for the *News* emphasized Roosevelt's personal characteristics—a "vigorous" handshake, strong face, and alert mind. "If elected," Milton wrote, "the country can look forward to him being a good president."[6]

Johnson's columns criticized the nation in general for the absence of leadership and new ideas. "No other factor of the depression," he wrote, "is quite as depressing as is the sterility of ideas which it has uncovered in our political and economic leadership." During the presidential campaign he gave a halfhearted salute to Roosevelt for at least refusing to offer panaceas to the voters but, in his column preceding election day, he declared that regardless of which candidate won, conditions would remain much the same: "It may be slightly better, but it is a million-to-one that the difference either way will hardly be perceptible to the naked eye."[7]

Four hard months passed between the election and Roosevelt's inauguration, during which the nation's economy verged on disintegration. Johnson's pessimistic postelection comparison of the depression to a head cold—not usually fatal but incurable and highly irritating to the sufferers—daily seemed more and more an understatement. President Hoover and President-elect Roosevelt refused to cooperate, and the lame-duck session of Congress, highlighted by a filibuster from Senator Huey Long, only added to the confusion of voices. In February, exhausted banks began to fail and frightened people rushed to remove their deposits from the banks that were still solvent. On inauguration day, 4 March 1933, thirty-eight states had declared "bank holidays" to halt the panic.[8]

After taking his oath of office on Saturday afternoon, FDR announced on Sunday a national bank holiday and called Congress into session. "Monday morning," Johnson declared on Thursday, "the country awoke to find the air so full of dust and feathers, that ordinary citizens were completely befogged and had to feel their way about. . . . We didn't know exactly whose heads were being cracked, but we were getting it!" And so it continued, until Congress adjourned in June—after passing legislation committing the nation to ambitious programs of government action—and newspapermen finally caught their breath.[9]

So swiftly did Roosevelt pour out his mixed bag of legislation that editorial judgment could hardly keep pace. In May, Johnson asserted that "it is no great risk to say that out of every dozen men who say they have kept up with all that has happened since March 4, 1933, more than eleven are lying." The journalists joined most Americans in grateful appreciation for FDR's helmsmanship. Indeed, the sudden and unexpected overhauling of the government to meet the economic emergency exhilarated them. "It is the Second American Revolution," Hodding Carter declared. "Truly, it is a privilege to live through such times as these."[10]

Roosevelt's policies gained the journalists' assent largely because he grasped the reins of government and took action. As Johnson wrote, "We can forgive Mr. Roosevelt a great deal just for his flat and unequivocal assertion of authority." Above all, though, they appreciated FDR's flexible, experimental approach to reform. Milton declared that "it is a delightful thing to find in the White House a man who is not such a slave to outworn slogans and shibboleths that he shudders at the thought of doing things which actual situations imperatively demand."[11]

Significantly, the New Deal seemed to them revolutionary in the changes it brought to American government, yet also in accord with the social and economic realities of the 1930s. Shortly after the close of the "Hundred Days," on 20 June 1933, Milton suggested to String-fellow Barr: "Why don't you get somebody to write you a piece for the Virginia Quarterly under the title 'Revolution—1933?'" As it happened, on the following day the *News* published the first installment of Milton's own three-part essay under that title. He argued that, at least since the Civil War, privilege and wealth had ruled the nation, under an ideology of extreme individualism. The New Deal began "a basic change" in a direction designed to bring "this tremendous economic power under social governance." In Milton's opinion, "this substitution of planning for social benefits rather than for individual profits is the most revolutionary change that has ever come to our American affairs."[12]

At the same time, he argued that the New Deal simply brought governmental principles and practices into line with social and economic reality. FDR's programs marked "an ending to our physical pioneering." The unrestrained individualism characteristic of the "frontier mind" no longer benefited society nor protected men's liberties. Under industrialism, wealth and power had concentrated in but a few hands and, Milton wrote, "this has set at naught most of our old precepts and policies of individual initiative, the dangers of monopoly, the desirability of unrestrained competition and other elements of the frontier philosophy from which our initial economic concepts sprang." He acknowledged that his argument for "limitations upon the individual's freedom of action" might seem "alien to the liberals of a generation ago"—but their principles had proven inadequate in the present. "Changing conditions seem to force us to change our ideology toward them," Milton concluded, "and to experiment with new techniques of adjusting our social controls to economic development."[13]

The other journalists also contended that New Deal programs, however revolutionary their appearance, actually constituted a more realistic approach to existing economic conditions than did the old doctrines of individualism and laissez-faire government. "America has learned its lesson from the great crash of 1929, or at least Mr. Roosevelt and his advisors have," Dabney wrote. "They have no intention of returning to the old laissez faire methods." Thus, Americans should judge policies by their results, not by their divergence from principle. "Remember the old economic doctrines turned out to be as inefficient as they were sacred," Hodding Carter pointed out.[14]

Roosevelt's sweeping legislation in the early years of the New Deal caused the journalists to revise swiftly their own ideas on American politics and government. The outlines of this change appear clearly in their redefinition of the Jeffersonian heritage. Almost from the beginning of Roosevelt's administration, conservative critics charged that New Deal legislation, which increased the power of the federal government and placed restrictions on entrepreneurial liberty, deviated from the Democratic party's Jeffersonian devotion to limited government. The journalists denied the charge and transformed Jefferson into a practical leader, sensitive to the realities of his day. "It is impossible to believe," Dabney wrote, "that so amazing a genius as the Sage of Monticello would prescribe the same governmental physic for the simple rural civilization of his day that he would recommend for the complex, highly developed and closely interwoven civilization of the twentieth century." Milton, too, concluded that there was "little merit to the insistence" that Jefferson would oppose the New Deal. In fact, Jefferson rather resembled Franklin D. Roosevelt. "While a philosopher," Milton said in 1936, "he was likewise a pragmatist: when a fact came into collision with a theory, he would adjust the theory to meet the fact." [15] However accurate his description of the two presidents, Milton's words aptly conveyed the changed views of the journalists. When the New Deal collided with doctrines that they had defended in the past, they leaped aboard FDR's bandwagon, dragging the malleable shade of Jefferson along with them.

By the close of FDR's first term, the journalists agreed that the New Deal essentially sought to benefit the majority. Johnson argued in 1936 that whereas the Democratic party no longer stood strictly for state rights, the party had remained consistent in its devotion to the spirit of Jefferson's philosophy. Today, Johnson explained, with the states feeble before the power of giant national businesses, only the federal government had the strength to protect the people. Thus the Democrats had diverged from Jefferson's techniques of government but not from his philosophy of government in the public interest. Like Johnson, Milton contended that, despite deviations from the "letter," the New Deal hewed consistently to the "spirit" of Jefferson. All the vicissitudes of the years could not "extinguish the enduring spark of a Democracy committed to struggle for the common man." Similarly, Dabney wrote that the Democratic party's sweeping victory in the 1936 election demonstrated "that a party founded in the interest of the masses, and operated in their interest, is practically indestructible."[16]

They well knew, however, that claims of devotion to the common man mixed with practical politics also served as the stock-in-trade of demagogues and charlatans. Huey P. Long may have revealed the discontents of the common man, but none of the journalists ever suggested that he deserved the mantle of Jefferson. In their discussions of government and politics during the 1930s they sought to distinguish proper leadership in democracy, guided by reason and realism, from the dangerous emotional frenzies that brought demagogues and tyrants to power. By 1936, they had joined other southern liberals in plans to create such a political system in the South and the nation. The journalists desired what Milton called a Rational Democracy.

Near the close of the Hundred Days, Gerald W. Johnson referred in his weekly column to the fast pace of change in American attitudes since the Great Crash in 1929. One need only consider the 1928 presidential campaign to appreciate the alteration, he said. "The argument over [the issues] that seemed so vital then now resembles the sort of conversation one hears in dreams."[17] Through the early 1930s, Johnson and the other journalists emphasized to their readers that the times called for change—in government, in society, and in ideology. Freed by the crisis of Depression, they could now envision a South transformed by reform as the New Deal's example inspirited a vigorous and ambitious southern liberalism.

George Fort Milton's *The Eve of Conflict* well documents basic elements of the journalists' thought in the 1930s. Certainly Milton intended for the book to address larger issues than Civil War causation. He explained to an interviewer at the time of the book's publication that he studied the past because "it enables one to penetrate beneath the surface of events to find out something about the real forces which move social developments." In a proud letter to a friend, he employed a similar image to describe his achievement: "In this one I think I have penetrated beneath the surface to find, or try to find, the mainsprings of the power conflict of the 'Fifties, and have really given an interpretation of the struggle between emotion and intelligence that may endure." Indeed, Milton built his life of Douglas on the framework of what he considered "the basic philosophical conflict of all American history, the battle between rational and mystic democracy." Through the concept of competing democracies, he proposed to explain war, politics, and race relations in the past while illuminating a wise and liberal course of action for the South and the nation in the present.[18]

Ironically, because of the book's influence on professional historians' interpretations of the Civil War, Milton is probably better remembered today as a historian than as a newspaper editor or a southern liberal. One student of writing on the Civil War declares that Milton's contention that the war need not have occurred "stands as a salient landmark" in the development of what became known as "Civil War revisionist" historiography. Questions of historical inevitability stand beyond proof, and therefore scholars have sought external explanations for this school of interpretation. For one thing, they note, the revisionists exhibited a definite antiwar, even pacifistic outlook that apparently reflected general American attitudes after World War I. Milton, too, abhorred war and, as he told a correspondent, intended in *The Eve of Conflict* "to show that the Civil War was needless, as all wars are needless." Some scholars also give weight to the southern backgrounds of leading revisionists, but they acknowledge that revisionism differed from the pro-South arguments of those who wholeheartedly defended the Confederacy. The revisionists excoriated the southern fire-eaters and admired the Unionists who sought to prevent secession. Thomas J. Pressley suggests that the difference resulted from the fact that many leading revisionists came from border states, such as Milton's Tennessee. In Milton's case, however, the best single explanation for his interpretation is that he wrote as a southern liberal.[19]

In January 1933 Milton began sending chapter drafts from the Douglas biography to friends for comment on his "new philosophy of American history." In the published book, however, he necessarily concentrated on the details of Douglas's political struggles; he employed his philosophy as an implicit backbone to the narrative, referring specifically to it only in order to set the scene for the Little Giant's emergence as an exemplar of Rational Democracy.[20]

Nevertheless, during 1933 Milton made extensive use of his philosophy to explain contemporary politics and race relations. In fact, his editorial essay on FDR's "Revolution—1933" marked the philosophy's first appearance in print. Milton asserted that Thomas Jefferson's victory over the Federalist party in 1800 had established "a Rational

Democracy, a government of philosophers seeking to supply an ar-bitrament of intelligence to the problems of our growing nation." For a generation "the intellectual elite" ruled, but in 1828 Andrew Jackson led "an emotion-driven campaign" from the frontier West into the presidency. With Old Hickory's election, Milton continued, "Rational Democracy was subordinated to the mysticism inherent in frontier life. Until the present, Rational Democracy has never regained control."[21]

A fortnight later, Milton expanded on this conception of strife be-tween rational and mystic democracy in lectures to the Institute of Race Relations at Swarthmore. Rather than beginning with Jefferson and the election of 1800, however, Milton opened his lectures with a description of the amiable compromises on the issue of slavery at the Constitutional Convention. No one should be surprised that the dele-gates from the North and the South had shared "this mutually sympa-thetic and understanding attitude," he declared; they also shared "the philosophy regnant at the birth of the republic," that of Rational De-mocracy. "In essence," he explained, "it meant the rule of the elite in intellect and character, not for their own benefit but for that of the many."[22]

This elite fell from power in the early nineteenth century, an age of sudden and unsettling economic changes in the industrializing North and in the expanding cotton South. Uncertain Americans sought se-curity in simple explanations and absolute convictions. As before, Milton contended that "the Rational Democratic spirit was over-whelmed, and the Irrational Democracy took command" with Andrew Jackson's advent in 1828. His focus on race relations, however, influ-enced him to identify a source for Jackson's "Irrational Democracy" other than the mysticism of the frontier. The spirit of Jacksonianism, he said, "insisted on a literal interpretation of the Declaration of Inde-pendence, and was firmly persuaded that 'the voice of the people is the voice of God.'" Similarly, he wrote in *The Eve of Conflict* that Old Hickory commanded "an emotional democracy, bottoming itself on Rousseau's mystic claims of innate rights, looking on Liberty as a spontaneous creation and asserting rights unconnected with respon-sibilities, among these the universal manhood competence for self-government." The irrational pell-mell of the era dissolved the reason-able foundations for government laid down in the years of Rational Democracy.[23]

This period spawned the antislavery movement, "a manifestation of emotional democracy." Milton conceded that Jackson himself "reprehended" the movement, but he linked the frontiersmen of Jackson's West with the abolitionists of the North: both founded their protest against the order of Rational Democracy on the principle of equality. "The formula of [abolitionist] attack was almost standard," he declared at Swarthmore; "the Negro was God's image in ebony. White and black were brothers, equals, thus slavery was a sin against God. The Declaration of Independence asserted a self-evident truth that all men were created equal. The establishment of slavery was, therefore, a breach of the Declaration as well as an affront to Almighty God." [24]

Milton's thesis exposed core beliefs of his southern liberalism. Untrammeled emotions and the concomitant transformation of political questions into moral issues blinded men to reality and prevented "the arbitrament of intelligence." Only leaders who relied on reason could guide the people through times of social change without exposing them to the dangers of conflict and violence. The example of the Civil War taught him that. It also taught him that, regardless of the consequences, people all too easily cast off any sense of their social responsibility and surrendered to the simple comforts of emotion. Thus, in defense of reason and progress, Milton rejected as dangerous the egalitarian tenets of popular democracy.

His arguments also exposed the limits of Milton's racial liberalism. The antislavery movement, of course, served as a cautionary example of emotions run wild rather than a positive model for modern reformers. A Rational Democrat would have condemned slavery as an outmoded labor system but not as a denial of the rights of man. The slaves were no more ready for responsible citizenship than were the frontiersmen of Tennessee.

Although he preferred to leave the future possibilities of southern race relations open, Milton was the product of a racist culture, and never in his writings did the idea of a racially egalitarian society appear realistic to him. Instead, he considered egalitarianism emotional and illegitimate. This conclusion and his insistence that reason must govern race relations hint at an internal struggle in regard to the Negro. It is irresistible to speculate that racial egalitarianism challenged his own emotions. Perhaps Milton's ban on emotion reflected an effort to down his own prejudices. At any rate, rather than confronting racism, he sacrificed egalitarianism to control it. [25]

To be sure, arguments for the necessity of personal and social control of emotion played a larger role in Milton's philosophy than simply a defense against race prejudice. Modern society, he believed, had grown too complex to risk the rule of mystic democracy. People must cooperate for the common welfare, and only reason made this possible. Emotions, inherently subjective, individualistic, and intolerant of compromise, prevented the arbitrament of intelligence. A liberal society required restraint, not passion.[26]

The hazardous antagonism of reason and emotion constituted the "Great Problem" of the modern age, an editorial on the New Deal contended in 1935. Human beings had not yet progressed to the point of rationally controlling their "instincts, emotional passions, [and] non-conscious influences." Times were changing, though, and the New Deal suggested that reason might gain ascendancy at last. "Now that Brain Trust has been put in the vocabulary, and its motives adjusted to the essence of thought," the editorial concluded, "there is hope that humankind will find its place in the sun."[27]

The editorial seemed a prophecy as 1935 continued. Milton's hopes that the New Deal might open the way to Rational Democracy soared as Chattanooga voted to purchase electric power from the Tennessee Valley Authority. The issue of public power in Chattanooga had arisen immediately after the TVA's creation during the Hundred Days. The private Tennessee Electric Power Company already served the city and announced its intention to fight the TVA with a strategic rate reduction in February 1934. Advocates of public power responded by forming the Public Power League. The voters would decide the issue on 12 March 1935, in an election on the question of issuing $8,000,000 in bonds to construct a municipal plant to take TVA electricity.[28]

Testimony before a congressional investigating committee in 1938 revealed the heavy-handed campaign of TEPCO's defenders. The anti-TVA forces, organized as the Citizen's and Taxpayer's League, also received significant financial aid—$20,000 of the $22,265.45 spent—from the Commonwealth and Southern Corporation, the holding company that owned TEPCO. Chattanooga's morning newspaper, the *Times*, contributed to the general tone of the campaign with editorials charging "that a favorable vote would be a vote for 'socialism, inefficiency, and graft.'"[29]

Public power advocates relied on the *Chattanooga News* to spread their message. From the beginning of the campaign, editorials emphasized that if Chattanooga rejected TVA electricity while neighboring cities took power at cheaper rates, the city's economic future was dim. "It's the day of cheaper power in the Tennessee Valley," the *News* proclaimed. Because the Public Power League had only $1,540 to spend—"they didn't have money enough to wad the gullet of a fish," Milton testified—the *News* also contributed a daily page of advertising to the cause during the final week before the voting. The paper's advocacy earned no praise from the city's elite, almost to a man sympathetic to TEPCO. At the campaign's peak, a *News* reporter later wrote, Milton "often lunched alone at the exclusive Mountain City Club."[30]

By February 1935, voter registration figures indicated widespread public interest in the coming election. Assuming a popular preference for public power, the *News* took this as an augury of victory. "If so," an editorial concluded, "it will be a very illuminating example of how ideas can rout both the money of Wall Street and the predatory power of the sinister political machine."[31]

Election day dawned cold and gray, with rain that turned to sleet before noon. The miserable weather seemed certain to diminish the turn-out; as Jonathan Daniels later wrote, "it looked as if God were a stockholder in the utilities." At midday, though, reports began to come in to the *News* of voters standing in line despite the elements to cast their ballots. By a margin of more than two to one, the bond issue passed.[32]

The victory seemed to Milton an example of democracy at its best. "The result of the election is a great tribute to Mr. John Citizen," the *News* declared. "It shows that he cannot be bought, influenced by selfish motives or swayed from the course he knows to be right. Democracy justified itself in Chattanooga Tuesday." Milton told a friend that the election "was a restorative of confidence in the general citizenship."[33]

Immediately after the election, TEPCO stopped advertising in the *News* and soon began "the virtual subsidizing" of a competing evening newspaper, the *Free Press*. This paper originated as a free weekly advertisement for a chain of grocery stores, but after an unidentified "outside interest" asked for advertising space in 1935 the *Free Press* became no longer free to grocery shoppers, and on 31 August 1936 it began daily publication. TEPCO aided the fledgling with discounts on electricity and paid advertising at rates in excess of regular advertising. Within five years of the election, the *Chattanooga News* closed down forever.[34]

For the time being, though, Milton and the *News* could look forward to a more rational democratic future in Chattanooga, the South, and the nation. Indeed, the power election provided a fine example for Milton's philosophy of American politics. As the overwhelming support for the bond issue demonstrated, the average voter would cast an intelligent ballot once he had been given sufficient information to understand the issues. Proper policy in a democracy, Milton argued, must always contribute to the general welfare rather than to the benefit of a privileged few. Under conditions of political health, then, the programs of Rational Democracy should obtain support from a majority of voters.

The later revelations of irregularities in the anti-TVA campaign of TEPCO and the Citizen's and Taxpayer's League came as no surprise to Milton. Unable to muster a majority through reason, they could only turn to shady tricks and clever attempts to arouse emotions with frightening references to socialism and other evils. Although defeated soundly in this case, TVA's opponents in Chattanooga resembled the interests who had benefited most from the campaigns of mystic democracy in the past.

American history, of course, amply demonstrated to Milton that Rational Democracy best served the common man's interests. For example, as the emotional cacophony of mystic democracy swelled before the Civil War, the heirs of Jefferson made a last stand for compromise and reason. These men, with Stephen A. Douglas at their head, managed to patch together the Compromise of 1850. "In essence," Milton explained in his lectures at Swarthmore, "it was a triumph of intelligence over emotion, a definite reassertion of control by economic realists. The emotion-driven Ultras, the sword dancers and side show freaks of both sections were rebuffed."[35]

In the following decade, the forces of mystic democracy returned to drive an unwilling nation into secession and civil war. Milton contended that the peaceful positions of Rational Democracy enjoyed majority support. Although Lincoln defeated Douglas in a four-way race for the presidency in 1860, Milton wrote, the election returns "indicated the general wish for Union and peace." Moreover, the South left the Union not by decision of the majority, but rather because of the alarms of "sincere but blind" ideologues and the work "of a small but powerful group of political exploiters, men . . . with a compelling interest to keep themselves in office and in power." By sacrificing the general welfare to their own special interests, this "radical minority" brought devastation and defeat down on the South.[36]

The rule of the Radicals in Reconstruction then displayed the inevitable fruits of mystic democracy. Under rhetorical banners of equality and justice, they forced Reconstruction legislation upon the unwilling southern white majority and thus created the hatreds that yet plagued the region. Moreover, while backed by emotional support in the North, Radicals steered the power of the federal government to the aid of special economic interests. The Republican party's clever "marriage of high tariff and 'Bloody Shirt'" enabled a minority, both political and economic, to dominate the nation until the collapse of the 1930s. "They talked of replacing the rule of the oligarchy by that of the people," Milton said, "but actually they designed government by the few, for the few."[37]

The emotional basis of mystic democracy produced a blindness to factual reality that enabled special interests to obtain power under the guise of "democracy," but Rational Democracy rested on reason and facts. An intellectual elite in government would fit policies to actual conditions and would direct them to securing the general welfare. In Milton's view, therefore, democratic government depended more on the quality of its leaders than on the extent of popular participation.

Although without employing Milton's concept of competing democracies, Gerald W. Johnson reached similar conclusions. A column on lynching, for example, referred to "the imbecility of lynchers as a class" and declared that "in a healthy society they are held under the domination of the intelligent." In 1936, Johnson discussed the quality of leadership in America and concluded that "the problem of linking power and responsibility" must be solved in order to ensure a liberal society. "No matter what the Declaration of Independence says," he went on, "all men are not born equal; some are better than others and when the able rule the nation prospers."[38]

Johnson, too, believed that the Civil War era demonstrated the necessity for wise leadership in a time of crisis. Like Milton, he described the antebellum period as a time of unsettling economic change when the North industrialized while the South committed itself ever more to plantation agriculture. At this critical juncture, the abolitionists proceeded to make slavery a moral issue, "and when a political question becomes a moral issue reason and sense promptly depart from it and emotion is all that counts." Although slavery and the tariff contributed to the Civil War, Johnson concluded that "the architect and builder was a statesmanship which had lost contact with the realities of the world; and this sort of statesmanship was almost equally distributed on both sides."[39]

Rather than as an irrepressible conflict between competing economic systems, therefore, Johnson and Milton interpreted the Civil War as the unnecessary result of irresponsible leadership. Failure to lead the nation through the difficult social adjustments required by the Industrial Revolution created secession and war. By clinging blindly to abstract principle, Johnson wrote, leaders of North and South "alike failed to discharge the highest duty of statesmanship, which is to reconcile the letter of the law with the spirit of the times." Milton made exception for Stephen A. Douglas, of course, but otherwise agreed. Indeed, he explained to a correspondent that "the main ideology" of _The Eve of Conflict_ was "that very few things are basically inevitable and irrevocable, that if only we are given men of good mind and goodwill the shocks of change can be cushioned and the shifts in our pattern accommodated without great group distresses."[40]

Milton continued to argue this thesis in his writings after _The Eve of Conflict_. Usually he began by citing the dictum that "change is the law of life" but—he went on—conflict is not; a sharp distinction must be made between the two. The former, he explained, "implies the orderly alteration and readjustment of social and economic patterns. Conflict implies clash, battle, strife and casualties. The fruit of change is progress. The fruit of conflict is desolation which it would be shameful to label peace." This argument suggested that social conflict originated from foolish attempts to hold back or to hurry social evolution. Again the Civil War era afforded him examples for contemplation. Blinded by emotions and absolute principles, the great antebellum reform movements evidenced neither "substantial trace of modern technique in social reconstruction, nor the proposal of a substitute mechanism to replace the organism to be destroyed." For their part, slavery's defenders responded with "subtleties of unrooted logic" that treated the Constitution "as a cadaver for verbal dissection rather than a living instrument, capable of organic growth." The result was a conflict for which both abolitionists and fire-eaters bore responsibility.

Society could not afford leadership from either radicals or reactionaries, both equally unwilling to face the facts of social evolution. "The task of statesmanship," Milton declared, "is to keep human situations unfrozen, so that society can constantly adjust itself to changing needs."[41]

The journalists judged Roosevelt, in his first term, a statesman—but by 1936 they had begun to measure him against the definitions of proper leadership that his New Deal programs had helped to shape. They expected Roosevelt, as a statesman, to stand above partisan squabbles and to lead the entire nation toward enjoyment of the fruits of progress. To do so, he would have to maintain a Rational Democracy while successfully competing with mystic democrats for support from the voters.

For all their qualms about the dangers of what Milton called mystic democracy, none of the journalists ever expressed any admiration for dictatorship. A government with dictatorial powers would make a Rational Democracy impossible. Because of their ability to coerce obedience, dictators never obtained the governmental discipline that the need to win consent for rational policies forced on democratic leaders. Johnson pointed out that whereas a dictator simply proclaimed his policy—assured by ideology of his infallibility regardless of actual conditions—and then jailed any dissenters, Roosevelt proposed to experiment. Reasonable men could support FDR, he continued, in the knowledge that if an experiment failed, no absolute principles prevented him from trying something else. Milton contended in speeches that the choice in governmental methods was between "duress or consent," between rule by external force or rule with "the consent and participation of the people themselves." Just as the Civil War had resulted from failure to steer "a middle course" between the contending abolitionist and proslavery extremes, failure to hold to the rational middle road in the present would result in dictatorship of the right or the left. "The best technique for ordered progress," the *News* declared, "is an abhorrence of extremes, and avoidance of absolutes, and a willingness to adopt workable plans for getting things done."[42]

The journalists realized that a hazardous gulf still yawned between their ideal and present political realities. The leaders of Rational Democracy must still appeal to emotions to win office. "The World is not ruled by reason and logic," Johnson wrote in 1931. The successful leader tended to be "not the intellectual, but the histrionic genius." Three years later he observed that, being "prone to indolence and stupidity," people looked on intelligent self-government as an unpleasant task, and their laziness left open the way for demagogues and criminals to grasp power. "The truth is," he said in 1941, "that men, while they may sometimes be reasoning beings, are always emotional beings." Realistic leaders and liberals must take these facts into account.[43]

In October 1934, as the Congressional elections neared, Milton privately expressed concern that "the mechanics of obtaining an intelligently given consent are extraordinarily great." At present all leaders must obtain consent "through the arousing of emotional agreements," which meant that the character of government depended on the quality of "the particular manipulator" who won office. A Huey Long eventually produced chaos, he continued, whereas "a man of fundamentally proper directives, like Roosevelt," benefited society. Two weeks later, on election day, he predicted to a friend that FDR would receive "a hearty cheer for the New Deal," but expressed skepticism about its significance. "Roosevelt has at the moment the emotional consent of the people," he wrote. "Neither he nor anyone else ever gets intellectual agreement sufficiently to make it matter. It is the ease with which the first is done and the difficulty in doing the last which makes the progress of democracy such a matter of fits and starts."[44]

A year later, in his signed column in the *News*, Milton addressed this problem again. A democratic government, responsive to public opinion and devoted to the common good, he explained, would prevent potential demagogues from gaining power through the exploitation of emotions. "Government by emotion is a grave danger to any nation," Milton warned. "Mystic democracy leads to Boss Tweeds, Big Bill Thompsons and Huey Longs. But a rational democracy is a public safeguard. Public opinion first informed, then discussed, then definitely expressed—this is the way Americans can safely choose."[45]

In 1936, as FDR's reelection victory neared, Virginius Dabney published a speculative essay on the course of history "if the Confederacy had triumphed in the Civil War." Rather than being an enthusiastic portrait of the glories that might have been, the essay revealed the fearful potential for mystic democracy that the journalists still saw in southern politics. At the beginning, Dabney pointed out that victory would have eliminated the "ordeal" of Reconstruction and permitted the continuation of antebellum patterns. Slavery, for example, probably would have been abolished within "a few decades," if only because "it would have been essential to the prosperity of the planters." He cited statistics on antebellum manufacturing and railroad mileage to support his claim that "the industrial advances achieved before the outbreak of hostilities would have been carried over into the post-war era." And he found it reasonable to conclude that "many of the industrial and educational advances which came to the North in the late nineteenth century would have come to the South instead, if the Confederacy had won."[46]

However, Dabney expressed no regret that the Confederacy had failed. Victory could not have "stemmed the rise of the so-called 'poor whites' to power," he contended. In the smaller "Confederate parliament," demagogic leaders of the masses, such as Tom Watson and Huey Long, would have gained greater influence than they held in the national Congress. "Indeed," Dabney wrote, "I greatly fear that we all should be vassals of Huey Long today if the Confederacy had won." After a passing attack on the Agrarians, "the neo-Confederates from Nashville," Dabney ended the essay with the conclusion that "perhaps the gods were kind when the gray wave spent itself on the scarred crest of Cemetery Hill, when Gettysburg was lost, and when Vicksburg fell."[47]

By the end of Roosevelt's first term, Dabney and his fellow journalists were ready to take up their duties in a Rational Democracy. They had joined other southern liberals in the creation of the Southern Policy Committee, an organization devoted to developing informed public opinion in the South "to prepare the way for intelligent political action."[48] They also endorsed Howard W. Odum's concept of "regionalism" and called for realistic regional planning as the foundation for liberal government in the South. Significantly, the journalists' work for these southern liberal programs revealed their criticisms of New Deal policies and their ambivalence about New Deal politics.

8 Southern Policy for the Southern Regions

On the afternoon of Friday, 26 April 1935, two "old slavery negroes" rode a mule-drawn buggy down Peachtree Street in Atlanta past crowds of appreciative spectators. As essential as the "southern belle" whose carriage they followed, octogenarian Aunt Lou and her companion, Ten-Cent Bill Yopp, were a part of the city's annual Confederate Veteran's Day parade. On the previous day, the Commission on Interracial Cooperation concluded its seventeenth annual meeting and the organizational meeting of the Southern Policy Committee began.[1]

The meetings in Atlanta on this southern holiday serve as a focal point for explaining the thinking of the journalists in the mid-1930s: discontent with the effects of the New Deal agricultural program on cotton tenancy, evidenced in resolutions adopted at both meetings, marked a beginning of their disengagement from the New Deal. The new Southern Policy Committee, intended to make southern and national politics more rational and more liberal, contributed to the separation. To be sure, the journalists continued to share many goals with the Roosevelt administration and expected support from the federal government for southern liberal programs. Nonetheless, they emphasized that reform in the South should conform to the principles and purposes that they espoused. The objectives of the SPC and the even grander prospects of Howard W. Odum's regionalism promised significant increases in economic security for southerners; they also revealed a distrust of political action for social change and the conviction that the federal government must defer to regional attitudes. The journalists shared this outlook. Examination of the SPC and of Odum's regionalism illuminates their thinking.

On 17 June 1938 Ralph McGill, the sports editor of the *Atlanta Constitution*, became the paper's executive editor. Readers who wondered if he was prepared to comment on matters weightier than the outcome of a prizefight did not realize that McGill had served a quiet intellectual apprenticeship during the 1930s. While continuing to write his popular daily column on sports, he joined social and agricultural scientists from Georgia Tech and Emory University in journeys around the state as they investigated social and economic conditions, gave speeches interpreting New Deal programs to small-town audiences, and talked and argued with one another. McGill listened and learned, and soon more than held his own in their discussions. For himself and for the South, he wrote forty years later, these were stimulating and educational years: "There was in the South an excitement about the early depression years of the early 1930's which ameliorated the harshness of them. There was a mighty surge of discussion, debate, self-examination, confession and release."[2]

McGill's articles on Georgia's agricultural conditions for the *Constitution* earned the respect of the paper's publisher and, in 1937, helped him win a $1,700 Rosenwald Fellowship. He used the money to travel to Scandinavia where he studied farming methods, farmers' cooperatives, and landownership programs that might afford models for agricultural reform in the South. Less than two weeks after his return he became the *Constitution*'s editor, responsible for a daily column of commentary.[3]

Other southern liberals shared McGill's concern for the future of southern agriculture. Years of drought and depression exposed the awful inadequacies of the region's agricultural economy, and the tenant farmer—insecure, ill-fed, and uneducated—became a symbol of the failure. Despite the urbanization and industrialization that so disturbed the Agrarians and heartened the journalists, the region's economy remained rooted in the soil, dependent on the production of market commodities such as tobacco and cotton.[4]

As the New Deal began, President Roosevelt believed that his program for agriculture would determine the success or failure of his administration. In essence, the Agricultural Adjustment Act sought to raise prices through restrictions on production but, as Paul E. Mertz points out, not necessarily to improve conditions for the people doing the producing. Reports from the South in 1933 indicated that few tenants benefited fairly, because many landlords counted existing debts against the federal payments for crop reductions, and some simply cheated their tenants. In addition, tenants faced the possibility of eviction as acreage reductions tempted landowners to eliminate unnecessary workers.[5] By April 1935, in the third year of the cotton program, southern liberals agreed that the New Deal had failed to help the tenant farmers.

No one deserved more of the credit for creating this consensus than Will Alexander of the Commission on Interracial Cooperation. In January 1934 the Rockefeller Foundation asked Alexander to organize a study of the effects of New Deal policies on blacks. He readily agreed to the study proposal and enlisted Edwin R. Embree, of the Rosenwald Fund, and Charles S. Johnson, of Fisk University, to create the Committee on Negroes in the Economic Reconstruction. Johnson, with his experience in field research, took charge of the committee's investigation of the rural South. Through the dry summer of 1934 his researchers examined the workings of the AAA cotton program. Johnson then compiled their data and reported to Alexander and Embree in October. The committee concluded that the AAA had compounded the problems of an already deteriorating system of agriculture.[6]

An important widening of vision had occurred. Rather than concentrating on the black cotton tenants, the Committee on Negroes in the Economic Reconstruction studied and criticized the tenancy system itself. The fact that the committee sought to reform an economic institution under which *both* white and black tenants suffered contributed importantly to the continuing retreat from racial distinctions in southern liberal thought. The emphasis on the economic factors behind the tenant system, of course, reflects the general—and natural—tendency during the Depression to perceive these forces as primary determinants of social conditions. For some southern liberals, this outlook implied that race constituted an artificial distinction that obscured the economic structure of southern society. As the committee itself pointed out, racism served only those who exploited the tenants. It followed that all tenants, white and black, shared a common economic, or class, interest that racism obscured. Indeed, the biracial Southern Tenant Farmers' Union already operated according to this principle.[7]

Relatively few southern liberals—and none of the journalists—embraced a class outlook. Instead, the journalists condemned tenancy for the damage that degraded material conditions inflicted on the tenants. The influence of the environment became a prominent theme in their editorial discussions of the southern poor. As Gerald W.

Johnson explained, "Southern vices, like Northern vices, thrive in an environment of poverty, ignorance and hopelessness, and Southern virtues are hard put to survive under such conditions."[8]

The fact that the tenants included both black and white southerners allied with environmentalism to challenge racist assumptions as well: if the condition of white tenants resulted from their material surroundings, so too did that of the black tenants. The committee's report stated the point flatly: "It is clear that meager and pinched living is not a racial trait but a result of the system of cotton tenancy."[9] Although such arguments never refuted racism as thoroughly as did arguments based on class analysis, by the late 1930s southern liberals had moved farther away from racist assumptions than perhaps some of them realized.

At the same time, however, the journalists' fear of the dangerous potential of the southern lower class for political mischief persisted. Environmentalism implied that the victims of tenancy lacked the ability to solve their problems themselves. Unfortunate though they were, these southerners still lynched, handled serpents in religious ecstasy, and backed demagogues. As Milton observed, "sharecropping and tenant farming—the form of slavery which we exchanged for chattel slavery—does not make sensitive cultured citizens of its victims." From this perspective, those who spoke of class consciousness and mass action as the means to social change seemed to romanticize the tenants. Effective organization by people who lived "like squirrels on an economic treadmill," as Dabney put it, seemed highly unlikely, and southern liberals sought governmental programs to uplift them. In the case of the tenants, they called for provision of land and training for self-sufficiency to make better citizens of them. Social planning and government-sponsored programs, not class conflict or political mobilization, would reform the South.[10]

The spread of environmentalism in southern liberal thought suggests the magnitude of the distress in the Cotton Belt. When Johnson, Embree, and Alexander met in October 1934 to study that summer's research, they decided to publicize their findings to the nation: the cotton tenancy system had collapsed, and heroic measures were essential to prevent social catastrophe. Some replacement must be created. The committee decided that a program of land-ownership to make small farmers of the tenants best suited their abilities and offered the greatest hope for easing rural poverty. Such a program would require action from the federal government, and Embree and Alexander went to Washington to lobby for the tenants.[11]

Alexander and Embree arrived at the right time, on the crest of a wave of liberal criticism directed against the AAA program in cotton. They produced a bill creating a government corporation to purchase land and sell it to former tenants. Their work bore results when Senator John H. Bankhead and Congressman Marvin Jones joined forces to introduce the Bankhead-Jones Farm Tenancy Bill on 26 March 1935.[12]

As the Bankhead-Jones Bill entered the slow process of congressional deliberation, Alexander worked to organize public opinion behind it. With the efficient help of a well-paid publicist he and Embree made the front pages of leading newspapers with their report of tenancy's collapse, while Johnson turned their data into a short and readable book, *The Collapse of Cotton Tenancy.* Alexander also mobilized southern liberals. In April, at the annual meeting, the CIC endorsed the bill, and two days later the new Southern Policy Committee issued a unanimous resolution of support. Under Alexander's leadership, southern liberals had organized to correct a misguided New Deal policy.[13]

Meanwhile, on 18 February, a week after Bankhead first introduced his bill in the Senate, President Roosevelt asked Rexford Tugwell, the liberal assistant secretary of agriculture, to head a new agency in charge of the government's land-use planning programs. Tugwell accepted the position eagerly and asked Will Alexander to join him as deputy administrator of the Resettlement Administration, as the new agency was called. Alexander apparently decided to accept the position during the April meetings in Atlanta. As his special assistant he chose Brooks Hays, a lawyer and a delegate to the SPC meeting from Arkansas. By the middle of May, Alexander was in Washington to begin his work in charge of matters related to tenancy; he would never return to lead the CIC. In October, the commission's board of directors asked Howard W. Odum to develop proposals for the CIC's future.[14]

In May 1934, as Charles S. Johnson's field researchers set out to assess the condition of cotton tenancy, Raymond Leslie Buell, the president of the Foreign Policy Association, asked Francis Pickens Miller to undertake a special project. Buell feared that the United States lacked a "sense of general national policy," as Miller recalled, and proposed that he organize "Committees of Correspondence" across the nation to generate policy discussion. Miller, a Virginian recently returned to the United States after several years of service in an international Christian organization, accepted Buell's offer enthusiastically. His labors led him to the South and to agricultural policy. [15]

Miller arranged meetings in various southern cities to present his plans. He told his audiences that narrow, special interests too often determined government policy, but that organized citizens' groups could develop policy in the "national interest" if they studied the issues and presented appropriate programs to the public and to government officials. Miller then extended an invitation to form a local Southern Policy Group within a regional organization. A persuasive man, he gained enthusiastic support, and the Southern Policy Committee's first conference, in April 1935, drew delegates from nine states. [16]

The SPC's origins as a project of the Foreign Policy Association, an organization favorable to free trade and internationalism, reflects another source of southern liberal dissatisfaction with the New Deal. The major New Deal recovery programs, the National Industrial Recovery Act and the AAA, were designed to raise domestic prices on American products and thus required a protectionist foreign policy. On the other hand, the secretary of state, Cordell Hull, boasted a reputation as an advocate of tariff reduction. These conflicting orientations caused the Roosevelt administration's foreign policy to remain problematic. The journalists generally favored the free-trade policies of Hull, and Francis Pickens Miller connected foreign policy and agriculture in his proposals for the Southern Policy Committee. Above all, he told his audiences in the South, the SPC should study the effects of crop controls and diminished cotton exports. Although Miller hoped that the policy committees would eventuate in a national organization, only in the South did his linkage of foreign policy and agricultural policy strike a responsive chord. [17]

Much of the credit for the SPC's concentration on policies for the South, however, belongs to a vocal minority within the organization: the Nashville Agrarians. Miller presented his plans for the SPC to those among the Twelve Southerners who sought to keep the cause of Agrarianism alive in Nashville, and they agreed to form a local policy group. Donald Davidson represented them at the organizational conference in Atlanta, and Allen Tate and Robert Penn Warren were delegates to the second meeting in Chattanooga. Lyle Lanier and Frank Lawrence Owsley also belonged to the Nashville group, and the latter prepared their statement on Agrarian policy for the Atlanta conference. In addition, H. C. Nixon—his views considerably modified since 1930—became chairman of the SPC.[18]

Though few in number, these men heavily influenced the discussions at the SPC conferences by measuring every policy proposal against their goal of an Agrarian South. Controversy erupted over and over, as the first SPC report put it, "between the predominant view expressed at the conference and a number of members of the Nashville group." In fact, a heated exchange between Allen Tate and William Amberson—a Socialist propounding collective farming—at the Chattanooga meeting, became almost legendary. Their shouting match went unrecorded, but numerous dissents and minority statements in the published SPC reports mark the course of the warfare. Should a policy statement fail to provoke the Agrarians, it elicited objections from the other delegates.[19]

The members of the SPC did agree on one issue—"and only one," Donald Davidson added—the Bankhead-Jones Farm Tenant Bill. Agrarians and liberals alike considered individual land-ownership the best solution to the collapse of tenancy. For their part, the Nashville group perceived the bill as a step toward an Agrarian society.[20]

The liberals in the SPC endorsed the bill for different reasons. A more diversified agriculture, with farmers obtaining income by selling their surpluses in local urban markets, would open a new market for the consumption of southern manufacturers while enabling city dwellers to have less expensive and better food. Industrial workers would benefit as well: so long as rural conditions remained bleak, southern employers could select from a large pool of desperate, powerless workers. "It isn't the mill owner—or even the militia—but the farmer, who makes Southern strikes so hopeless," George Fort Milton said. "Farm income is so pitifully low that almost any town or city payroll wage seems luxury to the farm boy or girl." With farming a realistic alternative, employers would have to improve wages and work conditions to hold their labor force. Thus, for the liberals in the SPC, agricultural reform represented a necessary first step toward general economic development in the South.[21]

The delegates at Atlanta declared that the primary purpose of the Southern Policy Committee was "to prepare the way for intelligent political action." The SPC's actual influence on contemporary politics, however, seems to have been quite limited. The fullest assessment of the organization appears in George B. Tindall's general history of *The Emergence of the New South, 1913–1945*. As do other historians, Tindall notes the SPC's endorsement of the Bankhead-Jones bill, the debates at the conferences, and the publication of policy reports, but he emphasizes the short life of the organization—"only about two years"—and concludes that "as a liaison between the intellectuals and the masses, the SPC failed."[22]

Examination of the SPC's outlook on politics and reform reveals the inevitability of this failure. The SPC based its program of public discussion and policy formation on the assumption that government in a democracy must represent the general interest. Although confident that this program would benefit the southern people, the SPC sought primarily to rationalize government and politics, not to establish a liaison with the masses.

Donald Davidson once expressed doubt that the delegates at the SPC conferences "included any dirt farmers, Fundamentalist preachers, business Tories, or actual mechanics, carpenters, salesmen, housewives, or philosophers." Despite his rhetorical flourishes, Davidson had perceived the homogeneity of the SPC's membership. In fact, more than half the delegates at both conferences came from either academia or journalism. Except for a few labor union officials, the other delegates came from the professions and business. Because Miller organized the SPC in the southern cities, the delegates represented primarily the professional class of the urban South. They were overwhelmingly white and male. In fact, with the single exception of Charles S. Johnson, who was designated a member-at-large to the committee in 1935, no blacks participated in the SPC's deliberations on the South's future.[23]

Davidson also charged that most delegates were "of a liberal-to-left-wing tendency." The Agrarian critic exaggerated the leftist sentiment in the SPC, but two other members, Virginius Dabney and

Jonathan Daniels, acknowledged that liberals constituted the main part of the membership. The SPC actually gave a formal structure to an existing informal network of southern liberals who shared a self-conscious southern identity and who judged policies first by their effect on the region.[24]

Nonetheless, the SPC declared its intention to represent the views of the "more general elements of opinion in the southern states." Members believed that the contemporary political system served the nation poorly. In a true democracy, the first conference declared, "the people themselves consciously directed governmental power" to serve "the common welfare," but representation in the United States had grown "increasingly irresponsible." In the South, in particular, "exclusive economic interests on the one hand or political sensa-tionalists on the other" had too often monopolized politics.[25]

The absence of references to the Democratic or Republican parties in the conference reports underlined the SPC's dissatisfaction with existing political practices. In fact, according to the policy committee ideal, the process of policy formation and implementation had no real place for political partisanship. Francis Pickens Miller envisioned the "democratic process" as a two-way flow of ideas and actions linking citizens and their government. The "voluntary opinions and activities of citizens" would converge on the government and then the govern-ment, both directly and indirectly through policy decisions, would "stimulate citizens to further thought and action." Clearly, politicians loyal only to party and office impeded and corrupted this process.[26]

The journalists shared this distaste for the governmental fruits of partisanship. Political machines, they complained, exerted dangerous power in American government; by their nature, these organizations served themselves, not the public, and self-interest spawned expedi-ent practices. "The real issues never follow party lines," Gerald W. Johnson contended. "The parties are organizations for the purpose of getting office, and fighting for real issues is a difficult and doubtful way to get office." Thus, the journalists praised every sign of prog-ress toward what Milton described as "that happy day, perhaps far in the future, when there comes a general and much-needed re-classification of American politics into liberal and conservative groups through the country as a whole."[27]

This vision of a rationalized political system, free from partisanship and machines, reappeared in the journalists' discussions of poll tax repeal. Without doubt the most important factor behind southern liberal campaigns against ballot restrictions was the New Deal's popularity among lower-class southerners, those whom the tax kept from the polls. Moreover, as the tenant farmer became the symbol of the South's most pressing problems of poverty and deprivation, further obscuring the stereotypes of degraded poor whites and ignorant Negroes, liberals could discuss expansion of the electorate without raising spectres of race or demagoguery. Comparisons of the statements on voting in the two SPC reports indicates the swift change of opinion that made poll tax repeal a major liberal cause in the late 1930s. At the 1935 meeting, the General Committee of the SPC addressed the suffrage issue cautiously and without reference to laws restricting the ballot. At the following year's meeting, however, the SPC adopted a straightforward resolution calling for "removal of those qualifications for voting which disfranchise the unpossessed, such as the poll tax and nonpermanent registration."[28]

Milton and Dabney endorsed the resolution, but their editorials against the poll tax justified repeal on the grounds that expansion of the electorate would make government in the South less subject to corrupt machines and irresponsible leaders. The tax kept worthy voters from the polls, reducing the electorate, while making it possible for machine leaders to pay poll taxes for a small number of pliant voters and thereby control elections. The *News* called the poll tax "the favorite tool of corrupt machines," and the *Times-Dispatch* claimed that the tax enabled unscrupulous politicians to buy the ballots of "venal voters."[29]

These arguments bore interesting implications for their opinion of voting by blacks. Critical references to political machines perpetuated long-standing southern complaints against black voters in the urban South. In a few cities, in fact, Negro political leaders acquired a degree of power through their ability to deliver votes to white politicians; the political power of these men seemed to the journalists typical examples of cynical machine politics and provided them with a ready explanation for white reluctance to enfranchise Negroes.[30]

Milton and Dabney objected to black political bosses for the same reason that they condemned white bosses: machine politicians hindered the efforts of responsible leaders to convince citizens to vote intelligently and independently. This conviction also made bloc voting by Negroes, with group interest the criterion for action, seem illegitimate and dangerous. Ironically, as Democrats and New Dealers, they interpreted the general shift of black voters nationally from the Republican to the Democratic party as evidence of a new, praiseworthy independence.[31]

These arguments assumed that political control should remain in the hands of the white majority. Rather than grasping power by voting as an organized group, Negroes must win admission to southern politics as disinterested, responsible citizens. The *Times-Dispatch* informed critics of its stand on the poll tax who feared for the future of "white man's government," that the newspaper favored "government largely by white men, but in which qualified Negro citizens are allowed the franchise, and given such opportunities as they can properly exercise as American citizens." Poll tax repeal would reform, not revolutionize, southern politics.[32]

The hatred for machine politics that appeared in discussions of poll tax repeal flowed from the journalists' self-proclaimed devotion to the common welfare. To be sure, they did not expect special interests to disappear from politics. The first SPC conference complained that "there are economic functional interests and general regional interests which are not at present afforded adequate expression" in government. Similarly, Francis Pickens Miller called for a national policy designed to ensure "justice as between regions and groups." Government could carry out this policy only by subordinating the desires of narrow interests to the greater claims of the general interest.[33]

Thus, the southern liberals in the SPC called for a rational government to balance legitimate interests within an American consensus that they labeled "the general interest." A healthy democratic process, which would assure to all Americans "a larger measure of social justice," would eliminate the danger to the nation posed by the external radicalism of fascism and communism. At home, too, extremists threatened democratic government. "The real danger to the country," the first conference declared, "is from the reactionaries, on the one hand, and the demagogues and political charlatans on the other." If responsible citizens failed to act, democracy could not survive.[34]

The outlook of the Southern Policy Committee, as put forth in the writings of its founder and in the organization's declared "Objectives," bore resemblances to Milton's concept of Rational Democracy. Milton argued that throughout American history, mystic democrats had aroused the emotions of the masses for political action; the ensuing clamor not only unseated the rational elite who provided government in the general interest, but also enabled selfish interests, under the cover of high-sounding rhetoric, to grasp power at the expense of the people. The language of the SPC's Objectives reveals similar qualms about the role of the masses in politics. The SPC hedged its commitment to expanded democracy with qualifying adjectives: the Objectives called for "intelligent political action," "desirable public policies," and "persons who possess the proper qualifications to undertake political activity." Rather than trying to establish a liaison between the southern intellectuals—the majority of them liberals—and the masses, the SPC sought to unify the southern intellectuals on matters of public policy. In essence, the SPC intended to replace the political bosses with liberal expertise. Achievement of the SPC's Objectives would bring about a political system in which, as Milton said of rule by the rational elite in Jefferson's day, "governments were shifted on issues, not impulses, and democracy involved reason and intelligence."[35]

In effect, therefore, the SPC proposed to become the arbiter of political legitimacy in the South. With the aid of their "impartial research agencies," the policy groups would not only define the issues but would also devise appropriate and practical policies on a framework of indisputable facts. Leaders who relied on reason could then drive the placemen and charlatans from politics. Most important, the Objectives of the SPC reflected the outlook of persons who perceived no fundamental conflict between the "general interest" and their own interests. As a result, these persons implicitly identified themselves and their reforms as the cutting edge of social change in the South. More militant advocates of change passed beyond the pale of responsibility and realism.

By the end of FDR's first term, the journalists had available a southern liberal alternative to the New Deal: Howard W. Odum's program of regional planning for the South. As director of the University of North Carolina's Institute for Research in Social Science and author of numerous studies of southern society, Odum epitomized the social scientist who provided citizens and their leaders with the facts necessary for development of public policies that served the general interest and protected the health of the democratic process. When the first SPC conference met in 1935, Odum was completing his most important project, an immense statistical survey of the South. Published in 1936 as *Southern Regions of the United States,* this study presented, in addition to a multitude of facts and figures, Odum's theory of rational reform through social planning on a basis of regionalism.[36]

The journalists had known and respected Odum since the 1920s, but the publication of *Southern Regions* won him further acclaim from them. Johnson even proposed "capital punishment for every [southern] newspaper reporter who could not prove within a specified time" that he had read *Southern Regions* and other works by the Chapel Hill regionalists.[37] In fact, though, *Southern Regions* proposed no revolution in southern liberal thinking.

Odum conceived of the Southeastern Region—the old Confederacy with Kentucky substituted for Texas—as one of six distinct regions within the United States, each of which required distinct policies of social planning that took into account regional needs, resources, and cultures. This accorded with the outlook of other southern liberals, who identified themselves with their region as much as they did with the particular state or city in which they resided. Their organizations invariably asserted a southern identity, in name and in practice. Above all, they perceived with Odum that the region's history, manifested "in a folk-regional culture of distinctive features," set it apart from the rest of the nation.[38] At the same time, they believed that the Depression demonstrated the economic interdependence of all the United States and that only the federal government could enforce and administer measures of the scope necessary for recovery. The federal government could provide the assistance essential for the South to escape its poverty by diversifying agriculture, expanding industry, and increasing the wages paid to labor.

Odum agreed that the South could not survive in isolation from the rest of the nation and proposed substitution of "the new regionalism for the old sectionalism in American life." Regionalism differed from sectionalism because it placed the national welfare first, ahead of the region's special interests. Thus, regionalism opened the way for cooperation and social planning. Sectionalism, "the group correspondent to individualism," led to its necessary corollary, "an inevitable coercive federalism."[39]

Unlike the journalists, Odum never mustered much enthusiasm for the New Deal. A consideration of timing may help to explain his attitude. When the Hundred Days began, Odum had been at work on his

"Southern Regional Study" for more than a year. Suddenly, a variety of far-reaching federal programs were under way in the South and the nation. The swift pace of events outdated his descriptive research while New Deal programs made his prescriptive proposals appear almost imitative. In 1934, he warned sourly that "the experimentation of the New Deal, because of its emergency nature and specialized motivation, can not meet the specifications of matured social planning." Although he conceded in *Southern Regions* that there were some "New Deal organizations in which were the beginnings of realistic planning," he expressed dismay at "many of the New Deal plans which ignored regional reality." Remarkably few references to "the Deal in Washington" appeared in *Southern Regions*, and even fewer were favorable.[40]

Social planners and politicians had little in common, in Odum's opinion. In *Southern Regions* he described government and politics as "the most critical of all regional social problems" and asserted that "the politics of the recent past and of the present stands as a closed door to any reasonably full opportunity for the southern people and their institutions." Although the book offered no clear alternative to the political system, Odum seemed to feel that careful social planning ought to replace partisan politics, with qualified administrators taking the place of office-seeking politicians. He even proposed that "during the special periods selected for civic education and planning there may be attempted a sort of moratorium on violent industrial and race conflict." This outlook constituted a major difference between Odum and the journalists. Despite their disgust at the corruptions that seemed typical of partisan politics, the journalists intended to reform the political system, not abandon it; they considered experts and their plans necessary resources upon which Rational Democracy would rely for facts and policy. For Odum, planning precluded politics; the Roosevelt administration, by its very nature, could never win his enthusiasm.[41]

The essential themes of Odum's regionalism, however, were balance and equilibrium. He argued that "in an expanding and complex urban industrial America" citizens must solve "the problem of balance between central and local control in democratic society." The alternatives of strict state rights or the "complete dominance of the central power" produced only dangerous imbalance. "Hence," Odum concluded, "logically comes this buffer of regional arrangements to seek equilibrium between centralization of power and the doctrine and practice of states' rights." His conception of regionalism confirmed his thesis. The states of the Southeast shared common characteristics of physical resources, culture, and history that transcended state boundaries while differentiating the region from the rest of the nation. In *The Wasted Land,* his "commentary" on *Southern Regions,* Gerald W. Johnson explained that regionalism meant the division of the nation into six "entities" rather than the artificial division of forty-eight states. Southerners must face facts, Johnson went on; "the interdependence of the States is such a fact, and where it comes into collision with the theory of States' Rights, the theory must give way to the fact."[42]

Odum's proposed buffer of regional arrangements between the Southeast and the federal government also provided him with a means to balance the divided purposes that his theory required. The region clearly lacked the ability to achieve optimal levels of development on its own, and Odum acknowledged that the Southeast must depend on federal assistance to carry out the program of regionalism. This strategy demonstrated that the material factors, such as expenditures on libraries or the value of farm land, that distinguished the Southeast, would be overcome through planning and regional development. The South of poverty and waste would disappear. Such a conclusion, however, threatened the very theory of regionalism itself, which depended on the existence of actual regional differences. Odum had to hold up the concept of the folkways, those time-encrusted customs of a distinct folk culture, as the primary justification for regional planning. Only persons sensitive to the nature and power of regional folkways could devise programs for healthy social change, and clearly the federal government lacked this knowledge. Odum insisted that patient social planning on a regional basis alone could make possible the development of southern resources within the gradual pace of change dictated by the folkways. Thus, Odum's regionalism had two faces: on the one hand, he would integrate the South into the nation, while on the other, he would protect regional distinctiveness against outside pressures.[43]

Odum's regionalism reinforced convictions that the journalists had long expressed. The South could not stand apart from the nation except at the price of poverty and provincialism. On the other hand, southern history warned that attempts to use federal power to bring about reforms that were in conflict with southern folkways would provoke opposition and conflict. Johnson asserted that the federal government, too, must face the fact of regionalism. Policies framed without consideration for regional realities would meet resistance. The result, as the sad case of Prohibition showed, would be disrespect for law and unnecessary turmoil. Johnson concluded that "the answer, obviously, lies in some form of region-State cooperation supervised by the national authority."[44]

On 24 April 1935, immediately before the first SPC conference, the annual meeting of the Commission on Interracial Cooperation endorsed the Costigan-Wagner Anti-Lynching bill, then suffocating under a southern filibuster in the Senate. The CIC had never before supported federal legislation against mob violence, and the endorsement caused dissent. The most prominent dissenter, Jessie Daniel Ames, director of the Association of Southern Women for the Prevention of Lynching, contended that only the traditional southern liberal method of education to improve public opinion could eliminate the causes of lynching. The federal bill struck at the prosecution of mob murderers, however, precisely where the southern judicial system, and southern liberals, had proved least effective. In its endorsement, the CIC pointed out that despite improved public attitudes, prosecution of lynchers remained "futile."[45]

The journalists remained dubious about the benefits of federal legislation against lynching, but their comments illustrate changes in opinion. On the whole, they continued to believe, as Ralph McGill said in 1939, that "public opinion is a stronger bulwark than law." Significantly, though, no one raised the principle of state rights against the legislation. John Temple Graves spoke for them all when he declared that "the only tenable basis for opposition to a federal bill is that it wouldn't work and isn't necessary."[46]

In defense of the New Deal, the journalists had repudiated the doctrine of state rights. Conservative opponents of the Roosevelt administration embraced state sovereignty as a sacred principle essential to the preservation of liberty, and the journalists scorned them for hypocrisy. "Time, and the Industrial Revolution, have taken the vessel of State's Rights and have poured from it all its oil and healing element," the *Chattanooga News* said. "It is this empty vessel which the Republicans hold before us as their newly discovered holy grail."[47]

Nonetheless, as the antilynching bill portended, the federal government might enact legislation obnoxious to the South and to southern liberals.

Significantly, in *Southern Regions* Odum often cited race relations as an example of the sort of condition, rooted in the folkways, that regionalism could best treat. He contended that no changes in race relations could be made "on any purely 'southern,' sectional basis," by which he meant in "the interests of the white South," nor could "complete federal coercion and control" bring about "immediate readjustments" in defiance of the powerful folkways. "What is needed," Odum concluded in characteristic prose, "is a comprehensive approach looking to the facts and welfare of the North and South, of white and Negro, all according to the regional-national approach inseparably involved both in ultimate ends and in methods of attainment." Skilled regional planners might "design events and practices" to begin transformation of the conditions that created and reinforced the folkways of race relations.[48]

Throughout *Southern Regions*, Odum seemed conscious of great impending changes in race relations. In particular, the black population's rising level of education and skills contrasted sharply with the Negro's present "proportionate part in southern life." Odum contended that erroneous premises of Negro inferiority had created "a supreme example of race tragedy under conditions which need not exist any more in civilized society." By his progress, the Negro had "earned in the hard school of social reality a better place than he now holds."[49]

On the other hand, the racial folkways of the region presented a barrier to swift social change. "Manifestly," Odum proclaimed, "it is asking too much of a region to change over night the powerful folk ways of long generations." The new day's dawning lay far in the future. He declared that "it is too big a burden to place upon one or two generations the task of changing the powerful folkways of the centuries at one stroke." Thus, southern liberals must give "hard-boiled realistic, evolutionary hope for the future" to impatient southern Negroes. Only careful regional planning could carry out this delicate yet essential program.[50]

Necessarily, then, social change in the South must occur gradually. "The objectives of the new planning envisage no Utopias or quick magic changes," Odum warned. Rather, southern development through planning meant "a goal ahead definitely to be achieved through gradual growth and through intelligence and skill." Indeed, planning itself required gradualism in method. He declared admiringly that "social planning is the most difficult and the least emotional and sentimental way, requiring time, skill, technical training, extraordinary ability, patience, courage."[51]

The idea of a direct attack on the Jim Crow system had no place in Odum's regionalism. In his discussions of education, for example, the South's dual school system represented an added expense for an already impoverished region, but never did he call it wasteful. Moreover, he concluded his discussion of reforming race relations with a lengthy quotation from an address that his colleague, Guy B. Johnson, had delivered to the CIC's annual meeting in 1935. According to Odum's summary, Johnson emphasized that Negro progress inevitably meant growing tensions over the issue of the participation of blacks in government and society. Southern liberals must recognize this progress and "take the inequalities out of the bi-racial system." Such a program posed no threat to "the integrity of the races," Johnson contended; "the races can go the whole way of political and civil equality without endangering their integrity."[52]

Thus, Odum's regionalism reasserted the southern liberal program of vertical segregation. His concepts rested on the same faith in evolutionary social progress as the only sure means to lasting reform. With the Negro treated as "an integral, normal, and continuing factor in the culture of the Southeast," regional planners would improve conditions for both blacks and whites without the need to challenge segregation.[53]

In *Southern Regions* Odum maintained that nonsoutherners, unfamiliar with regional folkways and impatiently insistent on social change, threatened rather than aided the work of planning. In 1936, however, the defensive qualities of regionalism remained latent. Odum declared confidently that "the time has come to follow up the earlier broadsides and critical appraisals of southern culture with something more nearly approaching functional analysis and working specifications." He proposed putting into effect "two six-year priority schedules" for regional planning. "Such a period," he explained, "is the minimum time within which the Southeast might attain its early maturity or, failing that, give evidence of what place it will henceforth hold in the nation." In his final sentence, Odum proclaimed that "this test of American Regionalism should be made before the turn of the mid-century."[54]

After the meetings in Atlanta, Will Alexander left the Commission on Interracial Cooperation to take up his new duties with the Re-settlement Administration. His departure presented Odum with the opportunity to set his regional planning program into motion. With the executive director in Washington, and with the foundation grants that funded the organization due to expire in 1938, the CIC's board asked Odum to develop a plan for the Interracial Commission's future.[55]

Odum proposed a new organization, designed to further the goals of regionalism, to supercede the CIC's concentration on interracial cooperation. Alexander gave his influential endorsement to the plan, and on 7 October 1937 Odum presented his proposal to the CIC's board of directors. The new organization would have four divisions—agriculture, industry, public administration–education, and inter-racial programs. The board conferred the presidency of the CIC on Odum and authorized him to look into funding for the new organiza-tion. He proceeded to create the "Interim Southeastern Regional Ad-visory Committee" and called for the committee to meet with him in Atlanta on 15 January 1938. Two delegates came from each state in the Southeastern Region, and Virginius Dabney joined Jonathan Daniels, John Temple Graves, and Mark Ethridge in a strong con-tingent of journalists on the committee. Odum presented his plan to this group of sympathetic southern liberals and, although disagreeing among themselves on priorities, they expressed general satisfaction. With the expectation that he would be able to incorporate both the CIC and the SPC into the new organization, in February 1938 Odum began raising funds for his Council on Southern Regional Development.[56]

None of the journalists yet realized it, but Odum's plan marked the high tide for their southern liberalism. The establishment of the Southern Policy Committee and the presentation of Odum's region-alism constituted the organizational expression of their outlook on the South. The SPC proposed to rationalize southern politics with the conviction that government would then serve the general welfare. Regionalism promised a further advance toward this goal. Social planners, dependent on facts and realistic because of the nature of their work, would provide the expertise necessary to frame proper policies. Perhaps by 1950, the journalists hoped, the South would be well along the way toward economic prosperity and social health.

Within six months, however, Odum's plan was in a shambles and the journalists were on the defensive. The Roosevelt administration seemed now in violation of the principles of Rational Democracy, and the journalists waxed critical at the apparent direction of the New Deal. As the threat of war in Europe cast ever darker shadows across the nation, they warned against impetuous reformers and the growing potential for conflict between classes, races, and sections.

9 The New Deal Is Dealt

Between the Right Honorable FD, the Southern Conference for Human Welfare, and twenty other groups that are literally taking the lead to do what the Council ought to do, I think I'll presently go heat-wave hay-wire," Howard W. Odum complained in mid-August 1938. On the eleventh, at Barnesville, Georgia, President Roosevelt announced the publication of the National Emergency Council's *Report on Economic Conditions of the South* and repeated his designation of the South as "the Nation's No. 1 economic problem." More importantly, he went on to criticize Georgia's Senator Walter F. George, seated on the stage near the president, and called on Georgians to vote against him in the upcoming primary election. Two days later, the invitations to the Southern Conference for Human Welfare, to meet in Birmingham in November, went out to liberals across the South.[1]

The journalists shared Odum's misgivings about these new developments. By the summer of 1938 they had grown angry with Roosevelt's stubborn insistence on continuing New Deal reform. Their dissatisfaction arose early in his second term with the president's apparent sympathy for labor militance and his devious effort to pack the Supreme Court, and climaxed with FDR's attempt to purge conservative Democrats from Congress in 1938.

Meanwhile, labor organization and New Deal reform had set in motion new currents in southern liberal thought. That some unions had successfully organized black and white workers seemed a sign that development of economic consciousness in the South would break down the racial barriers dividing workers. The idea of class divisions and conflicting economic interests within the South challenged the journalists' sense of the South as a distinct and unified region. These viewpoints constituted, in Richard H. King's phrase, "a new Southern intellectual liberalism" that envisioned significant social change resulting from a popular democratic movement for liberal reform backed by the power of the federal government. The Southern Conference for Human Welfare, with laborers, farmers, and a large minority of

Negroes among the delegates, seemed an institutional expression of the new southern liberalism.[2]

The journalists held firm to the ideas that they had pronounced for years and spurned invitations to join the SCHW. Examination of the context in which they encountered the new southern liberalism helps to explain their resistance. By the end of 1938 they believed that the New Deal had come to an end, and, even though the South's problems remained unsolved, the uproar surrounding the Southern Conference for Human Welfare seemed a demonstration that the new liberalism promised no solutions.

Organized labor's struggle to win collective bargaining rights climaxed early in FDR's second term with the tactic of sit-down strikes forcing employers to recognize the unions and with the enforcement of New Deal legislation protecting these rights. The journalists had welcomed labor unions to the South and applauded the National Industrial Recovery Act's Section 7A, which guaranteed the right to collective bargaining; nevertheless, they always emphasized southern economic development. Manufacturers, they argued, must recognize that better wages for workers would increase purchasing power in the South and would ensure their own prosperity in the long run. According to the journalists, then, labor and management should eschew conflict and seek compromises that would benefit the general interest of economic development.

In the final days of 1936, after Roosevelt's reelection triumph, militant members of the United Automobile Workers occupied the General Motors plant at Flint, Michigan. Workers at other GM plants swiftly followed suit. After a month's stalemate, the auto manufacturer surrendered to the union on 11 February 1937. The dramatic sit-down strike paved the way for organizers from the Committee of Industrial Organizations to gain union recognition from the United States Steel Corporation and other mass-production industries.[3]

The sit-downs shocked the journalists. "As much as we sympathize with Labor," the *Chattanooga News* said, "we can see no justification for seizure of private property." No liberal could countenance defiance of the laws. The *Times-Dispatch* warned against the dangerous implications of tolerating the sit-down tactic: "And what is to prevent any group—the Ku Klux Klan, the Silver Shirts, the *Amerika–Deutscher Volksbund,* or the lynching mob—from taking the law into its own hands whenever it sees fit to do so, if large groups of laborers are allowed to defy the courts?"[4]

In this context of liberal devotion to the law, President Roosevelt's bill to reorganize the federal judiciary caused trepidation among even those of the journalists who defended FDR. Hanging like a sword over Roosevelt's plans for his second term was the fact that the Supreme Court had already invalidated the NRA and the AAA and was likely to rule against other New Deal measures now moving upward through the courts. The Court's rulings against the New Deal programs had distressed the journalists, but their preferred method for FDR to fight back seemed to be through constitutional amendments limiting the Court's power.[5]

Thus, the announcement of FDR's court reorganization bill on 5 February 1937 came as a surprise. Although put forward as a measure to increase the efficiency of the federal courts, the bill would allow Roosevelt to appoint as many as six new justices to the Supreme Court, obliterating the present 5–4 conservative majority. The secrecy of the bill's preparation and the transparent attack on the Supreme Court hidden behind Roosevelt's pious concern for judicial efficiency caused even his most ardent supporters to swallow hard. After they recovered from their initial shock, though, most of the journalists did endorse the bill, arguing that it posed no threat to the Constitution.[6]

Virginius Dabney angrily opposed FDR's court plan. Significantly, Dabney's editorials connected the court fight with labor struggles in industry and expressed a fear of anarchy in the United States. "The constant and reiterated attacks on the Supreme Court from official sources must be considered in relation to the current wave of sit-down strikes," one editorial declared. Another pointed out that the courts protected "persecuted minorities" and civil liberties and warned that "repeated defiance of the courts can only mean chaos, mob psychology and the triumph of lynch philosophy."[7]

Dabney was not alone when he linked the sit-downs with criticism of the president. "When the 'stay-ins' are permitted to hold private property indefinitely," the *Chattanooga News* asked in January, "can we wonder that private industry has become bitter and that, blaming the New Deal for such things, it unleashed a campaign of unparalleled bitterness against the President in the last campaign?" Johnson complained that laws now forced corporations to act responsibly, but no restrictions on the unions existed. "Any group of men, whether laborers, capitalists, soldiers, or Ku Klux, ought to be held responsible as a group for their group activities," he declared.[8]

These initial months of FDR's second term, with labor conflicts creating the background to the stalled court bill, marked a turning away from the New Deal for the journalists. In the years preceding, they had given the president a crucial role in a liberal society. Protection of the general welfare depended on leaders who stood above partisan battles and defended the common interest. Now it appeared that FDR was choosing sides, favoring certain interests over others, and attempting to concentrate government power in his own hands.

As the political coalition of labor, farmers, blacks, and city-dwellers that gave Roosevelt his victory in 1936 pushed the government to serve their interests, the journalists suddenly began to essay definitions of liberalism. Dabney, for example, rejected the idea that liberalism inevitably favored human rights over property rights. Certainly liberals desired "the advancement of human rights," he said, but "the chief distinction between radical political thought, and liberalism in politics, is the respect that liberalism has for property rights." The sit-downs inspired John Temple Graves's definition as well: "If the word 'liberalism' has any meaning left in it now," he wrote, "it means playing fair, giving the devil his due, abiding by the rules, never saying the end justifies the means, respecting the law."[9]

As the conflict between New Deal reformers and obstinate conservatives intensified, the journalists tried to lift liberalism above the fray. The *Chattanooga News* decried the sort of thinking that labeled all advocates of social change Communists or Socialists but went on to condemn "the mis-named Liberal with a chip on his shoulder, who thinks all rich men are reactionary and bad at heart." In truth, it claimed, liberalism was "tolerance," a quality "badly needed in America."[10]

As the journalists reacted critically to the sit-downs, other southern liberals identified the labor unions as agents of liberal reform. In 1934, Will Alexander, Charles S. Johnson, and Edwin Embree—the Committee on Negroes in the Economic Reconstruction—arranged for Horace R. Cayton, a black sociologist who had studied with Robert Ezra Park at the University of Chicago, and George S. Mitchell, an economist at Columbia University, to investigate the effect on Negro workers of the upsurge of unionization inspired by the NIRA. The two men divided their tasks, with Cayton studying conditions in the North and Mitchell concentrating on the South.[11]

Mitchell took up his research for the committee with great interest. Unlike his older brother Broadus, whose studies concentrated on the process of industrialization in the South, Mitchell gave his attention to labor organization, writing his dissertation on unions in the cotton textile industry. In 1927 a Rhodes Scholarship took him to England where he studied the politically active labor unions in Lancastershire's cotton mills. The potential political power of American unions became a central theme in Mitchell's writing. If southern industrial workers could join with "the distressed cotton farmers" on a program for reform, he predicted, "a political rift of the first order would be in the making." Most important, he argued that although racism posed a potentially dangerous obstacle to the labor movement in the South, unionism held out the prospect of reducing racial prejudice and discrimination.[12]

Observers before Mitchell had recognized that Negro workers and white workers shared common interests, but the racially exclusive unionism condoned by the American Federation of Labor seemed to make such an alliance impossible and justified Booker T. Washington's conviction that the Negro must depend on white employers for racial advancement. As Kelly Miller said in 1925, "logic aligns the Negro with labor but good sense arrays him with capital." The Depression's harsh impact on blacks devastated the Washingtonian doctrine of self-help, but the idea of a workers' alliance still seemed unlikely. "It would seem that in the long run Negro workers cannot make their way apart from other workers," Will Alexander said in 1931. "At present this presents a difficulty, for white workers in this country are far more race conscious than they are class conscious."[13]

The New Deal reinvigorated the labor movement, and organizers spread out across the South. In June 1933 organizers from the United Mine Workers Union arrived in industrialized Jefferson County, Alabama, and swiftly enrolled some 18,000 miners into the union. Nearly half the mine workers in the Birmingham district were Negroes, and UMW campaigns in 1927 and 1930 had foundered on the race issue. The organizers in 1933 forthrightly signed up all miners, white or black. Members met in racially mixed meetings and, although whites customarily held "the more important places," officers came from both groups. [14]

Tough-minded practicality, not humanitarianism, dictated this strategy. The UMW knew that the division between white and black miners had crippled organizing campaigns in the past. At the same time, implementation of this strategy of "mixed unionism" required efforts to change racial attitudes. Prejudice was a powerful weapon in the arsenal of the employers. Thus, organizers emphasized the economic interests that workers shared. Inevitably, such arguments conveyed the idea that economic interests were more important than racial divisions, an intentional demotion of race as a value. [15]

Mitchell and Cayton completed their field work in March 1935, but in 1937 they began research in the field once again; the labor situation had changed dramatically. In November 1935, John L. Lewis of the United Mine Workers brought together eight unions from mass-production industries to form the Committee for Industrial Organization. The founders of the CIO believed that the AFL would fail to seize the opportunity to unionize presented by worker militance and the favorable political climate of the New Deal. Most important, the CIO followed the example of the UMW in Birmingham and enrolled all workers, regardless of race. Cayton studied the union in the steel industry, where U.S. Steel's collective bargaining agreement with the Steel Workers Organizing Committee marked the CIO's greatest victory, and he concluded that this policy was responsible for that success. Although he made it clear that racial antagonisms still lurked in the steel industry, the SWOC campaign impressed him nonetheless. "The effect of working together for a common goal, of facing a common enemy, and of day by day cooperation in union affairs," he wrote, "has been to draw white and Negro workers together to an extent perhaps never before equalled in this country." [16]

As FDR's second term got under way, George S. Mitchell's vision of southern workers organized as a political force for liberal reform seemed a distinct possibility. Moreover, the CIO's emphasis on the common economic interests of workers seemed a means to eliminate racial divisions. Economic consciousness might build a movement impervious to prejudice.

In his foreword to Cayton and Mitchell's *Black Workers and the New Unions*, Charles S. Johnson argued that race had divided workers in the past and had "seriously complicated" labor's campaign "for recognition and security in industry." At present, however, the "racial stratification in occupations" was undergoing a "process of transformation" as a result of the new vigor and activity of labor unions. The result was "a profound transition in Negro life as well as in the economic outlook of American workers generally." Johnson claimed that "class interests and class solidarity have measurably relaxed racial tensions and, by so doing, have mitigated the divisive effects of racial antagonism."[17]

Johnson's argument revised the concept of vertical segregation. In an article on "Race Relations and Social Change" he argued that southerners at the bottom of the social structure now understood that they would remain workers and were discovering class interests across racial barriers. Communication and common struggles in the labor unions indicated to Johnson "a progressive shifting of these racial relations, notably in the South, from a castelike structure to a class organization." He closed with the prediction that in the future "there will be less emphasis on the significance of race difference than upon the solidarity of class interests." The location of the vanguard for change had shifted from the best people of the CIC to the workers of the CIO.[18]

The journalists held to the methods of the CIC. Where Johnson's argument implied that southern employers used racism as a tool to divide the workers, the journalists continued to believe that the poor whites were the main exponents of anti-Negro prejudice. In addition, their conception of the sources of and solutions to southern economic problems caused them to give the labor movement little attention. The region's poverty began with agriculture, they believed, and reform must first solve the problems of the rural South.[19]

The journalists endorsed Howard W. Odum's prescription of regional planning as the cure for southern poverty. Significantly, nowhere in *Southern Regions* did Odum discuss labor unions. Instead, he advocated expert social planning to reorganize the southern economy as the preferred road to prosperity. Rather than conflict, Odum emphasized common regional interests; the South was a unit and all southerners shared an identity.

A focus on class divisions dissolved this concept of the South as a unified, distinct region. Not only did conflicting economic interests divide southerners but the South's problems resembled those found elsewhere in the nation. H. C. Nixon contended in 1938 that "the ills of the South are the ills of class more than of region or section." Thus, southern liberals must join with liberals outside the South to secure "a square deal" for farmers, laborers, and Negroes—"the three over-lapping groups who have been most consistently exploited by the 'American system'"—everywhere in the nation. "There can be no inter-regional justice without inter-class justice," Nixon concluded.[20]

With these arguments, Nixon divorced himself not only from the Regionalists but also from the Nashville Agrarians. As one of the original Twelve Southerners, Nixon did not repudiate "the 'agrarian' indictment of the American industrial system" but explained that he sought "a broader program of agricultural reconstruction" than the Agrarians seemed to favor. Most of all, he objected to the sectionalism of the Nashville group. Their argument had sense to it, he said, but failed "to recognize the limitations of regionalism in the face of class cleavage and class struggles, which transcend regional lines." He judged Odum's *Southern Regions* more favorably, declaring that the book "should ultimately form the basis of social action." The difficulty, he continued, lay in arousing that social action. The South could "not wait for long-range planning or for more difficult long-range action."[21]

Despite the use of phrases such as "class divisions" and "class conflict," Johnson, Nixon, and others did not endorse revolutionary methods of social change. Instead, they called for liberal reform through political action, emphasizing the necessity of obtaining support for these reforms from liberal forces outside the South. For example, C. Vann Woodward, a young historian at the University of Florida, echoed Nixon in 1939 with the contention that the South "must cooperate with the agricultural sections and other depressed classes for the purpose of seeking a national policy for the good of all sections and all classes, including Southern workers."[22]

In the previous year, Woodward had published a biography of Thomas E. Watson—Populist leader in Georgia and notorious as an anti-Semitic, anti-Catholic, and anti-Negro demagogue—in which he constructed an interpretation of southern history challenging that put forward by the journalists on nearly every count. Woodward bottomed his book on a thesis of economic conflict between industrialism and agrarianism, but the experience of the 1930s added complexity to his outlook. Rather than a unified agrarian South standing against the industrial Northeast and unanimously devoted to the Democratic party and white supremacy, the decade had revealed conflict between workers and their employers, between farmers and manufacturers, and between New Dealers and rigid conservatives. In his view, then, the Solid South was an artificial creation, obscuring actual divisions within the region.[23]

Historians had "strangely neglected" the two decades after Reconstruction, Woodward contended. "Out of the almost unanimous silence on this epoch had grown much erroneous thinking about the South and Southern history." The overthrow of Radical Reconstruction brought to the fore a "new type of Southern leader, the aggressive self-made business man," now triumphant in the South. These leaders rose to power on southern fears—"fear of the Negro menace, the scalawag menace, the Federal menace, menaces real and imaginary"—and politics in the one-party South became an empty charade. Meanwhile, these men of the New South trumpeted the glories of industrial and commercial development. Woodward kept his attention on the farms rather than the cotton mills, but he noted that northern visitors confirmed "rumors of cheap labor and fat profits." Outside the cities and mill villages, farmers slid ever further downward under the pressure of the crop lien system.[24]

Woodward's account not only set aside the traditional southern notion that the leaders who overthrew Reconstruction reinstituted the old order, but it devastated Broadus Mitchell's influential interpretation of *The Rise of the Cotton Mills in the South*: the advocates of industry were anything but ex-Confederates in spirit, and their motives were a mixture of greed and opportunism, not a patrician's sense of social responsibility toward the white masses.[25]

With the Democratic party in the hands of the businessmen, the distressed farmers had organized a new, third party, the People's or Populist party, and made the 1890s a period of wild political struggle. Woodward argued that Populism, despite the complexity of its constituency, recognized class distinctions and sought alliance with similar groups elsewhere against "the crushing oppression of capitalist finance and industrialism." Moreover, the Populists sought "a united front between Negro and white farmers," on a basis of common economic interests. "Here was a foundation of political realism upon which some more enduring structures of economic democracy might be constructed," Woodward declared. "Never before or since have the two races in the South come so close together as they did during the Populist struggles." In contrast to the traditional perception of the lower-class whites as the primary agents of white supremacy, Woodward presented racism—"the New South's perennial answer to a third party threat"—as the tool of the conservatives.[26]

On this historical stage, Woodward's Tom Watson played out his tragic role. As a Populist leader, the charismatic Watson fought for the lower classes and forthrightly challenged racial prejudices. The Georgia Democrats responded with electoral frauds that cheated him of his seat in Congress. Unjust defeats and the national collapse of Populism after 1896 made Watson a bitter and frustrated man. In an irony of ironies, Watson returned to power in Georgia politics as a cruel exploiter of prejudices after 1906, and even won election to the Senate in 1920, shortly before his death.[27]

Woodward acknowledged that Watson's life "was a paradox" and, despite his obvious admiration for the young Watson, refused to explain away the man's sordid final days. In his review of the book, Rupert B. Vance noted the paradox and said that Watson "could almost stand for all things to all men." The lessons drawn from the book, he predicted, "will prove as varied . . . as the politics of the reader."[28]

Political ideology did seem to determine the interpretations that southern liberals gave to the book. Those who favored expansion of the New Deal and endorsed the CIO's campaign to organize southern workers found Populism a heartening precedent. Woodward himself said that "in their political platforms the Populists made demands that one associates more with the 1930's than with the 1890's."[29]

The journalists read Woodward's biography of Watson, but his new interpretation caused little change in their thinking. Perhaps most important, where Woodward summarized Reconstruction in two pages and then turned to the developments that he believed actually made the modern South, the journalists continued to believe that all the South's sad modern history flowed directly from the evils of that period, for which the North bore primary responsibility. Rather than participating greedily in the "Great Barbecue," as Woodward contended, southerners remained passive victims.[30]

By the late 1930s, historians had begun to question whether that period had been as horrible as southern legend claimed. In effect, they looked backward from the conflicts of the 1890s and asked, if conservative supremacy led to the Populist revolt, could the overthrow of Reconstruction have been totally beneficial to all southerners? As Woodward's mentor, Howard K. Beale, declared in 1940, "some of the most condemned aspects of Radical Reconstruction were merely the manifestations of a democratic revolution in a region habituated to aristocratic control." Such a conclusion depended, as did Woodward's interpretation of the New South, on the perception of conflict—political and economic—in southern history. [31]

Rather than conflict, the journalists maintained their opinion that southern consensus, especially in regard to the folkways of race, had determined the region's postbellum history. As his title suggests, W. J. Cash's well-known *The Mind of the South* presents this view of a monolithic South in extreme form. Cash argued that the frontier conditions of the Old South caused the mind of the southerner to tend toward "unreality" and "romanticism." The antebellum defense of slavery and the war with the Yankees completed the process that transformed southerners into an unreflective, undifferentiated mass, devoted to what Cash called "the savage ideal," under which "dissent and variety are completely suppressed." [32]

As for Populism, which he described as essentially a response to southern agriculture's colonial relation to the industrial North, Cash noted that "some of the chief historians for the period" saw class awareness in the revolt, but he contended that this idea went "far beyond the fact." Certainly resentments existed, but the savage ideal remained strong; under the pressure of his "old captains" and appeals to white supremacy, Cash said, "the common white of the South did in overwhelming tide abandon his advance upon class consciousness and relapse into his ancient focus." [33]

Thus, in the twentieth century, for all the evidences of change that Cash described, the South remained true to the savage ideal. His account, however, now grew statistical, and the numbers provided grounds for concern over the future: the South had too many people, too few fertile farms, too little tax revenue, too much waste. Cash concluded his book with a discussion of the region's greatest tragedy, the lack of able leadership. [34]

This call for responsible, realistic leadership had been a theme with the journalists for years. Indeed, George Fort Milton's concepts of rational and mystical democracy, with his praise for rule by the rational elite, exalted this concern for leadership into a philosophy of American history. Whereas Woodward put forward the Populist leader, a man of the people who taught southerners their class interests and directed them to political action for social change, the journalists tended to look back to the southern aristocrat, whose sense of social responsibility ensured leadership in the common interest.[35]

In their reviews and comments on Woodward's biography, the journalists focused on Watson's last years of bigotry and demagoguery, not on his leadership of the Populists. Gerald W. Johnson praised Woodward's skill as a biographer, but rejected the author's interpretation for his own. He objected to Woodward's harsh treatment of the men who promoted the New South, declaring that perhaps they "did hand the South over to exploiters . . . , but after all, there is something to be said for economic reconstruction." The "true importance" of the book, he claimed, was "as a case study of a Southern liberal." Watson rose as the "champion of the tenant farmers of Georgia"— Johnson never mentioned Populism—and "an astute ruling class would have recognized this man's quality and would have taken measures to absorb him." Instead, the Bourbon Democrats "club[bed] him to his knees" and thus "turn[ed] him into an anarch whose frenzies swept Georgia back almost into the jungle." The book, Johnson said, provided "a much clearer understanding of why Southern liberalism has produced, not statesmen, but freaks."[36] In effect, he called on southern liberals not to emulate the Populists, but rather to enact sane reforms in order to forestall a repetition of the 1890s.

Living in Atlanta, Ralph McGill well knew the lasting devotion that many Georgians felt for Tom Watson. Without mentioning Woodward, in the summer of 1938 McGill told readers of the *Constitution* of new books appearing on Watson's life and declared him "a great man." During this summer, Eugene Talmadge, McGill's idea of the archetypical southern demagogue, was again a candidate for office—this time in the U.S. Senate. McGill considered "the political rabble-rouser" primarily responsible for southern problems such as "illiteracy, tenancy, inadequate health and all the associated fleas which he brought to the body politic." Thus, Watson's last years of bigotry, when he did "the common man a great injustice by giving him prejudices and inflaming some which already existed," loomed large in McGill's thinking. The ghost of Watson rose behind Talmadge's candidacy. "You may be sure the man from Sugar Creek has studied his Tom Watson," he warned.[37]

As McGill's example suggests, by the summer of 1938 events conspired to prevent the journalists from incorporating Woodward's interpretation of Populism into their thinking. Instead, that summer's hot political conflicts turned them even further against Franklin D. Roosevelt and the New Deal.

By early 1938 a stalemate had developed between FDR and his conservative congressional opponents. Both sides hoped to elect sufficient numbers of ideological soulmates in the fall elections to break the deadlock. Prospects for New Deal victory appeared brightest in the South: early primary victories for Lister Hill in Alabama and Claude Pepper in Florida seemed proof of the president's popularity below the Potomac. Two conservative Democratic incumbents, senators Walter George of Georgia and Ellison D. (Cotton Ed) Smith of South Carolina, were up for reelection and Roosevelt decided to oppose their candidacies.[38]

As he prepared for the purge, FDR agreed to a proposal by Clark Foreman, then head of the Public Works Administration's Power Division, that a pamphlet detailing New Deal accomplishments in the South be drawn up and publicized. In order better to serve his purposes in 1938, Roosevelt suggested that the pamphlet emphasize southern problems rather than advances. Foreman agreed and convened southern liberals in Washington, many of them associated with the Southern Policy Committee, to prepare the *Report on the Economic Conditions of the South*. FDR prefaced the report with a letter in which he declared his "conviction that the South presents right now the Nation's No. 1 economic problem."[39]

The *Report* aroused great interest, in the South especially, and more than 1,000,000 copies were distributed. Most of the factual information came from Howard W. Odum's *Southern Regions*, and the *Report*'s recommendations resembled Odum's plans for regional development. As Paul E. Mertz observes, the general argument of the *Report* was that southern poverty was due to the region's undeveloped potential; elimination of artificial sectional discriminations and national assistance to encourage economic progress would solve the problem. Compared to the platform of the old southern Populists, the *Report* seemed distinctly mild in its recommendations for regional development.[40]

Although southern patriots and anti–New Dealers predictably objected to the *Report*, the journalists generally gave it a hearty endorsement. Jonathan Daniels happily stated that the *Report* "should stir national interest in this one region which may drag the national advance or help propel it." W. J. Cash praised those liberal newspapermen who accepted the truth of the *Report* but damned "the greater part of the Southern press" and the "overwhelming majority" of politicians who rejected it. "The South faces pressing problems," Cash warned.[41]

These problems and the *Report* that described them disappeared from sight in the tumult that erupted after Roosevelt began his purge. In August, he went to Georgia and declared his support for Lawrence Camp, the little-known challenger to incumbent Senator George. On the way back to Washington, he halted in South Carolina to criticize Senator Smith, but by then the storm had broken about him.[42]

With one voice, the journalists condemned FDR's purge. The *Chattanooga News* claimed that Roosevelt exhibited surprisingly poor political sense. "It seems to us that he is blinking the fact that the people back home do not like to be told exactly what the White House wants them to do," the editorial said. "Furthermore, he seems blissfully unconscious that [Eugene] Talmadge [the third candidate in the race] and not Camp may be the beneficiary of his cracking the whip."[43]

Certainly Roosevelt had chosen a weak candidate on whom to stake his power and reputation, but the journalists objected primarily to the purge itself. McGill charged that Roosevelt had abandoned liberalism with his attack on George: "It is impossible to see how a government composed entirely of people who think only one way can be a liberal government." John Temple Graves announced that, if he lived in Georgia, he would cast his vote for George. "Something has become more important now than the New Deal, and that something is American democracy," he wrote.[44]

Two months earlier, in June 1938, a reader had written to Virginius Dabney and asked if the *Times-Dispatch*'s editorial policy was not "turning to the right?" In his editorial reply, Dabney acknowledged that opposition to New Deal policies put the paper in league with "all the ultra reactionaries in the country," and explained that this had caused the *Times-Dispatch* to hesitate before criticizing. Nonetheless, he said, the paper could not condone the administration's use of "unfair—even unethical—means to attain its ends." Dabney listed various issues such as policy toward private business and government spending, but returned in the end to disapproval of New Deal methods. "Since we are still in favor of what we understand to be the Administration's objectives," he concluded, "we do not consider that we have turned either to the Right or the Left." [45]

In fact, Dabney was correct. He and the other journalists planted themselves in the political center and criticized Roosevelt for moving to the left. "Democracies move slowly," McGill warned shortly before FDR spoke out against Senator George. "They move largely by trial and error, going to the left and then to the right, but staying, as far as progress is concerned, in the middle of the road." As FDR seemed to ally himself with the reform advocates in his administration and the CIO and other liberal pressure groups outside the government, the journalists spoke appreciatively of the middle road as the proper course for the nation. "This country is a middle class country," the *Chattanooga News* declared in 1937; "when anyone veers very far to either left or right of the middle of the road we begin to feel uncomfortable and seek the paddle in the woodshed." [46]

So the journalists interpreted Roosevelt's disastrous purge of 1938. On September 14 the voting took place, and Senator George overwhelmed Camp. "Read it any way you will," Gerald W. Johnson wrote, "the defeat of the Purge was a rebuke to the President." FDR's failure seemed to demonstrate again their conviction that the national government could not interfere in local southern affairs without provoking a stiff reaction. As Milton later said: "Hamilton's well-known thesis in the *Federalist*, about the power of localism as an antidote to central political control, was proved again." [47]

In the journalists' view, the failure of the purge marked the end of New Deal reform. "The New Deal, as such, really died from the blows of Court fight, Reorganization Bill and Purge," Milton later remarked, "and I didn't lament the event." In December 1938, John Temple Graves proclaimed that "the New Deal is dealt. For better or worse there isn't going to be any more now." [48]

Back in August, shortly after FDR's speech against Senator George, Francis Pickens Miller received an invitation from Louise O. Charlton, a judge in Birmingham and a member of the Alabama Policy Committee, and Luther Patrick, congressman from the Birmingham district. They spoke of the South's great problems, recently exposed to the nation in the National Emergency Council's *Report*. Because "issues affecting human welfare are of first consideration in arriving at our solutions," they proposed a Southern Conference for Human Welfare to be held in Birmingham. They asked Miller to join them "as a sponsor and as a member of the arrangements committee."[49]

Similar letters went out to other southern liberals. The list of sponsors for the SCHW included George Fort Milton, Virginius Dabney, Ralph McGill, Mark Ethridge, Jonathan Daniels, and John Temple Graves. In addition to the journalists, many other prominent liberals agreed to participate. As the SCHW's historian says, "the convention delegate and guest lists could have formed the nucleus for a who's who in Southern liberalism."[50] Despite the appearance of their names on the program, however, all of the journalists but Ethridge and Graves decided not to attend.

Conspicuous by his absence, also, was Howard W. Odum. Rather than perceiving the conference as an unusual gathering of southern liberals to whom he could present his plans for a Council on Southern Regional Development, Odum saw it as a threat. Where he conceived of the council as a planning agency staffed by experts drawn from academia, the organizers of the SCHW intended to unite southern liberals in a political program with mass appeal. The sociologist decided that attending the conference would imply an endorsement, and so he stayed home.[51]

Francis Pickens Miller shared Odum's institutional jealousies. Prominent among the SCHW's organizers were H. C. Nixon, chairman of the Southern Policy Committee, and W. T. Couch, head of the North Carolina Policy Committee. In addition, in official SCHW correspondence the Alabama Policy Committee appeared as the meeting's sponsor. The fact that neither Nixon nor Couch had managed to organize policy committees in their states, yet both were now "disgruntled at the fact that the Southern Policy Committee was not more active in a regional sphere," particularly aroused Miller's anger. The SCHW seemed an implicit criticism of the SPC and of himself. On the same day that he accepted the invitation to attend the conference, Miller wrote to Nixon telling him not to identify the SCHW with the Southern Policy Committee.[52]

Undoubtedly the journalists shared some of the feelings of Odum and Miller, but they had other reasons for misgivings, too. The conference appeared just as FDR's purge turned into a bitter draught for the president. Convinced as they were that grand schemes of reform should be held in abeyance until economic recovery arrived, they felt that the conference's hope to advance "the cause of political and economic democracy" struck a discordant note. Then came announcements that revealed a strong link between the conference and the New Deal. Claude Pepper of Florida and Aubrey Williams of Alabama, both ardent New Dealers, would attend; Eleanor Roosevelt would deliver a major address; and Supreme Court Justice Hugo Black would receive the SCHW's Thomas Jefferson Award, honoring "the Southerner who has done most to promote human and social welfare in line with the philosophy of Thomas Jefferson."[53]

The award to Black especially disturbed the journalists. Did not the SCHW realize that Black had been a member of the Ku Klux Klan? The revelation of Black's Klan background had come out in August 1937, immediately after FDR nominated him to the Supreme Court. In the context of the Court packing struggle, the nomination alone had raised eyebrows; Black's main qualification for the bench appeared to be his enthusiastic support for the New Deal. Then the stories of his Klan ties surfaced, and the journalists called for him to step down. The SCHW's award seemed to them an irresponsible declaration that loyalty to the New Deal was enough to wash away any sins. "While Justice Black was a Klansman we were fighting this racial hatred group," the *News* stated indignantly. The award so disturbed Dabney that he decided then, despite his agreement to serve as a sponsor, that he would not attend the conference.[54]

On Sunday, 20 November 1938, the Southern Conference for Human Welfare convened in Birmingham. More than a thousand delegates attended and observers remarked on the diversity of the crowd. The SCHW welcomed industrial workers, sharecroppers, union organizers, and students. Moreover, about one-fifth of the delegates were blacks. "The conference was literally a people's movement, representing every strata of society from capitalist to sharecropper," Lucy Randolph Mason reported. Sympathizers considered the SCHW a token of a new, more militant southern liberalism. The conference "marked a new stage in the development of southern progressive activities," claimed Katherine DuPre Lumpkin; "in it we see a tendency for liberal middle-class opinion to seek organized channels in company with labour."[55]

Despite the high hopes that the SCHW inspired in some southern liberals, by the time that the conference met, the tide of social reform had already begun to ebb. The conference itself originated in the hot summer of FDR's purge, when militant southern liberals looked forward to meeting in celebration of New Deal victories across the South. Instead, they met after a shocking defeat for the president and the uproar surrounding the purge had obscured the hard facts behind the NEC's *Report on the Economic Conditions of the South*, the text that gave the conference its sanction.[56]

Although a militant spirit was evident at the conference—George C. Stoney reported the scornful impatience of student delegates with the "old line liberals"—the SCHW's resolutions appear rather mild. Delegates called for more laws protecting labor and increased appropriations to the Farm Security Administration. They called for abolition of the poll tax, but endorsed extension of the right to vote only to citizens "of proper educational qualifications." The conference also endorsed the southern industrialists' campaign against freight-rate differentials. In addition, the conference's two stirring addresses—by Frank P. Graham, president of the University of North Carolina, on Sunday night, and by Eleanor Roosevelt on Tuesday night—emphasized improved public education as a cure for southern ills.[57]

Nonetheless, conservative critics pointed to Communists among the delegates and charged the SCHW with dangerous radicalism. A small number of Communists did attend the meeting, but they exerted little influence on the proceedings. In fact, one of them later complained that whenever the party members proposed militant action, moderates prevailed.[58]

More important than communism in blackening the conference's reputation was the race issue. Although city law required segregation, public meetings had been held in Birmingham before without the law being enforced, and delegates sat where they pleased during the first two days of the conference. Then, on Monday afternoon, fifteen city policemen arrived, ready to arrest those delegates not observing the segregation law. Hours of heated discussion followed, and the SCHW decided to obey the law but also resolved never to meet again in a city where segregated seating would be required, and denounced Birmingham officials for enforcing the law. The Associated Press reported the carefully phrased statement as "a resolution protesting 'Jim Crow' laws." The news story provoked angry reaction in the South, and the conference's supposedly radical attack on segregation appeared to verify the charges of Communist influence. As southern liberal politicians scrambled to distance themselves from the SCHW, the prospects for the conference as a force for political action in the South dissolved.[59]

Friendly observers tried to make the best of the situation. George C. Stoney explained that "one could not expect too much reserve from some of these people—steel workers, miners, and sharecroppers who have learned to sit in union halls beside Negroes in the past two years." Similarly, Charles S. Johnson noted that Birmingham's laborers had "recently discovered that class interests cut across race lines" and stated that "it was undoubtedly this submerged but solid sentiment that supported the racial philosophy of the Conference." They recognized that just as employers had used racism to divide workers against their interests, so, too, would the "bugaboo" of segregation be employed to obscure the SCHW's other resolutions. Nonetheless, the raising of the issue had some value. As Johnson said, "it gave emphasis . . . to the race tradition as the major challenge to any movement aiming at social reconstruction in the South."[60]

The police in Birmingham exposed the new southern liberalism's break from the old southern liberal doctrine of vertical segregation. Indeed, the authorities required only that the delegates separate themselves vertically, much as the CIC had done with the audience for Roland Hayes's performance in Atlanta thirteen years earlier. Those who desired collective action by southern workers saw that legal segregation represented a powerful weapon for opponents of social change. Jim Crow would have to die in order that workers could carry on the struggle for economic democracy in the South. The long debate on the issue at the SCHW meeting, of course, indicates that not all the delegates were yet prepared to reach this conclusion. Nonetheless, the controversy in Birmingham signified a dawning recognition that liberalism and segregation—even vertical segregation—might not be forever compatible.

The journalists reacted with anger to the resolution, which they interpreted as a general condemnation of Jim Crow laws. The *Chattanooga News* criticized the police for enforcing the segregation laws—"if the Southern liberals want to have Negroes sit with them, whose business is it but theirs?"—but it judged the SCHW's resolution a mistake in tactics. "Until the South is prepared of its own volition to level racial barriers," the *News* said, "no Conference resolutions are going to do anything but irritate and alienate the average Southerner." Foolish efforts to speed changes along only risked arousing reaction. "In a region as conservative as the South, reform moves slowly and through evolutionary processes," the *Times-Dispatch* said. "Attempts to drive the people into chaotic changes are almost uniformly unsuccessful."[61]

In addition, there were more pressing problems than segregation facing black southerners. "With Negroes needing decent living conditions, education, a chance to work at fair wages, the raising of the question of where they shall sit in streetcars was no service to them at all," the *News* contended. In similar fashion, Jonathan Daniels insisted in 1940 that "the need to eat is not racial." The real problem, he argued, "is not merely the protection of the Negro but the provision of an economic order in which all useful people can be decently employed at socially profitable tasks." Daniels concluded, therefore, that "in important regards we need less talk about the Negro problem."[62]

The journalists acknowledged that race presented an obstacle to reform but insisted that avoiding the issue was the only effective tactic. They remained committed to the promise of vertical segregation. As the South eliminated economic insecurity, prosperity would begin to dissolve racial fears and prejudices. As Milton said, "when these basic injustices are corrected, Jim Crow laws will vanish."[63]

Two weeks later, with Justice Hugo Black voting with the majority, the reorganized Supreme Court ruled that Lloyd L. Gaines must be admitted to the University of Missouri Law School because no law school for Negroes existed within the state. The Court did not outlaw the doctrine of separate but equal; rather, it insisted that segregation required provision of equal facilities. The NAACP's lawyers built their strategy on the fact that nowhere in the South did actual separate equality exist and, instead of challenging the legality of segregation, they insisted that the courts require southern states to obey the law.[64]

The *Gaines* decision bore especially powerful implications for the defense of vertical segregation. In 1939, Guy B. Johnson acknowledged that, at most, the color line had "begun to slant." The crucial question for the future was "how far and how fast can the horizontal line of caste shift toward the vertical line of a biracial society." If the shift continued at "a snail's pace," he said, no conflict would result. The *Gaines* decision, however, threatened a "show-down situation." Eventually a southern state would confront the question "of how much the color line is worth in dollars and cents," he predicted, and then "the color line must either swing to the vertical position or break." Whatever the result, Johnson concluded, the South faced "conflict, perhaps violence."[65]

The *Gaines* decision measured the limited achievements of southern liberals in tilting the color line. Ironically, just as the Court made its decision, the journalists had reaffirmed their conviction that vertical segregation alone could solve the South's Negro problem. The reaction in the South to the SCHW's resolution—reaction to which they had contributed—seemed to prove again the necessity of a long process of educating public opinion to accept changes.[66]

On the second night of the SCHW meeting, at the suggestion of Howard Odum, Mark Ethridge convened a small group of Southern Policy Committee members to consider the future of Odum's regional planning scheme in light of the new organization. The group decided, "after considerable discussion," to meet again in Atlanta on 14 and 15 January 1939, and authorized Francis Pickens Miller to send out the invitations. In his letter Miller explained that, with the publicity given to the NEC *Report*, he feared "a good deal of ill-considered legislation will be introduced at the next session of Congress," and proposed that "a selected group of responsible citizens should attempt to formulate a list of sound legislative measures which might be appropriately adopted at this time."[67]

About forty southern liberals gathered on that weekend to devise a "program to remedy ills" of the South. This meeting bore little resemblance to the diverse crowd at the SCHW. For one thing, Howard Odum participated. More importantly, though, the participants were from the same white professional group that made up the Southern Policy Committee. Of the thirty persons who signed the published statement, nineteen came from journalism or academia. Only one black southerner, the ubiquitous Charles S. Johnson, attended.[68]

In an implied rebuke to the militance of the SCHW, the group declared that "since our conditions are products of a long-existent economy, remedial action will require a relatively long period of time." The delegates here called for creation of Odum's Council on Southern Regional Development, which would "devote itself to long-range planning for the south." Otherwise, the group's program to treat the conditions exposed in the NEC *Report* resembled the resolutions approved in Birmingham. To justify federal assistance for southern development, however, the group asserted that the South's problems originated during Reconstruction and held the North largely responsible for them. "Failure to adopt a national policy looking toward reconstruction of the southern states and the rehabilitation of almost half her population after the War Between the States," they declared, "fastened upon her the one-crop system, the sharecropper system, and the credit 'furnishing' system, all of which have proved, for three generations, an unmitigated evil producing agricultural insecurity, low wages and poverty and all their attendant evils, such as illiteracy, physical deterioration and economic waste." Significantly, they said nothing of race in their "Recommendations," except for insistence on the "equitable distribution between the races" of funds for schools, a tacit endorsement of vertical segregation.[69]

Nothing came of their recommendations. Not only had the New Deal come to an end, but increasingly the nation's attention was on foreign affairs, not domestic reform. In May, Odum tried unsuccessfully to obtain an affiliation with the TVA for his Council on Southern Regional Development. By 1940, he had shelved his regional scheme.[70]

Pressure for reform in the South eased as President Roosevelt and all Americans turned their attention to foreign affairs. The journalists welcomed the shift. Within two years after the SCHW meeting, they were calling on Americans to recognize the war in Europe as a moral issue. In the crusade against Nazism, the journalists abandoned the antiwar doctrines that had sanctioned their gradualist approach to social reform and took up an emotion-charged rhetoric of democratic idealism. Where the new southern liberalism had failed to shake their thinking, Adolf Hitler succeeded.

10 Adolf Hitler and the American Way

As the United States entered the Second World War, John Temple Graves asked various southerners to essay explanations for the South's remarkable fighting spirit. More than in any other section of the country before Pearl Harbor, public opinion in the South expressed hostility toward Nazi Germany and favored American aid to England, even at the risk of war. Virginius Dabney offered to Graves a list of reasons for southern interventionism. He pointed to Anglo-Saxon homogeneity—a source of anglophilia and of greater consensus than in regions with large ethnic populations—to southern martial tradition, the region's dependence on foreign markets for agricultural exports, and the "realization of what it means to be conquered." Graves considered Dabney's last point most important: the Civil War and Reconstruction had a lasting psychological effect on southerners, breeding a resistance to change expressed in the form of defensive aggressiveness. He cited Howard W. Odum's lengthy response to back his opinion. Odum did declare that "the South has been invaded so often since the Civil War by thousands of reformers and accusers that it is automatically prepared to defend itself," but his answer raised other issues. [1]

Southerners tended to hold fast to ideals and honor, Odum told Graves, all too often as a substitute for doing the "difficult and concrete" things. Odum found southern anti-Nazi idealism ironic: "Hitler is anti-Christ, anti-individualistic, anti-American, and the fact that we ourselves in the South are fascistic and dogmatic has nothing to do with the logic of our believing in the principle of Americanism and fighting for it." Without his irony, other respondents echoed him. Mark Ethridge said that southerners knew that "war settles questions" and thus realized that "it is necessary to fight to preserve anything that is precious." Similarly, George Fort Milton contended that southerners remained close to "the true fundamentals of democracy," which explained the region's interventionist attitudes. [2]

These comments suggest the impact of Nazism and of the war

in Europe on the journalists' thinking. Here were realistic, practical liberals speaking of the "principle of Americanism" and the "true fundamentals of democracy." Here were men who had damned the Civil War as needless, pleased that southern bellicosity outstripped the nation's.

Adolf Hitler refuted the antiwar doctrines that served as an intellectual foundation for the southern liberal program of gradualism in reform. Moreover, the journalists now merged liberalism with ideals and ethics, a connection that they had opposed during the 1930s. At the same time, however, the contrast between Nazi Germany and the South reinforced their conviction that great progress had been made in improving race relations below the Potomac. The journalists yet retained their faith in southern liberalism.

In 1930, Virginius Dabney described in his column the friendly welcome that he had received in Germany while touring Europe three years before. He considered this further evidence that Americans had entered World War I as "crusaders for righteousness," their emotions aroused by propaganda that painted the Hun as an evil brute. A year later, he noted that a poll of clergymen revealed a majority opposed to church endorsement of any war. "This is distinctly encouraging," Dabney reported, "for the reason that the more sentiment against war we can build up in America and elsewhere, the less likely we are to have a repetition of 1917–1918."[3]

The tacit assumption that calm realism might have prevented the United States from entering this unnecessary war gave credence to the journalists' contention that the Civil War was also a needless conflict. "War always represents a collapse of statesmanship," Johnson maintained, "and the men who fight the war are paying the penalty for statesmen's negligence or incompetence." The World War also served as a frightening example of the dangers that self-righteous moralism and emotion-stirring propaganda posed in modern society. "The lessons of 1914–1918 should not be soon forgotten," Milton proclaimed.[4]

For this reason, Dabney refused to believe shocking reports from Germany of repressive violence as Adolf Hitler consolidated Nazi control in early 1933. There was "no excuse" for the Nazi persecution of the Jews, he said, but Americans should remember the false stories of atrocities that had preceded the World War. "That is why it is important for everyone to scrutinize the news from Germany today with the utmost care." Throughout 1933 Dabney continued to downplay reports of Nazi ruthlessness. Late in that year, he received a grant from the Oberlaender Trust of the Carl Shurz Memorial Foundation to tour Germany and Austria for six months.[5]

In Germany, Dabney discovered the truth behind the stories that he had disbelieved. On his return in October 1934 he told Louis I. Jaffé that he had developed "a deep-rooted detestation for the Nazis." Dabney summed up his experiences in a three-part essay for the *Times-Dispatch*. As for the atrocity reports, he said, by far the greater part were "accurate and reliable." In particular, no exaggerations of the anti-Semitic campaign had been made. "How can any Jew be happy in the Germany of today?" he asked. Moreover, Hitler's regime was "thoroughly militaristic" and the Nazis appeared to be preparing for war. Dabney expressed the "strongest possible dislike" for what he had seen of Hitler's methods of government.[6]

Unlike Dabney, the other journalists condemned Adolf Hitler from his first conquest of power. Rather than referring to the World War, however, they interpreted Hitler from a southern liberal perspective, as evidenced in comparisons of the Nazis to the Ku Klux Klan. "Hitler has accomplished the incredible," the *News* declared, "he has made an entire nation adopt the psychology of the organizations which Wizard Simmons and the Kleagles headed throughout the South some years ago."[7]

Similarly, the journalists condemned the German leader for exhibiting qualities that they had criticized in southern politics as well. "The campaign against the Jews is Hitler's method of rabble-rousing," Johnson said. "Had the Jews not been available, he would have used someone else." Dabney disagreed that Hitler's anti-Semitism was merely a cynical ploy but believed that it made him even more dangerous. "A completely sincere fanatic can sometimes do more harm than an insincere self-seeker," he explained; "Hitler is a sincere fanatic." Milton interpreted Nazism as further evidence of the constant struggle between reason and emotion. "Hitler's Germany affords us another of the all-too-frequent examples of the thin crust which separates our vaunted civilization from the brutalities of passion-driven force," he claimed.[8]

Perhaps most important, events in Germany showed conclusively that the World War had solved no problems. Contemporary Germany mocked those Americans who had gone to war in 1917 against the evils of the Kaiser's Germany. "It is not possible to say so and so is wrong, we will change it, that is the thing to do," the *News* explained. "The doctrine 'do right though Heavens fall' often causes the Heavens actually to fall upon us."[9]

Thus, although the journalists objected to Nazism, they insisted that it remained a problem for Germans themselves to solve. Despite his early recognition of the warlike nature of Nazism, Gerald W. Johnson insisted that the United States must avoid involvement in European conflicts. "It is not our affair," he said in 1933. Later that year, he noted the appearance of dictatorships in Russia, Eastern Europe, and Italy as well as in Germany, and declared that "it is not impossible that the ideal of individual liberty is destined to be extinguished in Europe in our time." Nonetheless, he concluded that liberty could not be imposed upon others and that Americans must allow it to "make its own way." Left alone, the journalists hoped, Hitler's regime might fall of its own weight. "A government which destroys liberty, which restricts intellectual life and freedom of thought, which rules by blood and iron, sooner or later must collapse," the *News* stated. Whatever happened in Europe, though, the United States must not go to war.[10]

War seemed the antithesis of liberalism. "War in itself is so evil a thing," Milton contended, "that whenever it is resorted to, one can expect the loosened hatreds of the governments to be put into policy, and the loosened passions of individuals to be permitted to have the freest rein." Moreover, the ill effects of war persisted long after peace returned. For the journalists, Radical Reconstruction proved this point. "The orgy of bloodshed released all the evils that customarily follow wars," Johnson said of that period. "Brute force, having replaced reason in the settlement of one problem, spread far afield."[11]

Consequently, the journalists warned Americans to hold their feelings about European developments in check. Wars would continue, Carter claimed, so long as "emotion and patriotism hold sway over reason." Johnson argued that merely "suppressing munitions makers and international bankers" would not prevent wars. Americans entered the World War "on a wave of fury, not on a wave of avarice," and even if economic motives for war were completely eliminated, "there would still remain the most dangerous of all explosives, the emotions of the people."[12]

The journalists rejected ethical pacifism as a potentially dangerous stand on absolute principle. "For the pacifist to let his case against war be compromised by moral complications, is for him to play into the hands of those who wage war for profit with moral battle cries," the *Times-Dispatch* said. "The pacifist must make intellectual war only against war, if he is to help end it." In like fashion, the *News* declared that "prevention of war, even at the risk of war, should not be attempted under the impulse of a moral or legal concept, but in defense of Reason." [13]

They also rejected isolationism in foreign policy as unrealistic and enthusiastically supported Secretary of State Cordell Hull in his efforts to obtain reciprocal trade agreements with other nations. In part, of course, their advocacy of free trade reflected the South's dependence on access to export markets for agricultural commodities. As Milton said, "every move this country makes toward isolation and self-sufficiency deals Dixie a blow." Beyond regional economic interests, however, the journalists believed that free international trade benefited the world. Policies that served the South's interests also served "the greater interest of world peace and world plenty," John Temple Graves contended. [14]

The journalists' view of foreign affairs in this period corresponded in many ways to their view of proper policy for the South. Just as they believed that the nations of the world must cooperate for the benefit of all, the journalists endorsed Odum's concept of regionalism that "envisage[d] the nation first, making the national culture and welfare the final arbiter." In fact, Odum described southern sectionalism as an isolationist policy, "analogous to the new economic nationalism as related to international economy." Regionalism contended that a general prosperity achieved through economic development would solve social problems peacefully. In particular, this was the best solution to racial problems, which had their origins in economic competition and insecurity. Similarly, Milton expected free trade to create international harmony through the elimination of "the psychic pressures, fears, insecurities, hungers and heartbreaks" that arose from poverty. Above all, social conditions requiring reform must not be interpreted as a moral issue—that way lay conflict and war. Instead, responsible men should plan practical methods of social amelioration. Only through the realistic application of reason could peace be maintained.[15] However, the threat of war grew ever greater, and after 1938 the journalists abandoned the convictions that seemed to prove the Civil War, and all wars, preventable.

The journalists considered Nazi domination in Germany but one more example of a general trend toward dictatorship in the world. In fact, long before Germany and the Soviet Union signed their nonaggression pact in 1939, they denied that fascism or communism differed in essence. As despotisms, both contrasted sharply with the New Deal in the United States. As governments seemingly on the extremes of right and left, Germany and the Soviet Union also reinforced the journalists' conviction that liberalism must hold the middle of the road.[16]

The major difference between democracy and dictatorship, the journalists contended, was that the latter employed force to compel obedience to government directives. Johnson argued that intelligent Americans recognized that men's minds cannot be coerced and so held to the basic belief that persuasion through reason best served liberty. Here was, of course, the mistake that the abolitionists and Radical Republicans had made in the South during the Civil War era. Milton referred to that period to explain the dangers still lurking for those Americans "struggling bravely to find a realistic middle path between rival Absolutes." He warned that by their nature, "group emotions" tended to "extremes." As evidence of what could happen when men abandoned the middle road, Milton pointed to the Civil War and to the World War, both of which might have been avoided had men reasoned together rather than choosing coercion.[17]

When the journalists looked outward to the dictatorships in Europe, they included all Americans—liberals and conservatives, Democrats and Republicans—within their definition of democracy. The characteristics that united Americans seemed more important than the specific policies over which they differed. In addition, in contrast to Germany or the Soviet Union, the United States now appeared remarkably excellent as a society and a government. "Democracy, it must be admitted, means an occasional buffoon in public office and an occasional thief in the public treasury, but at its rottenest it is a heaven on earth by comparison with any form of dictatorship," Johnson declared in 1936. "Its preservation is so important that all other issues sink into insignificance when weighed against it."[18]

This view of a nation united through liberal democratic consensus not only downplayed political differences but also lumped all Americans, regardless of race or religion, together against the dictatorships. Inevitably, then, the racist doctrines of Nazi Germany made racial and religious prejudice in the United States illegitimate and un-American. As the journalists became more satisfied with the American status quo politically and economically, their criticism of Nazi racialism raised sharp questions about the Jim Crow system in the South.[19]

None of them, however, concluded that Americans should therefore condemn southern racial practices. In fact, the persecution of Jews in Germany seemed to demonstrate the progressive improvement of race relations in the United States. As the number of lynchings steadily declined, and as economic issues pushed white supremacy from the political stage in the South during the 1930s, the journalists could proudly contrast southern race relations with anti-Semitic campaigns in Germany. "Leaders of Negro thought in America realize that in the South an experiment in gradual solution of racial problems is being made on a scale which might well be a model for the world," the *News* confidently stated. "There are hot-heads and bigots and lynchers, of course, but the progress of the Negro up from slavery is being solved, while in Germany, an alien race is being sold into a new slavery."[20]

Through the 1930s, the journalists had become much more open in their criticism of southern racial injustices. They declared race prejudice a falsehood and, by identifying it with the Nazis and the Klan, made it unrespectable. Even with tongue in cheek, Gerald W. Johnson would never have considered reasserting his 1932 call for "more and better race prejudice" as a means to prevent lynching. In fact, the historian of the Commission on Interracial Cooperation credits the southern liberals with "a vital role in preparing the minds of Southerners to accept a more liberal view of race relations."[21] Nonetheless, the journalists still considered segregation a problem for later generations to solve and objected to Negro protest against it. Two weeks before its proud editorial on racial progress, the *Chattanooga News* was part of the angry chorus of southern newspapers attacking the SCHW's resolution against segregation. The southern liberal program of gradualism had proved effective, and the journalists could see no justification for a direct assault on Jim Crow.

Through their contrasting of democracy and dictatorship, the journalists came to perceive an irreconcilable conflict between freedom and tyranny. The values that they invested in democracy led them toward the characterization of this conflict as a struggle between good and evil. Despite years of insistence that moralism and liberalism were incompatible, by the end of 1940 the journalists called on Americans to search their hearts and join the crusade against Hitler's evil.

The Spanish Civil War of the mid-1930s seemed a harbinger of general war in Europe, and even though they sympathized with the anti-Fascist Loyalists, the journalists cautioned Americans against policies other than neutrality. "The European catastrophe may take shape overnight," the *News* warned. "The time to make our desire for peace effective is now, before the passions of a great war drown out the voice of reason." Johnson declared that "the real European war" was "a clash between liberty and tyranny" and it was "raging now." The United States was "already committed to one side," he went on, "and if the actual fighting is not to spread to our shores, the preventive must be a government so good that no considerable number of our people will be tempted to change sides."[22]

Johnson maintained this conception of a struggle between liberty and tyranny and decided, by the end of 1937, that the United States could not stand aloof. In March, he stated that the "hostility is inevitable and eternal"; another column insisted that "liberty does not consist of a choice between tyrannies," and that Americans ought not to conceive of events in Europe as merely a conflict between fascism and communism. Finally, at the end of October he argued again that liberty and tyranny could not divide the world between them; one or the other must prevail. "So, whether we like it or not," he concluded, "in the end we shall have to fight or change our form of government—that is to say, fight abroad or at home."[23]

The other journalists followed him to the same conclusion. In December 1937 the Japanese attack on an American gunboat in China triggered Hodding Carter's decision that it was time for the United States and other nations "who still believe in the rights of man as man," to "get tough" with the dictators. Ralph McGill, touring Europe on a Rosenwald Fellowship, was in Vienna when Germany occupied Austria in March 1938. In his first report home, a month later, he wrote, "You may mark this down. Force is loose in the world. Brutality is loose. It is backed by intelligence and careful, methodical planning. The Democratic governments . . . alone stand in the way." Hitler's *Anschluss* also provoked John Temple Graves to criticize advocates of peace at any price. Peace might yet be saved, he said, "if those who love it will only dare to risk it." In July, Dabney cautioned against the hope that Germany desired peace; when "the German war machine is ready," he warned, "look out!" A month later, the *News* asserted that "America's hope for remaining aloof from the coming conflict" was "in vain."[24]

The journalists now began to reconsider the relevance of World War I to the present. "If [Woodrow] Wilson needed any justification," Johnson declared in 1937, "Hitler has furnished it; for Nazism is but a cruder and crazier form of the old Prussianism that was smashed in 1918." Those who dismissed warnings that Germany was "a terrible menace to civilization" as repetitions of "the old shibboleths which were heard in 1914–18" were mistaken, the *Times-Dispatch* contended in 1938; in fact, it went on, the Nazi rulers of Germany were demonstrably worse than the Kaiser.[25]

By September 1938, Hitler's campaign to wrest the Sudeten province away from Czechoslovakia had brought the world to crisis once again. "Czechoslovakia really means you and me," John Temple Graves warned in July; "that is something to remember." For several months he had been calling for a show of force to halt German aggressiveness, but he now advanced the argument. He admitted that the German people would not rise up against the Nazi regime and said that "the future of the world and of humanity demands that the German people be rescued from the ideology of Hitlerism." France and Britain decided to conciliate Hitler, however, and on 30 September at Munich, turned the Sudetenland over to Germany.[26]

The journalists scorned the Munich agreement. Dabney called it "a pious gesture," unlikely to deter Hitler from further aggression. Johnson bitterly observed that Americans, who rejected the League of Nations for Warren G. Harding, had no right to talk of betrayals, "but how anyone can doubt that the totalitarian system must eventually strike at us is beyond comprehension." He declared that "as Lincoln said of the nation, [the world] cannot permanently exist half slave and half free."[27]

Through 1939 the world slipped inexorably toward war. Germany occupied the rest of Czechoslovakia in March; Britain and France responded with a promise to defend Poland; and then, on 23 August, Germany signed a nonaggression agreement with the Soviet Union. The pact came as no surprise to the journalists. As McGill put it, they were "the Judy O'Grady and the Colonel's lady of totalitarian governments—sisters under their skins." The journalists also recognized that the pact meant war. "It is an anomalous circumstance when a newspaper as devoted to the cause of peace as *The Times-Dispatch*, regrets the approaching consummation of a nonaggression pact between two great powers," Dabney wrote. On 1 September Germany invaded Poland, and World War II began.[28]

Only the *Times-Dispatch* urged nonintervention in the war. As it said in December, "the way to destroy American democracy is for this country to be dragged into another World War." The war seemed to slow to a halt in early 1940, and Ralph McGill also decided that the United States should remain neutral. "It is the same old battle for trade and territory which Europe has had since the days when the Roman Legions ruled England," he contended. Through that spring, he regularly asserted that "this is not our war." Then, in May, Germany invaded the Netherlands and moved on toward France. When McGill heard the news, he said, "the vestigial muscles along the back crawled and the scalp prickled"; on 13 May he announced "a change of mind" and called on the United States to help the Allies defeat Hitler. Dabney hung back until England's survival seemed likely, and then in December 1940 he joined the other journalists in favor of aid to England at any cost. Asked by a reader to explain the change in editorial policy, Dabney responded, "anybody who didn't change his mind to some extent, in the face of such a world-wide cataclysm, would hardly change his mind about anything."[29]

The events of 1940 brought into the open a theme already implicit in the journalists' defense of democracy. Forgetting their criticism of the abolitionists and their conviction that the Civil War showed the futility of war fought for principle, they proclaimed the defeat of Hitlerism a moral issue. Editorials in the *Chattanooga News* between Munich and the opening of the war reveal the development of this ethical, emotional conception of America's duty in the struggle against totalitarianism. By the autumn of 1938, Milton had come to the conclusion that neutrality was impossible. "In the present state of world affairs," the *News* declared on 28 October, "those who are not with democracy are against it." Moreover, the struggle involved more than economic interests: "we cannot maintain our faith or even our self-respect and indorse what Hitler stands for." Milton addressed the students at the University of Chattanooga in February 1939, and told them that "judged by the things for which they struggle, the dictatorships are fundamentally wrong, and the democracies right."[30]

For years, Milton had insisted that reason alone could preserve liberal society, and those persons who chose instead to follow their emotions or to stand for absolute principles had abdicated their responsibility. His reputation as a historian rested on his contention that the Civil War, a product of blind emotion and abstract principles, need not have occurred had the reasonable compromises of the Unionists been enacted before Americans turned to arms. The threat of Nazism challenged these conclusions. On 16 October 1939, two months to the day before the *News* closed forever, Milton took his stand: "The average American would do well to consult his heart," his editorial said; "in the present situation, emotion has a value which may be even more reliable than cold intelligence."[31]

The other journalists moved in the same direction. Perhaps the most revealing evidence of their shift toward moralism was the appearance of religious references, absent from their writings previously. For example, Johnson described Hitler as "the protagonist of darkness" and declared that the difference between totalitarianism and democracy "is as high as heaven and as deep as hell." Likewise, Jonathan Daniels stated in 1941 that war was justified "to preserve democracy and Christian civilization on earth."[32]

As these comments predict, the journalists transformed the government, economy, and society of the United States into a moral abstraction. Johnson told Americans "to remember that the thing in America most worth defending is the American ideal of equal and exact justice for every man regardless of his race, nationality, religion, or politics." Democracy was a spirit as well as a government, he explained. "It consists of the ideals, the aspirations, the courage of the American people." At the end of 1940 the *Times-Dispatch* proclaimed that "more than ever it is apparent that the American way is a way worth fighting for, worth dying for, if need be." Jonathan Daniels expressed "elation" after the United States entered the war. "Here is the time," he said, "when a man can be what an American means, can fight for what American has always meant—an audacious, adventurous seeking for a better earth." Johnson summed up these views in 1942: "The man himself and his personal faith—that is the basis of Americanism, and you can call it religious or what you please, but that is the way it is."[33]

Most important, their identification of democracy with high idealism caused them to raise principle and emotion to an honored place beside reason. Milton explained in 1940 that, "in peacetime, we like to be a relativist, but in time of war danger there is a necessity that we become at least in part an absolutist." Similarly, Johnson observed that "pacifism, under some circumstances, may be no more than a denial that a man has any obligation to choose between right and wrong."[34]

Not surprisingly, then, the journalists looked back to the antiwar doctrines of the 1930s with bitter scorn and shame. Milton said that Americans should have seen the impossibility of compromise with dictatorships long before 1940. "Such, however, was the role of casualties, the burial of ideals, the loss of beliefs and faiths resulting from the World War that the peoples of the democracies almost en masse became pacifists in mind, completely unwilling under any circumstances to go to war again." Americans were now "beginning to realize the truth that in 1917 we stood in defense of human freedom, and that was, and is, worth defending," Johnson declared.[35]

The events of these years showed that good men could not stand by while evil existed in the world. "The world cannot endure half slave and halve [sic] free," Milton proclaimed. In Johnson's view, the fact that American interests were affected at every point in the conflict supported "the theory that the principle of freedom is a unit to the extent that when any man's freedom is attacked, every man's freedom is threatened." In 1941, he revised the doctrines that had guided him through the 1930s: "It is true that ideals cannot be established by force, but idealists can be protected by force. Hitler cannot be reformed by force, but he can be restrained by force."[36]

Comments along these lines bore obvious implications for the thesis that the Civil War need not have occurred. The events of 1940 made John Temple Graves's high praise in 1937 for Milton's "theory that the War Between the States was unnecessary, that all of the issues could have been settled peaceably and perfectly if it had not been for a few hotheads on both sides," sound naive. Indeed, critics of the Civil War revisionist school of historiography later cited the Second World War as evidence exploding the faith of the revisionists that the Civil War was not inevitable. Bernard De Voto opened his attack in 1946 with the observation that "people who are not historians have lived to learn that some wars are." More important, De Voto contended that the revisionists had pushed the slavery issue— "the core of the social, the economic, the political, and the constitutional conflicts"—to the periphery because of their conviction that it would disappear in time. Thus, they evaded the fundamental issue behind the war and, while casting blame on abolitionists and disunionists, refused to consider "even theoretically that the problem of slavery may have involved moral questions."[37]

In 1949 Arthur Schlesinger, Jr., carried this line of criticism to a thorough analogy between the Civil War and World War II. The revisionists, he charged, sought "in optimistic sentimentalism an escape from the severe demands of moral decision." The Old South became a "closed society" in defense of slavery that not only made internal reform impossible, but presented "the necessity for a moral judgment" to all Americans. "The democracies could not challenge fascism inside Germany any more than opponents of slavery could challenge slavery inside the South," he said, "but the extension of slavery, like the extension of fascism, was an act of aggression which made a moral choice inescapable." Slavery, like fascism, was "evil" and "also a betrayal of the basic values of our Christian and democratic tradition."[38]

These arguments, with their comparisons to World War II and Nazism, also represented a direct challenge to the southern liberal faith in gradualism as the only means to reform. Slavery was not merely a labor system soon to be outmoded but rather a violation of democratic ideals, and therefore a moral issue. Not only were the abolitionists justified, but so was the Civil War. As Schlesinger concluded, "the unhappy fact is that man occasionally works himself into a log-jam; and that the log-jam must be burst by violence."[39]

The journalists failed to see the connection. Johnson's columns afford a striking example of the disconnection between the past and present in their thinking as the war came. On 16 January 1941 he considered the claim that democracy inevitably suffered in wartime: not true, he said—the Woman Suffrage Amendment followed the First World War and the Thirteenth, Fourteenth, and Fifteenth Amendments emerged from the Civil War. "In both these cases," he concluded, "democracy, instead of being weakened by the experience, was extended." A week later, he essayed an explanation for the South's overwhelming support for aid to England: the region had experienced during Reconstruction something of what England faced with a Nazi victory. This era that had seen the extension of democracy in his preceding column, he now described in lurid terms. The Radical rulers "degraded all honor and decency, they outraged every instinct of the people, they gave . . . a new and sickening revelation of the depths to which humanity can sink." Even now, he said, "the South has a well-grounded terror of defeat and conquest." Because both columns served the cause of American aid to England, Johnson ignored the inconsistencies of his historical references.[40]

In fact, other analogies between the Civil War and World War II, in addition to the one that placed moral issues at the center of both, were possible. In 1942 George Fort Milton, now living in Washington, published a study of Abraham Lincoln's struggle with the Copperhead Democrats, northerners who sympathized with the South and sought a negotiated peace. Milton's title, *Abraham Lincoln and the Fifth Column*, evidenced his conviction that the study had contemporary applications. Indeed, he told friends that "the analogies to the present are most numerous and exciting." Rather than constructing a simple defense of Lincoln on the ground that "with the nation in danger, the safety of the people is the supreme law," Milton retained the old emphasis on the rational middle ground between extremists. Corresponding to the pro-Confederate Copperheads were the Radicals, "the agitation fringe" of the Republican party. As he told a correspondent, "the effect has been to portray the harmfulness of both extreme fringes—the Copperhead conspirators and their political allies on the extreme Right and the Joint Committee on the Conduct of the War and its shabby entourage, on the extreme Left."[41]

World affairs in the late 1930s challenged the journalists' interpretation of the Civil War but did not destroy it. Even as they denounced Nazi Germany and the Soviet Union as interchangeable forms of totalitarianism, the journalists still perceived them as ideological extremes of the right and the left. Not only was the United States the embodiment of democratic ideals in the crusade against evil dictatorship, it also remained the reasoned middle way between extremisms. When pressed to carry through reforms that moral imperatives supposedly demanded, the journalists could still retreat to practical middle ground and denounce the extremists.

Those uncomfortable and frightening years before Pearl Harbor saw the journalists introduce references to ideals and morality into their editorials, themes once banned as unrealistic and ultimately dangerous. That they did not carry out a revision of their interpretation of the Civil War and Reconstruction as a consequence of their repudiation of their antiwar doctrines, while hardly suprising, implies that the journalists' editorials against Nazism and in favor of American intervention in the war had a limited impact on their liberalism. In fact, however, the new themes of idealism and moral choice did bolster commitments to liberal principles and policies, especially for Hodding Carter and Ralph McGill. Their emphasis in the 1950s on issues of race as ethical problems had its source in the campaign against Nazi totalitarianism.[42]

George Fort Milton's unsuccessful struggle to maintain a liberal newspaper in Chattanooga provides a revealing example of how the introduction of moralism into foreign policy discussions flowed into other issues. Through 1938, the *News* continued to lose money. Then in August 1939 TEPCO finally sold its holdings to the TVA; the power fight, and the subsidies to the *Free Press*, came to an end. The *News* was operating in the black for the first time since 1937, and Milton now believed that he could win the war with the *Free Press*. His debts were too many and his borrowing power was exhausted, however, and in December his enemies took over the *News*.[43]

On 16 December Milton's farewell statement appeared on the front page of the *News*'s final edition. He explained that he had learned from his father that "it is better to lose a newspaper than to compromise with honor and sell your soul." Perhaps the *News* died because it had "believed in principles," he went on; regardless, "no newspaper is worthy of public trust and confidence unless it shall be ready and willing to sacrifice itself for what those who direct it believe the public good."[44]

Milton began preparing to create a new evening paper to challenge the ultraconservative *News–Free Press*. He decided to name it the *Evening Tribune*, "because of the old tribune of the people idea of the

Roman days," and went to "the people themselves" for his working capital. Shares in the *Tribune* sold for ten dollars, and, when the paper appeared in March 1940, Milton claimed more than seven hundred individual shareholders. "This is the People's Paper," he wrote in the first issue. "Only newspapers willing to subordinate counting-room to conscience are entitled to the respect and support of the people."[45]

The *Evening Tribune* continued the *News*'s campaign against Nazism and for aid to Britain. References to Christianity and moral principle proliferated. Editorials referred to the Allies "standing at Armageddon and battling against the host of evils which are represented by Adolf Hitler," and, as the Nazi invasion neared Paris, spoke fearfully of "the ascendancy of the Anti-Christ." Another editorial complained that too many Americans considered the question of American intervention "mentally, instead of spiritually," and the time had come "when America must consult not only her mind, but also her heart."[46]

The *Tribune*'s commitment to "the people," reinforced by the campaign against Hitler's evil, changed Milton's view of the New Deal and reform. Less than a year before, the *News* had complained of FDR's failure to consider "recovery as quite as important a thing as reform," and told the New Dealers to "cease any addictions to extremism." Now the *Tribune* damned "those journalistic panderers who revile persons on relief" and praised the president for increasing relief appropriations. In April, moreover, the *Tribune* welcomed "the great Southern Conference on [sic] Human Welfare" to Chattanooga for its second conference. It noted that "many Negro delegates attended" the unsegregated meeting and happily reported increased "good will between the races."[47]

Other editorials linked the war with liberal ideals. This was a presidential election year, and the Republican party nominated Wendell Willkie, the man whom Milton believed to have been behind the campaign against the *News*. The *Tribune* attacked the "selfish class-sense" of "Willkie-ism" that denied any responsibility for the poor and unemployed. With a reference to the fate of France, the editorial declared that "America will not be psychologically prepared to defend freedom until we recognize that we are one people and that the lowest among us has the same right to life, liberty and the pursuit of happiness as the highest."[48]

Five days later, the *Tribune* published its final issue. Milton simply had insufficient funds to keep the newspaper alive. Now in desperate financial straits, he accepted a part-time position with the National Resources Planning Board in Washington. In his spare time, he swiftly wrote a narrative history of the Civil War, *Conflict*, fulfilling a contractual obligation to a publisher, but the book sold poorly. In May 1941 he accepted a post in the Treasury Department, "writing material for the public acceptance for the Defense Savings Department." He took up residence at the Cosmos Club, where his old friend Will Alexander also lived, and completed *Abraham Lincoln and the Fifth Column* in 1942. Milton never returned to the South.[49]

Hodding Carter also left the South in 1940, but for different reasons, and, unlike Milton, he did return. In the spring of 1939, Carter learned that he had been awarded a Nieman Fellowship, under a program to afford talented newspapermen a year of study at Harvard University. The birth of their second son delayed the family's departure for Harvard until January 1940, and Carter spent less than a semester there. On the way to Cambridge he stopped in New York to visit the editor of an experiment in journalism, *PM*, which was to begin publishing in June. *PM* was to be a tabloid, filled with photographs and liberal opinions, but free from advertising. Journalists around the country watched with interest, and several thousand of them applied for the two hundred jobs available. Carter was one of the lucky few chosen and accepted the post of press editor. He left Harvard in May for New York and *PM*.[50]

Within a few months Carter had enjoyed all that he could stand of both. In his autobiography, he complained of *PM*'s "dreary, humorless, consecrated insistence upon conformity to a fixed and condescending liberalism" and reflexive hostility to businessmen and the South. He felt like a "misfit" there and left with no regrets. In the *Delta Democrat-Times*, however, Carter said nothing of the abrasive liberalism at *PM*. In fact, he stated that "we didn't come home because we disliked the job." Rather, he had concluded that Greenville was "a better place to live" than New York—"where the contrast between success and squalor is tragically inescapable, and where the premium one must pay for contentment is too high for all but a few"— and he preferred being his "own boss" to working "even for *PM*."[51]

Although Carter no doubt resented the complacently antisouthern attitudes of the liberals he met at *PM*, the experience also changed his own views. In 1938, his editorials had railed against "the thriftless, labor-courting, left-wing segment of the New Deal," but now he praised Roosevelt and liberal reform. Significantly, he described his stance in terms of the ethical democracy that the fight against Nazism had already inspired in his editorials.[52]

On 13 October 1940 Carter "set forth a personal philosophy." Better that no millionaires existed than that any family "should live at the sub-human level at which hundreds of thousands of families grovel today," he affirmed. Better that "a hundred drones be fed" than that men should lose self-respect and go hungry for lack of government relief and jobs. "We believe this is democracy," Carter declared, "and, if we have the right to say so, it is Christianity." Other editorials repeated these themes. "From this, the world's most hideous trial, will come a cooperative society of man," one predicted. Another discussed southern poverty and complained that white southerners took for granted the degradation in which too many blacks lived. "We are not prepared to say what does offer a solution," the editorial said. "We do believe, however, that it lies only in further travel along the road which the New Deal belatedly began, the road toward social responsibility."[53]

On 25 November 1940, Carter entered the Army for a year of training in Florida with the National Guard. "It is as small a thing as any American could want to do in return for the privilege of citizenship," he said. The following year, Carter injured his right eye during night maneuvers; infection set in, and despite an operation and a month in the hospital, he lost the sight in that eye. The Army transferred him to duty in Washington with the War Department's Public Relations Bureau, whence he expected to return to Greenville at the end of his one-year enlistment. The Japanese attack on Pearl Harbor changed his plans: "When we have whipped our enemies, I will come home, and not before unless the army decides otherwise," he told his readers.[54]

During the war, Carter served for a time in Cairo as editor of the Middle East edition of *Stars and Stripes* and saw, as an outsider, the bitterness and resentment that British colonial and racial attitudes inspired in the local population. Throughout his postwar editorials on race relations, Carter's sensitivity to race as a potent world issue appeared again and again. "Men with white skins are in the minority in this world," he wrote after Japan surrendered in 1945. "And in even smaller minority are white-skinned men who look upon darker skins with contempt." Nonetheless, the sources of Carter's racial liberalism lie in the period before the war, and his emphasis on the moral dimensions of race relations flowed out of the campaign against Nazism.[55]

Like Carter, Ralph McGill found a new language for southern liberalism at the beginning of World War II. Rather than leaving the South, however, McGill made his commitment during the 1942 Georgia governor's race as an outspoken opponent of Eugene Talmadge. In June 1941, Governor Talmadge called for the dismissal of the dean of the University of Georgia's School of Education and the president of South Georgia Teachers' College on the grounds that they favored interracial coeducation. In September, the Southern Accrediting Commission suspended Georgia's colleges because of Talmadge's interference and the Southern University Conference dropped the University of Georgia. Responding that "we credit our own schools down here," Talmadge continued to rail against threats to white supremacy.[56]

The journalists reacted with anger. Dabney called the ousters "a piece of domestic Fascism" and charged that Talmadge had "stooped to the lowest form of demagoguery and rabble-rousing." Jonathan Daniels warned that attacks on intellectual freedom could lead to destruction of all freedoms. Talmadge's action was a "dirty sign in a dark southern sky, and it is at least as big as Hitler's funny mustache looked ten years ago." McGill saw the episode as Talmadge's preparation for his reelection campaign. "He now indicates he is going to base his campaign on 'white supremacy,' which is not at all challenged, and a 'nigger! nigger!' appeal to ignorance and prejudice," McGill wrote in June. "There is absolutely no call for Georgia to have such a disgraceful campaign."[57]

Ellis Gibbs Arnall, the young attorney general, decided to run against Talmadge, "promising to free Georgia's education system, common schools and colleges alike, from every vestige of political interference." The *Constitution* backed Arnall's candidacy and McGill became "confidant and counselor" to him. In his columns, McGill linked the campaign to the war effort. Declaring that "the whole meaning of the war is bound up in the right to a free ballot," he implored Georgians to register to vote.[58]

The primary campaign began on the fourth of July, and McGill's column that day referred to the American Revolution, when "a belief and a faith" inspired the Founding Fathers "to defy a king and risk their lives." The current war had come "just in time," he went on. "It may give us back our faith and our idea." In another column, he envisioned "a great state, cleanly governed, its institutions respected and supported," and declared that "we can have it if we keep before us the fact that certain principles never change and always remain the eternal issues."[59]

On 22 July, he again recalled the day in 1938 when he had watched the Nazis triumphantly enter Vienna. "Standing there I took an oath," he wrote; "I promised myself that as long as I lived I would oppose in any way I could, small or great, those who taught hatred and intolerance, those who deceived the people for their own gain, those who would destroy the ideals of America with hatreds and intolerances."[60]

Through the month of August McGill's daily columns, except for an occasional note on the war or on victory gardens, maintained the attack on Talmadge. In fact, McGill made him the issue and rarely mentioned Arnall. "It is my opinion," he declared on election day, "that a vote for state dictatorship is a vote against our men in the Army who are fighting to kill one."[61]

Despite Georgia's county-unit system of voting that gave rural counties greater weight than their actual population would deserve, Arnall easily thrashed Talmadge. The *Richmond Times-Dispatch* described it as "a victory for decency over demagoguery, of sanity over sensationalism." With immense satisfaction, McGill stated that "Georgia won a great victory Wednesday."[62]

The successful campaign against Talmadge seems to have freed McGill to speak more openly against racial and religious prejudices. The war's legitimizing of democratic ideals and ethical principles also contributed to the tone of his editorials. One column discussed the escape of the Israelites from bondage in Egypt, which he associated with Nazi anti-Semitism. "Christianity," he continued, "is based on the brotherhood of man and the fatherhood of God and I guess that includes Jews and Catholics and all the other peoples which the Klan and all its associated societies denied." Against Talmadge, McGill took on the reputation of an opponent of race prejudice, but the campaign against Hitler gave him a broader perspective and a language of ethical judgment with which to express his opinions.[63]

"If this war is the cause of any people, it is the cause of the liberals," Jonathan Daniels wrote after Pearl Harbor. "Everything they believe in is at stake."[64] Indeed, the journalists had made the war their cause. In doing so, they rejected the antiwar doctrines and the distrust of idealism that had bottomed their thinking on southern problems during the 1930s. Rather than a method or a habit of mind, liberalism became a set of values, bound up with religious and ethical principles, and therefore less inclined to compromise with social evils.

Negro leaders took up this wartime rhetoric, too, and pointed out that if Nazi racism was evil, so was racism in the South. Americans must fight for the principles of democracy at home as well as abroad. Southern liberalism, however, still stopped at the color line. The journalists could not conceive of an end to Jim Crow in the South, whether it violated democratic ideals or not. Thus, they retreated to customary middle ground and damned the extremists on both sides of the issue. The middle ground, they soon realized, would grow ever more narrow.

11 The Conservative Course in Race Relations

In January 1942 an editor for *The American Scholar* asked George Fort Milton to write an essay on Talmadge's war against the colleges. Milton explained that his absence from the South for the preceding two years made him less than informed on southern matters but he promised to discuss the matter with Will Alexander. He reported that Alexander believed too little information was available "for any very useful presentation" but had observed that the controversy showed "that today there exists in the South a vigorous group of Liberals and/or progressives to challenge any such bigotted [sic] attitude or policy, and challenge it with some effectiveness."[1]

In late 1941, Lillian Smith and Paula Snelling, editors of the *North Georgia Review*, analyzed the controversy over Georgia's colleges. Talmadge's crucial mistake, they said, "lay not in using the racial club . . . but in using it on the wrong head." The governor's critics could accurately deny that the persecuted educators desired an end to segregation. Indeed, Daniels called it a "phony race attack," and Dabney's angry editorials assumed that Talmadge's claims were lies. The charges were "false, impossible and ridiculous," McGill sputtered. "In the first place, the state constitution forbids it, and in the second place, anyone willing to think about it would know there would be no one so foolish as to want to attempt it had there been, as there was not, someone who wanted so to do." In the opinion of Smith and Snelling, "if the Governor had been able to *make a case* . . . on the race issue the newspapers would have been about as talkative as a mute."[2]

Together these judgments sum up the achievements of southern liberalism in regard to race relations during the 1930s. No longer could southern politicians appeal to white racial fears without protest from articulate white southerners. On the other hand, the doctrine of vertical segregation yet promised that the South could have liberal reform without giving up the Jim Crow system. By the end of World War II, however, southern liberals faced a crisis: Jim Crow and liberalism had become incompatible.

As the journalists put away their antiwar convictions and exhorted the nation to prepare to fight for freedom and democracy, black Americans questioned the relevance of the war for themselves. Where the journalists held up France and England as the last bastions of Christianity and democracy in dictator-ridden Europe, Negroes looked on them as colonial rulers over nonwhite people. When the journalists set democratic ideals against the evils of Nazism, Negroes wondered whether racism in Germany differed significantly from that in the South. As defense preparations got under way, Negroes discovered discrimination in hiring for defense jobs and little more than hard labor or servants' work open to them in the military. Black spokesmen bitterly charged white Americans with hypocrisy; they would fight first for democracy at home.[3]

A. Phillip Randolph, head of the Brotherhood of Sleeping Car Porters, who understood well the effectiveness of mass organization, proposed in 1941 a march of Negroes on Washington to demand an end to discriminatory hiring practices and to segregation in the military. The proposal won enthusiastic support from blacks across the country and soon the National Association for the Advancement of Colored People and the Urban League endorsed the March on Washington Movement. After the MOWM's leaders convinced FDR that they expected 100,000 marchers, he agreed to issue Executive Order 8802 banning discrimination in hiring for defense work, and they called off the march. Although FDR had not met all their demands, MOWM leaders claimed a great victory.[4]

The journalists responded to the Negro protest with ambivalence that grew into frightened outrage. Discrimination, as Dabney pointed out, hampered "the arming of America" and had "serious" effects "on the prospects for national unity." Better jobs and wages for Negroes also would continue the progress that they perceived in race relations. That FDR appointed Mark Ethridge to head the Fair Employment Practices Commission set up to carry out Executive Order 8802 seemed an assurance that no foolhardy policies would result. At the same time, the journalists, like FDR, insisted that winning the war, not achievement of domestic reforms, came first. As Johnson put it, the country could have but one war aim: "Lick Hitler!" The war and its slogans gave the MOWM sufficient leverage to wrest action from FDR against discrimination in hiring, but these factors also gave further black protest the appearance of "weakening the republic" in time of crisis.[5]

A revealing comment came from Hodding Carter, reporting from Washington to the *Delta Democrat-Times*, who claimed that the Communists were behind the agitation. The charge was false—Randolph decreed the MOWM open only to blacks partly to block the Communists from participating—but it points to the deeper significance for southern liberalism of the Negro protest. The journalists had assumed that white southern liberals would determine the agenda and set the pace for racial reform; the MOWM revealed skillful black leaders with the organization and power behind them to set their own goals and move toward achieving them.[6]

Negroes seemed willing to take on Jim Crow himself. The protest had aroused the black masses, even more dissatisfied with the status quo than their leaders, and they pushed spokesmen to grow ever more militant. Even cautious men had to speak the language of protest or lose their following. By 1942, any Negro who endorsed segregation was sure to be labeled an "Uncle Tom."

Alarmed southern liberal journalists spoke out against the militance of the protest. Mark Ethridge, at the FEPC's first hearings in Birmingham, caused a sensation by charging that black leaders "who demand 'all or nothing'" were misleading their people and "playing into the hands of white demagogues." In a famous phrase, Ethridge declared that the Negro "must recognize that there is no power in the world—not even in all the mechanized armies of the earth, Allied and Axis—which could now force the Southern white people to the abandonment of the principle of social segregation." John Temple Graves proclaimed that "segregation is not an argument in the South. It is a major premise." Virginius Dabney warned that "if an attempt is made forcibly to abolish segregation throughout the South, violence and bloodshed will result."[7]

These statements called down a storm of criticism. "The highest casualty rate of the war to date seems to be that of Southern white liberals," Walter White observed. In the *New Republic*, Thomas Sancton contended that Dabney "and his colleagues" should stop worrying about outside agitators and address white southerners. "Educating these people for concessions on the race issue which the war demands—even though they don't want to be educated—is an editorial responsibility which rests on these Southern editors," he declared; "they should discharge it." Lillian E. Smith charged that, under stress, these men had reverted to the emotions of childhood "race-conditioning." The journalists had the power and the obligation "to turn the tide of southern opinion." Instead, she complained, "the southern liberal is busily concocting little recipes for sweetening the old segregation . . . and explaining all the while to a tired, puzzled world why this is not the right time for the freedom millions are dying for."[8]

Both Sancton and Smith were southerners and their criticisms belied the journalists' claims that the white South was united and willing to defend segregation with violence. Not many years before, Dabney and the others had performed a similar service: their protests against lynching and injustice encouraged other southerners to reject conformity and, by virtue of their dissent, exploded the image of a solidly anti-Negro South.

Not all southern liberals agreed with Ethridge, Graves, and Dabney, of course, but the trio became symbols of the breed. As a result, southern liberalism itself became discredited, the domestic equivalent of appeasement. The image of the southern liberal changed from that of a strong-hearted individual standing firm against southern bigotry to that of a person whose courage and liberalism evaporated at the color line. From this perspective, southern liberalism was inadequate to the task of racial reform in the South.

The publication in 1944 of Gunnar Myrdal's *An American Dilemma: The Negro Problem and Modern Democracy*, the Carnegie Corporation's massive report on the Negro and race relations in the United States, contributed importantly to southern liberalism's swiftly declining influence on racial reform thought. Myrdal echoed the critics. Southern liberals lacked popular support and power, he explained, and weakness taught them to evade principles, to approach problems by indirection, and to hail small changes as progressive triumphs. Although a bit gentler in his assessment of the Commission on Interracial Cooperation, "the organization of southern liberalism in its activity on the Negro issue," Myrdal contended that its achievements represented "capital" that must be "invested, even risked, in new ventures."[9]

Significantly, Myrdal rejected Robert E. Park's analysis of American race relations, the sociological doctrine in accord with southern racial liberalism. He quoted Park's diagram of vertical segregation from 1928 and said mildly that it contained "several overstatements." The color line had barely slanted from the horizontal, and rather than a corresponding social structure on the Negro side of the line, the black upper and middle classes were "*more than proportionately smaller than their lower class.*" Because the caste relationship of superior and inferior persisted, whites looked *down* on blacks rather than *across* the color line at them. Myrdal's criticisms of Park also measured southern liberalism's failure to bring about the separate but equal society that Dabney and his fellows promised to southern Negroes.[10]

On the other hand, Myrdal proved even more sanguine than Park in his conclusions. Where Park had assumed inevitable progress toward assimilation resulting from natural processes of social evolution, Myrdal proposed an activist "social engineering." He built his framework of research reports on the foundation of an assumption of American rationalism and moralism. Even conservative southerners believed in "the American Creed" of "liberty, equality, justice, and fair opportunity for everybody" and Christian brotherhood. Thus, the "American Dilemma" of his title resulted from the conflict between the tenets of this Creed and discriminatory treatment of the Negro. The Negro problem was a problem "in the heart of the American." Liberals must encourage all Americans to face this "moral struggle" and bring about "equalitarian reforms in line with the American Creed."[11]

Modern scholars have questioned Myrdal's assumptions, but as a document of the times, *An American Dilemma* remains a revealing work. The war against Hitlerism and the rhetoric of democratic ideals are pervasive influences in the book. Indeed, had Myrdal completed his writing before the war, his conclusions might have been very different. For this reason, however, *An American Dilemma* gave the sanction of social science to the contemporary Negro protest against Jim Crow.[12]

Ironically, as Lee A. Finkle points out, the journalists deserve much of the credit for publicizing the Negro protest. Because they made segregation the sticking point for reform, they also helped to narrow the debate to the Jim Crow laws rather than the broader issues of jobs and hiring practices over which the protest began. By entering the debates, the journalists swept away the haze of vagueness that had shrouded the doctrine of vertical segregation. For example, Ralph McGill welcomed FEPC investigators to Atlanta, telling his readers that the "Negro problem" was "economic almost entirely, and not at all a 'social equality' problem." White southerners, he went on, "must admit" that segregation "has come to mean not separation of the races, but exploitation and bad living conditions." McGill said nothing here that southern liberals, with varying degrees of frankness, had not said before. Now, however, McGill felt it necessary to preface his remarks with the assertion that "anyone with an ounce of common sense must see . . . that separation of the two races must be maintained in the South."[13]

Because the journalists remained desirous of improved conditions for blacks and expounded the democratic idealism of the war against Hitler, Negro protest against segregation forced them into a new and uncomfortable position, which manifested itself on their editorial pages. Some days they depicted a dangerous wave of black militance hovering over the South, while on others they expressed faith in the patriotism of the Negro and assured whites that the militance existed primarily in rumors, spread by enemy agents. By equating Negro protestors against segregation with race-baiting southern demagogues, they also tried to claim the rational middle ground for southern liberalism. McGill complained that the "most vocal voices" on the issue were "radical Negroes in the north" and "fanatics, Kluxers and demagogues" in the South. "The patriotic American," he declared, "must keep his balance and think things out."[14]

They invited black southern liberals to join them on middle ground. As Dabney put it, "the more level-headed members of both groups must not let these purveyors of hate steal the center of the stage and plunge the South into violence and bloodshed." In fact, Finkle argues that because southern liberalism depended on the cooperation of "moderate blacks" willing to accept, at least temporarily, the continuation of segregation, the journalists actually aimed their warnings of the strife that would follow assaults on Jim Crow not at the "northern radicals" whom they criticized but rather at southern Negroes. Certainly it was to these Negro leaders that they addressed their assertions that gradual reform with an emphasis on economic development of the whole South best served the interests of blacks. That southern liberalism must retain support from southern blacks also became a theme in their editorial warnings to white audiences. As Graves noted hopefully in 1942, "Southern Negro leaders have not made up their minds whether to follow the southern white liberals or the Northern crusaders for all-or-nothing."[15]

The journalists soon realized that obtaining the support of southern Negroes would be no easy task. During this period, the University of North Carolina Press—the publishing house of southern liberalism—asked Rayford Logan, a black historian, to edit a symposium on *What the Negro Wants*. Logan obtained essays by fourteen black writers, from the North and the South, holding opinions ranging from radical to conservative. To the horror of W. T. Couch, director of the press, every contributor condemned segregation. "If this is what the Negro wants," Couch wrote to Logan, "nothing is clearer than that what he needs, and needs most urgently is to revise his wants." After Logan responded to his attempt to cancel the book with a threat of legal action and publicity, Couch sent the manuscript to Dabney for his opinion. The editor told him that the authors accurately expressed black opinion. "Even the Southern conservatives among the Negroes are outspokenly critical," Dabney said, "lest they be considered 'Uncle Toms' or 'Handkerchief Heads.'" Couch had contracted for the book, he continued, in the mistaken conviction that some blacks did not desire the abolition of segregation. Dabney himself had so believed "in say, 1941," but events since then had revealed the unanimity of black opinion.[16]

Couch published the book, but added to it a "Publisher's Introduction" putting forward his views. With tortured reasoning, he charged advocates of Negro equality with valueless relativism and declared that democratic principles fully justified the white southern majority's treatment of blacks. Once more, a white southern liberal had stepped forward to defend segregation. Dabney, Johnson, and Ethridge all wrote to express their appreciation for Couch's "Introduction," but the controversy over *What the Negro Wants* revealed that white southern liberals could no longer expect black support if they made perpetual continuance of segregation a precondition for reform. As Logan put it, "conservatives, liberals and radicals alike want Negroes eventually to enjoy the same rights, opportunities and privileges that are vouchsafed to all other Americans."[17]

Meanwhile, southern liberals reorganized the Commission on Interracial Cooperation to salvage vertical segregation. After 1938, with Howard W. Odum's plans for a Council on Southern Regional Development stalled, the CIC had grown increasingly moribund. Will Alexander, who had learned in Washington the effectiveness of pressure-group tactics, seems to have concluded, at least privately, that the organization had lost its usefulness. Although Odum continued as president, by 1941 the CIC had become little more than the headquarters in Atlanta, where Jessie Daniel Ames, head of the Association of Southern Women for the Prevention of Lynching, was the dominant figure. She remained convinced that slow improvement of public opinion was the best route to improved race relations and stepped into the leadership vacuum in 1940 by taking the title of Director of Field Work and editing a monthly newsletter, *The Southern Frontier.*[18]

Ames warned readers of *The Southern Frontier* that "times had changed, and so have Southern Negroes," who now insisted on "the application of democratic principles to them," but the militant Negro protest outside the South still disturbed her. An editorial by Jonathan Daniels in the December 1941 issue, lamenting the absence of capable southern Negro leaders in this time of tension, expressed her own fears. That month she read an essay by Gordon Blaine Hancock, a Negro professor at Virginia Union University, warning that black militance threatened to produce a violent white backlash in the South. He called on the "better class of whites" and Negro leaders to meet the challenge and prevent disorder. Ames met with Hancock in early 1942, and convinced him to organize a conference of Negro southern liberals to draw up a "new charter of race relations" for presentation to white southern liberals.[19]

Scholars have treated Ames's appeal to Hancock as an attempt to reinvigorate the CIC and thereby expand her role in the organization, but her devotion to the southern liberal doctrines of the previous decade played a part in her action, too. Despite her ready insistence on the need for reforms, she emphasized the dangers of racial conflict. Yes, the nation did need to live up to its democratic professions, one editorial acknowledged, but "a law in a democracy is as strong as the people make it." "Remember the 18th Amendment," she warned. Indeed, in July 1942 she distributed reprints of Mark Ethridge's controversial attack on "Negro leaders who mislead" with that month's *Southern Frontier.*[20]

In Hancock, Ames believed she had found a man who shared her fears. He wrote to various other black southern liberals in May, telling them that an "interested white Southerner" had proposed that they present a program for race relations to whites, and received an enthusiastic response. These men—Charles S. Johnson, Horace Mann Bond, Benjamin Mays, P. B. Young, and others—perceived economic and political reforms as the necessary foundation for Negro advancement. Young spoke for them all when he declared that "the Negro's struggle is for bread."[21]

The organizing committee for the conference divided acrimoniously over whether to invite black delegates from outside the South. Hancock argued persuasively that if only southerners attended, whites could not dismiss their report as the work of northern radicals. Several organizers withdrew after this decision for fear of "adverse criticism from Northern Negroes." In fact, a leading black newspaper did charge Hancock with being "a stooge for Ethridge and Dabney." Significantly, even the cautious Hancock felt it necessary to protest to the paper's editor that he, too, opposed segregation.[22]

Ames, meanwhile, desired that the issue of Jim Crow not come up at all. She informed Virginius Dabney at the end of May 1942 that a plan was "afoot" and enclosed copies of her correspondence with Hancock. Once Hancock set a date for the conference, Ames said, she would meet with Dabney to choose the white delegates invited to respond to the new charter for race relations. That she chose Dabney, then speaking out against Negro militance, as a collaborator suggests her limited intentions for the conference. She also told Hancock "to think of the white people as well as the Negro group" in drafting the charter. It "must be interracial in philosophy and in policy," she went on. Above all, they ought to "avoid bringing in segregation, white supremacy and other loaded ideas."[23]

At their meeting in Durham on 20 October, the Negroes did bring segregation into their statement. Benjamin Mays proposed that they denounce Jim Crow forthrightly. Despite the nervousness that they all felt, those who disagreed with Mays's proposal argued only that the group must leave room for cooperation with white southern liberals, not that they should remain silent on the issue. Charles S. Johnson accepted the task of drafting their official statement, which appeared in December. Although they emphasized specific measures— abolition of the poll tax, improved education, and economic opportunities—that white southern liberals had endorsed for years and made it clear that they still accepted gradual reform as the most effective means to their goals, the Negroes unanimously declared themselves "fundamentally opposed to the principle and practice of compulsory segregation in our American society."[24]

Despite the fact that Dabney and McGill gave the Durham statement editorial endorsement, they evidenced their reluctance to acknowledge the import of the declaration against segregation. The former wrote that the statement "should aid markedly in promoting interracial harmony and sound Negro advancement," despite its "controversial aspects." McGill applauded the Negroes for their realistic recognition that segregation "will be retained for a long time to come." White southerners must cooperate with them to eliminate the needless "exploitation and mistreatment" from racial separation.[25]

The meeting of white liberals in response to the Durham conference went no further than McGill in its statement. In fact, Ames suggested the disparity between the two groups' intentions when she told Dabney that a whites-only meeting could attract people who would be "a little skittish" about an interracial gathering. The "Committee on Cooperation"—with McGill prominent among them—sent out some 500 invitations to "leaders of the Southland," but only about 100 appeared in Atlanta on 8 April 1943. McGill presided after Dabney turned down the post and guided the group to a statement endorsing better race relations through "evolutionary methods" of reform. Despite the Durham conference's declaration against Jim Crow, however, those meeting in Atlanta presented vertical segregation more as a goal than as a means. Condemning discriminatory treatment of blacks under the law, they proclaimed once again that the only justification for the Jim Crow laws "is that they are intended to minister to the welfare and integrity of both races."[26]

The delegates from the black and white conferences chosen to meet together on 16 June gathered uneasily in Richmond. Each group sat on its own separate side of the meeting place. Gordon Hancock, presiding because both Dabney and McGill had turned down invitations to chair the meeting, opened with a warning that if white southern liberals failed to cooperate with Negro southern liberals, northern black militants would step in. Hancock's address provoked M. Ashby Jones, a white founder of the CIC two decades earlier, to reply that blacks must restrain their desire for change or risk alienating white allies. As Hancock said later, Jones's angry speech "cold-watered" the already tense meeting. At this critical juncture, however, Howard W. Odum stepped into the breach. He convinced the divided delegates to endorse his prepared resolution emphasizing "the way of peace and planning rather than . . . conflict and revolution." Unlike the statement at the Atlanta conference, Odum's resolution skirted the issue of Jim Crow while giving solace to the Negroes with references to "equalizing opportunities" and to "our professed principles of Christianity and democracy."[27]

Six months earlier, Odum had expressed his hope that with a "successful charter of race relations" devised at the conferences, the CIC, "developed into a regional council, may have reasonable support." Until the Richmond meeting, though, he kept his distance, sending his proxy to McGill rather than attending the Atlanta conference. Naturally, Ames viewed his sudden participation with suspicion. When Hancock expressed his gratitude for Odum's rescue of the meeting, she bitterly acknowledged the coup with her reply that the resolution "was what the white man thought should come out of the meeting." For his part, Odum believed that Ames resented the independence of the Negro delegates, which had carried the conferences beyond her control.[28]

The Richmond meeting chose Charles S. Johnson and Dabney to chair the planning meeting in August to follow up Odum's resolution, but the editor wanted out. He explained to Jonathan Daniels that his work schedule on the *Times-Dispatch* and "reputation as a 'phoney liberal' in certain Northern circles" made him unsuitable. In addition, as he told Johnson, Odum had "a definite plan in mind." Shortly before the August meeting, with Ames reluctantly acceding, Dabney turned the chairmanship over to Odum.[29]

Now in command, Odum obtained agreement to organize a Southern Regional Council. Citing the CIC's decision of early 1938 to support his council, he absorbed the commission into the new SRC. On 11 February 1944, with McGill as one of the incorporators, the SRC formally began its work. That month's issue of *The Southern Frontier*—Jessie Daniel Ames's last as editor—carried a farewell editorial entitled "The Curtains Drop on the Old Order."[30]

Critics of southern liberalism expressed doubt that the old order had actually ended. Saunders J. Redding claimed that the SRC intended to compromise on the problems of racial prejudice and discrimination. Still "pretty effectively enslaved" by the issue of segregation, the SRC was little more than a duplication of the CIC, and its leaders were "worn gears in what is at best a reconditioned machine." Similarly, Lillian Smith charged the SRC with operating under false pretenses "as a race-relations movement" because of its failure to confront segregation, "the 'unfinished business' of southern liberals."[31]

Certainly, in contrast to the views of Smith and others, the new southern liberal organization chose, as McGill approvingly put it, a "conservative course in race relations." As they had since the 1920s, the southern liberals took up middle ground, calling on white southerners to concede improvements in conditions for black southerners in order to stave off "the northern radicals," while warning northerners that their misguided efforts at reform would only provoke a violent white backlash in the South. Not only did the organizers of the conferences leading to the SRC exclude northern—national—Negro leaders, but they also failed to invite their southern white critics, such as Lillian Smith. The only dissent from the official statements at the Atlanta and Richmond meetings came from whites who wanted a more definite endorsement of Jim Crow.[32]

Nonetheless, a crucial change had occurred. Despite the equivocation, the SRC tacitly accepted the dismantling of the Jim Crow system as its ultimate goal. In his reply to the criticisms of Redding and Smith, Guy B. Johnson, Odum's choice as the SRC's first executive director, argued that he would "rather help to capture the foothills which have to be captured sooner or later than merely to point out the distant peak and urge my comrades to storm it at once!" This statement—which failed to impress the critics—revealed that the clouds surrounding the goals of southern racial liberalism had cleared. Some day even these cautious men would confront segregation. As Johnson acknowledged, "I, too, can see the peak."[33]

Thus, although obscured by ambiguous language and overshadowed by the defensive rejection of northern radicalism, southern liberalism emerged from the racial crisis of World War II with the realization that segregation and liberalism, even southern liberalism, were ultimately incompatible. The achievement of a literal vertical segregation, an actual condition of separate but equal, was insufficient. For example, in 1944 John Temple Graves argued that blacks must endorse Jim Crow before whites could undertake reforms to tilt the color line, and he presented his program to Odum, whose writings in the 1930s had evidenced no desire to eliminate segregation; in his reply, however, Odum refused to join Graves. Referring to the findings of science, the ideals of democracy, and "the stated principles of Christianity," Odum declared that segregation violated all three. He could therefore commit no people to live "forever" under Jim Crow. The southern liberal program of making segregation vertical survived, but now only as a means, not as an end.[34]

The Negro southern liberals who met at Durham deserve most of the credit for this change: by declaring their opposition to segregation, they gave a clear destination to southern liberalism. At the same time, their cautious language and willingness to continue interracial cooperation with the whites obscured the significance of their declaration. Ironically, the Negro southern liberals, with their endorsement of the Southern Regional Council, helped to create a space enabling many white southern liberals to delay their confrontation with Jim Crow. The men who met at the Durham conference preserved southern liberalism. Nonetheless, they made their point. Their agreement to continue the methods of vertical segregation was, as Charles S. Johnson put it, "fundamentally a matter of expediency rather than conviction."[35]

In 1950, John Temple Graves published an essay on recent southern politics in the *Virginia Quarterly Review*. With obvious approval, he described the reaction against liberalism below the Potomac since the beginning of World War II that had led to the Dixiecrat campaign of 1948. He told the quarterly's editor that he had considered calling his article "The Ordeal of Virginius Dabney."[36]

Unlike Graves, who now insisted that blacks endorse segregation as a precondition for reform, Dabney had remained committed to southern liberalism during World War II. He acknowledged the validity of Negro protests against discrimination and even conceded privately that the defense of segregation conflicted with democratic principles. On the other hand, as early as 1942 he proposed a regional graduate university for Negroes as a means for the South to meet the Supreme Court's ruling in the *Gaines* case without permitting blacks to enter white universities. He told correspondents that if white southerners did not make a stand then, the whole system of segregation would crumble.[37]

The university proposal dropped from sight as Dabney joined the other journalists in their attack on Negro extremists and radicals. By the autumn of 1942, as Hancock organized the Durham conference, Dabney's fear of the Negro protest and its potential consequences inspired him to write an essay of warning to the nation, which appeared in the *Atlantic Monthly* for January 1943. He charged that "a small group of Negro agitators and another small group of white rabble-rousers" were pushing the country "nearer and nearer the precipice" of racial conflict and bloodshed. If this happened, he concluded, "there can be little doubt that the Negroes will be the worst sufferers."[38]

Blacks reacted with anger to Dabney's essay. Despite his references to "white rabble-rousers," he obviously held Negro protestors primarily responsible for the racial tensions. As did other white southern liberals, Dabney considered a violent white reaction to black militance inevitable, even natural. The new factor on the southern scene was Negro protest, not white racism, and Dabney directed his criticism in that direction. To blacks who objected to the *Atlantic* article, he reasserted that he, too, sought racial progress, but the first task was the prevention of racial violence. As he wrote to one critic who backed his argument with historical references: "Those who cite Patrick Henry's 'Give me Liberty, or Give me Death,' and who also say, 'Well, the abolitionists were radical, but they got rid of slavery' seem to ignore the fact that Patrick Henry helped to bring on an armed revolution and that the abolitionists were a major factor in bringing on the Civil War."[39]

Like the antebellum southern Unionists they admired, Dabney and the other journalists gave their highest priority to the prevention of conflict. Their program of gradual improvement of public opinion and faith in the progressive direction of social change had had a positive appearance in the 1930s, but the war's rhetoric of liberal idealism and the ensuing racial crisis stripped away this façade, exposing the defensive aspects of their positions. Reluctant themselves to imagine an unsegregated South, they assumed that years, even generations, of gradual public education must precede the change. So long as white southerners remained united in their devotion to Jim Crow, regardless of segregation's conflict with the tenets of liberalism, then northern liberals and Negroes must refrain from agitating the issue.

Suddenly, on 13 November 1943, Dabney wrote an editorial calling for the abolition of segregation on streetcars and buses. Wartime gasoline rationing had caused a vast increase in the use of public transportation, and crowded conditions made segregation an irritant.

The early response was favorable, and on 21 November he repeated his proposal in a long editorial entitled "The Conservative Course in Race Relations." Dabney summarized the meetings of Negroes and whites leading to the Southern Regional Council and explained that an end to Jim Crow on public transportation would demonstrate to southern blacks the willingness of whites to make concessions in the interest of better race relations. This would prevent more militant northern Negroes from securing "a large following in the South." In its conclusion, the editorial warned that "bitter racial clashes" would result if whites chose to ignore "the legitimate appeals of the Negroes for justice."[40]

Obvious reasons exist for Dabney's surprising editorial campaign to abolish segregation on the streetcars and buses. On a personal level, the proposal rehabilitated his reputation as a liberal, which had suffered during his previous year of attacks on Negro agitators. Public estimation mattered to Dabney as it does to all men, and editorials lumping him with Eugene Talmadge and other racist reactionaries had hurt. In addition, in light of his prominent part in its creation, the rehabilitation would give credibility to the Southern Regional Council as well. Finally, as he declared in his editorial, abolition of Jim Crow in public transportation would eliminate an irritant and serve as a token of white good will.[41]

Nonetheless, questions remain. The Southern Regional Council was well along the road to incorporation, and no crisis of southern Negro loyalty then required this action. The proposal could only raise blacks' expectations of further repeal of Jim Crow laws. During his editorial campaign, however, Dabney reiterated his desire for "equal, but separate accommodations, facilities and opportunities for our colored citizens." Repeal of the law in public transportation would not lead to the breakdown of segregation elsewhere. As he explained to one correspondent, "the Negroes have just grievances," and he sought to "do something tangible" for them. "It seems to me," he went on, "we can do this without destroying the Southern social pattern in any way."[42]

Above all, Dabney had contended over and over in the previous two years that attempts to eliminate Jim Crow would arouse white resistance, yet he chanced the very reaction that he feared. In fact, Dabney expected such a reaction. To his amazement, of the 114 published letters from white readers, 87 endorsed his editorials. He had expected, one editorial admitted, "that the reaction in our letter columns would be as strongly unfavorable as it has turned out to be favorable." Significantly, two years later Graves cited Dabney's streetcar proposal to prove overwhelming resistance to desegregation in the South: "Editor Virginius Dabney . . . had to call himself off a few months ago when his proposal . . . ran into a reaction more violent than any newspaper can meet and survive." As Graves's inaccurate assertion suggested, if whites were as adamantly opposed to changes in Jim Crow laws as he and Dabney claimed, there should have been a strong negative reaction to the proposal.[43]

In fact, it is irresistible to speculate that, perhaps unconsciously, Dabney sought such a reaction. In 1942, when proposing his regional university for Negroes, he had discussed the NAACP's stand against segregation and stated that "if a demonstration could be made that great and lasting interracial bitterness would be aroused through insistence by the association upon its legal rights . . . and it could be shown that most of the Negroes' white defenders and well-wishers in the South would be driven into the opposition by such tactics, the organization might modify its position." Perhaps Dabney's streetcar proposal was to have been such a demonstration as he called down the wrath of the white South on himself—a sacrifice to southern liberalism: with the claim then substantiated that white southerners were as one in their unbending devotion to Jim Crow, Dabney would have been able to warn northern agitators away, retain segregation, and still remain a southern liberal.[44]

Whatever his motives, with these editorials Dabney put his southern liberalism to the test. For decades, he and the others had reminded reformers of the disastrous Civil War and had warned that excessive pressure for change would result in a southern backlash, expressed in anti-Negro violence. At the same time, they strove to eliminate violence as a tool of racial subordination in the South. As the historian of the Commission on Interracial Cooperation points out, the relative absence of such violence in the South after World War II, compared to the Red Summer of 1919 that led to the commission's founding, measures the CIC's achievement. Ironically, at a time when segregationist southern liberals needed a white backlash to protect their liberalism against northern radicals, it did not occur.[45]

Dabney's proposal to abolish segregation in public transportation went nowhere. He sent copies of his editorials to "most" southern and Virginia editors, but, with the single exception of a newspaper in Kinston, North Carolina, none commented on the proposal. The Virginia General Assembly—the Jim Crow law was a state ordinance—refused to consider repeal, despite overwhelming support in the paper's letters column for the change. In the *Times-Dispatch* Dabney employed standard southern liberal doctrine to explain the legislature's inaction. Public opinion had not "been adequately prepared for such a step." After sufficient discussion to win the necessary "backing of local opinion," perhaps the legislative "session of 1946" would take up the proposal.[46]

Privately, he offered a more revealing explanation: the "average politician" feared to antagonize "the so-called 'poor whites,'" who were "pretty rabid on the Negro issue." The previous November, Dabney had referred to these people in order to downplay the significance of the surprising white support of his editorials. "The poor whites have hardly been heard from at all," he told P. B. Young, "and I am sure they would react overwhelmingly in the other direction."[47] For decades, southern liberals had brandished this bogeyman—the cruelly Negrophobic poor white—to drive away impetuous reformers. As Dabney's comments above suggest, this terrifying class of white southerners also paralyzed southern liberalism.

There was a deeper significance to the journalists' regular references to the meanness of the poor whites beyond the mere rationalization of their own caution. When Dabney proposed his regional university for blacks, he predicted that "hundreds, if not thousands, of Negroes" might suffer persecution should a black student insist upon admission to a white university. The agents of this persecution would not be the white students, but rather "the uneducated 'poor whites' in the remoter sections."[48] The Negro protest during World War II exposed the meaning of this warning. Dabney and other decent white southerners stepped forward to defend Jim Crow, yet references to the "rabid" poor whites enabled them to maintain their own innocence. Just as their histories of the Civil War era, filled with denunciations of the abolitionists and the fire-eaters, showed that the southern Unionists bore no responsibility for the conflict, southern liberalism ensured their freedom from blame for conditions in the South.

More important, though, was the failure of newspaper editors and state legislators to endorse Dabney's editorials. The southern liberals had rejected the poor whites as hopelessly lost in racial hatred and

had proposed instead to improve the attitudes of the white southerners who served in government and influenced public opinion—and
yet, whether one interprets Dabney's proposal as a sophisticated
scheme to defend segregation or as a sincere token of good will toward blacks, the fact remains that he won no support from the very
people whom southern liberalism claimed to address.

Dabney had hoped to sustain both segregation and liberalism. With
a choice now upon him, he tried to force the Southern Regional Council
to declare its loyalty to Jim Crow at the SRC's annual meeting in December 1944. Black members made clear their intention to resign in the
event of such a resolution, and so the SRC compromised with a study
of segregation in practice. Dabney gradually withdrew from the organization. He recognized that liberalism and segregation had become
incompatible and reluctantly cast his lot with the latter. By 1950, his
ordeal had ended, and he called himself a "conservative."[49]

The racial tension that aroused the journalists had eased tremen-
dously by the end of World War II. In part, as Finkle has argued,
much of the militant rhetoric was directed at encouraging black participation in the war effort, not at destroying Jim Crow. Wartime restrictions on travel also assured that no repetition to the threatened
March on Washington of 1941 might occur. In addition, as Charles
Eagles has shown, Jonathan Daniels, serving as a special assistant to
President Roosevelt, helped to carry out FDR's successful "efforts to
keep the lid on domestic racial difficulties during the war." The federal government's resistance to further change and a spate of racial
violence in cities across the nation caused Negro leaders to retreat
from militance after 1943. With black southern liberals cooperating
for gradual reform through the new Southern Regional Council, the
journalists could finally catch their breath.[50]

The Negro protest of the early 1940s, however, had taken the journalists by surprise and had exposed the limitations of their southern
liberalism. Because they relied on their interpretation of the Civil War
and Reconstruction to justify southern liberalism, the journalists simply did not conceive of the Negroes as a force for reform. Instead,
they saw themselves standing between modern-day abolitionists in
the North and fire-eaters in the South, and intersectional peace, not
racial reform, became their highest priority.

The doctrine of vertical segregation had promised that southern liberals could have racial reform without confronting racial segregation. Suddenly, opposition to the Jim Crow system had become the measure of a racial liberal. Sooner or later, white southern liberals would have to choose between segregation and liberalism. Whatever their choice, the southern liberalism of the 1920s and 1930s had come to an end.

Epilogue: Because Injustice Is Here*

I n 1948 Virginius Dabney won the Pulitzer Prize for editorial writing. The Prize committee, in an unusual decision, gave him the honor for his editorials as a group, and friends interpreted the award as recognition for his long career as a spokesman for southern liberalism. Significantly, a week before the announcement a prominent member of the Prize committee asked Dabney to send copies of recent *Times-Dispatch* editorials on race relations; since the award honored his work in the previous year, Dabney could only conclude that the committee wanted to ascertain that his current views were "acceptable." One conservative member of the committee still opposed his selection because the editor, as a leading southern liberal, must lack sufficient appreciation for the virtues of Virginia's conservative Senator Harry F. Byrd. By the time of the award, however, Dabney already labeled himself a "conservative" in his correspondence and expressed high admiration for Byrd.[1]

Although Dabney's swift rightward shift contributed to the confusion over his views, after World War II the meaning of the term southern liberal itself grew uncertain. The Negro protest during the war had made the middle ground of vertical segregation narrower than ever before and, as outside pressure for change and white southern resistance continually mounted, those southern liberals still trying to occupy that ground found their footing increasingly difficult to maintain. "Unless the Southerner measures up to the qualifications which the Northern liberals set for liberalism, he is considered no liberal at all," Hodding Carter complained in 1946. He defended those southerners who "work for racial amelioration, for orderly economic change in the South," and said that "for lack of a less misused definition, they might be described as Southern liberals." Though Carter wore the label proudly, his essays soon enclosed southern liberal within quotation marks, suggesting the problematic character of this program for reform in the South.[2]

---

* This phrase was Martin Luther King's explanation to critics who asked why he had come to Birmingham to lead demonstrations for civil rights in 1963 (King, *Why We Can't Wait*, p. 78).

After the Supreme Court outlawed racial segregation in the public schools in 1954, the journalists took up the more appropriate label of "moderates." Resistance to the Court's decision in the South and the rise of an effective Negro protest movement eventually forced the federal government into action against legal segregation. As the Jim Crow laws became a thing of the past, so, too, did the southern liberalism that had sought vainly to make their operation humane and equitable.

In the decade between the founding of the Southern Regional Council and the Supreme Court's *Brown* decision, advocates of civil rights for Negroes won allies in the northern liberal wing of the Democratic party and pressed for federal legislation against lynching, segregation, and discriminatory hiring practices. This situation reinvigorated the old analogy to the period before the Civil War when the agitation of northern abolitionists and the reaction of southern fire-eaters drowned out the wise counsel of the Unionists. Placing themselves on the middle ground sanctioned by history, the journalists again warned northerners of the dangers of laws enacted against local opinion, while telling white southerners that only by improving race relations could they ease the outside pressure for change.[3]

None of the journalists condemned Jim Crow; their goal remained the achievement of vertical segregation. Carter once cited "a caustically humorous comment" that the South "was the only place in the western world where a man could become a liberal simply by urging obedience to the law." He and the other journalists insisted openly now that southerners must make the separate-but-equal doctrine a reality. The principle of state rights, they contended, involved "state responsibilities," too. Although they continued to emphasize to reformers the social conflict that would inevitably flow from foolhardy attempts to abolish Jim Crow laws by fiat, references to white southerners' outrage at the prospect of intermarriage and social equality exposed their own deeper ambivalence about the attacks on segregation. "It is not easy to dismiss the beliefs with which one has grown up," Carter plaintively declared.[4]

They unanimously condemned President Truman's proposed civil rights legislation of 1948 as productive of conflict and politically motivated. The prominence of the civil rights issue inspired southern conservatives to mount a political revolt against the Democratic party in that year's presidential election. None of the journalists—except for John Temple Graves, now an avid segregationist—endorsed the Dixie-crats, as the political protesters became known. Secession failed in 1861, they told their readers, and it offered no solution in the present. Instead, they welcomed the political conflict as a sign that a two-party system might replace the old Solid South. At the same time, they advocated voting rights for black southerners as an effective means to gradual improvements in race relations. "Competition for that vote is an open sesame to rights," McGill explained. The rise of the Republican party in the South seemed a solution to their problem: political competition would reduce outside pressure for reform at the same time that it caused southerners to undertake reform themselves.[5]

The development of the cold war against the Soviet Union, however, kept the issue of segregation to the fore and added to the ambivalence of the journalists' southern liberalism. Jonathan Daniels explained President Truman's attention to civil rights with reference to "the world aspects of the situation in a cold war with the Communists, who everywhere make propaganda of any mistreatment of Negroes in the United States." Similarly, Carter warned southerners against racial discrimination "at a time when the appeal to race is the strongest which world Communism is making." Assertions of the transcendent necessity of preserving the free world against any communist threat coexisted uneasily with the insistence that compromise and caution remained the only safe course for obtaining civil rights in the South.[6]

The cold war also invigorated conservative criticism of the "socialistic" policies of the New Deal and made the "Popular Front liberalism" of the 1930s, with its emphasis on economic reform, illegitimate. The journalists joined the general rightward shift. Carter and Dabney, in fact, supported Republican presidential candidates in 1948 and 1952. McGill backed the Democratic candidates in those years but became a prominent critic of the "Communist-infiltrated" Southern Conference for Human Welfare and supported the campaign of 1950 in Florida against "the left-wing, long-in-office" Senator Claude Pepper. Conservatives in North Carolina that year also combined charges of racial and political radicalism to defeat Senator Frank Porter Graham, the SCHW's first president long ago in 1938. Jonathan Daniels, the most loyal of the journalists to the national

Democratic party, defended Graham—and the election results left him profoundly depressed about the prospects for liberalism in the South.[7]

The conservative shift and these bitter political campaigns only made segregation a more conspicuous issue. The old southern liberal arguments—that improved education and economic development better served the interests of southern blacks than did direct attacks on Jim Crow—now seemed evasions to other liberals. The conservative coalition in Congress blocked any expansion of federal assistance in these areas, while the journalists themselves grew reluctant to advocate an increased federal role in the South. Indeed, the antiradical atmosphere of the period made any calls for significant economic reform sound suspect. Thus, the issue of segregation, which could be put forward in terms of the worldwide struggle against communism, challenged Americans in a way that economic inequities no longer did. The issue would not go away.

The significance of the cold war for individual views, of course, depended on the particular journalist's endorsement of the crusade against communism. Virginius Dabney cautioned against American intervention to halt Soviet expansion everywhere and never found the competition for the hearts and minds of the world a compelling argument for racial reform in the South. Gerald W. Johnson, who resigned from the *Baltimore Evening Sun* in November 1943 to devote his time to free-lance writing, also refused to enlist in the crusade. His core conviction that liberalism above all required tolerance and skeptical realism served him well as a critic of the anticommunist hysteria during this period but made him slow to speak out on the issue of segregation.[8]

On the other hand, Carter and McGill invested the cold war with high moral purpose, keeping alive the rhetoric of democratic idealism from World War II. Inevitably, that flowed into discussions of race relations. Carter called on Americans to invigorate democracy with Christian brotherhood as a weapon against communism. Racial discrimination in the United States contradicted these ideals and provided "ammunition" for "the worldwide Red assault upon the minds of the undecided majority." Thus, he argued to Mississippians that equalization of facilities for blacks was a moral as well as a legal obligation. Although Carter advocated no more than vertical segregation, his emphasis on Christian brotherhood carried him to the verge of condemning Jim Crow. During this period, Ralph McGill's publisher censored his discussions of race relations in the *Constitution*, and the newspaper still defended vertical segregation. By the beginning of 1954, however, McGill declared in speeches that, "in a world torn by communism's battle to destroy the freedom and dignity of man," segregation "simply does not fit the concepts of our world today, neither political nor Christian."[9]

Perhaps more important in the long run, by endorsing the cold war in these terms Carter and McGill created for themselves a conflict between loyalty to the nation and loyalty to the South. Previously, by identification with the antebellum Unionists during the sectional conflict before the Civil War, the journalists had resolved these loyalties; they could be southerners *and* Americans. Sharing the fears of their fellow white southerners while understanding, even sympathizing with, the opponents of racial segregation, it is little wonder that they now tried to postpone declaring their loyalties as long as possible.

The central problem for southern liberal reform remained. As McGill put it to an impatient northern liberal: "The whole problem is one of means. How do we get there?"[10] Their long memory of the Civil War period, with reinforcement from the example of Prohibition, taught them that the federal government could not enforce reform in the South against the wishes of the white majority. The vicious primary campaigns of 1950 revealed that southern liberalism itself exerted little influence in southern politics. The idea of southern blacks as an independent force for reform certainly never occurred to them. Thus, even southern liberals who desired an end to segregation remained convinced that only through gradual change, acceptable to the white majority, could racial reform take place in the South.

After 1950 the NAACP's legal strategists, who had won case after case before the Supreme Court by contrasting the doctrine of separate-but-equal with its inequitable reality, determined to challenge the doctrine itself, and several test cases began moving through the courts. Vertical segregation had come to judgment. Late in 1951 the Southern Regional Council, which under the leadership of George S. Mitchell since 1947 had emphasized economic development in the South as the preferred means to eliminating racial prejudice, finally issued a public declaration against segregation. Virginius Dabney immediately submitted his resignation.[11]

Despite their differences on segregation, however, Dabney and

Mitchell favored much the same solution to the situation posed by the NAACP's legal campaign. Under pressure from the Supreme Court's rulings that the absence of equal facilities made segregation unacceptable, southern state governments began a belated effort to improve Negro schools and raise the salaries of black teachers. Recognizing that equalization would cost vast sums, Dabney and Mitchell both predicted that localities with few black students would eventually desegregate for economy's sake. Over time, economic logic and the evidence of successful desegregation elsewhere would lead more and more school districts to make this decision. With local opinion behind the change, no conflict need occur. This gradual process would take place whether or not the Supreme Court outlawed segregation, and a ruling against Jim Crow might even prove an obstacle. In fact, the journalists hoped that the Court would sustain the laws.[12]

On 17 May 1954 the Supreme Court declared racial segregation in public schools unconstitutional. The journalists responded to the decision without celebration. Segregation would survive for years to come, they told their readers, and calm deliberation better served the region than angry reaction. If only the extremists could be silenced, then some workable plan for the future might be devised.[13]

As the Court considered means to carry out its decision, resistance gathered in the South. On 31 May 1955 the Court proposed that local school districts be responsible for desegregation, which should take place "with all deliberate speed." To those opposed to Jim Crow, the decree seemed a step backward, whereas to those southerners promising resistance, it revealed the necessity of setting state power over local schools and enforcing white unity. To the journalists, the Court had exhibited wise moderation. Desegregation would come to the South because the region must obey the law, but the change could take place gradually, without conflict. The following years of defiance, violence, and struggle proved their optimism wrong. Until 1960 and the rise of Negro protest in the South, the situation seemed to set Dixie against the national authority, and the journalists, now calling themselves moderates, again occupied familiar middle ground.

Virginius Dabney alone among them became a defender of segregation. When James J. Kilpatrick, editor of Richmond's afternoon paper, introduced "interposition"—the notion that a state could inter-

pose its authority between its citizens and the federal government—
as a way to resist the Supreme Court's decision, Virginia took the lead
in the South's "massive resistance." Dabney privately considered interposition a "long-outmoded theory," but rather than opposing it he
"simply acquiesced in it silently" and allowed an associate to write the
Times-Dispatch's few editorials endorsing Kilpatrick's campaign.[14]

In his articles for national magazines, however, Dabney emphasized the unacceptable likelihood that "mixed schools" would lead to
"racial amalgamation." He also helped to publicize the similar arguments of Carleton Putnam, a northern segregationist. Assertions
that desegregation would lead to mongrelization and harm to white
civilization became a common theme in the southern case for continuing segregation. Most of these writers followed the example of Kilpatrick, who admitted that the question of the Negro's "innate" capabilities remained open but went on to assert that "whether these
characteristics are inherited or acquired, they *are*." Dabney, on the
other hand, always insisted that his argument implied nothing "of bigotry or prejudice, and nothing having to do with supposed racial superiority or inferiority." Rather, blacks and whites alike should desire
"to preserve the ethnic and cultural heritage of one's own race, and
not to have it diluted or destroyed through commingling with a race
that has a sharply contrasting background."[15]

In fact, Dabney still advocated vertical segregation. He described
again and again the Durham conference of southern Negroes in 1942,
the creation of the Southern Regional Council, and his editorial proposal to repeal segregation on public transportation during World War
II. Had white southerners then acted to lessen discrimination, he
claimed, the desegregation crisis would not exist.[16] Dabney incor-
rectly contended that the Durham conference endorsed vertical segregation as a permanent institution, but his assertion of the old southern liberal program—little more than a lament for opportunity missed
in the aftermath of the Court's decision—is revealing. The journalists
had recognized the contradiction between liberalism and racism, between southern progress and perpetuation of the Jim Crow system,
but only by suppressing these contradictions in the program of vertical segregation, they believed, could a liberal, progressive society
eventually be developed in the South. Through this compromise, they
had kept alive the spirit of liberalism, as Dabney's editorials in the

previous decades evidenced. The price of their achievement, however, was that, always proceeding by indirection, they and other southern liberals not only kept alive the malignancy of racism in the South and in themselves, but also failed to realize their highest goals. To seek a liberal South, southern liberals finally had to abandon compromises with racism. As Dabney's defense of segregation showed, not all of them managed to do that.

Those among the journalists who opposed the South's massive resistance could no longer defend vertical segregation, but they still justified their positions by the old southern liberal analogy to Unionism before the Civil War. While telling white southerners to eschew extremism in defense of segregation, they told northerners the pressure on the South would only aid the segregationists. By claiming the middle ground of moderation for themselves, they inevitably equated those who sought Jim Crow's immediate demise with white southern reactionaries and condemned both. Hodding Carter's response to the formation of the segregationist White Citizens' Council is revealing: "We've been battling the N.A.A.C.P.'s own angry racism for a long time," he declared. "We'll battle [Council founder Robert] Patterson's identical brand of hatred of dissimilar people just as hard." Such comments outraged the opponents of segregation, who questioned whether moderation meant anything except inaction in a time of crisis. "For what are the 'moderates'?" Carl Rowan asked angrily; "are they moderately *for* or *against* compliance with the United States Supreme Court's decision?"[17]

In fact, the main theme of the journalists' arguments was that the nation must not repeat the disaster of the Civil War and permit the extremists to sweep away moderate opinion. This interpretation of the past limited them as spokesmen for compliance with the Court's decision in the present. Because of their concentration on the Civil War era, they set the South against the North and ignored the blacks in their histories. As white southerners themselves, they recognized and even sympathized with the historical roots of massive resistance but were less able to appreciate the historical experience of blacks, experience that explained their impatience. With a segregated history as their guide, the journalists found it difficult to envision a desegregated future.[18]

Thus, they sought primarily to preserve and protect moderation in the South. Except for Carter, the moderate journalists backed

Adlai E. Stevenson's presidential candidacy in 1956, because only he among the party's hopefuls could hold the South for the Democratic party. Harry S. Ashmore, who advised Stevenson on his southern strategy, proposed that he present himself to the nation as "the Great Conciliator." Capture of the party by the "Abolitionists" in the North, Ashmore contended, would only deliver the South to the "racists."[19]

To an extent, then, the segregationists forced the journalists to oppose them. As Numan Bartley points out, the issue of segregation united a disparate coalition of southern political forces in a general conservative campaign. Whatever the journalists thought of the Supreme Court's decision, they could not accept the broader implications of the state rights argument. In addition, they considered southern racism harmful to America's course in the worldwide struggle against communism. Perhaps most important, the segregationists recognized that white southern unity was essential to overturning the *Brown* decision and treated the moderates as traitors. Whatever northern liberals thought of moderation's inadequacy, the segregationists saw it, in the words of a writer for *The Citizens' Council*, as no more than "gradual surrender to creeping integration as an alternative to the galloping variety."[20]

The moderates did play a crucial role. By their dissent from massive resistance, they not only kept alive a measure of debate in the South, but they also provided evidence to the rest of the nation that southern white unity was not total. At a time when President Eisenhower expressed doubts about the Supreme Court's wisdom, the assurances of a Ralph McGill that, despite the noise of battle, the resistance was but "fighting in the ruins, . . . and its denouement is sure," contributed significantly to the cause of desegregation. The regular complaints from segregationists that McGill and his fellow "pseudosoutherners" enjoyed ready access to the national media while the true "southern" side of the story went unheard, evidences the importance of their dissent during this period.[21]

In fact, by the end of the 1950s moderation seemed likely to carry the day in the South. The turning point came in 1957, when the governor of Arkansas blocked the desegregation of a Little Rock high school, and President Eisenhower sent federal troops to stop his defiance. Although segregationists conjured up visions of Reconstruction, the Little Rock crisis finally proved that the federal government would not permit noncompliance with the Court's ruling. As Bartley explains, white southerners now had to choose between desegregation and closing the public schools.[22]

Moderates emphasized that the issue was no longer segregation, but rather the preservation of public education and economic stability in the South. Closing the public schools would drive businesses and the middle class—the "backbone" of society—from the South, McGill warned. Because of residential segregation, he went on, few white schools would actually have any number of black students attending them. Better for the South to accept "token" desegregation than to continue defiance at great economic and social cost. After the courts rejected Virginia's interposition, Dabney began making similar arguments. "There are indications," he said in early 1960, "that it might be legally possible for Southern states to satisfy the Federal courts, keep open their public schools, and yet to hold mixing of the races in the schools to an absolute minimum." As the traumatic 1950s came to a close, none of the journalists expected significant racial reform in the South, especially the Deep South, to come for decades.[23]

With these arguments, McGill and other moderates necessarily looked for allies among those white southerners who valued social order and economic prosperity more than they did racial segregation. After examining the views of moderate newspapers in Tennessee during this period, Hugh Davis Graham concludes that these journalists better deserved the label of "enlightened conservatives" for their devotion to stability and their intent to accept but to limit racial change. Similarly, Bartley argues that the shift away from resistance after 1957, when "business conservatives" abandoned the segregationist coalition, was "conservative rather than reformist," seeking "social stability rather than social change."[24]

That the journalists looked to "computations on a balance sheet," to use Harry Ashmore's phrase, rather than to doctrines of social justice, as the force that would desegregate the South, involved no repudiation of their earlier views.[25] For years, they had argued that eventually white southerners would abandon racial discrimination as a matter of economic self-interest. Given the bitter conflict of the preceding years, that the journalists welcomed the shift away from massive resistance as a heartening sign of progress is hardly surprising. They remained convinced that the federal government could do little but put down blatant defiance; they could not imagine southern blacks organized as a force for reform; and they considered the mass of white southerners to be hopelessly racist and subject to the manipulation of reactionary politicians. They simply had nowhere else to turn for allies.

Early in 1960, Negro students began sit-in demonstrations at lunch counters in North Carolina and forced their desegregation, the first time that unwilling white southerners had lifted racial restrictions without federal pressure. The sit-ins galvanized young southern Negroes, and demonstrations spread across the South. With the rise of the Civil Rights protest movement, gradualism and moderation became anachronisms. Moreover, with southern blacks forcing change in the South, the Civil War analogy that had justified southern liberalism for decades no longer explained the situation below the Potomac. As blacks and the federal government—the two forces that the journalists had relegated to the sidelines in the struggle for reform in the South—dismantled the legal system of racial segregation, the southern liberalism of the Jim Crow era, its doctrines undermined by events, finally faded away.

George Fort Milton died before the Civil Rights movement began. After World War II he had returned to journalism, now in the North, as an editorial writer with the *Buffalo Evening News* from 1945 to 1950. The cold war reinforced the themes of morality and idealism that had first appeared in his editorials before World War II. He described the Soviets lost in an "Age of Hate" and proclaimed "our moral responsibility to succor freedom through the world." Thus, in 1949 he declared that "the conscience of America cannot ignore" the Negro's desire to become an American "in full." A year later, he welcomed the Supreme Court's "blows at segregation." Recent decisions, he contended, were "landmarks on the road to equal and exact justice." [26]

The past, however, had not changed. In reviews, Milton criticized historians who suggested that Stephen A. Douglas lacked "moral" sensitivity to the slavery issue. He retired in 1950 and returned to Washington where he began a biography of Thaddeus Stevens, the leader of the Radical Republicans during Reconstruction. Although he admired Stevens's skill as a congressional leader, Milton remained convinced of the evils that the Radicals had visited on the South. He still endorsed Abraham Lincoln's approach to Reconstruction, which "called for evolutionary, democratic progress, not the violence, fanaticism and torture the extremists of Civil War days insisted on." Ill health prevented him from completing the biography, and he died in 1955 without making public comment on the Supreme Court's ruling against segregation.[27]

In that year, Gerald W. Johnson wrote that the South had "experienced invasion, conquest and defeat." History made the region different from the rest of the nation and explained contemporary resistance to the Supreme Court's decision. Southerners lacked the "optimism" of other sections and hence, he claimed, were less tolerant of differences. There was one advantage to the South's peculiar history, though. "When a Southerner does evolve into a liberal," he concluded, "he is the sturdiest, most unshakeable liberal on earth." Indeed, as the Civil Rights movement grew, Johnson modified his interpretation of southern history and remained a sturdy liberal. He agreed now that conflict and struggle were necessary and healthy for both white and black southerners. By striving for freedom "under their own power," Negroes would truly liberate themselves and the whites as well. He argued that the overthrow of Reconstruction had required "subterfuge," and the "fraud" had caused white southerners to draw ever further away from reality in subsequent years. The Civil Rights movement could finally free the South from those falsehoods and open the way for the realism that he still insisted lay at the heart of liberalism. Johnson gave up his column for the *New Republic* in 1962, at the age of seventy-two, but remained a close observer of national affairs and continued publishing essays until well into his eighties. He died at his home in Baltimore in 1980.[28]

Hodding Carter retired from the *Delta Democrat-Times* in 1960 in order to write and lecture. Despite failing eyesight—he became blind in 1964—Carter wrote regularly for the *New York Times Magazine* and, with the assistance of his wife, completed three books. He continued to criticize northern intolerance toward white southerners who were struggling through a time of vast change, but he directed equally angry attacks at southern repression and violence. He expected the legacies of racial prejudice and discrimination to persist for long years but declared in January 1965 that "change will come because it has to come if ours is to be a nationwide democratic society." The events that followed the Civil Rights legislation in 1964 and 1965 dismayed Carter. Increased Negro militance and the Black Power movement's distrust for whites provoked him to write an unhappy essay in 1966, asserting that "The Old South Had Something Worth Saving." He referred wistfully to the "Old South" of only a few decades before, when Negroes considered him a friend and the barriers erected during the bitter struggle against segregation did not yet exist. The tragic death of a son compounded his sorrow as the nation seemed to come apart in 1968 and after. Periods of depression plagued him and he died, aged sixty-five, in 1972.[29]

Ralph McGill continued to write his daily column for the *Atlanta Constitution* and also became a national figure in the 1960s, writing and lecturing on the South. He maintained his moral interpretation of the race issue but now eschewed references to Abraham Lincoln, the man of compromise, and abandoned the analogy to the destruction of Unionism before the Civil War. The abolitionists had been right in their uncompromising attack on slavery, he argued, and the modern Negro protest organizers were heirs to the antislavery movement. The South, once again, had chosen the wrong side in a moral conflict. He told Americans that the Civil Rights Act of 1964 was but a beginning. With the ballot, and with jobs and education, Negroes would move against de facto segregation as well. The anger of Black Power seemed to McGill evidence of the work yet to be done, and he warned his audiences that when the majority failed to act, extremists would step in. For years he had emphasized the harm that racial discrimination did to America's global struggle against communism, and he supported the Viet Nam War without doubts. The antiwar movement angered McGill, and he feared that reaction would swing the nation to the right, destroying the prospects for further reform. Nonetheless, he continued to speak out against racial discrimination until his death, shortly before his seventy-first birthday, in 1969.[30]

When President Kennedy sent troops to protect the enrollment of James Meredith at the University of Mississippi in 1962, Virginius Dabney conceded defeat. "The cause is lost, as truly as it was at Appomattox," he wrote; now even the Deep South states must bow to superior force and join the rest of the region in "fighting a rearguard delaying action." Through the years of the "Second Reconstruction," Dabney's essays contended that Negroes would gain more concessions from whites by peaceful requests for gradual change than by protests and demonstrations. He retired from the *Times-Dispatch* in 1969, with the *New York Times* noting that he left journalism "with little notice or lament from the South's progressives and liberals, among whom the editor was once a hero." In the subsequent years of active retirement he has written popular histories of Virginia, Richmond, and the University of Virginia, a volume of memoirs, a defense of Thomas Jefferson against charges that he fathered mulatto children, and most recently, a history of the "last" Confederate reunion of 1932.[31]

In early 1965, as the Civil Rights movement neared its peak, the *Virginia Quarterly Review* celebrated its fortieth anniversary. One of the contributors, Gerald W. Johnson, reread the essay he had published in the quarterly's second issue in which he had contended that white southerners deserved sympathy for their efforts "to make an industrious, intelligent, socially competent citizen out of the negro." Now he wrote with respect for the Civil Rights movement's "demonstration of political maturity," a "feat," he noted with pride, "accomplished by the Southern Negro under Southern leadership." Had the South moved, "if only by an inch," in the direction of freedom for all during the past forty years? "The conclusive answer is supplied by the Negro revolution itself," he said.[32]

The contrast between Johnson's statements in the two essays measures the social and intellectual change in the South over those four decades, change that came most swiftly and completely with the Civil Rights movement. If Johnson's later essay may be read as a recognition of the fulfillment of southern liberalism's noblest ideals, the assertion in his earlier essay suggests why he and other southern liberals did not lead the way to that fulfillment. They began with the assumption that decent white southerners like themselves bore the responsibility for improving race relations, for improving "the negro." They thus denied independence—and hence equality—to black southerners. Should their own interests—a progressive South with peaceful race relations, economic development, and rationalized politics—not coincide with those of black southerners, the journalists expected the blacks to give way. The Negro protest during World War II first revealed that they would not, and the journalists reacted with shock and anger.

In the essay preceding Johnson's, Virginius Dabney argued that "the pace is important" in racial reform. He referred again to the crisis of southern liberalism during World War II when the Negro protest first appeared. Those who now demand "that everything be done overnight," he asserted, must give reluctant southerners "time to adjust their thinking." As an example, he cited Mark Ethridge's statement in 1942 that the combined armies of the Allied and Axis powers could not abolish Jim Crow in the South. "Today," Dabney continued, Ethridge was "one of the most militant advocates of full integration in the United States." His case showed that, with sufficient time to adjust, southerners would shift "steadily in the liberal direction."[33] Dabney's argument, belied by his own conservative course in the previous two decades, acknowledged that the southern liberalism he and the other journalists had advocated between the two world wars came to an end when black protest made segregation incompatible with liberalism. From that time, these men reacted and "adjusted" to the initiatives of others.

Southern liberalism shattered during World War II, yet, rather than leading to revision of the journalists' thinking, the following years of sectional and racial conflict found them vainly reasserting their old doctrines. To point to paternalism and persistent racism—even though these did flaw their thinking—as the sole explanation for their reluctance to endorse the protest, is inadequate. In fact, the protest exposed the particular issue of racial segregation as both the cornerstone and the stumbling block for southern liberalism.

The journalists perceived southern poverty, political perversity, and racial injustice as the unhappy products of the Civil War and Reconstruction, with their roots deepest in the rural, backward South. The processes of social change so evident in their own times promised to alleviate these evils. As the South urbanized and industrialized—progressed, by their definition—the competition, hatreds, and insecurity that had spawned the Jim Crow system would disappear. Racial justice and social reform would come to the South.

Continued progress, however, depended absolutely upon preventing a repetition of the sectional conflict, with northern pressure provoking southern reaction, that had distorted the South's development in the previous century. Rather than searching for the silent South, therefore, the journalists invested much of their energy in keeping the South silent. That required staving off premature reforms, and they brandished the danger of white southern reaction before more militant advocates of change. At the same time, southern refusal to make necessary reforms could only bolster militance and might justify outside intervention once again. The journalists used that danger to encourage white southerners to eliminate the most obvious injustices.

The Jim Crow system of racial segregation posed the gravest challenge for their divided program. It symbolized and perpetuated the white South's commitment to white supremacy while offering the most obvious target for those who sought an end to racial injustice. Segregation, like human slavery before it, presented an issue that defied compromise and threatened conflict. Southern liberals resolved the problem with their program of vertical segregation. They promised to blacks an eventual end to the Jim Crow system while promising to white southerners—and themselves—that segregation would survive as long as they desired. By presenting segregation made vertical as the instrument, in the course of continued southern progress, of its own ultimate demise, they denied it a legitimate place on the agenda of any reformer. The doctrine of vertical segregation expressed perfectly the divided program, and the ambivalence, at the heart of southern liberalism. The journalists necessarily perceived attacks on segregation as a threat to southern liberalism, as revolutionary and productive of chaos as the abolitionists and the Radical Republicans had been, rather than as a step toward liberal reform. To protect southern liberalism, they had to protect segregation.

As products of a region and society that they loved, the journalists viewed injustice and prejudice as aberrations, the legacies of an unnecessary Civil War. With the adjustments of southern liberal reform, they believed that race relations could become humane and equitable, political practices could become rationalized, and all southerners could enjoy economic security. Their interpretation of the southern past justified their cautious and indirect methods of reform. They recalled the past, though, primarily to point blame at those responsible for conflict and, less obviously, to establish their own innocence. In doing so, they pushed slavery, and the southerners whose ancestors had been slaves, to the periphery of their histories.

Thus, as the Civil Rights movement got under way, the journalists found themselves standing as their spiritual ancestors, the southern Unionists, had stood before the Civil War. Their doctrines—which had once challenged complacency, alerted southerners to the necessity for reform, and justified the methods of southern liberalism—

now sent them toward the same fate that the Unionists had suffered. Reluctantly, the journalists made their choices, between the South and the nation, between segregation and civil rights. That they had to choose marked, by their own definition, the end to the southern liberalism of the 1920s and 1930s.

Notes

Introduction

1. Alexander (unpub.), "Reminiscences," pp. 201–206; the quotation appears on pp. 205–206.

2. W. C. Johnson and Robb, *South and Its Newspapers*, p. 128.

3. Dykeman and Stokely, *Seeds of Southern Change*; the quotation is from p. xiii.

4. Myrdal, *American Dilemma*, pp. 470–73.

5. Eagles, *Jonathan Daniels*, pp. x, xiv.

6. Sosna, *Silent South*, pp. 37–38, 206, 174.

7. Ibid., p. viii; Dunbar, *Against the Grain*.

8. Sosna, *Silent South*, p. viii; Phillips, "Southern History."

9. Hartz, *Liberal Tradition*, p. 305.

10. Gaston, *New South Creed*, p. 32; "The Emperor's New Clothes" is the title to his Chapter 6.

11. O'Brien, *American South*; R. King, *Southern Renaissance*; Singal, *War Within*. The quoted phrase is from King's subtitle.

12. Singal, *War Within*, pp. xii, 8–10.

Chapter 1

1. Graves, *Fighting South*, p. 206; George Fort Milton to Ralph Snow, 3 May 1939, Milton Papers; Govan and Livingood, *Chattanooga Country*, pp. 111–13; *Appleton's Cyclopedia of American Biography*, 2:508; Virginius Dabney to Warren Chappell, 13 Apr. 1954, Dabney Papers; Fletcher M. Green, "Editor's Introduction," to Smedes, *Memorials*, pp. xi–xii; Carter, *First Person Rural*, p. 12; Carter, *Where Main Street Meets the River*, p. 6.

2. Ashmore, *Epitaph*, p. 175.

3. Faulkner, *Intruder in the Dust*, p. 194, as quoted in Davenport, *Myth of Southern History*, p. 104; Daniels, *Southerner Discovers*, p. 335.

4. For a recent discussion of southern Progressivism, see Grantham, "Contours," pp. 1035–1058.

5. "Mrs. Sarah Fort Milton Dies After Short Illness," *Chattanooga News*, 4 May 1932, p. 2; Milton to Kathryne Milton, 6 Sept. 1934, Milton Papers. Of his grandmother, Milton later declared that she "did more probably to stimulate and strengthen whatever of good and merit I have had, than any other person throughout my life" (Milton to Edward E. Hunt, 5 May 1943, Milton Papers).

6. Milton to Porter Warner, Jr., 13 Apr. 1942, Milton Papers. For biographical in-

formation on Tomlinson Fort, one of Chattanooga's leading citizens in the late nineteenth century, see Armstrong, *History of Hamilton County*, 1:411–12.

7. Dabney, *Story of Don Miff*, p. 9; Smedes, *Memorials*, p. lvii. For biographical information on the first Virginius Dabney, see *Dictionary of American Biography*, 5:22. Many years later, the younger Virginius Dabney unsuccessfully tried to convince the Lippincott Company to reissue *The Story of Don Miff* (author's interview with Virginius Dabney, 6 Aug. 1982).

8. For biographical information on Thomas Smith Gregory Dabney, see Smedes, *Memorials*, and *Dictionary of American Biography*, 5:21–22.

9. Carter, *Southern Legacy*, pp. 17, 19, 71; Carter, *First Person Rural*, p. 86. Carter reproduced his great-grandmother's presidential pardon in his history of Reconstruction, *The Angry Scar*, pp. 65–66.

10. Graves, *Fighting South*, p. 27; McGill, *Atlanta Constitution*, 1 Sept. 1947, p. 8; Martin, *Ralph McGill*, p. 10.

11. Freehling, *Prelude*; Tomlinson Fort to John C. Calhoun, 15 July 1831, and speech of Tomlinson Fort to "Fellow Citizens," 1831, copies in Milton Papers, Box 28.

12. Smedes, *Memorials*, pp. 105, 172.

13. Daniels, *End of Innocence*, p. 33; G. W. Johnson, "To Live and Die," p. 31; G. W. Johnson, *By Reason of Strength*, pp. 149, 151, 191–92; McGill, *South and the Southerner*, p. 53. In *Tar Heels*, Jonathan Daniels described *By Reason of Strength* as Johnson's "almost homesick novel about the beginnings of his own North Carolina people" (p. 68).

14. Mast, *History of the Movies*, p. 80; Sklar, *Movie-Made America*, p. 58; C. Higham, *American Film*, p. 11; Cripps, "Reaction of Negro," pp. 344–62.

15. McGill, *South and the Southerner*, p. 129; Morrison, *W. J. Cash*, p. 13; Carter, "Furl That Banner," p. 13. In his *Born to Rebel*, Benjamin Mays, a Negro, recalled seeing the film while a student at Bates College in Lewiston, Maine, and fearing for his safety in the aroused audience (p. 60). See also Lumpkin, *Making of a Southerner*, p. 200.

16. Screentitle from "Birth of a Nation," quoted in Sklar, *Movie-Made America*, p. 58.

17. William Archibald Dunning's best-known work is *Reconstruction: Political and Economic, 1865–1877* (New York: Harper & Brothers, 1907). The literature on Reconstruction historiography is vast. See, for instance, Vernon L. Wharton, "Reconstruction," in *Writing Southern History*, ed. Arthur S. Link and Rembert W. Patrick (Baton Rouge: Louisiana State University Press, 1965), pp. 295–315.

18. Grantham, "Southern Progressives," p. 78; Grantham discusses the varieties of southern Progressivism in this essay, but see also Bailey, *Liberalism*.

19. Dabney, *Virginia*, pp. 429–41; Moger, *Virginia*, pp. 192–94; Link, "Progressive Movement," pp. 179, 183–92. Also see Woodward's general discussion of disfranchisement in the south, *Origins of the New South*, pp. 321–49.

20. "Two Southern Views," pp. 810–12.

21. G. F. Milton, Sr., "Material Advancement," p. 39.

22. Cell, *White Supremacy*, pp. 172, 171–80 passim; Rabinowitz, *Race Relations*, pp. 331–32.

23. Kirby, *Darkness*, p. 95.

24. Watters, *South and Nation*, p. 186.

25. Milton to Charles T. Cates, Jan. 1931, Milton Papers.

26. Milton to Charles E. Clarke, 28 Apr. 1936, Milton Papers.

27. Dabney, "Richard Heath Dabney," pp. 93–94; Dabney, "History as Avocation," p. 136.

28. Dabney to H. Turner Jones, 22 Jan. 1957, Dabney Papers; Dabney, "Journalism as Career," 27 June 1957, Dabney Papers.

29. Carter, *Southern Legacy*, p. 75; Robinson (unpub.), "Hodding Carter," pp. 8–9.

30. "Mark Foster Ethridge," in *Current Biography, 1946*, p. 186; McGill, *Atlanta Constitution*, 1 Sept. 1947, p. 8; "Jonathan Daniels," in *Current Biography, 1942*, pp. 172–73; Graves, *Fighting South*, p. 24.

31. "Jonathan Daniels," in *Current Biography, 1942*, p. 173; "Louis I. Jaffé, 62, Editor of Virginian Pilot Dies," *Norfolk Virginian-Pilot*, 13 Mar. 1950, p. 1; Cash, "Possibilities," reprinted in Morrison, *W. J. Cash*, p. 13; G. W. Johnson et al., *Sunpapers*, p. 385. Johnson's father, Archibald Johnson, edited *Charity and Children* and his uncle, Livingston Johnson, edited the *Biblical Recorder* (see Gatewood, *Preachers*, p. 36).

32. McGill, *Atlanta Constitution*, 29 July 1938, p. 6; Logue, *Ralph McGill*, 1: 35–36; "Mark Foster Ethridge," in *Current Biography, 1946*, p. 186.

33. Giddens, "Grover C. Hall," p. 14; Hollis, "Hall Family," p. 121.

34. Grantham, "Southern Progressives," p. 98. Woodward employs the phrase as the title of the final chapter in *Origins of the New South*.

35. Dabney, "Richard Heath Dabney," p. 98; Moger, *Virginia*, p. 276.

36. Logue, *Ralph McGill*, 1:18; McGill, *South and the Southerner*, pp. 55, 104–5; "The President," in Alsop, *Greatness of Woodrow Wilson*, p. 82. See also Graves, *Shaft in the Sky*, pp. 274–75; G. W. Johnson, "Since Wilson," pp. 321–23, 336.

37. Isaac, *Prohibition and Politics*, p. 265; Moger, *Virginia*, pp. 218, 304, 318; Dabney, "Richard Heath Dabney," p. 115.

38. G. F. Milton, Sr., "Edward Ward Carmack," p. 811; Link, "Democratic Politics," pp. 107, 108, 109–10; Isaac, *Prohibition and Politics*, pp. 152, 191.

39. Link, "Democratic Politics," pp. 118–21, 122; *Chattanooga News*, 11 Apr. 1936, p. 4.

40. Milton to Joseph Pulitzer, 2 June 1944, Milton Papers.

41. Johnson, *Undefeated*, p. 58; Tindall, *Emergence*, p. 53. One likely source for this awareness of change was the newspaper. As did all Americans, southerners hungered for news from the war fronts and this resulted in a sharp increase in newspaper sales. Gerald W. Johnson said in *Number Thirty-Six* that the war made the people of the South "a newspaper reading public" (p. 190).

42. Dabney to Mrs. D. M. Roderick, 5 Apr. 1954, Dabney Papers; "Richard Heath Dabney," p. 96; G. W. Johnson et al., *Sunpapers*, pp. 385–86n; Chambers and Shank, *Salt Water*, p. 313.

43. Milton, "With the Guns of the Rainbow," pp. 5, 67, ms. in Milton Papers, Box 32. (He wrote these war memoirs in 1920, but never found a publisher for them; see

Milton to Thomas R. Coward, 29 Oct. 1929, and to Monte F. Bourjaily, 29 Mar. 1930, Milton Papers); G. W. Johnson, "For Ignoble Pacifism," p. 727; G. W. Johnson, "Religious Refugee," pp. 399–400.

44. Johnson, "For Ignoble Pacifism," p. 727; Milton, "Guns of the Rainbow," p. 67 (see n. 43 above). See also Jonathan Daniels to Josephus Daniels, 24 Feb. 1923, Josephus Daniels Papers, Reel 17, Container 30.

45. On the war's effect on Progressive intellectuals, see Rochester, *American Liberal Disillusionment.*

Chapter 2

1. Dabney, *Across the Years*, p. 122; G. W. Johnson, "Woodrow Wilson," p. 41. Hobson, *Serpent in Eden*, provides an account of those southern critics, like Johnson, who came under Mencken's influence. However, see also the more general discussion of southern writing during the 1920s in Tindall's *Emergence*, pp. 285–317.

2. Dabney, *Liberalism*, p. 412.

3. Tindall, *Emergence*, p. 215; Mencken, "South Rebels Again," p. 249. The essay originally appeared on 7 Dec. 1924.

4. Purcell, *Crisis of Democratic Theory*, pp. 11, 97–100, 42, 21.

5. Ibid., p. 11. With their reportorial methods and their illusionless attitude toward society, newspapermen would find this approach and outlook congenial. Dabney's description of his swift education as an innocent new reporter suggests as much: "In six months, I learned more about actually what was going on and what made things tick and who was what, than I learned in the previous six years" (Dabney interview, 16 Aug. 1982; see also Dabney, *Across the Years*, p. 106).

6. Lippmann, *Public Opinion*, pp. 13, 25. In 1922 also, Gerald W. Johnson proposed to Howard Odum an essay—Odum published it as "Mr. Babbitt Arrives at Erzerum"—that had "to do with Lippmann's notion of the pseudo-environment and the process of its modification by intelligent publicity—in other words, the creation of public opinion" (Johnson to Odum, 18 May 1922, Odum Papers).

7. Lippmann, *Public Opinion*, pp. 248–49, 378, 313, 123, 234, 358, 365.

8. Lippmann, "H. L. Mencken," p. 413; Hobson, *Serpent in Eden*, p. 50; Mencken, "Sahara," pp. 136–54.

9. Nathan and Mencken, *American Credo*, p. 103.

10. Ibid., pp. 39, 73, 8–9, 39, 91, 95.

11. In "The Sahara of the Bozart," for example, Mencken described the Old South as "a civilization of manifold excellences—perhaps the best that the Western Hemisphere has ever seen—undoubtedly the best that these states have ever seen" (p. 137). Then the Civil War came and "left the land to the harsh mercies of the poor white trash, now its masters" (p. 143).

12. Waskow, *From Race Riot*, pp. 1–60.

13. M. A. Jones, "Interracial Commission," p. 1. On the origins of the CIC, see Burrows (unpub.), "Commission on Interracial Cooperation," pp. 49–72; Dykeman

and Stokely, *Seeds of Southern Change*, pp. 52–76; and Ellis (unpub.), "Commission on Interracial Cooperation," pp. 7–22.

14. J. D. Hall, *Revolt Against Chivalry*, pp. 62–63; Sosna, *Silent South*, p. viii; Burrows, "Commission on Interracial Cooperation," p. 134.

15. Dykeman and Stokely, in *Seeds of Southern Change*, note that "the commission's press service reached a thousand newspapers, magazines, and specialized journals, both black and white, and occasionally double that number" (p. 119).

16. Baker, *Following the Color Line*, pp. 9–10.

17. Dabney, *Liberalism*, pp. 240–42; J. D. W. [John Donald Wade], "John Temple Graves," in *Dictionary of American Biography* (New York: Charles Scribner's Sons, 1931), 7:509; Cash, *Mind of the South*, p. 309.

18. Daniels, *End of Innocence*, p. 289; Graves, *Shaft in the Sky*, pp. 81–82.

19. Graves, *Fighting South*, p. 30. A year later Graves discovered that his father had, in fact, left the *Atlanta Evening News* for the *Georgian* eight months before the riot and thus bore no direct responsibility for the sensationalism. See Graves, *Birmingham Age-Herald*, 25 May 1944, p. 1, and Graves to W. E. B. DuBois, 7 July 1944, DuBois Papers, Reel 56, Frame 147.

20. Carter, *Where Main Street*, p. 228; Robinson, "Hodding Carter," p. 6. In *Making of a Southerner*, Katherine DuPre Lumpkin told of creating a neighborhood Klan with her childhood friends. What struck her as most significant about the play at Klan was the children's sense of nobility while members of their secret order. In fact, they next played at being Knights of the Round Table without modifying their feeling of chivalric purity (pp. 136–37).

21. Carter, *Southern Legacy*, pp. 16–17.

22. Carter, *First Person Rural*, p. 48.

23. Dabney, *Liberalism*, pp. 240–41.

24. Garson, "Political Fundamentalism," pp. 219–33.

25. Hobson, *Serpent in Eden*, pp. 83, 98; Tindall, *Emergence*, p. 215; Hohenberg, *Pulitzer Prizes*, p. 77.

26. Hobson, *Serpent in Eden*, p. 100; Dabney, *Liberalism*, pp. 327, 350, 390, 406. Historian William E. Dodd had eight titles in Dabney's bibliography, the same number as Johnson. On Johnson's prominence, also see Tindall, *Emergence*, p. 214.

27. G. W. Johnson, et al., *Sunpapers*, pp. 385–86n; E. Clark, *Innocence Abroad*, pp. 253–54; Mencken, "South Rebels Again," pp. 252–53. Johnson sought greater opportunities, too. As he wrote to Howard Odum in 1923, "I am quite frankly on the make right now; I am trying to sell some stuff, and everything and anything that will bring my name to the attention of editors will give me a better chance of selling" (Johnson to Odum, 28 Feb. 1923, Odum Papers).

28. G. W. Johnson: "Mr. Babbitt," p. 206; "Woodrow Wilson," pp. 38, 42; *Andrew Jackson*, pp. 221, 264; "Third Republic," pp. 342, 343–44; "Tarheel," pp. 242, 239, 240; "Rise of Cities," p. 250; "Tilt With Southern Windmills," p. 190; "Religious Refugee," pp. 402–4.

29. G. W. Johnson: "Third Republic," p. 343; "Ku-Kluxer," p. 211; "Onion Salt," p. 61; "Cadets at New Market," p. 119.

30. G. W. Johnson: "Fourteen Equestrian Statues," p. 22; "Onion Salt," p. 63.

31. G. W. Johnson: "Critical Attitudes," p. 578; "Ku-Kluxer," p. 208.

32. G. W. Johnson, "Battling South," pp. 304, 305, 307, 305. Edwin Mims described this essay as "a veritable trumpet-blast in the war for liberation" in the South (*Advancing South*, p. 125).

33. G. W. Johnson: "South Takes Offensive," p. 75; "Tilt With Southern Windmills," p. 187; "South Takes Offensive," pp. 74–75; "Tilt With Southern Windmills," pp. 188–89.

34. Tindall credits the Congressional debates over Dyer's antilynching bill with awakening southern opinion to the need for action against lynching (*Emergence*, p. 174).

35. Grantham, "Southern Progressives," p. 105.

36. Johnson, "Mr. Babbitt," p. 209. See also Johnson: "Journalism Below the Potomac," pp. 77–79, 82; "Southern Image-Breakers," pp. 515, 512.

37. Mathews, "Julian L. Harris," pp. 483–98; Louis I. Jaffé to Julian Harris, 2 July 1927, Jaffé Papers; Mugleston, "Julian Harris," p. 289.

38. Mathews, "Julian L. Harris," p. 409; Mugleston, "Julian Harris," p. 298; Harris, quoted in Mims, *Advancing South*, p. 187.

39. "Grandma Married," *Time*, 16 Dec. 1940, p. 50; Grover C. Hall to "Dear Cody," 2 June 1939, Hall Papers.

40. Mencken, "South Rebels Again," p. 254.

41. Hobson, *Serpent in Eden*, p. 109.

42. Dabney, "Virginia," pp. 349–56; Mencken to Dabney, 5 Nov. 1925 and 18 Mar. 1926, Dabney Papers; Mencken, "South Looks Ahead," p. 506; Dabney, *Across the Years*, pp. 116, 120. Dabney also credits Mencken with the recommendation to the University of North Carolina Press that he write *Liberalism in the South* (Dabney interview, 16 Aug. 1982).

43. McGill, *South and the Southerner*, p. 77.

44. Johnson et al., *Sunpapers*, pp. 390–91, 385, 386; Dabney to Hamilton Owens, 4 Apr. 1956, Dabney Papers; Dabney, *Across the Years*, pp. 114–15. Hollis, in "Hall Family," reports that Owens encouraged Grover C. Hall in his fight against the Ku Klux Klan (p. 130).

45. Clark, *Innocence Abroad*, tells *The Reviewer*'s story; Mencken is quoted on page 121.

46. Singal, *War Within*, pp. 122–23, 125–28.

47. *Virginia Quarterly Review* I (April 1925), pp. ii, iv; Lambert Davis to Jonathan Daniels, 9 Mar. 1938; James Southall Wilson to Grover Hall, 24 Sept. 1929; Hall to Wilson, 26 Sept. 1929, *Virginia Quarterly Review* Papers.

48. See Jaffé Papers, 9924e, Box 1, and "Virginius Dabney" file in 9924b, Box 3.

49. Jaffé to Grover C. Hall, 16 Oct. 1929; Hall to Jaffé, 18 Oct. and 19 Oct. 1929; Gerald W. Johnson to Jaffé, 14 Oct. and 16 Oct. 1929; Jaffé to Lenoir Chambers, 15 Oct. 1929, Jaffé Papers.

50. Carter, *First Person Rural*, p. 50.

51. G. W. Johnson, "Southern Image-Breakers," p. 515.

Chapter 3

1. Dabney to Jaffé, 4 May 1931; Johnson to Dabney, 29 May 1931; Hall to Dabney, 11 May 1931, Dabney Papers.

2. Hall to Dabney, 11 May 1931, Dabney Papers.

3. Hall, *Baltimore Evening Sun*, 27 July 1928, p. 21.

4. McGill, *Atlanta Constitution*, 20 Feb. 1941, p. 6; Milton to Dudley V. Haddock, [?] 1931, Milton Papers.

5. Milton described his father's Prohibition battle in the final issue of the *News* and declared that from it he had learned "that it is better to lose a newspaper than to compromise with honor and sell your soul" (*Chattanooga News*, 16 Dec. 1939, p. 1); Taylor, *Woman Suffrage Movement*, pp. 43, 108, 38, 108, 140n.15. A laudatory biographical sketch of Abby Crawford Milton appeared in the *Atlanta Journal*, 20 Dec. 1925, 4:7.

6. *Chattanooga News*, 1 Jan. 1924, p. 9; 5 Jan. 1924, p. 2; 8 Jan. 1924, p. 1. On McAdoo, see Stratton, "Splattered With Oil," p. 63, and Murray, *103rd Ballot*, pp. 41–42. In John Temple Graves's novel, *The Shaft in the Sky*, the Wilsonian hero attended the 1920 Democratic convention and "believed that the fate of Wilson and of the League hung upon the nomination of McAdoo" (p. 275).

7. Milton, "Henry Ford Boom," p. 5; G. W. Johnson, "Ku-Kluxer," p. 209. See also Milton, "What Mr. McAdoo," p. 488, and "Muscle Shoals," p. 8.

8. G. W. Johnson, "Southern Image-Breakers," p. 510; Johnson, "Cadets at New Market," p. 119; Milton, "Muscle Shoals," p. 8.

9. Stratton, "Splattered with Oil," p. 64; Bates, "Teapot Dome Scandal," pp. 306–307; "Will Ask M'Adoo to Stay in Field," *New York Times*, 18 Feb. 1924, p. 1; Allen, "McAdoo Campaign," p. 221. Milton unsuccessfully tried to declare the $1300 he spent in this campaign as a business expense in his tax return for 1924 (Milton to "Collector of Internal Revenue," 14 Oct. 1925, Milton Papers).

10. On Smith, see Handlin, *Al Smith*, and Matthew and Hannah Josephson, *Al Smith*. On the Democratic party, see Buenker, *Urban Liberalism*; Huthmacher, *Senator Robert F. Wagner*; and especially Burner, *Politics of Provincialism*.

11. Allen, "McAdoo Campaign," p. 225; Murray, *103rd Ballot*, p. 87. McAdoo's leading rivals, Senator Oscar Underwood of Alabama in the South and Smith in the North, made their distaste for the Klan well known.

12. Murray, *103rd Ballot*, pp. 153–61, 202–6. In "William Gibbs McAdoo," Prude argues that McAdoo hoped to secure the nomination by calling for repeal of the "two-thirds" rule as soon as he gained a majority of the votes, and so bore primary responsibility for prolonging the balloting (pp. 621–28).

13. Murray, *103rd Ballot*, pp. 222, 246–47; Allen, "McAdoo Campaign," p. 227; Milton, handwritten draft, dated 1924 (on stationery from the Madison Square Hotel), Milton Papers; Milton, "What Will McAdoo Democrats Do," p. 22; Milton to Joseph S. Myers, 18 Nov. 1931, Milton Papers.

14. "George F. Milton Dies," *New York Times*, 24 Apr. 1924, p. 19; *Chattanooga News*, 28 Apr. 1924, p. 4. The senior Milton's will divided his ownership of the *News* among his heirs and associates, giving 51% of the stock to his wife and 31% to his

son, who became the paper's editor. The will also set $5,000 aside to fund annual prizes to the best southern editorial on international peace and to the southern woman writer "who has done the most for her sex" ("Will of G. F. Milton," *Chattanooga News*, 28 Apr. 1924, p. 5).

15. Milton to J. P. Watson, 10 June 1925; Milton to William H. Seward, 9 Feb. 1928, Milton Papers. In the book itself, Milton credited a local banker with the suggestion that Johnson's career deserved "a careful study and reappraisal" (*Age of Hate*, p. ix).

16. The most complete description of the trial and events leading to it is Ginger's *Six Days or Forever*. Julian Harris, who attended the trial, exemplified the outrage of southern liberals at the Tennessee law. See Pekor, "Adventure," p. 413; Mathews, "Julian L. Harris," pp. 492–93.

17. Milton to Theo. D. Jervey, 4 Aug. 1925, Milton Papers; Milton, "Testing 'Monkey Bill,'" p. 661; Milton, "Dayton Postscript," pp. 550, 551; *Chattanooga News*, 6 June 1925, p. 4.

18. Milton, "Dayton Postscript," p. 550.

19. Tindall, *Emergence*, p. 208; Dabney, *Liberalism*, p. 290; G. W. Johnson, "Journalism Below the Potomac," p. 80; Ginger, *Six Days or Forever*, p. 113. Journalists presenting their credentials to Virginius Dabney for *Liberalism in the South* emphasized their opposition to "clericalism in politics," as Grover C. Hall put it (Hall to Dabney, 14 June 1931; Ethridge to Dabney, 27 Oct. 1931, Dabney Papers).

20. Mims, *Advancing South*, pp. vii, 16, 257; Stewart, *Burden of Time*, p. 110; Davidson, *Southern Writers*, p. 30; Rock (unpub.), "Making and Meaning," pp. 202–6, 208.

21. *Chattanooga News*, 11 July 1925, p. 4; Mencken to Milton, 25 July, 27 July, and 6 Aug. 1925, Milton Papers. Milton called off the barrage of anti-Mencken missives in an editorial, *Chattanooga News*, 1 Aug. 1925, p. 4.

22. *Chattanooga News*, 11 Apr. 1936, p. 4; Milton, "Dayton Postscript," p. 550; Milton to Mary Baird Bryan, 8 Mar. 1926, Milton Papers. Milton's attitude toward Bryan may be compared to that of Jonathan Daniels, who shared the critical southern liberal view toward Prohibition and fundamentalism and objected to Bryan's crusade against evolution (see Daniels to "Dearest Mother," undated [1923?], Josephus Daniels Papers, Reel 20, Container 34).

23. Milton, "Planks," p. 492; Jaffé, "Democracy and Al Smith," p. 331; Dabney, *Liberalism*, p. 275; Milton, "New Tennessee," p. 577; Dabney, *Liberalism*, pp. 267–68.

George Brown Tindall has argued that behind the furor over the Klan, fundamentalism, and Prohibition, state government in the South during the 1920s better deserves the description of "business progressivism." Governors accepted as the duty of government a narrowed legacy of efficiency and public services from the broader agenda of the Progressive Era. Tindall's thesis accords with Blaine Brownell's account of the "urban ethos" put forward by the "commercial-civic elite" of the southern cities, which emphasized planning and public services rather than growth at all costs (Tindall, "Business Progressivism," pp. 142–62; Brownell, *Urban Ethos*). The journalists welcomed these developments but because they devoted their attention to issues of intellectual and cultural liberty, with the accompanying conviction that demagogues and their rural, lower-class followings posed the gravest threat to southern liberalism, they never considered "business progressivism" or the "urban ethos" a dominant trend in southern politics.

24. See, for example, G. W. Johnson, "Onion Salt," p. 62; Milton, "Can We Save," p. 94; Dabney, *Liberalism*, p. 164.

25. G. W. Johnson, "Dead Vote," pp. 39, 41, 40–42.

26. Julian Harris to Jaffé, 24 June 1927; Dabney to Jaffé, 28 July 1927, and 17 Aug. 1929, Jaffé Papers.

27. Jaffé, "Democracy and Al Smith," pp. 332, 325, 326, 328.

28. Ibid., pp. 334–35, 341, 339–40, 327.

29. Milton to James Southall Wilson, 12 May 1926, *Virginia Quarterly Review* Papers; "M'Adoo Quits Race for the Presidency to Harmonize Party," *New York Times*, 18 Sept. 1927, pp. 1, 24; Milton, "'Al' Smith," pp. 271, 276; Milton, "Smith's Southern 'Gains,'" pp. 406, 405; "Smith Cannot Win, Says M'Adoo Man," *New York Times*, 21 Jan. 1927, p. 5.

30. Jaffé, "Democracy and Al Smith," p. 336.

31. Peel and Donnelly, *1928 Campaign*, p. 71; Moore, *Catholic Runs for President*, p. 195; Burner, *Politics of Provincialism*, p. 217; Murray, *103rd Ballot*, p. 276; Hall to Jaffé, 25 Apr. 1927, Jaffé Papers. In his analysis of voting outside the South, *Prejudice and the Old Politics*, Lichtman concludes that "differences between Catholics and Protestants best explain the unique shape of electoral politics in the presidential contest" (p. 76).

32. For an indication of the themes and the volume of these anti-Smith editorials, see *Chattanooga News*, 2, 3, 5, 6, 7, 9, 10, 11, 12, 13, 17, 19, 21, 23, and 27 Jan. 1928. The satirical editorial appears in *Chattanooga News*, 22 May 1928, p. 4.

33. *Chattanooga News*, 11 Feb. 1928, p. 4; 23 Aug., p. 4; 10 May, p. 4.

34. *Chattanooga News*, 3 Jan. 1928, p. 4; 19 Jan., p. 4; 21 Jan., p. 4; 10 Sept., p. 4. As the campaign passed Labor Day, the *News* indulged in a fit of antiimmigrant prejudice and then returned to the liquor issue (24 Aug.; 5, 6 Sept.; and 12 Sept. 1928, p. 4).

35. *Norfolk Virginian-Pilot*, 2 Nov. 1928, p. 6. See also *Norfolk Virginian-Pilot*, 9 July 1928, p. 6; 12 Sept., p. 6; 22 Sept., p. 6; and 30 Oct., p. 6; Johnson, *Baltimore Evening Sun*, 17 May 1928, p. 31; 7 June, p. 29; 28 June, p. 29, and 12 July, p. 25; and Dabney, *Richmond Times-Dispatch*, 24 June 1928, 3:2; 2 Sept., 2:2, and 9 Sept., 2:2.

36. Jaffé, "Democracy and Al Smith," p. 327.

37. Milton, "Black Ballots," pp. 907, 911.

38. Ibid., pp. 912–13; Milton, "Can We Save," p. 95.

39. *Norfolk Virginian-Pilot*, 24 July 1928, p. 6; *Baltimore Evening Sun*, 17 May 1928, p. 31.

40. *Baltimore Evening Sun*, 26 July 1928, p. 23; Hall, *Baltimore Evening Sun*, 27 July 1928, p. 21. In a report to the *Evening Sun*, Dabney said that "the race issue is being worked overtime in Virginia" (25 Oct. 1928, p. 29).

41. Burner, *Politics of Provincialism*, p. 224; Peel and Donnelly, *1928 Campaign*, p. 121; Hall to Dabney, 14 June 1932, Dabney Papers. Clarence Cason, a professor of journalism at the University of Alabama, said in 1935 that "it was only through

appeal to the mythical dread of the Emperor Jones that the Democrats were able to offset the temporary menace of Romanism in 1928" (*90° in the Shade*, pp. 79–80). See also Key, *Southern Politics*, pp. 318–29.

42. *Norfolk Virginian-Pilot*, 6 Nov. 1928, p. 6; Cash, "Mind of the South," p. 191; Johnson, *Baltimore Evening Sun*, 29 Nov. 1928, p. 29. "I died a little when Al Smith was defeated," Jonathan Daniels recalled in *Time Between the Wars* (p. 347).

43. *Chattanooga News*, 18 Jan. 1928, p. 4, and 27 Feb., p. 4; Hoover, *New Day*, pp. 98–107; *Norfolk Virginian-Pilot*, 7 Oct. 1928, p. 6; *Chattanooga News*, 8 Oct. 1928, p. 4.

44. *Chattanooga News*, 26 Oct. 1928, p. 4; 2 Nov., p. 4.

45. Milton to Howard K. Beale, 18 Jan. 1929, Milton Papers; *Chattanooga News*, 28 Dec. 1929, p. 4. The title page to *The Age of Hate* bore Thomas Carlyle's declaration: "The history of mankind is the history of its great men; to find out these, clean the dust from them, and place them on their proper pedestal, is the true function of a historian."

46. G. W. Johnson, *Andrew Jackson*, p. 263. See also Johnson, *Randolph of Roanoke*, pp. 125–26.

47. Johnson, *Randolph of Roanoke*, p. 207. Milton's concentration on state rights developed from his efforts to explain Senator Charles Sumner's claim that, in a meeting after Lincoln's death, Andrew Johnson had endorsed Sumner's plans for black suffrage in the South. Unwilling to believe that Johnson might have changed his mind or that he misled Sumner, Milton turned to the philosophy of state rights as a means to explain both Johnson's apparent agreement with Sumner and his later vetoes of suffrage legislation (see Milton to David R. Barbee, 12 Aug. 1929, Milton Papers; Milton, *Age of Hate*, pp. 177–79).

48. Dabney, undated note, file "Literature and Journalism," Dabney Papers, 7690-j, Box 3; Dabney, *Liberalism*, pp. 404–5; *Chattanooga News*, 22 Sept. 1928, p. 4.

49. See Dabney, *Liberalism*, pp. 24–40, 190–200, and 280–308. In his original prospectus for the book, Dabney declared that "the tremendous power wielded by pastors of the evangelical sects seems . . . to have been the greatest single obstacle to the growth of liberal thought below the Potomac" (Dabney to Addison Hibbard, 4 May 1930, V. Dabney, "Liberalism in the South" file, University of North Carolina Press Papers).

50. Dabney, *Liberalism*, pp. 2, 9.

51. Ibid., pp. 99, 97.

52. Ibid., pp. 123–24, 125, 416–17.

53. In *Advancing South*, Edwin Mims avoided this problem by beginning his tale of progress in 1865 after Appomattox.

54. Milton, *Age of Hate*, pp. 90–91, 100.

55. Ibid., p. 291.

56. Dabney, *Liberalism*, pp. 268–69, 253.

57. Dabney, *Richmond Times-Dispatch*, 30 Aug. 1931, 2:2.

58. Jaffé to Dabney, 22 Oct. 1932, Jaffé Papers.

59. Dabney, *Liberalism*, pp. 419–20.

Chapter 4

1. T. D. Young, *Gentleman in a Dustcoat*, p. 204; Davidson, *Correspondence*, pp. 191, 193.

2. Davidson, *Correspondence*, p. 233. Although scholars justly give attention to the arguments of the Nashville Agrarians, as the group became known, they have neglected the impact of *I'll Take My Stand* on southern thought, especially southern liberal thought, during the 1930s. Some scholars, who follow the southern liberals in treating the book as a program for the South, conclude that the Agrarians never resolved the dilemmas that creating an Agrarian South involved and their ideas "had little appeal" to other southerners (Stewart, *Burden of Time*, p. 172; Rock [unpub.], "Making and Meaning," p. 412). Louis D. Rubin, Jr., on the other hand, argues in the "Introduction" that the book's "assertion of the values of humanism and its rebuke of materialism," a message that "has become increasingly relevant over the years," makes the question of its contemporary effects less important (Twelve Southerners, *I'll Take My Stand*, pp. xvii–xviii; hereafter cited as *ITMS*). George B. Tindall gives the fullest account of the controversy that the Twelve Southerners provoked, but he keeps his focus on the Agrarians themselves and concludes that Agrarian thought had most significance for southern literature (*Emergence*, pp. 576–83, 588).

3. Mims, *Advancing South*, p. 198; Davidson, *Correspondence*, p. 174. The literature on the Fugitive poets is large. On the history of the group, see, for example, Young, *Gentleman in a Dustcoat*, pp. 107–146; and Purdy, *Fugitives' Reunion*.

4. *ITMS*, pp. ix–xx.

5. Ibid., p. ix. See also pp. 52–53.

6. McGill, "Agrarianism vs. Industrialism," p. 1.

7. Davidson, "'I'll Take My Stand': A History," pp. 313–14; Davidson, *Correspondence*, pp. 221–22; Rock, "Making and Meaning," p. 233n; Stewart, *Burden of Time*, pp. 140–41; *ITMS*, p. xxxviii.

8. Davidson, *Correspondence*, p. 253; *Chattanooga News*, 4 Sept. 1930, p. 4.

9. G. W. Johnson, "No More Excuses," p. 333. In this essay, Johnson argued that just when labor clashes in southern industry, which were impossible to blame on the Civil War and Reconstruction, promised to force southerners to face their problems instead of making excuses, now came the Agrarians, holding up "Industrialism" as another excuse (pp. 331–37). Milton gave the essay an editorial endorsement in the *Chattanooga News* (17 Jan. 1931, p. 4). See also *Macon Telegraph*, 24 Sept. 1930, p. 4 (quoted in Davidson, "'ITMS': A History," p. 316); and Dabney, *Richmond Times-Dispatch*, 4 Jan. 1931, 3:2.

10. Barr, "Shall Slavery Come South?" pp. 481–94; Young, *Gentleman in a Dustcoat*, p. 218.

11. Lambert Davis to Donald Davidson, 27 Sept. 1930, *Virginia Quarterly Review* Papers; Young, *Gentleman in a Dustcoat*, p. 218; *Chattanooga News*, 18 Oct. 1930, p. 4.

12. Young, *Gentleman in a Dustcoat*, p. 220 (Davidson's report appeared in the *Chattanooga News*, 15 Nov. 1930, p. 25); Milton to Barr, 4 Nov. 1930, *Virginia Quarterly Review* Papers.

13. Barr to Clarence Cason, 21 Apr. 1931, *Virginia Quarterly Review* Papers; T. D. Young, "Prescription to Live By," p. 614.

14. *Norfolk Virginian-Pilot,* 10 Nov. 1930, p. 4.

15. *Richmond Times-Dispatch,* 15 Nov. 1930, p. 1.

16. Young, *Gentleman in a Dustcoat,* pp. 222–27; Ransom to Tate, 4 Dec. [1930] and 5 Dec. [1930], Tate Papers; Davidson, *Correspondence,* pp. 258–59; *Atlanta Constitution,* 12 Feb. 1931, p. 1; Woody, "Second Annual Meeting," p. 83.

17. Dabney, "Crusade in Dixie," *Baltimore Evening Sun,* 16 Dec. 1930, p. 27 (Jaffé reprinted this essay in the *Norfolk Virginian-Pilot,* 18 Dec. 1930, p. 6); G. W. Johnson, "No More Excuses," p. 336.

18. Young, *Gentleman in a Dustcoat,* pp. 218–19; *Richmond Times-Dispatch,* 15 Nov. 1930, p. 2; Barr, "Shall Slavery Come South?" p. 487; *Chattanooga News,* 3 Sept. 1930, p. 4.

19. Dabney, *Richmond Times-Dispatch,* 4 Jan. 1931, 3:2; *Chattanooga News,* 3 Sept. 1930, p. 4; *Norfolk Virginian-Pilot,* 10 Nov. 1930, p. 4.

20. B. Mitchell, *Rise of Cotton Mills,* p. 102. Milton named Mitchell along with Barr as leaders of the "Young Virginians" whom he set against the Agrarians for debate (*Chattanooga News,* 18 Oct. 1930, p. 4).

21. Mitchell, *Rise of Cotton Mills,* pp. 132, 132n, 103–4, 127.

22. Mitchell and his brother, George Sinclair Mitchell, published their essays together in *The Industrial Revolution in the South* (the quoted phrase appears on p. 237); Dabney, *Liberalism,* p. 311. Gerald W. Johnson borrowed Mitchell's interpretation for two essays on the textile mills: "Behind the Monster's Mask" and "Service in the Cotton Mills."

23. Davidson, *Correspondence,* p. 235. On the strikes, see G. S. Mitchell, *Textile Unionism,* pp. 63–83, and Marshall, *Labor in the South,* pp. 101–20.

24. Milton, "South Fights the Unions," p. 202; Johnson, *Baltimore Evening Sun,* 15 Sept. 1929, p. 31; Dabney, *Richmond Times-Dispatch,* 24 Aug. 1930, 3:2.

25. Milton, "Duties," p. 68. See also Cash, "War in the South," p. 169; Cash employed Mitchell's interpretation for the background to his discussion (pp. 164–65).

26. Ethridge, "South's New Industrialism," pp. 253, 254; Dabney, *Liberalism,* pp. 332, 323–24. In his essay, Ethridge noted that "editors had accepted, without question, the tradition that the cotton mills were instituted in the South after the Civil War to take care of unfortunate white people" (p. 252).

27. Young, *Gentleman in a Dustcoat,* p. 220; Barr, "Shall Slavery Come South?" p. 494; *Chattanooga News,* 18 Oct. 1930, p. 4.

28. Johnson, "No More Excuses," p. 336.

29. Ibid., p. 337.

30. *Chattanooga News,* 27 Sept. 1930, p. 4.

31. *ITMS,* pp. i–xiii. In his introduction to the 1977 Louisiana State University Press edition of *ITMS,* Rubin modifies this analysis. Some of the Twelve, he says, did envision their book as a practical program for the South, whereas others employed a conscious literary strategy of metaphor to develop a philosophical argument for Agrarianism (pp. xvi–xxii).

32. Tindall, *Emergence,* p. 581; *ITMS,* pp. 190–91, 16.

33. *Richmond Times-Dispatch,* 15 Nov. 1930, p. 1; Dabney, *Baltimore Evening*

Sun, 16 Dec. 1930, p. 27; *Richmond Times-Dispatch,* 22 Feb. 1931, 2:2; G. W. Johnson, "South Faces Itself," p. 157.

34. Davidson, "'ITMS': A History," p. 302.

35. Purdy, *Fugitives' Reunion,* pp. 206–7.

36. Davidson, *Southern Writers,* p. 51; Davidson, *Correspondence,* p. 280; Rubin, *Wary Fugitives,* pp. 225–26. Michael O'Brien shows how interpretations of the South, very different for Agrarians and liberals, paradoxically created a sense of intellectual community in which all the disputants seemed to talk of the same things (*American South,* pp. 226–27).

37. This summary follows Owsley's "Irrepressible Conflict," in *ITMS,* pp. 61–92. Quotations are from pp. 69, 72, 90, 71. For similar sentiments, see *ITMS,* pp. 12–15, 48, 52, 96, 99, 112, 153, 202, 213, 271, and 328.

Two of the Twelve—Robert Penn Warren (see n. 42 below) and Herman Clarence Nixon—deviated from this Agrarian interpretation. Nixon's history of the Old South corresponded more closely to that of the journalists. He wrote that the South "was working toward a balanced industry, a reformed agriculture, . . . when the war upset the orderly process of evolution." Unlike the other Agrarian theses, Nixon's essay, as its title, "Whither Southern Economy?" suggests, concentrated on conditions in the modern South. Admitting that "there is no point in a war with destiny or the census returns," he used facts and figures to argue that industrial development required "a supporting agrarian economy." Nixon concluded that by protecting its farmers, the industrializing South could preserve the Agrarian spirit essential for a healthy human culture and avoid the economic problems of industrialization at the expense of agriculture (*ITMS,* pp. 176–200; quotations are from pp. 188, 176, 200). Privately, Gerald W. Johnson acknowledged that Nixon "wrote sensibly" (Johnson to Barr, 27 Oct. 1930, *Virginia Quarterly Review* Papers).

38. *ITMS,* p. 7; Davidson, "'Mystery' of the Agrarians," p. 7; Davidson, *Southern Writers,* p. 44; *ITMS,* pp. 14, 76.

39. Dabney, *Richmond Times-Dispatch,* 4 Jan. 1931, 3:2; Johnson, "No More Excuses," p. 334; Barr, "Shall Slavery Come South?" p. 484; Dabney, *Liberalism,* pp. 310–12. Also see Dabney, *Richmond Times-Dispatch,* 27 Dec. 1931, 2:2, and Johnson, "South Faces Itself," p. 157.

In *The Mind of the South* (1941), W. J. Cash made a slightly different but equally anti-Agrarian argument. He described the Old South as frontierlike and hence too new for any "establishment" to have existed. Then, following Broadus Mitchell, he argued that after the Civil War southerners themselves brought industry to the South and did so without "any Yankee model or any other." In fact, Cash asserted, Agrarianism "had never, the facile assumptions of Allen Tate and the Southern Agrarians to the contrary notwithstanding, got to be a fundamental constituent of the Southern mind" (*Mind of the South,* pp. 10–11 and 184–85).

40. Dabney, *Richmond Times-Dispatch,* 27 Dec. 1931, 2:2; Johnson, "South Faces Itself," p. 157; Johnson, *Randolph of Roanoke,* p. 39.

41. Dabney, *Liberalism,* p. 356; *Chattanooga News,* 18 Oct. 1930, p. 4; Milton, "Impeachment," p. 248. See also *Baltimore Evening Sun,* 16 Dec. 1930, p. 27; *Richmond Times-Dispatch,* 4 Jan. 1931, 3:2, and 27 Dec. 1931, 2:2; *Chattanooga News,* 7 Jan. 1931, p. 4.

42. Lanier's essay in *ITMS* appears on pp. 122–54 (the first two quotations are on p. 123); *ITMS*, pp. xvi–xvii, 8. This general refutation of "Progress" as a false and dangerous concept made Robert Penn Warren's essay on the Negro an anomaly in *ITMS*. Warren argued that race relations would be most equitable in an Agrarian society, and his description of black farmers, still segregated but independent on their own land, accorded with the highest Agrarian principles. Nonetheless, his essay provoked a controversy among the Twelve Southerners. Davidson, the unofficial general editor of the symposium, at first thought of rejecting the essay and said that he could hardly believe that Warren himself had written it. He feared that the essay would offend their desired southern audience, and indicated that Warren's racial attitudes were much too egalitarian for his taste. Certainly Warren's essay granted an independence and dignity to black southerners that contrasted sharply with many racist statements in the other essays. More important, though, his essay, alone among the twelve in *ITMS*, described a history of progress since 1865. Given the existence of slavery in the Old South, he could hardly have done otherwise. Scholars today contend that on the issue of race, "the Agrarians were most vulnerable," and Warren's acquiescence to Jim Crow has received criticism. Ironically, Warren's essay, so different from the other essays, probably ensured that contemporary critics would not object to the Agrarian manifesto on the issue of race. At least, race relations did not figure in the debates with the southern liberal journalists ("Briar Patch," *ITMS*, pp. 246–65 [the quotation is from p. 263]; Davidson, *Correspondence*, pp. 250–51; Rock, "Making and Meaning," pp. 263, 408, 437; Stewart, *Burden of Time*, p. 165 [see also Rubin, *Wary Fugitives*, pp. 232–35, 339, 356–57]). For examples of anti-Negro attitudes of the Agrarians, see *ITMS*, pp. 62, 68, 77, 83.

43. Davidson, *Richmond Times-Dispatch*, 15 Feb. 1931, 2:2; Tate, "View of the Whole South," pp. 411, 429.

44. Johnson, *Baltimore Evening Sun*, 19 Jan. 1939, p. 21; Davidson, "Where Are the Laymen?" p. 478; Johnson to Lambert Davis, 25 Mar. 1935, *Virginia Quarterly Review* Papers.

45. *Richmond Times-Dispatch*, 8 Jan. 1940, p. 6. See also Cash, *Mind of the South*, p. 393, and Tindall, *Emergence*, pp. 575–606.

46. Rock (unpub.), "Making and Meaning," pp. 331–32; Graves, "Wilson and South," p. 384; Graves, *Atlanta Constitution*, 9 Mar. 1939, p. 9, and 3 Mar. 1937, p. 4; Woodward, "Why the Southern Renaissance?" p. 233.

47. Cash, *Mind of the South*, pp. 391, 392.

48. *Richmond Times-Dispatch*, 8 and 15 June; 13 and 27 July; 7, 14, and 21 Sept.; 19 Oct.; 23 Nov. 1930.

49. Johnson, *Baltimore Evening Sun*, 12 Mar. 1931, p. 27; Milton, *Chattanooga News*, 26 Mar. 1931, p. 6, and 27 Apr. 1931, p. 4.

Chapter 5

1. Ellis, "Crusade," p. 27; Dykeman and Stokely, *Seeds of Southern Change*, pp. 158–59. In his "Commission on Interracial Cooperation," Burrows (unpub.) reports that the CIC raised "over $1,000" from the concert (pp. 163–64).

2. M. A. Jones, "Approach to South's Race Question," p. 41; Odum, "Fundamental Principles," p. 282. Jones's essay represented a quasi-official statement from the Commission on Interracial Cooperation (see Will W. Alexander to Odum, 14 Mar. 1922, Odum Papers).

3. Tindall, *Emergence*, pp. 170–75; Grant (unpub.), "Anti-Lynching Movement," pp. 120–21, 246; Zangrando, *NAACP Crusade*, pp. 35, 51–71. Statistics on lynching appear in Raper, *Tragedy of Lynching*, pp. 480–81.

4. *Chattanooga News*, 18 Sept.; 12 Dec. 1924, p. 4; G. W. Johnson, "Tilt With Southern Windmills," p. 190; Johnson, "Critical Attitudes," p. 577.

5. *Chattanooga News*, 12 Dec. 1924, p. 4; Johnson, "Tilt With Southern Windmills," p. 189.

6. Chambers and Shank, *Salt Water*, pp. 315–18; Hohenberg, *Pulitzer Prize Story*, pp. 78–79.

7. Harris, quoted in Mims, *Advancing South*, p. 188, and in White, *Rope and Faggot*, p. 33. On black leaders' view of lynching, see Grant, "Anti-Lynching Reform Movement," pp. v, 32, 240, 326, and White, *Rope and Faggot*, p. 82. For a typical defense of lynching, see Raper, *Tragedy of Lynching*, p. 19.

8. Villard, "Crumbling Color Line," pp. 163, 159, 160; *Chattanooga News*, 30 Dec. 1929, p. 4.

9. Raper, *Tragedy of Lynching*, tells the story of the Ocilla lynching (pp. 141–71; the quotation is from p. 154). Ethridge's abortive investigation made it impossible for Arthur Raper to obtain information on the lynching ten months later. Blessed with researcher's luck, however, he picked up a garrulous hitchhiker on his return to Atlanta who not only described the lynching, but also proudly exhibited the toe he had saved as a souvenir (Raper, *Tragedy of Lynching*, pp. 144–45; Ellis [unpub.], "Commission on Interracial Cooperation," p. 73).

10. Raper, *Tragedy of Lynching*, pp. 319–55, describes the violence at Sherman.

11. Ellis, "Commission on Interracial Cooperation," pp. 69–70; Dykeman and Stokely, *Seeds of Southern Change*, pp. 136–37.

12. Alexander to Milton, 26 July; Milton to Alexander, 29 July; Alexander to Milton, 31 July; Milton to Alexander, 6 Aug. 1930, Milton Papers; Dykeman and Stokely, *Seeds of Southern Change*, p. 137. Although early correspondence and press releases referred to the Negroes as "advisory members," the distinction disappeared after the SCSL began its work and, in its publications, members' names appeared in alphabetical order, without racial labels.

13. Milton to Mrs. Sylvia Metcalf, 24 Sept. 1930, Milton Papers; *Chattanooga News*, 26 Sept. 1930, p. 4; and 13 Sept., p. 4.

14. *Chattanooga News*, 14 Nov. 1931, p. 4; Milton, "South Do Move," p. 143.

15. Ellis, "Commission on Interracial Cooperation," pp. 363, 358.

16. Milton to Raper, 30 June, and Raper to Milton, 2 July 1931, Raper Papers, Series II, File 785.

17. The best account of the case is Dan T. Carter's *Scottsboro*.

18. *Chattanooga News*, 27 Mar., and 6 May 1931, p. 6; Wilson, "Freight Car Case," p. 39; Milton to Bruce Bliven (editor of *The New Republic*), 25 Aug. 1931, Milton Papers; Minutes to SCSL meeting, 20 July 1931, Milton Papers, Box 88. See also Milton to Arthur Raper, 23 June 1931, Milton Papers.

19. Milton to Alexander, 25 Aug. 1931, Milton Papers; Milton to Walter White, 4 Jan. 1932, Milton Papers; *Chattanooga News*, 10 Apr. 1933, p. 4. In *They Shall Be Free*, Dr. Allen K. Chalmers, chairman of the Scottsboro Defense Committee, mentions the assistance of Milton (pp. 57–58), John Temple Graves (p. 63), Virginius Dabney (pp. 151–53), and, above all, Grover C. Hall, to whom he dedicated his book. After the first trial Dabney expressed doubts about "the validity of the jury's findings" (*Liberalism*, p. 257), and the second trial convinced him, like Milton, that "they are innocent" (*Richmond Times-Dispatch*, 16 Apr. 1933, 3:2).

20. *Chattanooga News*, 21 Dec. 1932, p. 4; Milton to Harry M. Ayers, 21 Aug. 1933, Milton Papers. Virginius Dabney, ardent in his defense of civil liberties, criticized southern persecution of Communist organizers. Nonetheless, he warned that liberals must guard against the agitators' gaining the ear of the masses. His complaint, like Milton's, was that persecution aided the Communist party by creating martyrs such as Angelo Herndon (*Richmond Times-Dispatch*, 13 Sept. 1931, 2:2; 29 Jan. 1933, 3:2).

21. See minutes to SCSL meetings of 22 Dec. 1930 and 20 July 1931, Milton Papers, Box 88; Milton to Raper, 25 Jan. 1932, Milton Papers. On the magazine campaign, see, for example, Milton to Oswald Garrison Villard, 27 Oct. 1931, Milton Papers.

22. *Lynchings and What They Mean*, pp. 19–20, 56; Barr to Milton, 7 Dec. 1931, *Virginia Quarterly Review* Papers; Dabney, *Liberalism*, pp. 249–50.

23. *Lynchings and What They Mean*, pp. 15, 31, 33, 37, 18, 56, 12, 46, 35–36. See also Raper, *Tragedy of Lynching*, for the case studies that led to the SCSL's conclusions.

24. *Chattanooga News*, 12 Nov. 1931, p. 4. On the connection between hard times and lynching, see, for example, Johnson, *Baltimore Evening Sun*, 3 Dec. 1931, p. 25; *Chattanooga News*, 13 Jan. 1931, p. 4; and Mark Ethridge to Stringfellow Barr, 4 Nov. 1930, *Virginia Quarterly Review* Papers.

25. *Lynchings and What They Mean*, p. 63.

26. Johnson, *Baltimore Evening Sun*, 3 Dec. 1931, p. 25; *Norfolk Virginian-Pilot*, 11 Nov. 1931, p. 6.

27. *Lynchings and What They Mean*, pp. 45–46.

28. Ibid., pp. 23, 53.

29. Ellis, "Commission on Interracial Cooperation," p. 80; Johnson, "Note on Race Prejudice," p. 226. Alexander next asked Milton to write the book but, busy with his biography of Stephen A. Douglas, he declined. Subsequently, Arthur Raper accepted the assignment and produced his excellent *Tragedy of Lynching*.

30. G. W. Johnson, "Note on Race Prejudice," pp. 227, 228, 232, 233.

31. *Lynchings and What They Mean*, pp. 18, 56, 57; the quotation is from p. 57.

32. In *The Basis of Ascendancy*, Edgar Gardner Murphy wrote: "There would be no problem if the negro were not a negro; there would be no problem if this age, and this country—which is its characteristic institutional expression—were not distinctly democratic" (p. 226). Murphy's certainty of black inferiority allowed him to advocate segregation as a "liberal" solution to the race problem. Without black inferiority, Jim Crow was difficult to defend without giving up liberal principles. In 1924 Gerald W. Johnson subordinated liberalism to social order to justify segregation: "the

South has the knowledge, born of bitter experience, that if it permits one educated, cleanly and entirely inoffensive Negro to enjoy facilities provided for whites, a horde of the other kind will demand the same privilege with an insistence that will yield to nothing but shotguns. Why precipitate rioting and bloodshed upon an entire community simply for the convenience of an individual?" ("South Takes Offensive," p. 77).

33. Banton, *Idea of Race*, p. 109; Gossett, *Race*, p. 416; Matthews, *Quest for an American Sociology*, pp. 164, 173; Park, "Bases of Race Prejudice," pp. 11–20 (the quotations are from p. 16).

34. G. W. Johnson, "Note on Race Prejudice," p. 226. For a striking example of the new racial concepts combining uneasily with older verities in southern liberal thought, see M. A. Jones, "Negro and the South," pp. 1–12.

35. Milton to Raper, 14 Sept. 1931, Milton Papers. In *Liberalism in the South*, Dabney placed his discussion of schools for Negroes in his chapter on the Negro rather than in his chapter on education; segregation simply seemed the natural order.

36. Woodward, *Strange Career*, pp. 103–4; Giddings, *Principles of Sociology*, pp. 17–19; Sumner, *Folkways*, pp. 87, 94–95. Banton suggests that in the United States, unlike western Europe, race relations have always been primarily a "domestic" problem, and therefore Americans have pioneered the sociological approach to race relations (*Idea of Race*, pp. 101–2). For a striking example of Giddings's "consciousness of kind," which he treated as the psychological element of nationalism, made to apply to southern race relations, see Murphy, *Basis of Ascendancy*, pp. xviii–xx.

37. Matthews, *Quest for an American Sociology*, p. 2.

38. Milton to Odum, 31 Oct. 1931; Odum to Milton, 5 Nov. and 11 Nov. 1931, Milton Papers. On Odum, see the editors' introduction to Odum, *Folk, Region, and Society*, pp. vii–xiv, and Tindall, "Howard W. Odum."

39. Odum, "Lynchings, Fears, and Folkways," *The Nation*, 30 Dec. 1931, reprinted in *Folk, Region, and Society*, pp. 36–41.

40. Sumner, *Folkways*, pp. iv, 77–78.

41. Odum, "Lynchings, Fears, and Folkways," p. 39.

42. See Odum, "Folk and Regional Conflict as a Field of Sociological Study," in *Folk, Region, and Society*, pp. 241–42; and Odum, *Understanding Society*, pp. 225–34 and 363–74. See also George L. Simpson's "Introductory Note," in *Folk, Region, and Society*, pp. 219–21.

43. Park, "An Autobiographical Note," in *Race and Culture*, pp. vii–viii; Matthews, *Quest for an American Sociology*, pp. 77–78, 81.

44. Embree, *13 Against the Odds*, p. 55. In addition to Johnson, Park's students Bertram W. Doyle, E. Franklin Frazier, and Horace Mann Bond taught for a time at Fisk. Other Park students included Guy B. Johnson of the University of North Carolina, Edgar T. Thompson of Duke University, Everett C. Hughes, Horace Cayton, John Dollard, and Everett V. Stonequist.

45. Park, "Our Racial Frontier on the Pacific" (1926), in *Race and Culture*, pp. 138–51; Park, "Race Relations and Certain Frontiers" (1934), in *Race and Culture*, pp. 117–37. The quotation is from *Race and Culture*, p. 167.

46. Park: "Negro Race Consciousness as Reflected in Race Literature" (1923), in

Race and Culture, pp. 284–300; "The Negro and His Plantation Heritage" (1934), in *Race and Culture*, pp. 66–78; "The Bases of Race Prejudice" (1928), in *Race and Culture*, pp. 230–43. The quotations are from *Race and Culture*, pp. 297, 233.

47. Park, "Our Racial Frontier on the Pacific," pp. 138–51; Park, "The Concept of Social Distance" (1924), in *Race and Culture*, pp. 256–60. The quotations are from *Race and Culture*, pp. 150, 233. As Michael Banton points out, Park devoted little attention to the study of social structure. Perhaps part of the explanation for that is found in his remark that "race relations have everywhere so largely determined the structure of human society." No doubt this outlook made it easier for him to reach his grandly optimistic conclusions. One of his critics complains that Park had too much influence: "Park's race relations cycle had provided the essential sociological imagination for successive generations of American scholars. Thereafter they would pursue the dream of a racially homogeneous world to be ushered in by the gradual operation of social evolution" (Banton, *Idea of Race*, p. 106; Park, *Race and Culture*, p. 190; Lyman, *Black American*, p. 35).

48. Park, "Bases of Race Prejudice," in *Race and Culture*, p. 243.

49. Wright, "Southern White Man," pp. 193, 183; Ethridge, *America's Obligation*, p. 11; Weatherford and Johnson, *Race Relations*, pp. 444–45. Wright, the owner and editor of the *Columbia Record* from 1916 to his retirement in 1929, earned a reputation as a liberal in the 1920s (see G. W. Johnson, "Journalism Below the Potomac," p. 81; Johnson, "Southern Image-Breakers," p. 511; and Dabney, *Liberalism*, p. 410).

50. Ethridge, *America's Obligation*, p. 6. In the Preface to the reprinting of his 1934 book, *The Education of the Negro in the American Social Order* (New York: Octagon Books, 1966), Horace Mann Bond declared that "when this book was written more than thirty years ago, the institution of racial segregation appeared to be an immutable feature of the American social order" (p. x).

51. Ethridge, *America's Obligation*, p. 5; Dabney, *Richmond Times-Dispatch*, 9 Apr. 1933, 3:2.

52. Milton, "Lecture II: The Two Slaveries," Institute of Race Relations, Swarthmore, Pa., 12 July 1933, pp. i, 3–4, typescript in Milton Papers, Box 31. In his *Silent South*, Sosna cites these lectures and says that Milton "exemplified the typical outlook of the white Southern liberals who worked with the Interracial Commission" (p. 27). See also G. W. Johnson, *Secession*, p. 132.

53. Park, *Race and Culture*, pp. 234–35, 150–51, 177–79. In *Race Relations*, Charles S. Johnson echoed Park: "The process of individual manumissions . . . revealed in its spread and variety and intensity much of the nature of human nature itself. It reflected the long contest between material advantage, by which survival was possible, and those intimate and humane sentiments by which survival is made worthwhile. It foreshadowed the troublesome problems to be faced in our democracy by the presence of a free population of Negroes now numbering twelve million, for whom neither extinction, nor fixed and universal subordination, nor colonization is a solution" (p. 258).

54. Ramsdell, "Natural Limits," pp. 151–71; the quotation is from p. 171. Ramsdell revealed the importance of his thesis to a defense of the South with his statement that "there is no question but that our generation must, if the fears of the anti-

expansionists were well founded, sympathize with the opposition to slavery expansion" (p. 152).

55. Sumner, *Folkways*, pp. 90, 306. Almost hopefully, Sumner pointed to the treatment of Africans in the Republic of South Africa and the German colonies as potential proof that "the humanitarians of the nineteenth century did not settle anything" (p. 306).

56. Milton, "Lecture II," pp. 8, 13, 7 (see n. 52 above).

57. Milton, "Lecture III: Reconstruction," 13 July 1933, pp. 2–3, 6–8, 18.

58. Milton, "Lecture II," pp. 7–8.

59. Alexander, "Negroes and Economic Structure," p. 277. Lyman criticizes Park's race relations cycle on similar grounds (*Black American*, pp. 50, 68).

60. M. A. Jones, "Negro and the South," p. 12.

61. White, *Man Called White*, p. 141. In 1935 Guy B. Johnson told the annual meeting of the CIC that "we must hammer home over and over again the idea that the South is holding itself down by holding the Negro down" ("Some Methods," p. 274). See also, for example, letters from Daniels and Couch to *The Nation*, 17 Jan. 1934, pp. 74, 76.

62. See, for example, *Lynchings and What They Mean*, p. 23. Park wrote that "generally speaking, there was no such thing as a race problem before the Civil War and there was at that time very little of what we ordinarily call race prejudice, except in the case of the free Negro" (*Race and Culture*, p. 185).

63. J. B. Kirby, *Black Americans*, p. 35. Kirby suggests, as an explanation for the prominence of southern interracialists in the Roosevelt administration, that liberalism in the South had become linked with the race issue, whereas "most northern progressives had no articulated position on the question in the early 1930s" (p. 48).

Chapter 6

1. Daniels, *Southerner Discovers*, p. 339. Eagles, in his *Jonathan Daniels*, concludes that Daniels's experiences on this tour "stimulated him to think about racial matters" (p. 51). The main topic of the conversations reported in Daniels's book and in his "Notes Made On Southern Tour" (Daniels Papers, Box 82), however, was southern politics.

2. Sosna, *Silent South*, pp. 86–87; Tindall, *Emergence*, pp. 632–33; R. H. King, *Southern Renaissance*, pp. 242–43. An early and influential analysis of southern liberalism and popular democracy appears in Myrdal, *American Dilemma*, pp. 470–73.

3. See, for example, Johnson, *Baltimore Evening Sun*, 27 Nov. 1930, p. 31, and 12 Nov. 1931, p. 27; Dabney, *Richmond Times-Dispatch*, 23 Nov. 1930, 3:2; and *Chattanooga News*, 1 Jan. 1931, p. 4, and 18 Sept. 1931, p. 6.

4. *Chattanooga News*, 6 Jan. 1931, p. 4, 26 Mar., p. 6, and 27 Apr., p. 4; Milton to H. A. Moehlenpah, 20 June 1931, and to Hinkeley Lyon, 2 Dec. 1931, Milton Papers.

5. *Chattanooga News*, 20 Apr. 1932, p. 4; Milton to Roy F. Nichols, 27 July 1932, and to Vance McCormick, 15 Sept. 1932, Milton Papers.

6. Dabney, *Richmond Times-Dispatch*, 31 Dec. 1933, 3:4.

7. Johnson, *Baltimore Evening Sun*, 17 Aug. 1933, p. 21. The label "moralists" is

Johnson's (*Baltimore Evening Sun*, 24 Nov. 1932, p. 23), and the term "political parsons" comes from Dabney (*Richmond Times-Dispatch*, 1 Jan. 1933, 3:2).

8. Dabney, *Dry Messiah*, pp. 48, 84–85, 132, 133, 317. Dabney actually wrote the original manuscript two decades earlier with the intention of exposing the then-puissant bishop for the hypocritical charlatan that the young reporter believed his evidence proved him to be. Publishers, wary of libel suits, turned him away, and he only returned to the manuscript after Cannon's death in 1944. On the Cannon manuscript, see Mencken to Dabney, 28 Jan. 1931, and Dabney to Wm. B. Smith, 8 Sept. 1944, Dabney Papers; Dabney, *Across The Years*, pp. 120–22, 177, 212–13. For a recent, and very different, interpretation, see N. H. Clark, *Deliver Us From Evil*.

9. *Chattanooga News*, 16 Sept. 1930, p. 4; Milton, "Stimulate and Organize," p. 23.

10. Milton to Wellington Wright, 5 Jan. 1932, Milton Papers; Milton, *Eve of Conflict*, pp. 1, 155–56, 157. Milton argued that the Industrial Revolution produced similar effects in western Europe as evidenced by Karl Marx's "Communist Manifesto" and the revolutions of 1848 (*Eve of Conflict*, p. 155).

11. Milton to James E. Babb, 9 Feb. 1932, Milton Papers.

12. *Chattanooga News*, 16 July 1932, p. 4; 1 May 1933, p. 4.

13. Milton, *Eve of Conflict*, pp. 157–58. See also Milton to James K. Pollock, 19 Dec. 1932, Milton Papers. In 1854, Michigan and Wisconsin also endorsed prohibition in referenda. Milton asked friends—Pollock at the University of Michigan and W. B. Hesseltine at the University of Wisconsin—to check the vote in those states. They reported inconclusive figures, and Milton relegated their information to a footnote (*Eve of Conflict*, p. 158 n. 4).

14. *Chattanooga News*, 19 Apr. 1933, p. 4; 7 Aug. 1933, p. 4. See also 15 July 1933, p. 4.

15. Milton, *Eve of Conflict*, p. 2; G. W. Johnson, *Secession*, pp. 86–89.

16. Milton, *Eve of Conflict*, pp. 149, 153–54, 8, 149–50. Although Milton referred in his acknowledgments to Charles W. Ramsdell, "one of the South's shrewdest students on ante-bellum economics and politics," he presented his version of the "natural limits" thesis through citations of antebellum opinion (pp. vii, 149). In this way, he could show that Douglas's "realistic" approach to the slavery issue accorded with unemotional opinion in the nation at large. Moreover, the conviction that slavery expansion had reached its "natural limits" enabled Milton to describe Lincoln's "House Divided" position as no more than a clever formula to bind the people's "emotional consent" to the Republican party (p. 456).

17. Ibid., pp. 343–44, 81.

18. Milton to Roy F. Nichols, 30 Nov. 1933, Milton Papers.

19. Milton, "Douglas' Place," pp. 343, 344–45. See also "Douglas and the Needless War," address to Atlanta Lawyers' Club, 13 July 1934, Milton Papers, Box 30.

20. Milton to Mrs. Isabel S. Johnson, 11 Jan. 1933, Milton Papers.

21. G. W. Johnson, "After Appomattox," p. 132; Johnson, *Secession*, p. 115.

22. G. W. Johnson, "Villains," p. 226. In this essay, Johnson argued that American history revealed no "villains" on the evil scale of a Hitler and, in fact, the worst disasters in the nation's history had resulted from the work of people who intended to do

good. His criticism of these do-gooders' intolerance implied criticism of the contemporary anti-Communist witchhunters. See also Johnson, *Secession*, p. 156.

23. Milton to Norton McGiffen, 6 Nov. 1934, Milton Papers; Dabney, "Dixie Rejects Lynching," p. 580; Graves, *Atlanta Constitution*, 26 Nov. 1937, p. 6.

24. McGill, "Civil Rights," p. 65 (in this essay, McGill argued that southern blacks could more effectively gain their civil rights through exercise of the ballot than through pressure on the federal government); *Greenville Delta Democrat-Times*, 22 Aug. 1954, p. 1. C. Vann Woodward's thesis in *Strange Career* that the enactment of the segregation laws changed race relations from the flexible, ambiguous conditions of the 1880s to a rigid, monolithic system of segregation and discrimination after 1900—that is, that stateways did change folkways—may be read in part as an antisegregationist southern liberal's response to these arguments against swift desegregation.

25. The most complete account of Long's life and career is T. H. Williams, *Huey Long*, but see also Alan Brinkley's analysis of Long and his followers in *Voices of Protest*. Long contended that, properly, one dunked rather than crumbled one's cornpone in the potlikker. Julian Harris responded with an editorial in the *Atlanta Constitution* advocating the greater merits of crumbling. The controversy gained national attention in 1931, perhaps as a humorous respite from the Depression. Significantly, Franklin D. Roosevelt told Harris that he preferred to crumble his cornpone (Williams, *Huey Long*, pp. 460–62).

26. Carter, *Where Main Street*, p. 57. In "Hodding Carter," Robinson observes that Carter "thrived on controversy, would have been miserable without it, and often went out of his way to provoke it" (p. 335).

27. *Hammond Courier*, 26 Aug. 1932, p. 2; 3 Jan., and 10 May 1934, p. 1. See also 14 June 1932, p. 2; 16 Nov. 1933, p. 2; and 10 Aug. 1934, p. 1.

28. Carter, "Kingfish to Crawfish," p. 305; Carter, "How Come Huey Long?" p. 12; *Hammond Courier*, 10 May 1934, p. 1. See also Carter, "Huey Long," pp. 26–27.

29. *Hammond Courier*, 17 Jan. 1934, p. 1. See also Carter, *Where Main Street*, p. 51; *Hammond Courier*, 17 Aug. and 21 Aug. 1931, p. 1; and 1, 2, and 10 Aug. 1934, p. 1. Carter apparently decided at this point that actions spoke louder than words. He devoted his time to anti-Long activities and was a member of the Square Deal Association, a quasi-military anti-Long organization. During this murky period, the *Courier* regularly used canned editorials, sent to newspapers by special-interest organizations, attacking high taxes and public utilities or extolling self-help and private charity (Carter, *Where Main Street*, p. 62). On the Square Deal Association, see T. H. Williams, *Huey Long*, pp. 822–29.

30. *Hammond Courier*, 10 Feb. and 10 May 1934, p. 1.

31. *Hammond Courier*, 13 Sept. 1935, p. 1.

32. *Hammond Courier*, 23 Sept. 1935, p. 1, and 7 Nov., p. 6; Carter, *Southern Legacy*, p. 137; *Hammond Courier*, 23 Jan. and 24 Jan. 1936, p. 1. Later Carter ruefully compared his campaign to "a one-legged man running a race with the Twentieth Century Limited" (quoted in MacKaye, "South's Fighting Editor," p. 107).

33. Carter, *Where Main Street*, pp. 188–90, 69, 66.

34. *Richmond Times-Dispatch,* 21 Aug. 1932, 3:4; *Chattanooga News,* 10 Apr., and 20 Aug. 1934, p. 4. See also Dabney, *Across The Years,* pp. 136–37; *Chattanooga News,* 7 Apr. 1933, p. 6; 5 Aug. 1933, p. 4; 1 Sept. 1933, p. 4; and 13 Sept. 1934, p. 4.

35. G. W. Johnson to Lambert Davis, 25 Mar. 1935, *Virginia Quarterly Review* Papers.

36. Johnson to Davis, 22 Sept. 1935, *Virginia Quarterly Review* Papers.

37. Johnson, "Live Demagogue," pp. 9, 10, 11.

38. Ibid., pp. 12, 13, 14. For similar conclusions from other journalists, see *Chattanooga News,* 10 Sept. 1935, p. 4; *Richmond Times-Dispatch,* 11 Sept. 1935, p. 8; 13 May 1937, p. 12; Cash, *Mind of the South,* pp. 291n, 292, 294; McGill, *Atlanta Constitution,* 27 Oct. 1938, p. 6; Mark Ethridge, "Long Leads Real Revolt Though a Demagogue," undated [c. 1934?] clipping, Miller Papers, 9760, Box 24.

39. Milton, "Also There Is Politics," p. 125.

40. Ibid., p. 117. In *Liberalism,* Dabney described events in South Carolina as typical (pp. 205–7). For a bald statement of this thesis, see Clarence Cason, "Alabama's Growing Wetness," *Baltimore Evening Sun,* 1 Apr. 1932, p. 33; Cason to Milton, 20 Jan. 1932, Milton Papers; Cason, *90° in the Shade,* p. 58.

41. Dabney, *Liberalism,* pp. 216, vii; Hicks, *Populist Revolt,* p. vii.

42. Hicks, *Populist Revolt,* pp. 251–54, 410–12. In his brief for the southern demagogue, "From Tillman to Long," Daniel M. Robison also held the Populists responsible for disfranchisement of black voters (pp. 308–9).

43. Dabney, *Liberalism,* pp. 215, 268–69, 238, 269.

Chapter 7

1. Dabney, *Liberalism,* pp. 423–25.

2. Johnson, *Baltimore Evening Sun,* 16 July 1930, p. 29; 26 Nov. 1930, p. 25; 19 Mar. 1931, p. 25; *Chattanooga News,* 22 Sept. 1930, p. 4; 1 Jan. 1931, p. 4. See also Milton to Homer S. Cummings, 21 Apr. 1933, Cummings Papers; *Chattanooga News,* 22 Sept. 1930, p. 4; and Johnson, *Baltimore Evening Sun,* 16 July 1931, p. 29.

3. Dabney, *Richmond Times-Dispatch,* 8 Mar. 1931, 2:2; *Chattanooga News,* 20 Jan. 1932, p. 4; Johnson, *Baltimore Evening Sun,* 14 Apr. 1932, p. 25, and 20 May, p. 31.

4. Hodding Carter, whose "personal choice" for the nomination was Governor Albert Ritchie of Maryland, distrusted Roosevelt because of his political association with Huey Long. After the election, the *Courier* grudgingly allowed that "Mr. Roosevelt will make a pretty good president despite the caliber of those who have attached themselves to him" (*Hammond Daily Courier,* 2 July 1932, p. 2, and 7 Nov., p. 1).

5. Dabney, *Richmond Times-Dispatch,* 8 May 1932, 3:4, 11 Sept., 3:2, and 6 Nov., 3:2.

6. Milton to Alexander W. Spence, 16 July 1932, Milton Papers; *Chattanooga News,* 29 June 1932, p. 4, and 25 Oct., p. 4. See also Milton to William B. Hesseltine, 22 Oct. 1932, and to Thomas P. Martin, 31 Oct. 1932, Milton Papers. Gerald W.

Johnson also experienced Roosevelt's legendary charm when he once delivered to him a political message of "slight importance." Johnson recalled: "He uttered no word of flattery, but his bearing and tone during the interview subtly and delightfully conveyed the impression that the visitor was a person of tremendous importance; so the visitor naturally went away ready at a moment's notice to whoop for Franklin Roosevelt for anything from constable to Pope" (*Baltimore Evening Sun*, 2 Oct. 1930, p. 29).

7. Johnson, *Baltimore Evening Sun*, 16 July 1931, p. 29; Johnson, "Bryan," pp. 389–90; *Baltimore Evening Sun*, 16 Sept. 1932, p. 33, and 3 Nov., p. 25.

8. Johnson, *Baltimore Evening Sun*, 10 Nov. 1932, p. 23; Leuchtenburg, *FDR and the New Deal*, pp. 18–32, 38–40.

9. *Baltimore Evening Sun*, 9 Mar. 1933, p. 15; Leuchtenburg, *FDR and the New Deal*, pp. 41–62. In *Incredible Tale*, Johnson said that in the "dreary history" of his generation there was "an episode of such pure delight that the young fellows of today can hardly be expected to understand it, much less to experience anything like it. This episode was the first year of the New Deal" (p. 155).

10. Johnson, *Baltimore Evening Sun*, 18 May 1933, p. 21; *Hammond Daily Courier*, 10 Apr. 1933, p. 2. See also Dabney, *Richmond Times-Dispatch*, 4 Mar. 1934, 3:4.

11. Johnson, *Baltimore Evening Sun*, 6 July 1933, p. 23; Milton to Homer S. Cummings, 21 Apr. 1933, Cummings Papers. See also Johnson, *Baltimore Evening Sun*, 6 July 1933, p. 23, and 3 Aug., p. 21; *Chattanooga News*, 19 Jan. 1934, p. 6.

12. Milton to Stringfellow Barr, 20 June 1933, *Virginia Quarterly Review* Papers; *Chattanooga News*, 21 June 1933, p. 4, 24 June, and 25 June, p. 6.

13. *Chattanooga News*, 21 June 1933, p. 4, 24 June, and 25 June, p. 6. Milton's association of the frontier with a wasteful, antisocial individualism was a characteristic theme of southern liberal arguments for government planning, especially in regard to the use of natural resources. See, for example, Miller, *Blessings of Liberty*, pp. 8 and 35, and G. W. Johnson, *Wasted Land*, p. 38.

14. Dabney, *Richmond Times-Dispatch*, 23 July 1933, 3:4; *Hammond Daily Courier*, 29 Mar. 1934, p. 2. See also, for example, Cash, *Mind of the South*, p. 373; "Advertiser," *Newsweek*, 16 Jan. 1937, p. 35 (Grover C. Hall).

15. Dabney, *Richmond Times-Dispatch*, 23 July 1933, 3:4; Milton, "Jefferson, Practical Idealist," *Chattanooga News*, 10 Oct. 1936, p. 4. See also *Chattanooga News*, 27 Nov. 1933, p. 4.

16. Johnson, *Baltimore Evening Sun*, 18 June 1936, p. 25; *Chattanooga News*, 9 May 1935, p. 4; *Richmond Times-Dispatch*, 8 Nov. 1936, 4:2.

17. Johnson, *Baltimore Evening Sun*, 25 May 1933, p. 27.

18. "Editor Turns Historian," *Bulletin of the American Society of Newspaper Editors* (17 Oct. 1934), pp. 4–5, clipping in Milton Papers, Box 96; Milton to J. Glenn McFarland, 24 Sept. 1934, Milton Papers; Milton, *Eve of Conflict*, p. 156.

19. Pressley, *Americans Interpret*, pp. 301, 305–6; Fehrenbacher, "Disunion and Reunion," p. 119; Milton to Charles Edward Russell, 17 June 1936, Milton Papers; Bonner, "Civil War Historians," pp. 205–6; Fehrenbacher, "Disunion and Reunion," p. 112; Pressley, *Americans Interpret*, pp. 318, 294, 297. Kirk Jeffrey, Jr., notes

Milton's emphasis on Douglas's "realism" and declares that "published in the heyday of the New Deal, Milton's biography reflected the intellectuals' new-found admiration for pragmatic politicians" ("Stephen A. Douglas," p. 260).

20. Milton to Thomas P. Martin, 13 Jan. 1933, Milton Papers; Milton, *Eve of Conflict*, p. 156.

21. *Chattanooga News*, 24 June 1933, p. 4.

22. Milton, "Lecture I: The Historical Approach to Slavery," Institute of Race Relations, Swarthmore, Pa., 12 July 1933, pp. 7–8, Milton Papers, Box 31.

23. Ibid., p. 9; *Eve of Conflict*, p. 156.

24. *Eve of Conflict*, p. 156; "Lecture II," p. 2 (see n. 22 above).

25. During the early 1930s, issues of white supremacy and racism remained suppressed. Roosevelt himself maintained "a position of benevolent neutrality" on racial issues, and the New Deal made no direct challenges to the Jim Crow system. Milton and other southern liberals continued to work for the separate-but-equal race relations of vertical segregation as they strove to ensure that New Deal programs provided to blacks "benefits commensurate" with whites (Freidel, *F.D.R. and the South*, p. 97; Ellis (unpub.), "Commission on Interracial Cooperation," p. 288). For more detailed discussions of southern liberal activities under the New Deal, see Ellis, pp. 288–311, and Sosna, *Silent South*, pp. 60–87.

26. See, for example, *Chattanooga News*, 18 Apr. 1933, p. 4.

27. Ibid., 23 Jan. 1935, p. 4.

28. Bennett (unpub.), "Struggle for Power," pp. 172–82; McCraw, *TVA and the Power Fight*, pp. 128–30.

29. Bennett, "Struggle for Power," pp. 182–87, summarizes the campaign, but see also U.S. Congress, "Hearings." The quotation is from Bennett, "Struggle for Power," p. 182.

30. *Chattanooga News*, 7 Sept. 1934, p. 6; U.S. Congress, "Hearings," p. 2913; Gaskill, "Newspaper Is Killed," p. 80.

31. *Chattanooga News*, 20 Feb. 1935, p. 4.

32. Daniels, *Southerner Discovers South*, p. 95. Of 50,000 persons registered, 27,162 voted and approved the referendum by a count of 19,056 to 8,091 (Bennett, "Struggle for Power," p. 187).

33. *Chattanooga News*, 14 Mar. 1935, p. 4; Milton to W. B. Hesseltine, 15 May 1935, Milton Papers.

34. Bennett, "Struggle for Power," pp. 188–90. Privately, Milton attributed the *Free Press*'s appearance to a change in the *Chattanooga Times*'s editorial position on TVA power. Julian Harris left the *Atlanta Constitution* to become editor of the *Times* and, Milton said, changed the paper from an opponent of TVA to "a tepid neutral" in the power fight. Desirous of a more enthusiastic "mouthpiece," he went on, "the private power group" aided the *Free Press* (Milton to Silas Bent, 13 Sept. 1938, Milton Papers).

35. Milton, "Lecture I," p. 14 (see n. 22 above).

36. Milton, *Eve of Conflict*, pp. 501, 478, 503, 478–79. The phrase "radical minority" is from Milton's speech, "Douglas and the Needless War," to the Atlanta Lawyer's Club, 13 July 1934 (Milton Papers, Box 30). In an interview, Milton declared that in history "one finds extra-ordinary examples of the techniques by which minor-

ities enforce decisions upon majorities, elites cling to power and the masses are emotionalized into doing things which are against their best interests" ("Editor Turns Historian," p. 5 [see n. 18 above]).

37. Milton, "Lecture III," pp. 3, 6 (see n. 22 above).

38. Johnson, *Baltimore Evening Sun*, 22 Feb. 1934, p. 19; 26 Mar. 1936, p. 23.

39. Johnson, *Secession*, pp. 31, 82, 41, 14, 27.

40. Ibid., p. 117; Milton to Alexander Sachs, 29 Mar. 1938, Milton Papers.

41. Milton, speech, "The Press and Social Conflict," to the "Conference on Social and Economic Problems of the South," 27 Oct. 1935, Milton Papers, Box 30; Milton, *Eve of Conflict*, pp. 157, 156; *Chattanooga News*, 22 Jan. 1936, p. 11. See also Milton, abstract of speech, "What Is Ahead for America," South Georgia State Teachers College, Collegeboro, Ga., 10 Jan. [?], Milton Papers, Box 30, and "Trade Barriers," p. 46.

42. Johnson, *Baltimore Evening Sun*, 3 Aug. 1933, p. 21; Milton, speech, "Duress or Consent," Judson College, Marion, Ala., 5 Dec. 1934; Milton, abstract of speech, "What Is Ahead for America," Milton Papers, Box 30; *Chattanooga News*, 10 Dec. 1934, p. 4, 23 Jan. 1934, p. 4, and 25 Mar. 1935, p. 4. See also Milton, "This Changing World," *Chattanooga News*, 30 Nov. 1935, p. 4; Johnson, *Baltimore Evening Sun*, 9 Aug. 1934, p. 23; and *Chattanooga News*, 7 Nov. 1934, p. 6 (Milton wrote a signed column called "This Changing World" that appeared irregularly in the *News* between 27 Nov. 1935 and 28 Apr. 1936).

43. G. W. Johnson, "Bryan," pp. 387, 389; *Baltimore Evening Sun*, 15 Feb. 1934, p. 21; Johnson, *American Heroes*, p. 271. See also Johnson, *Liberal's Progress*, pp. 204–5.

44. Milton to William E. Dodd, 24 Oct. 1934, and to Norton McGiffen, 6 Nov. 1934, Milton Papers.

45. Milton, "This Changing World," *Chattanooga News*, 30 Nov. 1935, p. 4. Similarly, an editorial in the *Richmond Times-Dispatch* declared: "What many of the Southern States that have drifted along, governmentally, since the War Between the States, without party programs, need, is not dictators like Huey Long, but men capable of an intelligent mass appeal and of retiring politicians who have governed merely by appealing to the passions and prejudices of unschooled voters" (13 May 1937, p. 12).

46. Dabney, "If the South Had Won," pp. 199–201.

47. Ibid., pp. 201–5.

48. *Southern Policy*, p. 3.

Chapter 8

1. *Atlanta Constitution*, 25 Apr. 1935, p. 14, and 26 Apr., pp. 1, 3.

2. Ibid., 17 June 1938, p. 1; McGill, *South and Southerner*, pp. 159–60, 166–67, 159. See also Martin, *Ralph McGill*, pp. 39, 42.

3. Martin, *Ralph McGill*, pp. 56–59; *Atlanta Constitution*, 23 Nov. 1937, p. 7. On the Rosenwald Fellowships, see Embree and Waxman, *Investment in People*, pp. 147–51. Southern liberals had great influence on the selection of Rosenwald Fellows; both

Will W. Alexander, of the CIC, and Charles S. Johnson, of Fisk University, served as permanent members of the Committee on Fellowships, and in 1937 committee member Mark Ethridge, of the *Louisville Courier-Journal*, helped push McGill's candidacy.

4. On southern agriculture, see Mertz, *New Deal Policy*, pp. 1–19, and Tindall, *Emergence*, pp. 111–42.

5. Leuchtenburg, *FDR and the New Deal*, p. 72; Mertz, *New Deal Policy*, pp. 21, 68, 20–67 *passim*; Tindall, *Emergence*, pp. 409–14.

6. Dykeman and Stokely, *Seeds of Southern Change*, pp. 198–99; Mertz, *New Deal Policy*, pp. 93–94.

7. Mertz, *New Deal Policy*, p. 109; C. S. Johnson, Embree, and Alexander, *Collapse of Cotton Tenancy*, pp. 10–11. On the Southern Tenant Farmers' Union, see Grubbs, *Cry From the Cotton*.

8. Johnson, *Baltimore Evening Sun*, 9 June 1938, p. 29.

9. Johnson, Embree, and Alexander, *Collapse of Cotton Tenancy*, p. 14.

10. *Chattanooga News*, 6 May 1936, p. 4; *Richmond Times-Dispatch*, 11 Sept. 1935, p. 8.

11. Mertz, *New Deal Policy*, pp. 96–98; Dykeman and Stokely, *Seeds of Southern Change*, pp. 200–201. Mertz contends that this program "wisely refused to idealize the poor by overestimating their own abilities," but he notes that "the emphasis on landownership also meant an increasingly narrow concern only with those among the poor who had sufficient ability and resources to become small owners."

12. Baldwin, *Poverty and Politics*, pp. 81–84, 132–33, 136–39; Mertz, *New Deal Policy*, pp. 104–6, 116–17.

13. Baldwin, *Poverty and Politics*, pp. 130–31, 145–48; Dykeman and Stokely, *Seeds of Southern Change*, pp. 213–14; Mertz, *New Deal Policy*, pp. 144–46; *Atlanta Constitution*, 26 Apr. 1935, p. 3; *Southern Policy*, p. 4.

14. Baldwin, *Poverty and Politics*, pp. 92–94, 145–46; Mertz, *New Deal Policy*, pp. 119–21; Dykeman and Stokely, *Seeds of Southern Change*, p. 216; Ellis (unpub.), "Commission on Interracial Cooperation," p. 333; O'Brien, *American South*, p. 72.

15. Miller, *Man From the Valley*, pp. 78–79.

16. Ibid., pp. 82, 80. Mertz, *New Deal Policy*, explains the SPC's origins through Miller's organizing in North Carolina (p. 143). Donald Davidson describes Miller's organizing in North Carolina (p. 143). Donald Davidson describes Miller's recruitment in Nashville, in "Where Are the Laymen?" (pp. 463–65). No delegates from Alabama, Florida, or Mississippi attended the 1935 conference, nor did any from the latter two states attend the 1936 meeting.

17. Dallek, *FDR and American Foreign Policy*, pp. 33, 38. Miller expressed surprised pleasure at the southern response to his proposals (Miller to Jonathan Daniels [copy], 10 Nov. 1934, and to Frank P. Graham, 13 Nov. 1934, Graham Papers).

18. Davidson, "Where Are the Laymen?" pp. 463–65; *Southern Policy*, pp. 2, 26; Miller, *Second Southern Policy Conference Report*, p. 23.

19. *Southern Policy*, p. 11. Jonathan Daniels describes the argument between Tate and Amberson in *Southerner Discovers South*, pp. 81–88.

20. *Southern Policy*, pp. 7–8, 18. On the Agrarian view of issues during the 1930s, see also Shapiro, "Southern Agrarians."

21. *Southern Policy*, p. 16; Miller, *Second Southern Policy Conference Report*,

pp. 13–14. Gerald W. Johnson diverged from this general southern liberal conception of economic reform. Neither the tenant farmer nor the Bankhead-Jones bill inspired his pen. He continued to view the farmer as inevitably a dependent peasant, regardless of reforms, and criticized government aid to agriculture. Nonetheless, his views on desirable economic development in the South accorded with those of the other journalists. While giving all the credit to industrial development, he approvingly pointed out the growth of diversified farming in regions around southern urban centers. Any improvement in the farmer's situation, he predicted, would result from further expansion of industrialization below the Potomac. See Johnson: _Baltimore Evening Sun_, 19 Mar. 1931, p. 25, and 7 Sept. 1933, p. 25; to Lambert Davis, 29 Mar. 1935, _Virginia Quarterly Review_ Papers; and _Wasted Land_, p. 34.

22. _Southern Policy_, p. 3; Tindall, _Emergence_, pp. 592–93. Mertz, _New Deal Policy_, pp. 142–46, and Baldwin, _Poverty and Politics_, pp. 146–47, discuss the SPC in connection with the Farm Tenant bill. Mertz provides the most complete account in the historical literature of the SPC's founding. Virginia Jean Rock (unpub.), in "Making and Meaning," summarizes the debates between the Agrarians and the liberals at the SPC conference, but without analysis (pp. 362–68). Sosna, in his _Silent South_, associates the SPC with Herman Clarence Nixon, its chairman, and suggests inaccurately that the SPC merged both intellectually and institutionally with the Southern Conference on Human Welfare, which Nixon helped to organize in 1938 (p. 89).

23. Davidson, "Where Are the Laymen?" p. 476. Of the twenty-seven delegates in 1935, nine identified themselves with universities and eight with journalism (the numbers in 1936, of fifty-three delegates, were nineteen and nine respectively). Other professions represented in 1935 included law (3), labor unions (2), and business (3); the other two delegates were Miller and Alexander. Those attending in 1936 included seven from government, four from labor unions, a judge, three businessmen, two lawyers, a clergyman, and seven others who gave unidentifiable addresses and for whom no information is available in standard reference works. On the difficult decision to add a Negro member to the SPC, see Miller to Members of the Southern Policy Committee, 5 July 1935, National Policy Committee Papers, Box 11; Miller to H. C. Nixon, 30 Sept. 1935, and Nixon to Miller, 2 Oct. 1935, Box 2; and Minutes of Southern Policy Committee, New Orleans, 27 Oct. 1935, Box 11.

24. Davidson, "Where Are the Laymen?" p. 476; Daniels, _Southerner Discovers South_, p. 83; Dabney, _Below the Potomac_, p. 308. See also Miller to Delegates to the Atlanta Policy Conference, undated, Daniels Papers, Folder 33, Box 2; Hays, _Politics Is My Parish_, p. 119.

25. _Southern Policy_, pp. 3, 7.

26. Miller, _Blessings of Liberty_, pp. 62–63.

27. Johnson, _Baltimore Evening Sun_, 29 Oct. 1936, p. 29; Milton, "Also There Is Politics," in Couch, _Culture in South_, pp. 120–21. See also _Chattanooga News_, 4 Aug. 1934, p. 4, and 6 Nov. 1936, p. 6; Johnson, _Baltimore Evening Sun_, 9 Aug. 1934, p. 23; Dabney, _Richmond Times-Dispatch_, 4 Feb. 1934, 3:4.

28. _Southern Policy_, p. 5; Miller, _Second Southern Policy Conference Report_, p. 3. Miller later claimed that the discussion of the poll tax at the 1936 conference convinced Dabney to come out for repeal in the _Times-Dispatch_ (_Man From the Valley_, p. 84).

29. *Chattanooga Tribune*, 5 Apr. 1940, p. 4; *Richmond Times-Dispatch*, 6 May 1938, p. 14; *Chattanooga News*, 23 Aug. 1938, p. 4; *Richmond Times-Dispatch*, 3 Jan. 1940, p. 6. After the demise of the *News* on 16 Dec. 1939, Milton attempted unsuccessfully to establish a new evening paper, the *Tribune*, which published between 25 Mar. and 4 Sept. 1940.

Hodding Carter and Ralph McGill remained unsympathetic to poll tax repeal until after World War II. Significantly, during these years both men fought hard editorial campaigns against demagogic politicians—Theodore Bilbo in Mississippi and Eugene Talmadge in Georgia—who employed appeals to prejudice to mobilize their predominantly rural, white supporters. The editors feared that, as McGill claimed in 1942, repeal of the poll tax "would strengthen immeasurably the hands of the demagogues" (*Atlanta Constitution*, 20 Nov. 1942, p. 8).

Gerald W. Johnson said little one way or the other on the suffrage issue. His conviction that the quality of government depended far more on the small number who led than on those who voted, no doubt diminished the issue's importance for him. "To demand intelligence of twenty-five million people is, to be sure, to demand what is patently impossible," he wrote in *The Wasted Land*, "but, fortunately, to shape the polity of a nation it is not necessary to transform the entire population into philosophers. All that is requisite is intelligence in a relatively small group of leaders. Regardless of the form of government under which they live, the destinies of men have always been determined by a minority of mentally alert individuals" (p. 20).

30. For examples of references to "Negro bosses" in discussions of black voting, see Dabney, *Richmond Times-Dispatch*, 30 Aug. 1931, 2:2, *Chattanooga News*, 2 May 1931, p. 4, and 28 Aug. 1934, p. 4. On Negro voters, see, for example, Dabney to Jonathan Daniels, 15 Apr. 1935, and Daniels to Dabney, 16 Apr. 1935, Daniels Papers.

31. *Chattanooga News*, 31 Oct. 1936, p. 4.

32. *Richmond Times-Dispatch*, 29 Jan. 1938, p. 6. "Let the Negro prove himself a self-respecting, self-voting citizen," the *News* had proclaimed. "Then his pleas will gain the favor they will then deserve" (2 May 1931, p. 4).

33. *Southern Policy*, p. 7; Miller, *Blessings of Liberty*, p. 57.

34. Miller, *Second Southern Policy Conference Report*, p. 5; *Southern Policy*, p. 7. The phrase quoted from the *Report*, appears in an amendment to the statement on "Democratic Institutions" proposed by Virginius Dabney and accepted by the Conference.

35. Milton, *Eve of Conflict*, p. 156. The "Objectives of the Southern Policy Committee" appear in *Southern Policy*, p. 4, and Miller, *Second Southern Policy Conference Report*, pp. 16–17.

36. Odum, *Southern Regions*. In his introductory note, Odum explained that "approximately a year" passed between completion of the study and publication in order to check data against current government research and to prepare comparisons with other regions (p. x). On Odum, see also Sosna, *Silent South*, pp. 42–59; O'Brien, *American South*, pp. 31–93; G. B. and G. G. Johnson, *Research in Service*, pp. 3–31, 36–48, 160–76; and Singal, *War Within*, pp. 115–52.

37. Johnson, *Baltimore Evening Sun*, 30 July 1936, p. 21, and 19 Jan. 1939, p. 21. Hodding Carter offered a striking tribute to Odum's achievement in his second novel,

Flood Crest, published a decade after the heyday of regionalism. In this story of demagogic politics in Mississippi, Carter created a visiting professor of sociology from the University of North Carolina as his spokesman for southern liberalism.

38. Odum, *Southern Regions,* p. 11; Odum discussion his indices and the boundaries of the Southeast and the Southwest on pp. 5–11. For Odum, the South long preceded the abstractions of regionalism. His colleague Rupert B. Vance observes that "just as other sociologists were to choose urban or rural society as specialities, Odum started with an attempt to understand his own region," in Odum, *Folk, Region, and Society,* p. 109.

39. Odum, *Southern Regions,* pp. 2, 253–59. See also Odum, *Regional Approach,* p. 19. The SPC circulated this pamphlet to the local Policy Groups for their study during the winter of 1934–35 (*Southern Policy,* p. 26).

40. Odum: *Regional Approach,* p. 7n; *Southern Regions,* pp. 579, 582, 287. Sosna suggests that the failure of New Dealers to take advantage of Odum's regional studies caused him to break with them (*Silent South,* p. 62). In fact, Odum exhibited a protective jealousy toward his project that led him to see any effort to bring reform to the South as a threat. For evidence of this attitude toward the Southern Policy Committee, see Odum to Jonathan Daniels, 25 Feb. 1935, Daniels Papers.

41. Odum, *Southern Regions,* pp. 525, 203.

42. Odum, *Southern Regions,* p. 533; G. W. Johnson, *Wasted Land,* p. 102. See also Kantor, "Howard W. Odum," p. 284. Johnson told Odum that with *The Wasted Land,* he was "merely playing Huxley to your Darwin" (Johnson to Odum, 4 Dec. 1937, Odum Papers).

43. Odum, *Southern Regions,* pp. 582–85. Odum's colleagues at North Carolina, Guy Benton Johnson and Guion Griffis Johnson, report that "these concepts [of regionalism and regional planning] had at their core his philosophy of the role folkways play in human society" (*Research in Service,* p. 169).

44. Johnson, *Baltimore Evening Sun,* 14 Jan. 1937, p. 23.

45. Ellis, "Commission on Interracial Cooperation," pp. 89–90; J. D. Hall, *Revolt Against Chivalry,* pp. 238–43; Tindall, *Emergence,* pp. 551–52; *Atlanta Constitution,* 26 Apr. 1935, p. 3.

46. McGill, *Atlanta Constitution,* 28 Jan. 1939, p. 4; Graves, *Atlanta Constitution,* 26 Nov. 1937, p. 6. See also Carter, *Greenville Delta Star,* 21 Nov. 1937, p. 2, and 26 Nov., p. 4; Cash, *Baltimore Evening Sun,* 11 Sept. 1935, p. 17; Johnson, *Baltimore Evening Sun,* 4 Apr. 1935, p. 25; *Chattanooga News,* 6 May 1935, p. 4; 15 Apr. 1937, p. 4.

47. *Chattanooga News,* 24 June 1935, p. 4.

48. Odum, *Southern Regions,* pp. 255, 235. See also pp. 586–87.

49. Ibid., pp. 479–80, 483, 485.

50. Ibid., p. 483.

51. Ibid., pp. 189, 578.

52. Ibid., pp. 111, 487. In *The Wasted Land,* Johnson similarly said that the biracial school system led "to some duplication of effort and increase of expenditure" but never condemned it as wasteful (p. 68). Guy B. Johnson addressed the CIC as a last-minute substitute for Odum, and the latter may have quoted from his own prepared remarks in *Southern Regions;* Johnson said that he used Odum's notes as a foundation

for his own extended remarks (Johnson, "Some Methods," p. 272n; Will W. Alexander to Odum, 23 Apr. 1935, Odum Papers).

53. Odum, *Southern Regions*, p. 481.

54. Ibid., pp. 203, 596, 603, 601, 603.

55. Ellis, "Commission on Interracial Cooperation," p. 333; O'Brien, *American South*, p. 72; G. B. and G. G. Johnson, *Research in Service*, p. 115.

56. Ellis, "Commission on Interracial Cooperation," pp. 333–35; O'Brien, *American South*, pp. 72–75; Tindall, *Emergence*, pp. 585–86; Odum to Will W. Alexander, 17 Jan. 1938, Odum Papers.

Chapter 9

1. Odum to Emily Clay, 15 Aug. 1938, Odum Papers; Tindall, *Emergence*, p. 627; National Emergency Council, *Report on Economic Conditions*.

2. R. H. King, *Southern Renaissance*, pp. 242–44. King associates this "new" liberalism with the work of H. C. Nixon, C. Vann Woodward, V. O. Key, and Robert Penn Warren. Because he links it to the rediscovery of the Populist legacy, King sees hope for "agrarian insurgency" in the 1930s, rather than the labor movement, as the contemporary source of the "new southern liberalism." Although his contention that these ideas had little impact on southern thinking in the 1930s is correct, King's conclusion that "the usable past it sought to discover lacked contemporary resonance" results from his inattention to the labor movement. Dunbar's recent *Against the Grain* examines activism in the rural South, especially the Southern Tenant Farmers' Union, and finds its sources in Protestant Christianity.

3. Fine, *Sit-Down*; Bernstein, *Turbulent Years*, pp. 519–51.

4. *Chattanooga News*, 9 Jan. 1937, p. 4; *Richmond Times-Dispatch*, 31 Mar. 1937, p. 10. See also *Greenville Delta Democrat-Times*, 21 Jan. 1938, p. 4; Graves, *Atlanta Constitution*, 8 Mar. 1937, p. 4. In his "Southern Newspapers View Organized Labor in the New Deal Years," Wyche reports unanimous condemnation of the sit-down tactic in the southern press (pp. 189–90).

5. Leuchtenburg, *FDR and the New Deal*, pp. 231–33. See also *Chattanooga News*, 30 May 1935, p. 4; *Richmond Times-Dispatch*, 7 Jan. 1936, p. 8; Miller, *Second Southern Policy Conference Report*, p. 11; *Richmond Times-Dispatch*, 1 June 1936, p. 8; and the editorials collected in Miller, *Southern Press*.

6. See Johnson, *Baltimore Evening Sun*, 11 Feb. 1937, p. 21, and 25 Feb., p. 21; *Chattanooga News*, 11 Feb. 1937, p. 4; Graves, *Atlanta Constitution*, 16 Feb. 1937, p. 4, and 23 Feb., p. 4. Patterson, *Congressional Conservatism*, pp. 77–127, explains the relationship between the court bill and the rise of the conservative coalition in Congress.

7. *Richmond Times-Dispatch*, 24 Mar. 1937, p. 10, and 31 Mar., p. 10. See also 6 Feb. 1937, p. 6, and 11 Feb., p. 10.

8. *Chattanooga News*, 9 Jan. 1937, p. 4; Johnson, *Baltimore Evening Sun*, 10 June 1937, p. 25. See also *Richmond Times-Dispatch*, 25 June 1937, p. 14; *Greenville Delta Democrat-Times*, 21 Jan. 1938, p. 4; Graves, *Atlanta Constitution*, 25 Mar. 1937, p. 8.

9. _Richmond Times-Dispatch_, 21 Aug. 1937, p. 6; Graves, _Atlanta Constitution_, 21 Apr. 1937, p. 4. See also Graves, _Atlanta Constitution_, 2 July 1937, p. 9.

10. _Chattanooga News_, 1 May 1937, p. 4. See also Milton to Felix Morley, 15 May 1937, Milton Papers.

11. Dykeman and Stokely, _Seeds of Southern Change_, pp. 199–200. See also Cayton and Mitchell, _Black Workers_.

12. Weltner (unpub.), "George Sinclair Mitchell," pp. 15–16; G. S. Mitchell, "Organization of Labor," pp. vi–vii.

13. Sitkoff, _New Deal for Blacks_, p. 170; Alexander, "Negroes and Economic Structure," p. 271. For a more optimistic view, based on the existence of biracial organizations such as the CIC, see Hill, "Negroes in Southern Industry," p. 179.

14. Cayton and Mitchell, _Black Workers_, pp. 323–27; Marshall, _Labor in South_, pp. 143–46, 150–52.

15. G. S. Mitchell, "Negro in Southern Trade Unionism," pp. 26–33.

16. Bernstein, _Turbulent Years_, pp. 400–404; Cayton and Mitchell, _Black Workers_, pp. 198–212 (the quotation is from p. 212). See also Brody, "Emergence."

17. Cayton and Mitchell, _Black Workers_, Foreword by Charles S. Johnson, pp. vi, vii, vi. See also Fullinwider, _Mind and Mood_, pp. 173–77.

18. C. S. Johnson, "Race Relations," pp. 291, 294–95, 298, 300, 303.

19. See, for example, _Richmond Times-Dispatch_, 6 Mar. 1937, p. 6; Odum to Ethridge, 6 Dec. 1938, Odum Papers; _Chattanooga News_, 23 Jan. 1936, p. 4; Daniels, "Democracy Is Bread," pp. 481–91.

20. Nixon, _Forty Acres_, pp. 95–96.

21. Nixon, "Two Schools of Southern Critics," undated newspaper clipping in Miller Papers, 9760, Box 24; Nixon, _Forty Acres_, p. 96.

22. Woodward, "Hillbilly Realism," p. 681. For similar arguments, see also Lumpkin, _South in Progress_.

23. Woodward, _Tom Watson_. See also Potter, "C. Vann Woodward," pp. 375–77; Roper, "Woodward's Early Career," pp. 7–21.

24. Woodward, _Tom Watson_, pp. 52, 56, 66, 73, 67, 129–31, 86.

25. Ibid., pp. 117, 119; B. Mitchell, _Rise of Cotton Mills_, pp. 102–3, 104, 132.

26. Woodward, _Tom Watson_, pp. 135–39, 143–44, 217, 219–22, 276. Woodward still maintains this view of the Populists and race; see _Strange Career_, p. 64.

27. Woodward, _Tom Watson_, pp. [ii], 330–31, 401–2, 418–19.

28. Ibid., p. [ii]; Vance, "Rebels and Agrarians," p. 42.

29. Woodward, _South in Search_, p. 11. See also Lumpkin, _South in Progress_, p. 138 (and pp. 34 and 205); Collier, "Heritage of Defeat," p. 22; Hall, "What Tom Watson," p. 13; Kennedy, _Southern Exposure_, p. 47.

30. Milton, _Chattanooga News_, 29 Sept. 1937, p. 4; Woodward, _Tom Watson_, p. 65. See also McGill, _Atlanta Constitution_, 14 Dec. 1939, p. 24; _Richmond Times-Dispatch_, 6 Feb. 1938, 4:2; Johnson, _Baltimore Evening Sun_, 9 Jan. 1936, p. 19; Hall, _Atlanta Constitution_, 2 Feb. 1936, p. 7B. In _Angry Scar_, Carter grafted Woodward's account of the years after 1877 onto a traditional interpretation of Reconstruction, which, Carter said, southerners remembered "as a nightmare is remembered" (p. 387). The political conflicts of the 1890s, then, merely ratified the heritage of Reconstruction.

31. Beale, "On Rewriting," p. 826. Beale followed Woodward's account faithfully in his discussion of Georgia (pp. 815, 817–18). Jonathan Daniels did revise his view of Reconstruction but, in doing so, merely reversed his judgment. That is, where Milton and others claimed that had Radical Reconstruction not occurred, the modern South would have been more liberal, Daniels believed that had Radical Reconstruction succeeded, the modern South would be more liberal. Woodward, however, rejected this idea. He praised the Populists for regarding the Negro "neither as the incompetent ward of White Supremacy, nor as the ward of military intervention, but as an integral part of Southern society with a place in its economy" (Daniels, *Tar Heels*, pp. 125–26, 336; Woodward, *Tom Watson*, p. 221).

32. Cash, *Mind of the South*, pp. 46, 93–94.

33. Ibid., pp. 162, 165, 175. In his account of the textile industry's rise, Cash followed Broadus Mitchell's interpretation (pp. 180, 175–83 *passim*).

34. Ibid., pp. 429–35, 439.

35. See, for example, Daniels, "Letter to Yankees," *Raleigh News & Observer*, 22 Mar. 1936, reprinted in Miller, *Southern Press*, pp. 3, 9. See also Daniels, *Southerner Discovers*, pp. 330–33; Eagles, *Jonathan Daniels*, pp. 19, 78–79. Johnson endorsed Daniels's "Letter" in the *Baltimore Evening Sun*, 26 Mar. 1936, p. 23.

36. G. W. Johnson, "Vinegar Tree," p. 338. Similarly, in *The Angry Scar*, Hodding Carter contended that Watson's career "exemplified the frustration of Southern liberalism because of the racial dilemma" (p. 366).

37. McGill, *Atlanta Constitution*, 7 July 1938, p. 6; 19 Mar. 1939, p. 2K; 18 Aug. 1938, p. 12.

38. Patterson, *Congressional Conservatism*, pp. 211–49.

39. Davis, "South as Economic Problem," pp. 119–21; National Emergency Council, *Report on Economic Conditions*, p. 1.

40. Mertz, *New Deal Policy*, pp. 235–36.

41. Daniels, *Greenville Delta Democrat-Times*, 25 Sept. 1938, 2:1; Cash, "South Hides Its Eyes," *Charlotte News*, 2 Oct. 1938, reprinted in Morrison, *W. J. Cash*, pp. 244–45. Cash praised the *Richmond Times-Dispatch*, the Norfolk papers, the *Montgomery Advertiser*, *Atlanta Constitution*, *Raleigh News & Observer*, *Charlotte News*, *Greensboro News*, *Chattanooga News*, "and a few others" (p. 243).

42. Patterson, *Congressional Conservatism*, pp. 277–80.

43. *Chattanooga News*, 12 Aug. 1938, p. 6. See also Jonathan Daniels to Josephus Daniels, undated [Sept. 1938?], Josephus Daniels Papers, Reel 20, Container 34.

44. McGill, *Atlanta Constitution*, 19 Aug. 1938, p. 7. See also Daniels, *Time Between the Wars*, p. 299; *Greenville Delta Democrat-Times*, 10 July 1938, p. 4.

45. *Richmond Times-Dispatch*, 20 June 1938, p. 8.

46. McGill, *Atlanta Constitution*, 5 Aug. 1938, p. 6; *Chattanooga News*, 7 Sept. 1937, p. 4.

47. G. W. Johnson, *Roosevelt*, p. 265; Milton, *Use of Presidential Power*, p. 283. See also *Richmond Times-Dispatch*, 16 Sept. 1938, p. 12.

48. Milton to Miss Rothschild, 3 May 1944, Milton Papers; Graves, *Atlanta Constitution*, 1 Dec. 1938, p. 11.

49. Louise O. Charlton and Luther Patrick to Francis Pickens Miller, 13 Aug. 1938, Miller Papers.

50. Krueger, *And Promises to Keep*, p. 22. A list of sponsors may also be seen in Miller Papers, Box 103. Among the sponsors from Florida was C. Vann Woodward.

51. Krueger, *And Promises to Keep*, pp. 24–25; Sosna, *Silent South*, pp. 90–91. See also Odum to Charles S. Johnson, 21 Sept. 1938, to H. C. Nixon, 8 Oct. 1938, and to Dr. A. R. Mann, 24 Oct. 1938, Odum Papers; and Nixon to Francis P. Miller, 16 Sept. and 19 Oct. 1938, National Policy Committee Papers, Box 3.

52. Krueger, *And Promises to Keep*, pp. 16–19; Miller, *Man from the Valley*, p. 151; Miller to Louise O. Charlton, 13 Sept. 1938, to the Chairman of the National Policy Committee, 29 Nov. 1938, and to Brooks Hays, 13 Sept. 1938, Miller Papers. On Nixon's and Couch's roles in organizing the SCHW, see Singal, *War Within*, pp. 291, 293n.

53. "Southern Conference for Human Welfare: Plans and Purposes," copy in Miller Papers, Box 103; Krueger, *And Promises to Keep*, p. 22.

54. *Chattanooga News*, 25 Nov. 1938, p. 4; Dabney to Miller, 2 Dec. 1938, Miller Papers. See also McGill to Miller, 28 Feb. 1939, National Policy Committee Papers, Box 4; Eagles, *Jonathan Daniels*, p. 72. On Black's nomination, see *Richmond Times-Dispatch*, 13 Aug. 1937, p. 12; *Chattanooga News*, 15 Sept. 1937, p. 4; *Richmond Times-Dispatch*, 15 Aug. 1937, 4:2; *Greenville Delta Star*, 3 Oct. 1937, p. 4; Graves, *Atlanta Constitution*, 24 Sept. 1937, p. 10. The reaction of the journalists may be compared to the opinion of Walter White, of the NAACP, who said that he viewed Black as "an advance guard of the New South we dreamed of," and supported his nomination (*Man Called White*, pp. 177–78).

55. Mason, "Southerners Look at South," p. 17; Lumpkin, *South in Progress*, p. 228. See also Couch, "Southerners Inspect South," p. 168; C. S. Johnson, "More Southerners Discover South," p. 14; Stoney, "Southerners Write Prescription," p. 42.

56. Davis, "South as Economic Problem," pp. 128–29. The SCHW "represented not so much the peak of the New Deal as the epilogue," observes Tindall, *Emergence*, p. 639.

57. Krueger, *And Promises to Keep*, pp. 29–31, 28.

58. Ibid., pp. 22–23; Painter, *Narrative of Hosea Hudson*, pp. 289–91. Francis Pickens Miller spotted a party member from Virginia among the delegates on Tuesday and immediately departed from Birmingham. He said afterward that the Communist policy of rule-or-ruin made cooperation with them impossible and the incident confirmed his worst suspicions about the people behind the SCHW. In addition, Miller had political ambitions and feared that association with the Communist party could ruin his career. Despite his early departure, Miller's political enemies during the McCarthy era made much of his supposed fellow-traveling at Birmingham (see Krueger, *And Promises to Keep*, p. 38; Dunbar, *Against the Grain*, pp. 191–95; Miller, *Man from the Valley*, pp. 151–52; Miller to Brooks Hays, 25 Nov. 1938, Miller Papers; Daniels to Odum, 20 Dec. 1938, Daniels Papers; Nixon to Graham, 17 Jan. 1939, Graham Papers). Singal, *War Within*, p. 293, contends that in the period after the Birmingham meeting, members of the Communist party did infiltrate the leadership of the SCHW, and he charges that they "managed to stop dead whatever momentum the SCHW might have achieved had it remained in liberal hands." Both the infiltration

and the lost "momentum," however, have their source in the initial, swift defection of the southern liberals.

59. Couch, "Southerners Inspect South," p. 169; Krueger, *And Promises to Keep*, pp. 29–30, 37–38. For the AP story, see "First Lady Strikes at Sectionalism," *Atlanta Constitution*, 23 Nov. 1938, p. 12. Stoney, "Southerners Write Prescription," noted that the SCHW lacked a press department and gave out no press releases, thus contributing to the unfavorable coverage (p. 42). Brooks Hays told Miller that "the public reaction, at least in Arkansas, is so unfavorable (in fact, explosive) that the only explanation which satisfies my *'political'* friends is that I was in New Orleans on Wednesday when the resolutions were passed" (to Miller, 3 Dec. 1938, Miller Papers). See also Hays, *Politics Is My Parish*, pp. 131–32; Johnson to Odum, 25 Nov. 1938, Odum Papers; James K. Feibleman to Roger Baldwin, 28 Nov. 1938, ACLU Archives, V. 2118, pp. 149–50; Graham to Dr. L. A. Crowell, Jr., 22 Dec. 1938, Graham Papers; Nixon to Daniels, Jan. [?] 1939, and Daniels to Nixon, 20 Jan. 1939, Daniels Papers.

60. Stoney, "Southerners Write Prescription," p. 42; Johnson, "More Southerners Discover South," p. 15. Stoney reported that enforcement of racial segregation changed the spirit of the conference: "In the sessions after that participants became increasingly race conscious. It was 'my people' and 'your people.' Negro speakers became concerned largely with the welfare of their race and white speakers made a special category for 'the black man' in their plans for southern improvement" (p. 42).

61. *Chattanooga News*, 25 Nov. 1938, p. 4; *Richmond Times-Dispatch*, 26 Nov. 1938, p. 8. See also *Greenville Delta Democrat-Times*, 28 Nov. 1938, p. 2; Graves, *Birmingham Age-Herald*, 24 Nov. 1938, p. 1; Eagles, *Jonathan Daniels*, pp. 72–73. Neither McGill nor Johnson commented on the SCHW.

62. *Chattanooga News*, 25 Nov. 1938, p. 4; Daniels, "Need to Eat," pp. 1, 4.

63. *Chattanooga News*, 25 Nov. 1938, p. 5.

64. Tindall, *Emergence*, pp. 561–62; Kluger, *Simple Justice*, pp. 134–37, 212–13.

65. G. B. Johnson, "Patterns of Racial Conflict," pp. 147, 150–51.

66. On the *Gaines* decision, see *Greenville Delta Democrat-Times*, 28 Nov. 1938, p. 2; *Richmond Times-Dispatch*, 13 Dec. 1938, p. 8; Eagles, *Jonathan Daniels*, pp. 68–69; Odum to Thomas Cooper, 24 Jan. 1939, Odum Papers; Daniels to James E. Shepard, 25 Jan. 1939, Daniels Papers; Couch, "Negroes and the University," 21 Feb. 1939, Couch Papers, Box 1, Folder 10.

67. Miller, *Man from the Valley*, p. 151; Odum to Ethridge, 3 Nov. 1938, Ethridge Papers; Ethridge to Odum, 10 Dec. 1938, Odum Papers; Barry Bingham to Miller, 28 Nov. 1938, Miller to H. C. Nixon, 5 Dec. 1938, and Miller to Nixon, 10 Dec. 1938, National Policy Committee Papers, Box 3; Miller to Chairman of the National Policy Committee, 29 Nov. 1938, Miller Papers; Odum to Daniels, 12 Dec. 1938, Daniels Papers.

68. *Atlanta Constitution*, 16 Jan. 1939, pp. 1, 2. The other eleven signers included five from politics or law, four from labor unions, one businessman, and Josephine Wilkins of the Georgia Citizens Fact-Finding Committee. Dabney, McGill, and Julian Harris were among the journalists present.

69. Ibid., p. 2.

70. Ellis (unpub.), "Commission on Interracial Cooperation," pp. 338–39; O'Brien, *American South*, pp. 73–79.

Chapter 10

1. Graves, *Fighting South*, pp. 8, 12–15. Graves requested these opinions before Pearl Harbor. See, for example, Graves to Ethridge, 1 Oct. 1941, Ethridge Papers. For public opinion polls on foreign policy issues during the prewar period, see Hero, *Southerner and World Affairs*, pp. 91–103.

2. Ibid., pp. 17, 8, 9.

3. Dabney, *Richmond Times-Dispatch*, 6 July 1930, 3:2; 3 May 1931, 2:2.

4. Johnson, *Baltimore Evening Sun*, 29 June 1933, p. 23; *Chattanooga News*, 11 Nov. 1931, p. 4.

5. Dabney, *Richmond Times-Dispatch*, 23 Apr. 1933, 3:2; Dabney, *Across the Years*, p. 123. Other southern liberal journalists who received Oberlaender grants included Julian Harris (1931) and Mark Ethridge (1933).

6. Dabney to Jaffé, 7 Oct. 1934, Jaffé Papers; *Richmond Times-Dispatch*, 30 Sept. 1934, pp. 1, 18, 1 Oct., p. 4, and 2 Oct., p. 4. On his return to Richmond, Dabney became the chief editorial writer for the *Times-Dispatch* with the promise of becoming editor.

7. *Chattanooga News*, 9 Oct. 1933, p. 4. See also *Chattanooga News*, 29 June 1933, p. 4; Johnson, *Baltimore Evening Sun*, 16 Apr. 1933, p. 33, and 27 July, p. 21; Dabney, *Richmond Times-Dispatch*, 19 Aug. 1934, 3:2; Carter, *Hammond Courier*, 25 Mar. 1933, p. 2, and 9 July 1934, p. 2; Ethridge to Harry S. Strozier, 30 Mar. 1933, Ethridge Papers.

8. Johnson, *Baltimore Evening Sun*, 5 Oct. 1933, p. 29; Dabney, *Richmond Times-Dispatch*, 30 Sept. 1934, p. 18; *Chattanooga News*, 7 Aug. 1933, p. 4. Not surprisingly, Hodding Carter saw parallels between his enemy, Huey Long, and the German dictator. "Today seems to be the age of the rabble-rousing dictator, who preys upon the prejudices, the hatreds and the cupidity of men," he said in 1934 (*Hammond Courier*, 3 Aug. 1934, p. 2. See also 10 July 1934, p. 1, 16 Aug., p. 1, and 20 Aug., p. 1; and 3 Aug. 1935, p. 4).

9. *Chattanooga News*, 30 Oct. 1933, p. 4.

10. Johnson, *Baltimore Evening Sun*, 6 Apr. 1933, p. 33, and 5 Oct., p. 29 (see also 27 July 1933, p. 21); *Chattanooga News*, 2 July 1934, p. 4. See also *Chattanooga News*, 16 July 1934, p. 4, 22 Aug., p. 4, and 12 Sept., p. 4; Dabney, *Richmond Times-Dispatch*, 2 Oct. 1934, p. 9, and 11 Nov. 1936, p. 10; *Hammond Courier*, 27 July 1934, p. 2.

11. *Chattanooga News*, 26 Sept. 1935, p. 4; G. W. Johnson, *America's Silver Age*, p. 149. See also *Chattanooga News*, 10 May 1935, p. 4.

12. *Hammond Courier*, 28 Feb. 1934, p. 2; Johnson, *Baltimore Evening Sun*, 10 Sept. 1936, p. 25. See also *Chattanooga News*, 23 Mar. 1935, p. 4, and 4 Dec. 1936, p. 4; Johnson, *Baltimore Evening Sun*, 12 Dec. 1935, p. 31; *Richmond Times-Dispatch*, 3 June 1937, p. 8, and 26 May 1938, p. 12.

13. *Richmond Times-Dispatch*, 12 May 1937, p. 12; *Chattanooga News*, 2 Aug. 1936, p. 4.

14. Milton, "The South Do Move," p. 141; Graves, *Atlanta Constitution*, 27 Oct. 1937, p. 7. See also Johnson, *Baltimore Evening Sun*, 13 Jan. 1938, p. 21; McGill, *Atlanta Constitution*, 27 May 1938, p. 11.

15. Odum, *Southern Regions*, pp. 253, 259; Milton, "Trade Barriers," p. 46. During the 1930s, the common concept of the South as an economic "colony" to the Northeast contributed to the linkage between the situation of the South and world affairs. For example, John Temple Graves offered a revealing definition of these terms: "Colonialism, in the unhappy sense of the word, is the removal of a land's natural wealth without regard to what becomes of that land and its people. Regionalism, on the other hand, is the development of a land's natural wealth in a way that preserves and increases it to great benefit of its people" (*Atlanta Constitution*, 24 June 1937, p. 9).

16. See, for example, Johnson, *Baltimore Evening Sun*, 5 Oct. 1933, p. 29, 15 Feb. 1934, p. 21, 24 Sept. 1936, p. 25, 11 Mar. 1937, p. 25, and 12 May 1938, p. 23; *Chattanooga News*, 5 Mar. 1934, p. 4, and 10 June 1935, p. 4; *Hammond Courier*, 3 Apr. 1936, p. 2; McGill, *Atlanta Constitution*, 27 Feb. 1938, p. 4A, and 23 Sept. 1938, p. 8.

17. Johnson, *Baltimore Evening Sun*, 13 June 1935, p. 25; *Chattanooga News*, 23 Jan. 1934, p. 4.

18. Johnson, *Baltimore Evening Sun*, 1 Oct. 1936, p. 27.

19. See, for example, Dabney, *Richmond Times-Dispatch*, 19 Aug. 1934, 3:2; *Chattanooga News*, 29 June 1933, p. 4, 4 Dec. 1933, p. 4, and 15 Sept. 1937, p. 4; McGill, *Atlanta Constitution*, 30 July 1938, p. 4; Johnson, *Baltimore Evening Sun*, 28 Oct. 1937, p. 33; Graves, *Atlanta Constitution*, 17 Jan. 1939, p. 9, and 24 Mar. 1939, p. 10.

20. *Chattanooga News*, 6 Dec. 1938, p. 4.

21. Ellis (unpub.), "Commission on Interracial Cooperation," pp. 380–81.

22. *Chattanooga News*, 4 Dec. 1936, p. 4; Johnson, *Baltimore Evening Sun*, 24 Sept. 1936, p. 25. On the Spanish Civil War, see also *Richmond Times-Dispatch*, 31 Dec. 1936, p. 8, and 2 May 1937, 4:2; Johnson, *Baltimore Evening Sun*, 13 Aug. 1936, p. 23.

23. Johnson, *Baltimore Evening Sun*, 11 Mar. 1937, p. 25, 18 Mar., p. 25, and 21 Oct., p. 27.

24. *Greenville Delta Star*, 14 Dec. 1937, p. 4; McGill, *Atlanta Constitution*, 12 Apr. 1938, p. 5; Graves, *Atlanta Constitution*, 24 Mar. 1938, p. 6; *Richmond Times-Dispatch*, 24 July 1938, 4:2; *Chattanooga News*, 18 Aug. 1938, p. 6.

25. Johnson, *Baltimore Evening Sun*, 15 May 1937, p. 6; *Richmond Times-Dispatch*, 3 Oct. 1938, p. 6. See also *Chattanooga News*, 4 Aug. 1937, p. 4.

26. Graves, *Atlanta Constitution*, 24 July 1938, p. 4. Graves at first viewed Munich as a victory over Hitler. See *Atlanta Constitution*, 4 Oct. 1938, p. 5, 6 Oct., p. 7, and 8 Oct., p. 7.

27. *Richmond Times-Dispatch*, 1 Oct. 1938, p. 10; Johnson, *Baltimore Evening Sun*, 22 Sept. 1938, p. 2. See also *Chattanooga News*, 19 Sept. 1938, p. 4; *Greenville*

Delta Democrat-Times, 14 Nov. 1938, p. 2; McGill, *Atlanta Constitution*, 13 Sept. 1938, p. 6.

28. McGill, *Atlanta Constitution*, 28 Aug. 1939, p. 4; *Richmond Times-Dispatch*, 22 Aug. 1939, p. 10. See also *Greenville Delta Democrat-Times*, 17 May 1939, p. 2; *Chattanooga News*, 30 Aug. 1939, p. 4; Johnson, *Baltimore Evening Sun*, 24 Aug. 1939, p. 27.

29. *Richmond Times-Dispatch*, 14 Dec. 1939, p. 10; McGill, *Atlanta Constitution*, 28 Jan. 1940, p. 4B, 14 Mar., p. 6, 11 May, p. 4, and 13 May, p. 4; *Richmond Times-Dispatch*, 5 Dec. 1940, p. 12, and 24 Feb. 1941, p. 6.

30. *Chattanooga News*, 28 Oct. 1938, p. 4, 31 Oct., p. 4, 1 Dec., p. 4, and 8 Feb. 1939, p. 1. See also 7 Sept. 1939, p. 4, and 9 Sept. 1939, p. 4.

31. Ibid., 16 Oct. 1939, p. 4.

32. Johnson, *Baltimore Evening Sun*, 20 Oct. 1938, p. 27, and 9 Feb. 1939, p. 23; Daniels, "A Native at Large," *The Nation*, 8 Mar. 1941, p. 271 (Daniels wrote a weekly column, "A Native at Large," for *The Nation* between 10 Aug. 1940 and 21 Feb. 1942). See also McGill, *Atlanta Constitution*, 13 May 1940, p. 4, and 24 May, p. 8; *Greenville Delta Democrat-Times*, 20 Nov. 1938, p. 2.

33. Johnson, *Baltimore Evening Sun*, 18 Apr. 1940, p. 31, and 19 Sept., p. 31; *Richmond Times-Dispatch*, 16 Dec. 1940, p. 8; Daniels, "A Native at Large," *The Nation*, 20 Dec. 1941, p. 643; Johnson, *Baltimore Evening Sun*, 20 Aug. 1942, p. 23.

34. *Chattanooga Evening Tribune*, 20 May 1940, p. 4; Johnson, *Baltimore Evening Sun*, 7 May 1942, p. 29.

35. *Chattanooga Evening Tribune*, 16 May 1940, p. 4; Johnson, *Baltimore Evening Sun*, 2 Oct. 1941, p. 29. See also McGill, *Atlanta Constitution*, 15 June 1942, p. 4.

36. *Chattanooga Evening Tribune*, 17 June 1940, p. 4; Johnson, *Baltimore Evening Sun*, 26 June 1941, p. 29, and 3 July, p. 11. See also *Richmond Times-Dispatch*, 9 Dec. 1940, p. 8; McGill, *Atlanta Constitution*, 8 Dec. 1941, p. 8; *Greenville Delta Democrat-Times*, 27 Oct. 1940, p. 2.

37. Graves, *Atlanta Constitution*, 15 May 1937, p. 9; De Voto, "Easy Chair," Mar. 1946, p. 237, and Feb. 1946, pp. 125, 126.

38. Schlesinger, "Causes of the Civil War," pp. 976, 976–77, 978, 979. Schlesinger and De Voto concentrated their attack on the work of James G. Randall, a professional historian, and neither mentioned the histories by Johnson and Milton. Both critics, however, did describe Stephen A. Douglas, whom Schlesinger said "always thought that the great moral problems could be solved by moral sleight-of-hand" (p. 978), as the "hero" of the revisionist historians (De Voto, "Easy Chair," p. 274).

39. Schlesinger, "Causes of the Civil War," p. 979.

40. Johnson, *Baltimore Evening Sun*, 16 Jan. 1941, p. 25, and 23 Jan., p. 25.

41. Milton to Nicholas Wreden, 7 May 1942, Milton Papers; Milton, *Abraham Lincoln*, pp. 175, 212; Milton to John H. Cramer, 3 Sept. 1942, Milton Papers.

42. In his *In Search of the Silent South*, Morton Sosna observes that before 1954, Virginius Dabney and Ralph McGill expressed similar opinions on the issue of segregation, yet once the Civil Rights movement began they moved in diametrically different directions. Sosna perceives a strong religious element in McGill's writing that

was absent in Dabney's. "Is it possible that the differing attitudes of the two men toward religion accounted for their dissimilar reaction on this most difficult issue for liberals to confront?" Sosna asks. "At any rate," he continues, "it can be said that the white Southern liberals who eventually adopted antisegregationist outlooks were more often than not the ones who exhibited a strong evangelical orientation" (p. 174).

When Sosna identifies McGill and Hodding Carter with evangelical religion, he reads their editorials too literally. In fact, they expressed an ethical liberalism that invested high morality in democracy and the American way. Out of the crusade against Nazism, then reinforced by the Cold War struggle against communism, Carter and McGill advocated not a specifically religious creed but rather, the "American creed" of postwar liberalism.

43. Gaskill, "Newspaper Is Killed," pp. 81–82. See also Milton to William Gibbs McAdoo, 21 Aug. 1939, Milton Papers; J. H. Jones, *Fifty Billion Dollars*, p. 233; Lilienthal, *Journals*, 1 : 153–54.

44. *Chattanooga News*, 16 Dec. 1939, p. 1.

45. *New York Times*, 28 Dec. 1939, p. 19; Gaskill, "Newspaper Is Killed," p. 82; Milton to Homer S. Cummings, 6 Jan. 1940, Cummings Papers; *Chattanooga Evening Tribune*, 25 Mar. 1940, pp. 4, 1; *New York Times*, 26 Mar. 1940, p. 19.

46. *Chattanooga Evening Tribune*, 11 Apr. 1940, p. 4, 5 June, p. 4, 17 June, p. 4.

47. *Chattanooga News*, 10 June 1939, p. 4; *Chattanooga Evening Tribune*, 28 Mar. 1940, p. 4, 15 Apr., p. 4, 17 Apr., p. 4. See also Krueger, *And Promises To Keep*, pp. 53–64. At this meeting, the SCHW made no challenge to segregation and the resolutions instead indicated a desire, Krueger says, "to refurbish Jim Crow's cage until it resembled the white dove's aviary" (p. 58).

48. *Chattanooga Evening Tribune*, 30 Aug. 1940, p. 4. The demise of the *News* became a minor campaign issue that year. Willkie had been the president of the Commonwealth and Southern Corporation, the holding company that controlled the Tennessee Electric Power Company, and Democratic party spokesmen assailed him for TEPCO's subsidies to the *Free Press* (*New York Times*, 24 Sept. 1940, p. 15, 3 Oct., p. 22, and 5 Oct., p. 27).

49. *New York Times*, 5 Sept. 1940, p. 48; Milton to Carl Cartinhour, 15 Jan. 1941, Milton Papers; Milton, *Conflict*; Milton to James Henle, 27 Nov. 1941, and to Porter Warner, 20 Feb. 1942, Milton Papers.

50. Carter, *Where Main Street*, pp. 108–14; *Greenville Delta Democrat-Times*, 16 Jan. 1940, p. 2, and 17 May, p. 1. On *PM*'s short existence, see Kobre, *Development of American Journalism*, pp. 612–14. While in New York, Carter also obtained the contract to write his first book, *Lower Mississippi*.

51. Carter, *Where Main Street*, pp. 115, 117–19, 122–23; *Greenville Delta Democrat-Times*, 3 Oct. 1940, p. 2, and 9 Oct., p. 6.

52. *Greenville Delta Democrat-Times*, 10 Nov. 1938, p. 4.

53. Ibid., 13 Oct. 1940, p. 2, 20 Oct., p. 4, 18 Nov., p. 2.

54. Ibid., 24 Nov. 1940, p. 2; Carter, *Where Main Street*, p. 134; *Greenville Delta Democrat-Times*, 19 Dec. 1941, p. 1.

55. Carter, *Where Main Street*, pp. 147–74, 161; *Greenville Delta Democrat-Times*, 16 Aug. 1945, p. 4.

56. On the controversy, see Anderson, *Wild Man*, pp. 196–201; McGill, "It Has Happened Here," pp. 449–51.

57. *Richmond Times-Dispatch*, 15 July 1941, p. 8; Daniels, "Native At Large," *The Nation*, 2 Aug. 1941, pp. 93–94; McGill, *Atlanta Constitution*, 22 June 1941, p. 10A.

58. Arnall, *Shore Dimly Seen*, p. 42; Martin, *Ralph McGill*, p. 80; McGill, *Atlanta Constitution*, 22 Apr. 1942, p. 6.

59. McGill, *Atlanta Constitution*, 4 July 1942, p. 4, and 12 July, p. 4B.

60. Ibid., 22 July 1942, p. 4.

61. Ibid., 9 Sept. 1942, p. 6.

62. *Richmond Times-Dispatch*, 11 Sept. 1942, p. 2; McGill, *Atlanta Constitution*, 11 Sept. 1942, p. 8.

63. McGill, *Atlanta Constitution*, 28 Nov. 1943, p. 6D.

64. Daniels, "Native At Large," *The Nation*, 27 Dec. 1941, p. 670.

Chapter 11

1. Ruth E. Campbell to Milton, 16 Jan. 1942, and Milton to Campbell, 21 Jan. and 24 Jan. 1942, Milton Papers.

2. "Georgia Folklore," p. 23; Daniels, "Native At Large," *The Nation*, 2 Aug. 1941, p. 93; *Richmond Times-Dispatch*, 26 June 1941, p. 10; McGill, *Atlanta Constitution*, 13 Oct. 1941, p. 4; "Georgia Folklore," p. 23.

3. Dalfiume, "'Forgotten Years,'" pp. 92–95; Sitkoff, *New Deal for Blacks*, pp. 298–302.

4. Garfinkel, *When Negroes March*, pp. 37–61; Sitkoff, *New Deal for Blacks*, pp. 314–23.

5. *Richmond Times-Dispatch*, 13 Apr. 1941, p. 6, and 9 Jan. 1942, p. 12; Johnson, *Baltimore Evening Sun*, 29 Jan. 1942, p. 25, and 18 Sept. 1941, p. 31. See also *Richmond Times-Dispatch*, 17 Dec. 1940, p. 8, 18 Jan. 1941, p. 6, 10 Nov. 1941, p. 10, 14 Apr. 1942, p. 8; Jonathan Daniels, "Native At Large," *The Nation*, 8 Feb. 1941, p. 158; Johnson, *Baltimore Evening Sun*, 13 Mar. 1942, p. 31; McGill, *Atlanta Constitution*, 6 Aug. 1940, p. 4.

6. *Greenville Delta Democrat-Times*, 30 June 1941, p. 2. Years later, Jonathan Daniels repeated the charge in his *Time Between the Wars*, p. 326.

7. Mark Ethridge, "Fairness Based on Reason, Not Emotion, Is Racial Problem's Need," *Louisville Courier-Journal*, 21 June 1942, 3:3; Graves, *Fighting South*, p. 120; Dabney, "Nearer and Nearer," p. 100.

8. White, "Decline of Southern Liberals," p. 43; Sancton, "Trouble in Dixie," p. 14; Smith, "Are We Not Confused?" pp. 31–32, 33; Smith, "Buying a New World," p. 24. See also Cy W. Record, "What's Happened to the 'Southern Liberals,'" *New Leader*, 3 July 1943, p. 5.

9. Myrdal, *American Dilemma*, pp. 466–73, 844, 849. Howard Odum read a draft of Myrdal's discussion of the CIC and objected strongly to his conclusions (Odum to Myrdal, 7 Aug. 1942, Odum Papers).

10. Myrdal, *American Dilemma*, pp. 691–92. See also pp. 1049–50.

11. Ibid., pp. xliv, 461n, xliii, xiv, 1015. Southern, in *"American Dilemma* Revisited," has argued that southern liberals wisely viewed Myrdal's optimistic conclusions with "skepticism" (p. 184). Because he assumes that these men "could have easily acquiesced in an integrated society" (p. 187), Southern exaggerates their prescience and downplays their fears.

12. In regard to the war's influence on Myrdal's argument, see his final chapter, "America Again At The Crossroads," pp. 907–1024. For recent assessments of *An American Dilemma*, see Lyman, *Black American*, pp. 110–19; Wacker, "American Dilemma," pp. 117–25; Matthews, *Quest for American Sociology*, pp. 184–89; Banton, *Idea of Race*, pp. 126–28.

13. Finkle, *Forum for Protest*, pp. 63, 79; McGill, *Atlanta Constitution*, 24 Oct. 1942, p. 4.

14. McGill, *Atlanta Constitution*, 24 Oct. 1942, p. 4.

15. *Richmond Times-Dispatch*, 24 Aug. 1942, p. 6; Finkle, *Forum for Protest*, p. 72; Graves, "Southern Negro," p. 510.

16. Singal, *War Within*, pp. 296–301; Couch to Rayford W. Logan, 9 Nov. and 14 Dec. 1943, Logan to Couch, 18 Dec. 1943, Couch to Dabney, 20 Dec. 1943, and Dabney to Couch, 10 Jan. 1944, in "Logan, R. W. (ed.) What The Negro Wants" files, University of North Carolina Press Records. See also Logan, "Introduction to the Reprint," *What the Negro Wants*, pp. 2–3; and Langston Hughes to Arna Bontemps, 6 Jan. 1944, in Bontemps, *Bontemps–Hughes Letters*, pp. 150–51.

17. Couch, "Publisher's Introduction," in Logan, *What The Negro Wants*, pp. ix–xxiii; Dabney to Couch, 26 Feb. 1944, Ethridge to Couch, 11 Apr. 1944, and Johnson to Couch, 9 Oct. 1944, "Logan, R. W. (ed.), What the Negro Wants" files, University of North Carolina Press Records.

18. Gavins, *Perils and Prospects*, pp. 118–19; Dykeman and Stokely, *Seeds of Southern Change*, pp. 249, 272–73, 279; J. D. Hall, *Revolt Against Chivalry*, p. 257.

19. "Times Have Changed and So Have Southern Negroes," *Southern Frontier*, May 1941, p. 2; Daniels, "Negro Leadership Moves North"; Gavins, *Perils and Prospects*, pp. 117–18.

20. "Remember the 18th Amendment," *Southern Frontier*, Apr. 1942, p. 2; "Mark Ethridge Speaks," ibid., July 1942, p. 1. On Ames's motives, see Hall, *Revolt Against Chivalry*, pp. 256–60; Gavins, *Perils and Prospects*, pp. 118–19.

21. Gavins, *Perils and Prospects*, p. 119; P. B. Young, "No Armistice."

22. Gavins, *Perils and Prospects*, pp. 121–22; *Baltimore Afro-American*, 1 Aug. 1942, pp. 1, 4.

23. Jessie Daniel Ames to Dabney, 26 May 1942, and Ames to Gordon Hancock, 24 July 1942 (copy), Dabney Papers.

24. Mays, *Born to Rebel*, p. 219; Gavins, *Perils and Prospects*, pp. 124–25. The text of the Durham statement appears in Odum, *Race and Rumors*, pp. 185–95; the quotation is from p. 186.

25. *Richmond Times-Dispatch*, 17 Dec. 1942, p. 10; McGill, *Atlanta Constitution*, 18 Dec. 1942, p. 8.

26. Ames to Dabney, 10 Feb. 1943, and Dabney to Ames, 25 Mar. 1943, Dabney Papers; Gavins, *Perils and Prospects*, p. 138; *Southern Frontier*, Apr. 1943, p. 3.

27. Hancock, "Writing 'New Charter,'" p. 20; "Resolutions of Collaboration Committee," reprinted in *New South*, 19 (Jan. 1964), pp. 16–17.

28. Odum to Jackson Davis, 8 Jan. 1943, and to William C. Cole, 15 Apr. 1943, Odum Papers; Ames to Hancock, 1 July 1943 (copy), Dabney Papers; Odum to Cole, 25 June 1943, Odum Papers.

29. Dabney to Jonathan Daniels, 24 and 30 July 1943, to Charles S. Johnson, 30 July 1943, and to Ames, 3 July 1943, and Ames to Dabney, 12 July 1943, Dabney Papers.

30. *Southern Frontier*, Aug. 1943, p. 3, Sept. 1943, p. 2, Mar. 1944, p. 1, Feb. 1944, p. 2.

31. Redding, "Southern Defensive—I," pp. 39–40; Smith, "Southern Defensive—II," pp. 44–45.

32. McGill, *Atlanta Constitution*, 17 Feb. 1944, p. 16; Lillian Smith to Guy B. Johnson, 12 June 1944, copy in ACLU Archives, V. 2597, pp. 151–54.

33. G. B. Johnson, "Southern Offensive," p. 91. On Johnson's views, see also Singal, *War Within*, pp. 324–27.

34. Tindall, "Howard W. Odum," pp. 90–91. For Graves's views, see, for example, Graves, "Chance-Taking South," p. 168.

35. C. S. Johnson, "Present Status," p. 29.

36. Graves to Charlotte Kohler, 31 Jan. 1950, *Virginia Quarterly Review* Papers. See also Graves, "Revolution in South," pp. 199–200.

37. *Richmond Times-Dispatch*, 10 Nov. 1941, p. 10, 9 Jan. 1942, p. 12, 14 Apr. 1942, p. 8; Dabney to Lillian E. Smith, 20 Aug. 1942, and to Beverley D. Tucker, 29 July 1942, Dabney Papers; Dabney, *Below the Potomac*, pp. 220–23; Dabney, "Negro and Schooling," pp. 459–68; Dabney to Major Osmond T. Jamerson, 4 Aug. 1942, and to Phillis Judau, 22 May 1942, Dabney Papers.

38. Dabney interview, 16 Aug. 1982; Dabney to Edward Weeks, 21 Oct. 1942, Dabney Papers; Dabney, "Nearer and Nearer," pp. 94, 100.

39. Dabney to P. B. Young, 14 Jan. and 21 Jan. 1943, and to Fletcher P. Martin, 16 Jan. 1943, Dabney Papers.

40. *Richmond Times-Dispatch*, 13 Nov. 1943, p. 4, and 21 Nov., 4:2. The second editorial is reprinted in Dabney's autobiography, *Across the Years*, pp. 391–96.

41. On the criticism, see Dabney to Park Rouse, Jr., 10 Nov. 1942, and to Gordon Hancock, 3 Aug. 1942, Dabney Papers. In connection with the Southern Regional Council, see Dabney to Daniels, 30 July 1943, Dabney Papers.

42. Gavins, *Perils and Prospects*, pp. 147–48; *Richmond Times-Dispatch*, 27 Nov. 1943, p. 6; Dabney to Allen J. Saville, 4 Dec. 1943, Dabney Papers.

43. *Richmond Times-Dispatch*, 9 Dec. 1943, p. 10 (24 black letter-writers also backed his proposal), and 30 Nov. 1943, p. 8; Graves, "Chance-Taking South," p. 168. Dabney pointed out Graves's inaccuracy to the *Quarterly*'s editor, but said that he "did not attach great importance to his error" (to Charlotte Kohler, 6 Apr. 1945, *Virginia Quarterly Review* Papers).

44. Dabney, *Below the Potomac*, p. 224.

45. Ellis (unpub.), "Commission on Interracial Cooperation," pp. 380–81.

46. Armstrong (unpub.), "Study of Attempt," p. 59; Dabney, *Across the Years*, pp. 164–65; *Richmond Times-Dispatch*, 23 Jan. 1944, p. 2D.

47. Dabney to Lee Morris, 11 Feb. 1944, and to P. B. Young, 29 Nov. 1943, Dabney Papers.

48. Dabney, *Below the Potomac*, pp. 217–18.

49. Dabney to George Watts Hill, 3 May 1945, and to Guy B. Johnson, 11 May 1945, Dabney Papers; Gavins, *Perils and Prospects*, pp. 155–56; Dabney to Jenkins L. Jones, 29 Jan. 1948, and to Irving Dillard, 16 Feb. 1948, Dabney Papers. See also Miller, *Man From the Valley*, pp. 171–72.

50. Finkle, *Forum for Protest*, pp. 9–10; Eagles, *Jonathan Daniels*, p. 119; Gavins, *Perils and Prospects*, pp. 103–4. Both Harvard Sitkoff, in "Racial Militancy and Inter-racial Violence," and Lee Finkle, in "Conservative Aims of Militant Rhetoric," have argued that the Negro protest actually had little effect and dissipated soon after. Thus, they contend, historians should not treat it as the beginning to the Civil Rights movement. These arguments indicate that the significance of the wartime protest is to be found in the changes that occurred in racial liberalism as a result.

Epilogue

1. Dabney, *Across the Years*, pp. 202–3; Hohenberg, *Pulitzer Prizes*, p. 196. On Byrd, see Dabney to James C. Derieux, 14 Jan. 1948, Dabney Papers; Dabney, "What We Think," pp. 30–31, 92–94. Jonathan Daniels spoke to the Richmond Forum on 8 January 1951 and, with Dabney seated on the stage next to him, declared, "I am sure that he would maintain that I have as much right to my opinions as he does to Harry Byrd's" (Daniels, speech, "Have the New Deal and Fair Deal Helped or Hurt America?" copy in Miller Papers, 9760, Box 51).

2. Carter, "Chip on Shoulder," pp. 145–46; "Civil Rights Issue," p. 53; "New Rebel Yell," pp. 13, 15.

3. Sitkoff, *Struggle for Black Equality*, pp. 12–19. On the analogy to the Civil War era, see, for example, Dabney, "Is South That Bad?" pp. 87–88; Carter, "Chip on Shoulder," pp. 18–19; McGill, "Can We Solve," pp. 1–2.

4. Carter, *Greenville Delta Democrat-Times*, 7 Nov. 1948, p. 4; Carter, "Chip on Shoulder," p. 19.

5. McGill, "Civil Rights," p. 64. On Truman's proposals, see, for example, Carter, "Civil Rights Issue," p. 15; Ashmore, "Plea for Affirmative Action," *Greenville Delta Democrat-Times*, 14 Mar. 1948, p. 4 (Ashmore gained prominence as a southern liberal spokesman after becoming editor of the *Little Rock Arkansas Gazette* in 1947). Jonathan Daniels defended Truman by arguing that he actually favored no more than vertical segregation (Eagles, *Jonathan Daniels*, p. 139). On the Dixiecrats, see Carter, "Southern Liberal," p. 10; Carter and Ashmore, "What Should We Do," p. 11; Dabney to J. Strom Thurmond, 17 Sept. 1948, Dabney Papers. On a "two-party" South, see Carter, *Greenville Delta Democrat-Times*, 26 Sept. 1950, p. 4; McGill, "What Are Real Campaign Issues?" pp. 4, 6.

6. Daniels, *Man of Independence*, p. 336; Carter, *Greenville Delta Democrat-Times*, 13 Aug. 1950, p. 4.

7. Carter, *Greenville Delta Democrat-Times*, 20 Oct. 1948, p. 4; Carter and Graves, "Change of Administration," pp. 7–8; Dabney to James P. C. Southall, 3 Nov. 1948,

Dabney Papers; *Richmond Times-Dispatch*, 2 Nov. 1952, p. 2B; McGill, *Atlanta Constitution*, 2 Sept. 1947, p. 10, and 15 Nov. 1947, p. 4 (under the threat of a libel suit, McGill retracted his charges on 30 Jan. 1948, p. 8); McGill, "Can He Purge," p. 32; Ashby, *Frank Porter Graham*, pp. 256–71; Eagles, *Jonathan Daniels*, pp. 147–53. On the turn away from "Popular Front Liberalism," see Hamby, *Beyond New Deal*, pp. 148–68 and *passim*.

8. *Richmond Times-Dispatch*, 6 Feb. 1948, p. 6, 28 Apr. 1948, p. 12, 24 Sept. 1949, p. 6, 2 May 1954, p. 2B; G. W. Johnson: "Liberal of 1946," pp. 154–59, "Devil Is Dead," pp. 395–403, and "Villains," pp. 221–28. These essays are reprinted in Johnson, *America-Watching*.

9. *Greenville Delta Democrat-Times*, 14 Mar. 1946, p. 4, and 9 Sept. 1951, p. 4 (see also 20 May 1946, p. 4, 26 Jan. 1947, p. 4, 11 Nov. 1948, p. 4, 31 May 1949, p. 4, 25 May 1952, p. 4, and 7 June 1953, p. 4); McGill, speech, Daytona Beach Open Forum, 3 Jan. 1954, in Logue, *Ralph McGill*, 2:50 (see also McGill, *Fleas Come With Dog*, p. 120). On the censorship, see Logue, *Ralph McGill*, 1:82; Martin, *Ralph McGill*, pp. 134–36.

10. McGill, "Can We Solve," p. 5.

11. Kluger, *Simple Justice*, pp. 290–94; Weltner (unpub.), "George Sinclair Mitchell," pp. 37–38.

12. Weltner, "George Sinclair Mitchell," p. 45; Dabney, "Southern Crisis," pp. 40–41, 104. See also *Greenville Delta Democrat-Times*, 13 Feb. 1952, p. 4, 16 Mar. 1952, p. 4, 10 Nov. 1953, p. 4, 4 Dec. 1953, p. 4, and 15 Mar. 1954, p. 4; Dabney to Mrs. Lillian Money Read, 22 Dec. 1952, and to Ernest W. Goodrich, 29 Sept. 1953, Dabney Papers; Eagles, *Jonathan Daniels*, pp. 155, 165, 167; Martin, *Ralph McGill*, p. 151.

13. Ashmore, "Desegregated Schools," p. 9; Carter, *Greenville Delta Democrat-Times*, 18 May 1954, p. 1; *Richmond Times-Dispatch*, 18 May 1954, p. 14; Eagles, *Jonathan Daniels*, p. 169; Logue, *Ralph McGill*, 1:65; Martin, *Ralph McGill*, pp. 151–52.

14. Dabney, *Across the Years*, pp. 232–33. Kilpatrick's editorials may be seen in *Interposition*.

15. Dabney, "School Crisis," p. 30; Dabney, "Frank Talk," p. 114; Dabney, "School Integration," p. 378; Dabney, "Virginia's 'Peaceable, Honorable Stand,'" pp. 52, 55; Putnam, *Race and Reason*, pp. 4–10; *Richmond Times-Dispatch*, 16 Oct. 1958, p. 14, and 7 Jan. 1959, p. 10; Kilpatrick, *Southern Case*, p. 71. See also Graves, "South Won't Surrender," pp. 39–46; Sass, "Mixed Schools," pp. 45–49; Waring, "Southern Case," pp. 39–45; Workman, *Case for South*.

16. Dabney: "School Crisis," pp. 26–28; "School Integration," p. 378; *Richmond Times-Dispatch*, 21 Aug. 1958, p. 22.

17. *Greenville Delta Democrat-Times*, 18 Dec. 1954, p. 4; Rowan, *Go South*, p. 204. See also Carter, "Court's Decision," p. 56; "'Middle Ground' Urged for the South [by Carter]," *New York Times*, 7 June 1955, p. 35; Daniels to Arthur Krock, 21 Oct. 1955, Arthur Krock Papers, Box 23; "Southerner Faces Facts," [Mark Ethridge] p. 21; McGill, "Angry South," pp. 31–34; McKnight [editor of the *Charlotte Observer*], "Troubled South," pp. 29, 31; Johnson, "Superficial Aspect," *New Republic*, 25 Apr. 1955, p. 16, 29 July 1957, p. 8, 16 Sept. 1957, p. 10, 14 Oct. 1957,

p. 10, 9 June 1958, p. 9, and 29 Sept. 1958, p. 13; Ashmore, *Epitaph*, pp. 70–78; Hays, *Southern Moderate*, pp. 223, 228. For contemporary liberal criticisms of "moderation," see, for example, "The Fallacy of 'Moderation,'" *Southern Patriot* XIV (April 1956): 1; Boyle, *Desegregated Heart*, p. 215.

18. C. Vann Woodward's argument, in *Strange Career*, that the Jim Crow system first appeared in the 1890s as the bitter fruit of economic and political struggle among white southerners, with its strong implication that these laws did change customary behavior, challenged this southern liberal interpretation of the past's meaning for the present. Those among the journalists who incorporated Woodward's account into their own books, however, emphasized the elements that fit their own views. Carter, for example, accepted Woodward's description in his *Angry Scar*, but treated the segregation laws as the final act of the more important drama, Reconstruction (see also "Editor Sees Signs of a 'Healed South,'" *New York Times*, 9 Mar. 1956, p. 18). Similarly, Ashmore cited Woodward's description of the surprisingly flexible race relations during the 1880s under Conservative rule in his *Epitaph for Dixie* and concluded with a wistful expression of hope that the South could recapture "the original Southern concept of aristocracy" that emphasized social responsibility (pp. 51–54, 183–84, 187).

19. Ashmore, "Memorandum," 30 Mar. 1956, Adlai E. Stevenson Papers, Box 427. See also Daniels to Stevenson, 18 Apr. 1956, Box 428; Johnson to Stevenson, 8 June 1956, 7 Aug. 1956, Box 433; Ashmore to Stevenson, 2 Aug. 1956, 24 Aug. 1956, Box 425, Stevenson Papers; Martin, *Ralph McGill*, pp. 138–41; Ashmore, *Hearts and Minds*, pp. 226–36.

20. Bartley, *Rise of Massive Resistance*, pp. 26–27; Tom Ethridge, "Mississippi Notebook," *Citizens' Council*, May 1956, p. 2. For similar comments, see also Debnam, *Old Kentucky Home*, pp. 120, 125–26; Workman, *Case for South*, pp. 270, 274.

21. McGill, "Angry South," p. 31; *Citizens' Council*, Oct. 1957, p. 1. For similar complaints, see also, *Citizens' Council*, July 1957, p. 3; Mar. 1958, p. 1; June 1958, p. 2; Kilpatrick, "Conservatism in South," in Rubin and Kilpatrick, *Lasting South*, p. 195; Workman, *Case for South*, pp. 66–67.

22. Bartley, *Rise of Massive Resistance*, p. 320. Ashmore and the *Arkansas Gazette* won Pulitzer Prizes for their roles during the Little Rock Crisis. Ashmore's editorials are reprinted in Hohenberg, *Pulitzer Prize Story*, pp. 102–4.

23. McGill, *Atlanta Constitution*, 2 Dec. 1958, p. 1; McGill, speech, Emory University, 21 Jan. 1959, in Logue, *Ralph McGill*, 2:175; *Atlanta Constitution*, 21 Jan. 1959, p. 1; *Richmond Times-Dispatch*, 20 Jan. 1959, p. 12, 23 Jan., p. 12, and 31 Jan., p. 6; Dabney, "Next in South's Schools," pp. 92, 94. See also Ashmore, *Epitaph*, pp. 170–71; Eagles, *Jonathan Daniels*, pp. 193–200; Carter, quoted in Peters, *Southern Temper*, p. 117; "Carters in Mississippi," pp. 78–79.

24. Graham, *Crisis in Print*, p. 299; Bartley, *Rise of Massive Resistance*, p. 320.

25. The phrase serves as the title for Chapter 7 of *An Epitaph for Dixie*, pp. 113–32.

26. *Buffalo Evening News*, 6 Mar. 1950, 20 Jan. 1949, 19 July 1949, and 6 June 1950, clippings in Milton Papers, Box 100.

27. Milton, review of Angle, *Lincoln Reader,* Milton Papers, Box 99; Milton, rev. of Nichols, *Disruption,* p. 163; Milton to Paul Bartley, 6 Apr. 1950, and rev. of Randall, *Lincoln, Liberal Statesman,* Milton Papers, Box 99; "George F. Milton, Newsman, Is Dead," *New York Times,* 13 Nov. 1955, p. 88.

28. G. W. Johnson, "Superficial Aspect," *New Republic,* 25 April 1955, p. 16; Johnson, "To Live and Die," pp. 29–34; Johnson, "Meditation," pp. 161–71; "Gerald W. Johnson, Reporter–Historian," *New York Times,* 24 Mar. 1980, 2:9. A selection of Johnson's essays on the South are available in Johnson, *South-Watching.*

29. "Carters in Mississippi," pp. 78–79; Carter, "Double Standard," p. 30; Carter, "Old South," pp. 50–51, 170, 172–74, 176–77, 179; Lyons, "Other Carters," p. 92.

30. McGill, "South Will Change," pp. 13, 16, 18; McGill, *South and Southerner,* pp. 225, 238; McGill, speech, Greater Boston Chamber of Commerce, 28 May 1968, in Logue, *Ralph McGill,* 2: 488–94; Martin, *Ralph McGill,* pp. 250–51, 256, 268–69. A colleague recalled that McGill "went back and read some of [his writings on the race issue before 1954], and it was pretty pale tea. He was not proud of it. He wished that he had been even more forward." See Eugene Patterson interview in Raines, *My Soul Is Rested,* p. 367.

31. *Richmond Times-Dispatch,* 2 Oct. 1962, p. 12, and 11 Oct., p. 16; Dabney, "Richmond's Quiet Revolution," pp. 18–19, 28; Dabney to Arthur Krock, 19 Feb. 1964, Krock Papers; Ben A. Franklin, "An Early Backer of Negro Rights Retires as Editor in Richmond," *New York Times,* 5 Jan. 1969, p. 66; Dabney: *Virginia; Richmond; Mr. Jefferson's University; Jefferson Scandals; Last Review.*

32. G. W. Johnson, "Tilt With Southern Windmills," p. 189; Johnson, "After Forty Years," pp. 194, 195, 201.

33. Dabney, "Pace Is Important," pp. 180–81.

Bibliography

Newspapers

Atlanta Constitution, 1937–45, 1954, 1957, 1958.
Baltimore Evening Sun, 1928–43.
Chattanooga News, 1924–39.
Chattanooga Evening Tribune, 1940.
Greenville Delta Star, 1937–38.
Greenville Delta Democrat-Times, 1938–42, 1945–54.
Hammond Courier, 1932–36.
Norfolk Virginian-Pilot, 1928, 1930, 1931.
Richmond Times-Dispatch, 1928–45, 1948, 1954, 1958, 1959.

Manuscript Collections

Amherst, Massachusetts
  University of Massachusetts
    W. E. B. DuBois Papers
Chapel Hill, North Carolina
  University of North Carolina: Southern Historical Collection
    William Terry Couch Papers
    Jonathan Worth Daniels Papers
    Mark Foster Ethridge Papers
    Frank Porter Graham Papers
    Howard Washington Odum Papers
    Arthur Franklin Raper Papers
    University of North Carolina Press Papers
Charlottesville, Virginia
  University of Virginia: Alderman Library
    Homer S. Cummings Papers
    Virginius Dabney Papers
    Louis I. Jaffé Papers
    Francis Pickens Miller Papers
    Virginia Quarterly Review Papers
Montgomery, Alabama
  Alabama State Archives
    Grover Cleveland Hall, Sr., Papers

Princeton, New Jersey
  Princeton University: Firestone Library
    Allen Tate Papers
  Princeton University: Mudd Library
    American Civil Liberties Union Archives
    Arthur Krock Papers
    Adlai E. Stevenson Papers
Washington, D.C.
  Library of Congress
    Josephus Daniels Papers
    George Fort Milton Papers
    National Policy Committee Papers

Unpublished Sources

Alexander, Will W. "Reminiscences." Columbia University Oral History Collection, 1952.

Armstrong, Nancy. "The Study of an Attempt Made in 1943 to Abolish Segregation of the Races on Common Carriers in the State of Virginia." University of Virginia Phelps-Stokes Fellowship Papers, No. 17, 1950.

Bennett, James David, II. "Struggle for Power: The Relationship Between the Tennessee Valley Authority and the Private Power Industry, 1933–1939." Ph.D. dissertation, Vanderbilt University, 1969.

Burrows, Edwin Flud. "The Commission on Interracial Cooperation, 1919–1944: A Case Study in the History of the Interracial Movement in the South." Ph.D. dissertation, University of Wisconsin, 1954.

Ellis, Ann Wells. "The Commission on Interracial Cooperation, 1919–1944: Its Activities and Results." Ph.D. dissertation, Georgia State University, 1975.

Grant, Donald Lee. "The Development of the Anti-Lynching Movement in the United States: 1883–1932." Ph.D. dissertation, University of Missouri–Columbia, 1972.

Robinson, James E. "Hodding Carter: Southern Liberal, 1907–1972." Ph.D. dissertation, Mississippi State University, 1974.

Rock, Virginia Jean. "The Making and the Meaning of *I'll Take My Stand*: A Study in Utopian-Conservatism, 1925–1939." Ph.D. dissertation, University of Minnesota, 1961.

Weltner, Susan Martin. "George Sinclair Mitchell: Gradualism and the Changing South." Honors Thesis, University of Virginia, 1979.

Published Sources

"Advertiser: New Print Dress Smartens Up a Local Character." *Newsweek* 9 (16 January 1937): 34–35.

Alexander, Will W. "Negroes and the Economic Structure." *Southern Workman* 60 (June 1931): 269–77.

Allen, Lee N. "The McAdoo Campaign for the Presidential Nomination in 1924." *Journal of Southern History* 29 (May 1963): 211–28.

Alsop, Em Bowles, ed. *The Greatness of Woodrow Wilson, 1856–1956.* New York: Rinehart & Co., 1956.

Anderson, William. *The Wild Man from Sugar Creek: The Political Career of Eugene Talmadge.* Baton Rouge: Louisiana State University Press, 1975.

Armstrong, Zella. *The History of Hamilton County and Chattanooga Tennessee.* Chattanooga: Lookout Publishing Co., 1940.

Arnall, Ellis Gibbs. *The Shore Dimly Seen.* Philadelphia: J. B. Lippincott Co., 1946.

Ashby, Warren. *Frank Porter Graham: A Southern Liberal.* Winston-Salem, N.C.: J. F. Blair, 1980.

Ashmore, Harry. "Desegregated Schools." *University of Chicago Round Table* 862 (17 October 1954).

———. *An Epitaph for Dixie.* New York: W. W. Norton & Co., 1958.

———. *Hearts and Minds: The Anatomy of Racism from Roosevelt to Reagan.* New York: McGraw-Hill Book Co., 1982.

Bailey, Hugh C. *Liberalism in the New South: Southern Social Reformers and the Progressive Movement.* Coral Gables: University of Miami Press, 1969.

Baker, Ray Stannard. *Following the Color Line: An Account of Negro Citizenship in the American Democracy.* New York: Doubleday, Page & Co., 1908.

Baldwin, Sidney. *Poverty and Politics: The Rise and Decline of the Farm Security Administration.* Chapel Hill: University of North Carolina Press, 1968.

Banton, Michael. *The Idea of Race.* London: Tavistock Publications, 1977.

Barr, Stringfellow. "Shall Slavery Come South?" *Virginia Quarterly Review* 6 (October 1930): 481–94.

Bartley, Numan V. *The Rise of Massive Resistance: Race and Politics in the South During the 1950's.* Baton Rouge: Louisiana State University Press, 1969.

Bates, J. Leonard. "The Teapot Dome Scandal and the Election of 1924." *American Historical Review* 60 (January 1955): 303–22.

Beale, Howard K. "On Rewriting Reconstruction History." *American Historical Review* 45 (July 1940): 807–27.

Bernstein, Irving. *Turbulent Years: A History of the American Worker, 1933–1941.* Boston: Houghton Mifflin Co., 1970.

Bond, Horace Mann. "A Negro Looks At His South." *Harper's Magazine* 163 (June 1931): 98–108.

Bonner, Thomas N. "Civil War Historians and the 'Needless War' Doctrine." *Journal of the History of Ideas* 17 (April 1956): 193–216.

Bontemps, Arna Wendell. *Arna Bontemps–Langston Hughes Letters, 1925–1967.* Selected and edited by Charles H. Nichols. New York: Dodd, Mead & Co., 1980.

Boyle, Sarah Patton. *The Desegregated Heart: A Virginian's Stand in Time of Transition.* New York: William Morrow & Co., 1962.

Brinkley, Alan. *Voices of Protest: Huey Long, Father Coughlin, and the Great Depression.* New York: Alfred A. Knopf, 1982.

Brody, David. "The Emergence of Mass Production Unionism." In *Change and Continuity in Twentieth-Century America*, edited by John Braeman, Robert H. Bremner, and Everet Walters, pp. 221–62. Columbus: Ohio State University Press, 1964.

Brownell, Blaine A. *The Urban Ethos in the South 1920–1930*. Baton Rouge: Louisiana State University Press, 1975.

Buenker, John D. *Urban Liberalism and Progressive Reform*. New York: Charles Scribner's Sons, 1973.

Burner, David. *The Politics of Provincialism: The Democratic Party in Transition, 1918–1932*. New York: Alfred A. Knopf, 1968.

Carter, Dan T. *Scottsboro: A Tragedy of the American South*. Baton Rouge: Louisiana State University Press, 1969.

Carter, Hodding. *The Angry Scar: The Story of Reconstruction*. Garden City, N.Y.: Doubleday & Co., 1959.

———. "Chip on Our Shoulder Down South." *Saturday Evening Post* 219 (2 November 1946).

———. "The Civil Rights Issue As Seen in the South." *New York Times Magazine*, 21 March 1948.

———. "The Court's Decision and the South." *Reader's Digest* (September 1954): 51–56.

———. "A Double Standard for Murder?" *New York Times Magazine*, 24 January 1965.

———. *First Person Rural*. Garden City, N.Y.: Doubleday & Co., 1963.

———. *Flood Crest*. New York: Rinehart & Co., 1947.

———. "Furl That Banner?" *New York Times Magazine*, 25 June 1965.

———. "How Come Huey Long?" *New Republic* 82 (13 February 1935): 11–14.

———. "Huey Long: Louisiana Limelighter." *Review of Reviews* 91 (March 1935): 23–28, 64.

———. "Kingfish to Crawfish." *New Republic* 77 (24 January 1934): 302–5.

———. "The Old South Had Something Worth Saving." *New York Times Magazine*, 4 December 1966.

———. *Southern Legacy*. Baton Rouge: Louisiana State University Press, 1950.

———. "A Southern Liberal Looks at Civil Rights." *New York Times Magazine*, 8 August 1948.

———. *Where Main Street Meets the River*. New York: Rinehart & Co., 1953.

Carter, Hodding, and Ashmore, Harry. "What Should We Do About Race Segregation?" *Bulletin of America's Town Meeting of the Air* 14 (9 November 1948).

Carter, Hodding, and Graves, John Temple. "How Will a Change of Administration Affect Our World Position?" *Bulletin of America's Town Meeting of the Air* 18 (17 June 1952).

"The Carters in Mississippi." *Newsweek* 60 (11 January 1960): 78–79.

Cash, W. J. "The Mind of the South." *American Mercury* 18 (October 1929): 185–92.

———. *The Mind of the South*. New York: Alfred A. Knopf, 1941.

———. "The War in the South." *American Mercury* 19 (February 1930): 163–69.

Cason, Clarence. *90° in the Shade*. Chapel Hill: University of North Carolina Press, 1935.

Cayton, Horace R., and Mitchell, George S. *Black Workers in the New Unions*. Chapel Hill: University of North Carolina Press, 1939.

Cell, John W. *The Highest Stage of White Supremacy: The Origins of Segregation in South Africa and the American South*. Cambridge: Cambridge University Press, 1982.

Chalmers, Allan K. *They Shall Be Free*. Garden City, N.Y.: Doubleday & Co., 1951.

Chambers, Lenoir, and Shank, Joseph E. *Salt Water and Printer's Ink: Norfolk and Its Newspapers, 1865–1965*. Chapel Hill: University of North Carolina Press, 1967.

Clark, Emily. *Innocence Abroad*. New York: Alfred A. Knopf, 1931.

Clark, Norman H. *Deliver Us From Evil: An Interpretation of American Prohibition*. New York: W. W. Norton & Co., 1976.

Collier, Tarleton. "Heritage of Defeat." *North Georgia Review* 3 (Spring 1938): 8, 22.

Couch, W. T., ed. *Culture in the South*. Chapel Hill: University of North Carolina Press, 1934.

———. "Southerners Inspect the South." *New Republic* 70 (14 December 1938): 168–69.

Cripps, Thomas R. "The Reaction of the Negro to the Motion Picture *Birth of a Nation*." *Historian* 25 (May 1963): 344–62.

Dabney, Virginius (1835–1894). *The Story of Don Miff*. 2d ed. Philadelphia: J. B. Lippincott Co., 1886.

Dabney, Virginius. *Across the Years: Memories of a Virginian*. Garden City, N.Y.: Doubleday & Co., 1978.

———. *Below the Potomac: A Book About the New South*. New York: D. Appleton–Century Co., 1942.

———. "Dixie Rejects Lynching." *Nation* 145 (27 November 1937): 579–80.

———. *Dry Messiah: The Life of Bishop Cannon*. New York: Alfred A. Knopf, 1949.

———. "A Frank Talk to North and South About 'Integration.'" *U.S. News & World Report* 42 (15 March 1957): 112–18.

———. "History as an Avocation." *Virginia Magazine of History and Biography* 76 (April 1968): 136–41.

———. "If the South Had Won the War." *American Mercury* 39 (October 1936): 199–205.

———. "Is the South That Bad?" *Saturday Review of Literature* 29 (13 April 1946): 9–10, 84–88.

———. *The Jefferson Scandals: A Rebuttal*. New York: Dodd, Mead & Co., 1981.

———. *The Last Review: The Confederate Reunion, Richmond, 1932*. Chapel Hill: Algonquin Books, 1984.

———. *Liberalism in the South*. Chapel Hill: University of North Carolina Press, 1932.

———. *Mr. Jefferson's University: A History.* Charlottesville: University Press of Virginia, 1981.

———. "Nearer and Nearer the Precipice." *Atlantic Monthly* 171 (January 1943): 94–100.

———. "The Negro and His Schooling." *Atlantic Monthly* 169 (April 1942): 459–68.

———. "Next in the South's Schools: 'Limited Integration.'" *U.S. News & World Report* 48 (18 January 1960): 92–94.

———. "The Pace Is Important." *Virginia Quarterly Review* 41 (Spring 1965): 176–91.

———. "Richard Heath Dabney: A Memoir." *Magazine of Albemarle County History* 33–34 (1975–76): 53–140.

———. *Richmond: The Story of a City.* Garden City, N.Y.: Doubleday & Co., 1976.

———. "Richmond's Quiet Revolution." *Saturday Review of Literature* 47 (29 February 1964): 18–19, 28.

———. "School Crisis in Dixie." *American Magazine* 162 (August 1956): 26–30, 100.

———. "School Integration: Effect of the Interracial Controversy Upon the Public Schools." *Vital Speeches of the Day* 23 (1 April 1957): 376–80.

———. "Southern Crisis: The Segregation Decision." *Saturday Evening Post* 225 (8 November 1952).

———. "Virginia." *American Mercury* 9 (November 1926): 349–56.

———. *Virginia: The New Dominion.* Garden City, N.Y.: Doubleday & Co., 1971.

———. "Virginia's 'Peaceable, Honorable Stand.'" *Life* 45 (22 September 1958): 51–52, 55–56.

———. "What We Think of Senator Byrd's Machine." *Saturday Evening Post* 222 (7 January 1950).

Dalfiume, Richard M. "The 'Forgotten Years' of the Negro Revolution." *Journal of American History* 55 (June 1968): 90–106.

Dallek, Robert. *Franklin D. Roosevelt and American Foreign Policy, 1932–1945.* New York: Oxford University Press, 1979.

Daniels, Jonathan. "Democracy Is Bread." *Virginia Quarterly Review* 14 (Autumn 1938): 481–90.

———. *The End of Innocence.* Philadelphia: J. B. Lippincott Co., 1954.

———. *The Man of Independence.* Philadelphia: J. B. Lippincott Co., 1950.

———. "The Need to Eat Is Not Racial." *Southern Frontier* 1 (August 1940): 1, 4.

———. "Negro Leadership Moves North." *Southern Frontier* 2 (December 1941): 2, 4.

———. *A Southerner Discovers the South.* New York: Macmillan Co., 1938.

———. *Tar Heels: A Portrait of North Carolina.* New York: Dodd, Mead & Co., 1941.

———. *The Time Between the Wars: Armistice to Pearl Harbor.* Garden City, N.Y.: Doubleday & Co., 1966.

Davenport, F. Garvin, Jr. *The Myth of Southern History: Historical Consciousness in Twentieth-Century Southern Literature*. Nashville: Vanderbilt University Press, 1970.

Davidson, Donald. "'I'll Take My Stand': A History." *American Review* 5 (Summer 1935): 301–21.

———. *The Literary Correspondence of Donald Davidson and Allen Tate*. Edited by John Tyree Fain and Thomas Daniel Young. Athens: University of Georgia Press, 1974.

———. "The 'Mystery' of the Agrarians." *Saturday Review of Literature* 26 (23 January 1943): 6–7.

———. *Southern Writers in the Modern World*. Athens: University of Georgia Press, 1958.

———. "Where Are the Laymen?: A Study in Policy-Making." *American Review* 9 (October 1937): 456–81.

Davis, Steve. "The South as 'the Nation's No. 1 Economic Problem': the NEC Report of 1938." *Georgia Historical Quarterly* 62 (Summer 1978): 119–32.

Debnam, W. E. *Then My Old Kentucky Home Good Night!* Raleigh, N.C.: W. E. Debnam, 1955.

De Voto, Bernard. "The Easy Chair." *Harper's Magazine* 192 (February 1946): 123–25.

———. "The Easy Chair." *Harper's Magazine* 192 (March 1946): 234–37.

Dunbar, Anthony P. *Against the Grain: Southern Radicals and Prophets, 1929–1959*. Charlottesville: University Press of Virginia, 1981.

Dykeman, Wilma, and Stokely, James. *Seeds of Southern Change: The Life of Will Alexander*. Chicago: University of Chicago Press, 1962.

Eagles, Charles W. *Jonathan Daniels and Race Relations: The Evolution of a Southern Liberal*. Knoxville: University of Tennessee Press, 1982.

Ellis, Ann Wells. "A Crusade Against 'Wretched Attitudes': The Commission on Interracial Cooperation's Activities in Atlanta." *Atlanta Historical Journal* 23 (Spring 1979): 21–44.

Embree, Edwin R. *13 Against the Odds*. New York: Viking Press, 1944.

Embree, Edwin R., and Waxman, Julia. *Investment in People: The Story of the Julius Rosenwald Fund*. New York: Harper & Brothers, 1949.

Ethridge, Mark. *America's Obligation to Its Negro Citizens*. Atlanta: Conference on Education and Race Relations, 1937.

———. "The South's New Industrialism and the Press." *Annals of the American Academy of Political and Social Science* 153 (January 1931): 251–56.

Fehrenbacher, Don E. "Disunion and Reunion." In *The Reconstruction of American History*, edited by John Higham, pp. 98–118. New York: Harper & Row, Publishers, 1962.

Fine, Sidney. *Sit-Down: The General Motors Strike of 1936–1937*. Ann Arbor: University of Michigan Press, 1969.

Finkle, Lee. "The Conservative Aims of Militant Rhetoric: Black Protest During World War II." *The Journal of American History* 65 (December 1973): 692–713.

———. *Forum for Protest: The Black Press During World War II*. Rutherford, N.J.: Fairleigh Dickinson University Press, 1975.

Freehling, William W. *Prelude to Civil War: The Nullification Controversy in South Carolina, 1816–1836*. New York: Harper & Row, 1966.

Freidel, Frank. *F.D.R. and the South*. Baton Rouge: Louisiana State University Press, 1965.

Fullinwider, S. P. *The Mind and Mood of Black America: 20th Century Thought*. Homewood, Ill.: Dorsey Press, 1969.

Garfinkel, Herbert. *When Negroes March: The March on Washington Movement in the Organizational Politics for FEPC*. Glencoe, Ill.: Free Press, 1959; reprint ed., New York: Atheneum Publishers, 1969.

Garson, Robert A. "Political Fundamentalism and Popular Democracy in the 1920s." *South Atlantic Quarterly* 76 (Spring 1977): 219–33.

Gaskill, Gordon. "A Newspaper Is Killed." *New Republic* 102 (15 January 1940): 80–82.

Gaston, Paul M. *The New South Creed: A Study in Southern Mythmaking*. New York: Alfred A Knopf, 1970.

Gatewood, Willard B., Jr. *Preachers, Pedagogues & Politicians: The Evolution Controversy in North Carolina, 1920–1927*. Chapel Hill: University of North Carolina Press, 1966.

Gavins, Raymond. *The Perils and Prospects of Southern Black Leadership: Gordon Blaine Hancock, 1884–1970*. Durham, N.C.: Duke University Press, 1977.

"Georgia Folklore." *North Georgia Review* 6 (Winter 1941): 22–24.

Giddens, Lucia M. "Grover C. Hall." *Editor and Publisher* (30 June 1928): 14.

Giddings, Franklin Henry. *The Principles of Sociology*. 3d ed. New York: Macmillan Co., 1907.

Ginger, Ray. *Six Days or Forever: Tennessee v. John Thomas Scopes*. Boston: Beacon Press, 1958.

Gossett, Thomas F. *Race: The History of an Idea in America*. Dallas: Southern Methodist University Press, 1963.

Govan, Gilbert E., and Livingood, James W. *The Chattanooga Country, 1540–1962: From Tomahawks to TVA*. Chapel Hill: University of North Carolina Press, 1963.

Graham, Hugh Davis. *Crisis in Print: Desegregation and the Press in Tennessee*. Nashville: Vanderbilt University Press, 1967.

"Grandma Married." *Time* 36 (16 December 1940): 50.

Grantham, Dewey W. "The Contours of Southern Progressivism." *American Historical Review* 86 (December 1982): 1035–1058.

———. "Southern Progressives and the Racial Imperative." In *The Regional Imagination: The South and Recent American History*, pp. 77–106. Nashville: Vanderbilt University Press, 1979.

Graves, John Temple. "The Chance-Taking South." *Virginia Quarterly Review* 21 (Spring 1945): 161–73.

———. *The Fighting South*. New York: G. P. Putnam's Sons, 1943.

———. "Revolution in the South." *Virginia Quarterly Review* 26 (Spring 1950): 190–203.

———. *The Shaft in the Sky*. New York: George H. Doran Company, 1923.

———. "The South Won't Surrender." *American Mercury* 83 (July 1956): 39–46.

————. "The Southern Negro and the War Crisis." *Virginia Quarterly Review* 18 (Autumn 1942): 500–517.

————. "Wilson and the South Today." *Virginia Quarterly Review* 6 (July 1930): 382–88.

Grubbs, Donald H. *Cry from the Cotton: The Southern Tenant Farmers' Union and the New Deal.* Chapel Hill: University of North Carolina Press, 1977.

Hall, Jacquelyn Dowd. *Revolt Against Chivalry: Jessie Daniel Ames and the Women's Campaign Against Lynching.* New York: Columbia University Press, 1979.

Hall, R. F. "What Tom Watson Taught the South." *New South: A Journal of Progressive Opinion* 1 (June 1938): 12–13.

Hamby, Alonzo L. *Beyond the New Deal: Harry S. Truman and American Liberalism.* New York: Columbia University Press, 1973.

Hancock, Gordon B. "Writing a 'New Charter of Southern Race Relations.'" *New South* 19 (January 1964): 18–21.

Handlin, Oscar. *Al Smith and His America.* Boston: Little, Brown and Co., 1958.

Harlan, Louis R. *Booker T. Washington: The Making of a Black Leader, 1856–1901.* New York: Oxford University Press, 1972.

Hartz, Louis. *The Liberal Tradition in America.* New York: Harcourt, Brace and Co., 1955.

Hays, Brooks. *Politics Is My Parish.* Baton Rouge: Louisiana State Univeristy Press, 1981.

————. *A Southern Moderate Speaks.* Chapel Hill: University of North Carolina Press, 1959.

Hero, Alfred O., Jr. *The Southerner and World Affairs.* Baton Rouge: Louisiana State University Press, 1965.

Hicks, John D. *The Populist Revolt: A History of the Farmers' Alliance and the People's Party.* Minneapolis: University of Minnesota Press, 1931.

Higham, Charles. *The Art of the American Film.* Garden City, N.Y.: Anchor Press/Doubleday, 1974.

Higham, John. *History.* Englewood Cliffs, N.J.: Prentice-Hall, 1965.

Hill, T. Arnold. "Negroes in Southern Industry." *Annals of the American Academy of Political and Social Science* 153 (January 1931): 170–81.

Hobson, Fred C., Jr. *Serpent in Eden: H. L. Mencken and the South.* Chapel Hill: University of North Carolina Press, 1974.

Hohenberg, John. *The Pulitzer Prize Story.* New York: Columbia University Press, 1959.

————. *The Pulitzer Prizes: A History.* New York: Columbia University Press, 1974.

Hollis, Daniel W., III. "The Hall Family and Twentieth-Century Journalism in Alabama." *Alabama Review* 32 (April 1979): 119–40.

Hoover, Herbert. *The New Day: Campaign Speeches of Herbert Hoover, 1928.* Stanford, Cal.: Stanford University Press, 1928.

Huthmacher, J. Joseph. *Senator Robert F. Wagner and the Rise of Urban Liberalism.* New York: Atheneum Publishers, 1969.

Interposition: Editorials and Editorial Page Presentations, 1955–1956. Richmond: *Richmond News Leader,* 1956.

Isaac, Paul E. *Prohibition and Politics: Turbulent Decades in Tennessee, 1885–1920.* Knoxville: University of Tennessee Press, 1965.

Jaffé, Louis I. "The Democracy and Al Smith." *Virginia Quarterly Review* 3 (July 1927): 321–41.

Jeffrey, Kirk, Jr. "Stephen Arnold Douglas in American Historical Writing." *Journal of the Illinois State Historical Society* 61 (Autumn 1968): 248–68.

Johnson, Charles S. "More Southerners Discover the South." *Crisis* 46 (January 1939): 14–15.

———. "The Present Status of Race Relations in the South." *Social Forces* 23 (October 1944): 27–32.

———. "Race Relations and Social Change." In *Race Relations and the Race Problem: A Definition and an Analysis,* edited by Edgar T. Thompson, pp. 271–303. Durham, N.C.: Duke University Press, 1939.

Johnson, Charles S.; Embree, Edwin R.; and Alexander, Will W. *The Collapse of Cotton Tenancy: Summary of Field Studies & Statistical Surveys 1933–1935.* Chapel Hill: University of North Carolina Press, 1935.

Johnson, Gerald W. "After Appomattox." *Virginia Quarterly Review* 6 (January 1930): 129–33.

———. "After Forty Years—Dixi." *Virginia Quarterly Review* 41 (Spring 1965): 192–201.

———. *America-Watching: Perspectives in the Course of an Incredible Century.* Owings Mills, Md.: Stemmer House Publishers, 1976.

———. *American Heroes and Hero-Worship.* New York: Harper & Brothers, 1941.

———. *America's Silver Age: The Statecraft of Clay—Webster—Calhoun.* New York: Harper & Brothers, 1939.

———. *Andrew Jackson: An Epic in Homespun.* New York: Minton, Balch & Co., 1927.

———. "The Battling South." *Scribner's Magazine* 77 (March 1925): 302–7.

———. "Behind the Monster's Mask." *Survey* 50 (April 1923): 20–22, 55–56.

———. "Bryan, Thou Shouldst Be Living: A Plea for Demagogues." *Harper's Magazine* 163 (September 1931): 385–91.

———. *By Reason of Strength.* New York: Minton, Balch & Co., 1930.

———. "The Cadets at New Market: A Reminder to the Critics of the South." *Harper's Magazine* 160 (December 1929): 111–19.

———. "Critical Attitudes North and South." *Social Forces* 2 (May 1924): 575–79.

———. "The Dead Vote of the South." *Scribner's Magazine* 78 (July 1925): 38–43.

———. "The Devil Is Dead, And What a Loss!" *American Scholar* 16 (Autumn 1947): 395–403.

———. "For Ignoble Pacifism." *Harper's Magazine* 163 (November 1931): 727–32.

———. "Fourteen Equestrian Statues of Colonel Simmons." *Reviewer* 4 (October 1923): 20–25.

———. *Incredible Tale: The Odyssey of the Average American in the Last Half Century.* New York: Harper & Brothers, 1950.

———. "Journalism Below the Potomac." *American Mercury* 9 (September 1926): 77–82.

————. "The Ku-Kluxer." *American Mercury* 1 (February 1924): 207–11.

————. "The Liberal of 1946." *American Scholar* 15 (Spring 1946): 154–59.

————. *Liberal's Progress.* New York: Coward-McCann, 1948.

————. "Live Demagogue, or Dead Gentleman?" *Virginia Quarterly Review* 12 (January 1936): 1–15.

————. "Meditation on 1963." *Virginia Quarterly Review* 39 (Spring 1963): 161–71.

————. "Mr. Babbitt Arrives at Erzerum." *Social Forces* 1 (March 1923): 206–9.

————. "No More Excuses: A Southerner to Southerners." *Harper's Magazine* 162 (February 1931): 331–37.

————. "Note on Race Prejudice." *North American Review* 233 (March 1932): 226–33.

————. *Number Thirty-Six.* New York: Minton, Balch & Co., 1933.

————. "Onion Salt." *Reviewer* 5 (January 1925): 60–63.

————. *Randolph of Roanoke: A Political Fantastic.* New York: Minton, Balch & Co., 1929.

————. "The Religious Refugee." *Century Magazine* 3 (February 1926): 399–404.

————. "The Rise of the Cities: A Pessimistic Note." *Harper's Magazine* 157 (July 1928): 246–50.

————. *Roosevelt: Dictator or Democrat?* New York: Harper & Brothers, 1941.

————. *The Secession of the Southern States.* New York: G. P. Putnam's Sons, 1933.

————. "Service in the Cotton Mills." *American Mercury* 5 (June 1925): 219–23.

————. "Since Wilson." *Virginia Quarterly Review* 8 (July 1932): 321–36.

————. "The South Faces Itself." *Virginia Quarterly Review* 7 (January 1931): 152–57.

————. "The South Takes the Offensive." *American Mercury* 2 (May 1924): 70–78.

————. *South-Watching: Selected Essays by Gerald W. Johnson.* Edited by Fred Hobson. Chapel Hill: University of North Carolina Press, 1983.

————. "Southern Image-Breakers." *Virginia Quarterly Review* 4 (October 1928): 508–19.

————. "A Tarheel Looks at Virginia." *North American Review* 228 (August 1929): 238–43.

————. "The Third Republic—And After: Meditations Upon Our Plutocratic Government." *Harper's Magazine* 156 (February 1928): 339–44.

————. "A Tilt with Southern Windmills." *Virginia Quarterly Review* 1 (July 1925): 184–92.

————. "To Live and Die in Dixie." *Atlantic Monthly* 206 (July 1960): 29–34.

————. *The Undefeated.* New York: Minton, Balch & Co., 1927.

————. "The Villains." *Harper's Magazine* 201 (October 1950): 221–28.

————. "Vinegar Tree." *New Republic* 94 (20 April 1938): 338.

————. *The Wasted Land.* Chapel Hill: University of North Carolina Press, 1938.

————. "Woodrow Wilson." In *Southern Pioneers in Social Interpretation*, edited by Howard W. Odum, pp. 29–49. Chapel Hill: University of North Carolina Press, 1925.

Johnson, Gerald W.; Kent, Frank R.; Mencken, H. L.; and Owens, Hamilton. *The Sunpapers of Baltimore.* New York: Alfred A. Knopf, 1937.

Johnson, Guy B. "Patterns of Racial Conflict." In *Race Relations and the Race Problem,* edited by Edgar T. Thompson, pp. 125–51. Durham, N.C.: Duke University Press, 1939.

———. "Some Methods of Reducing Race Prejudice in the South." *Southern Workman* 64 (September 1935): 272–78.

———. "Southern Offensive." *Common Ground* 4 (Summer 1944): 87–93.

Johnson, Guy B., and Johnson, Guion Griffis. *Research in Service to Society: The First Fifty Years of the Institute for Research in Social Science at the University of North Carolina.* Chapel Hill: University of North Carolina Press, 1980.

Johnson, Walter C., and Robb, Arthur T. *The South and Its Newspapers, 1903–1953.* Chattanooga: Southern Newspaper Publishers Association, 1954.

Jones, Jesse Holman. *Fifty Billion Dollars: My Thirteen Years with the RFC, 1932–1945.* New York: Macmillan Co., 1951.

Jones, M. Ashby. "The Approach to the South's Race Question." *Social Forces* 1 (November 1922): 40–41.

———. "The Interracial Commission: An Experiment in Racial Relations." *Southern Frontier* 5 (February 1944): 1.

———. "The Negro and the South." *Virginia Quarterly Review* 3 (January 1927): 1–12.

Josephson, Matthew, and Josephson, Hannah. *Al Smith: Hero of the Cities.* Boston: Houghton Mifflin Co., 1969.

Kantor, Harvey A. "Howard W. Odum: The Implications of Folk, Planning and Regionalism." *American Journal of Sociology* 79 (September 1973): 278–95.

Kennedy, Stetson. *Southern Exposure.* Garden City, N.Y.: Doubleday & Co., 1946.

Key, V. O. *Southern Politics in State and Nation.* New York: Alfred A Knopf, 1949.

Kilpatrick, James J. "Conservatism in the South." In *The Lasting South: Fourteen Southerners Look at Their Home,* edited by Louis D. Rubin, Jr., and James J. Kilpatrick, pp. 188–205. Chicago: Henry Regnery Co., 1957.

———. *The Southern Case for School Segregation.* N.p.: Crowell-Collier Publishing Co., 1962.

King, Martin Luther, Jr. *Why We Can't Wait.* New York: Harper and Row, Publishers, 1964.

King, Richard H. *A Southern Renaissance: The Cultural Awakening of the American South, 1930–1950.* New York: Oxford University Press, 1980.

Kirby, Jack Temple. *Darkness at the Dawning: Race and Reform in the Progressive Era South.* Philadelphia: J. B. Lippincott Co., 1972.

Kirby, John B. *Black Americans in the Roosevelt Era: Liberalism and Race.* Knoxville: University of Tennessee Press, 1980.

Kluger, Richard. *Simple Justice: The History of Brown v. Board of Education and Black America's Struggle for Equality.* New York: Alfred A. Knopf, 1976.

Kobre, Sidney. *Development of American Journalism.* Dubuque, Iowa: Wm. C. Brown Co. Publishers, 1969.

Krueger, Thomas. *And Promises to Keep: The Southern Conference for Human Welfare, 1938–1948.* Nashville: Vanderbilt University Press, 1967.

Leuchtenburg, William E. *Franklin D. Roosevelt and the New Deal, 1932–1940*. New York: Harper & Row, Publishers, 1963.

Lichtman, Allen J. *Prejudice and the Old Politics: The Presidential Campaign of 1928*. Chapel Hill: University of North Carolina Press, 1979.

Lilienthal, David E. *The Journals of David E. Lilienthal*. Vol. 1. New York: Harper & Row, Publishers, 1964.

Link, Arthur S. "Democratic Politics and the Presidential Campaign of 1912 in Tennessee." *East Tennessee Historical Society's Publications* 18 (1946): 107–30.

———. "The Progressive Movement in the South, 1870–1914." *North Carolina Historical Review* 23 (April 1946): 172–95.

Lippmann, Walter. "H. L. Mencken." *Saturday Review of Literature* (11 December 1926): 413.

———. *Public Opinion*. New York: Harcourt, Brace and Co., 1922.

Logan, Rayford W., ed. *What the Negro Wants*. Chapel Hill: University of North Carolina Press, 1944; reprint ed., New York: Agathon Press, 1969.

Logue, Calvin McLeod. *Ralph McGill: Editor and Publisher*. 2 vols. Durham, N.C.: Moore Publishing Co., 1969.

Lumpkin, Katharine DuPre. *The Making of a Southerner*. New York: Alfred A. Knopf, 1947.

———. *The South in Progress*. New York: International Publishers, 1940.

Lyman, Stanford M. *The Black American in Sociological Thought*. New York: G. P. Putnam's Sons, 1972.

Lynchings and What They Mean: General Findings of the Southern Commission on the Study of Lynching. Atlanta: The Commission, 1931.

Lyons, Gene. "The Other Carters." *New York Times Magazine*, 18 September 1977.

McCraw, Thomas K. *TVA and the Power Fight, 1933–1939*. New York: J. B. Lippincott Co., 1971.

McGill, Ralph. "Agrarianism vs. Industrialism Question Skillfully Debated by Anderson and Dr. Ransom." *Atlanta Constitution*, 12 February 1931, p. 1.

———. "The Angry South." *Atlantic Monthly* 197 (April 1956): 31–34.

———. "Can He Purge Senator Pepper?" *Saturday Evening Post* 222 (22 April 1950).

———. "Can We Solve the Civil Rights Issue Now?" *University of Chicago Round Table* 621 (12 February 1950).

———. "Civil Rights for the Negro." *Atlantic Monthly* 184 (November 1949): 64–66.

———. *The Fleas Come With the Dog*. Nashville: Abingdon Press, 1954.

———. "It Has Happened Here." *Survey Graphic* 30 (September 1941): 449–53.

———. "The President." In *The Greatness of Woodrow Wilson, 1856–1956*, edited by Em Bowles Alsop, pp. 81–128. New York: Rinehart & Co., 1956.

———. *The South and the Southerner*. Boston: Little, Brown and Co., 1963.

———. "The South Will Change." *Saturday Evening Post* 234 (30 September 1961).

———. "What Are the Real Campaign Issues?" *Bulletin of America's Town Meeting of the Air* 18 (1 July 1952).

MacKaye, Milton. "The South's Fighting Editor." *Saturday Evening Post* 219 (14 June 1947).

McKnight, C. A. "Troubled South: Search for a Middle Ground." *Collier's* 137 (22 June 1956): 25–31.

Marshall, F. Ray. *Labor in the South*. Cambridge, Mass.: Harvard University Press, 1967.

Martin, Harold H. *Ralph McGill, Reporter*. Boston: Little, Brown and Co., 1973.

Mason, Lucy Randolph. "Southerners Look at the South." *North Georgia Review* 3 (Fall and Winter 1938–39): 17.

Mast, Gerald. *A Short History of the Movies*. Indianapolis: Bobbs-Merrill Co., 1971.

Mathews, John M. "Julian L. Harris: The Evolution of a Southern Liberal." *South Atlantic Quarterly* 75 (Autumn 1976): 483–98.

Matthews, Fred H. *Quest for an American Sociology: Robert E. Park and the Chicago School*. Montreal and London: McGill-Queen's University Press, 1977.

Mays, Benjamin E. *Born to Rebel*. New York: Charles Scribner's Sons, 1971.

Meier, August. "Toward a Reinterpretation of Booker T. Washington." *Journal of Southern History* 23 (May 1957): 220–27.

Mencken, H. L. "The Sahara of the Bozart." In *Prejudices: Second Series*, pp. 136–54. New York: Alfred A. Knopf, 1920.

———. "The South Looks Ahead." *American Mercury* 8 (August 1926): 506–9.

———. "The South Rebels Again." In *The Bathtub Hoax and Other Blasts and Bravos from the Chicago Tribune*, edited by Robert McHugh, pp. 249–54. New York: Alfred A. Knopf, 1958; reprint ed., New York: Octagon Books, 1977.

Mertz, Paul E. *New Deal Policy and Southern Rural Poverty*. Baton Rouge: Louisiana State University Press, 1978.

Miller, Francis Pickens. *The Blessings of Liberty*. Chapel Hill: University of North Carolina Press, 1936.

———. *Man From the Valley: Memoirs of a 20th-Century Virginian*. Chapel Hill: University of North Carolina Press, 1971.

———, ed. *Second Southern Policy Conference Report*. Chapel Hill: University of North Carolina Press, 1936.

———, ed. *The Southern Press Considers the Constitution*. Chapel Hill: University of North Carolina Press, 1936.

Milton, George Fort, Sr. "Edward Ward Carmack." *North American Review* 187 (June 1908): 806–12.

———. "The Material Advancement of the Negro." *Sewanee Review* 3 (November 1894): 37–47.

Milton, George Fort. *Abraham Lincoln and the Fifth Column*. New York: Vanguard Press, 1942.

———. *The Age of Hate: Andrew Johnson and the Radicals*. New York: Coward-McCann, 1930.

———. "'Al' Smith and the Solid South." *North American Review* 225 (March 1928): 269–76.

———. "Also There Is Politics." In *Culture in the South*, edited by W. T. Couch, pp. 115–26. Chapel Hill: University of North Carolina Press, 1934.

_____. "Black Ballots in the White South." *Forum* 78 (December 1927): 906–13.

_____. "Can We Save the Democratic Party?" *Century Magazine* 110 (May 1925): 94–100.

_____. *Conflict: The American Civil War.* New York: Coward-McCann, 1941.

_____. "A Dayton Postscript." *Outlook* 140 (19 August 1925): 550–52.

_____. "Douglas' Place in American History." *Journal of the Illinois State Historical Society* 26 (January 1934): 323–48.

_____. "The Duties of an Educated Southerner." *Sewanee Review* 38 (January 1930): 61–70.

_____. *The Eve of Conflict: Stephen A. Douglas and the Needless War.* Boston: Houghton Mifflin Co., 1934.

_____. "Henry Ford Boom in the South Held to Resemble Hoover's." *Baltimore Evening Sun*, 13 July 1923, p. 5.

_____. "The Impeachment of Judge Lynch." *Virginia Quarterly Review* 8 (April 1932): 247–56.

_____. "Muscle Shoals and Dry Issue Loom in South." *New York Times*, 16 December 1923, 8:8.

_____. "The New Tennessee." *Independent* 117 (20 November 1926): 577–79.

_____. "Planks in a Liberal Platform." *Outlook* 142 (31 May 1926): 492–95.

_____. Review of *The Disruption of American Democracy* by Roy F. Nichols. *American Historical Review* 54 (October 1948): 163.

_____. "Smith's Southern 'Gains.'" *Outlook* 146 (27 July 1927): 405–6.

_____. "The South Do Move." *Yale Review* 29 (September 1939): 138–52.

_____. "The South Fights the Unions." *New Republic* 59 (10 July 1929): 202–3.

_____. "Stimulate and Organize." *Crisis* 42 (January 1935): 22–23.

_____. "Testing the 'Monkey Bill.'" *Independent* 114 (13 June 1925): 659–61.

_____. "Trade Barriers and Their Consequences." *Annals of the American Academy of Political and Social Science* 198 (July 1938): 43–47.

_____. *The Use of Presidential Power, 1789–1943.* Boston: Little, Brown and Co., 1944.

_____. "What Mr. McAdoo Stands For." *Outlook* 135 (21 November 1923): 488–89.

_____. "What Will the McAdoo Democrats Do?" *Outlook* 139 (7 January 1925): 22–24.

Mims, Edwin. *The Advancing South: Stories of Progress and Reaction.* Garden City, N.Y.: Doubleday, Page & Co., 1926.

Mitchell, Broadus. *The Rise of Cotton Mills in the South.* Baltimore: Johns Hopkins University Press, 1921.

Mitchell, Broadus, and Mitchell, George Sinclair. *The Industrial Revolution in the South.* Baltimore: Johns Hopkins University Press, 1930.

Mitchell, George Sinclair. "The Negro in Southern Trade Unionism." *Southern Economic Journal* 2 (January 1936): 26–33.

_____. "Organization of Labor in the South." *Annals of the American Academy of Political and Social Science* 153 (January 1931): 182–87.

_____. *Textile Unionism and the South.* Chapel Hill: University of North Carolina Press, 1931.

Moger, Allen W. *Virginia: Bourbonism to Byrd, 1870–1925*. Charlottesville: University Press of Virginia, 1968.

Moore, Edmund A. *A Catholic Runs for President: The Campaign of 1928*. New York: Ronald Press Co., 1956.

Morrison, Joseph L. *W. J. Cash: Southern Prophet*. New York: Alfred A. Knopf, 1967.

Mugleston, William F. "Julian Harris, the Georgia Press, and the Ku Klux Klan." *Georgia Historical Quarterly* 59 (Fall 1975): 284–95.

Murphy, Edgar Gardner. *The Basis of Ascendancy*. New York: Longmans, Green, and Co., 1909.

Murray, Robert K. *The 103rd Ballot: Democrats and the Disaster in Madison Square Garden*. New York: Harper & Row, Publishers, 1976.

Myrdal, Gunnar. *An American Dilemma: The Negro Problem and Modern Democracy*. New York: Harper & Brothers, 1944.

Nathan, George Jean, and Mencken, H. L. *The American Credo: A Contribution Toward the Interpretation of the National Mind*. New York: Alfred A. Knopf, 1920.

National Emergency Council. *Report on Economic Conditions of the South*. Washington, D.C.: U.S. Government Printing Office, 1938.

Nixon, Herman Clarence. *Forty Acres and Steel Mules*. Chapel Hill: University of North Carolina Press, 1938.

O'Brien, Michael. *The Idea of the American South, 1920–1941*. Baltimore: Johns Hopkins University Press, 1979.

Odum, Howard W. *Folk, Region, and Society: Selected Papers of Howard W. Odum*. Edited by Katherine Jocher, Guy B. Johnson, George L. Simpson, and Rupert B. Vance. Chapel Hill: University of North Carolina Press, 1964.

———. "Fundamental Principles Underlying Inter-racial Cooperation." *Social Forces* 1 (March 1923): 282–85.

———. *Race and Rumors of Race: Challenge to American Crisis*. Chapel Hill: University of North Carolina Press, 1943.

———. *The Regional Approach to National Social Planning*. New York: Foreign Policy Association; Chapel Hill: University of North Carolina Press, [1935].

———. *Southern Regions of the United States*. Chapel Hill: University of North Carolina Press, 1936.

———. *Understanding Society: The Principles of Dynamic Sociology*. New York: Macmillan Co., 1947.

Painter, Nell Irvin. *The Narrative of Hosea Hudson: His Life as a Negro Communist in the South*. Cambridge: Harvard University Press, 1979.

Park, Robert Ezra. "The Bases of Race Prejudice." *Annals of the American Academy of Political and Social Science* 140 (November 1928): 11–20.

———. *Race and Culture*. Glencoe, Ill.: Free Press, 1950.

Patterson, James T. *Congressional Conservatism and the New Deal: The Growth of the Conservative Coalition in Congress, 1933–1939*. Lexington: University of Kentucky Press, 1967.

Peel, Roy V., and Donnelly, Thomas C. *The 1928 Campaign: An Analysis*. New York: Richard R. Smith Co., 1931.

Pekor, Charles F., Jr. "An Adventure in Georgia." *American Mercury* 8 (August 1926): 408–13.

Peters, William. *The Southern Temper.* Garden City: N.Y.: Doubleday & Co., 1959.

Phillips, Ulrich Bonnell. "The Central Theme of Southern History." *American Historical Review* 34 (October 1928): 30–43.

Potter, David M. "C. Vann Woodward." In *Pastmasters: Some Essays on American Historians,* edited by Marcus Cunliffe and Robin W. Winks, pp. 375–407. New York: Harper & Row, Publishers, 1969.

Pressly, Thomas J. *Americans Interpret Their Civil War.* Princeton: Princeton University Press, 1954; reprint ed., New York: Free Press, 1965.

Prude, James C. "William Gibbs McAdoo and the Democratic National Convention of 1924." *Journal of Southern History* 38 (November 1972): 621–28.

Purcell, Edward A., Jr. *The Crisis of Democratic Theory: Scientific Naturalism and the Problem of Value.* Lexington: University Press of Kentucky, 1973.

Purdy, Rob Roy, ed. *Fugitives' Reunion: Conversations at Vanderbilt, May 3–5, 1956.* Nashville: Vanderbilt University Press, 1959.

Putnam, Carleton. *Race and Reason: A Yankee View.* Washington, D.C.: Public Affairs Press, 1961.

Rabinowitz, Howard N. *Race Relations in the Urban South, 1865–1890.* New York: Oxford University Press, 1978.

Raines, Howell. *My Soul Is Rested: Movement Days in the Deep South Remembered.* New York: G. P. Putnam's Sons, 1977.

Ramsdell, Charles W. "The Natural Limits of Slavery Expansion." *Mississippi Valley Historical Review* 16 (September 1929): 151–71.

Raper, Arthur W. *The Tragedy of Lynching.* Chapel Hill: University of North Carolina Press, 1933.

Redding, J. Saunders. "Southern Defensive—I." *Common Ground* 4 (Spring 1944): 36–42.

Robison, Daniel M. "From Tillman to Long: Some Striking Leaders of the Rural South." *Journal of Southern History* 3 (August 1937): 289–310.

Rochester, Stuart I. *American Liberal Disillusionment in the Wake of World War I.* University Park: Pennsylvania State University Press, 1977.

Roper, John Herbert. "C. Vann Woodward's Early Career—The Historian as Dissident Youth." *Georgia Historical Quarterly* 64 (Spring 1980): 7–21.

Rowan, Carl T. *Go South to Sorrow.* New York: Random House, 1957.

Rubin, Louis D., Jr. *The Wary Fugitives: Four Poets and the South.* Baton Rouge: Louisiana State University Press, 1978.

Sancton, Thomas. "Trouble in Dixie: The Returning Tragic Era." *New Republic* 158 (January 1943): 11–14.

Sass, Herbert Ravenel. "Mixed Schools and Mixed Blood." *Atlantic Monthly* 198 (November 1956): 45–49.

Schlesinger, Arthur, Jr. "The Causes of the Civil War: A Note on Historical Sentimentalism." *Partisan Review* 16 (October 1949): 969–81.

Shapiro, Edward. "The Southern Agrarians and the Tennessee Valley Authority." *American Quarterly* 22 (Winter 1970): 791–806.

Singal, Daniel Joseph. *The War Within: From Victorian to Modernist Thought in the South, 1919–1945.* Chapel Hill: University of North Carolina Press, 1982.

Sitkoff, Harvard. *A New Deal for Blacks: The Emergence of Civil Rights as a National Issue.* New York: Oxford University Press, 1978.

———. "Racial Militancy and Interracial Violence in the Second World War." *The Journal of American History* 63 (December 1971): 661–81.

———. *The Struggle for Black Equality, 1954–1980.* New York: Hill and Wang, 1981.

Sklar, Robert. *Movie-Made America: A Cultural History of American Movies.* New York: Vintage Books, Random House, 1976.

Smedes, Susan Dabney. *Memorials of a Southern Planter.* Edited by Fletcher M. Green. New York: Alfred A. Knopf, 1965.

Smith, Lillian E. "Are We Not Confused?" *South Today* 7 (Spring 1942): 30–34.

———. "Buying a New World With Old Confederate Bills." *South Today* 7 (Autumn–Winter 1942–43): 7–30.

———. "Southern Defensive—II." *Common Ground* 4 (Spring 1944): 43–45.

Sosna, Morton. *In Search of the Silent South: Southern Liberals and the Race Issue.* New York: Columbia University Press, 1977.

Southern, David W. "*An American Dilemma* Revisited: Myrdalism and White Southern Liberals." *South Atlantic Quarterly* 75 (Spring 1976): 182–97.

"Southern Leaders Out to Track Down Judge Lynch." *Literary Digest* 107 (18 October 1930): 24–25.

Southern Policy: Report of the Southern Policy Conference in Atlanta, 25–28 April 1935. N.p.: 1935.

"A Southerner Faces Facts." *Time* 67 (5 March 1956): 21.

Stewart, John L. *The Burden of Time: The Fugitives and Agrarians.* Princeton, N.J.: Princeton University Press, 1965.

Stoney, George C. "Southerners Write Their Own Prescription." *Survey Graphic* 28 (January 1939): 42–43.

Stratton, David H. "Splattered with Oil: William G. McAdoo and the 1924 Democratic Presidential Nomination." *Southwestern Social Science Quarterly* 44 (June 1963): 62–75.

Sumner, William Graham. *Folkways: A Study of the Sociological Importance of Useages, Manners, Customs, Mores, and Morals.* Boston: Ginn and Co., 1906.

Tate, Allen. "A View of the Whole South." *American Review* 2 (February 1934): 411–32.

Taylor, A. Elizabeth. *The Woman Suffrage Movement in Tennessee.* New York: Bookman Associates, 1957.

Tindall, George Brown. "Business Progressivism: Southern Politics in the Twenties." In *The Ethnic Southerners,* pp. 142–62. Baton Rouge: Louisiana State University Press, 1976.

———. *The Emergence of the New South, 1913–1945.* Baton Rouge: Louisiana State University Press, 1967.

———. "Howard W. Odum: A Preliminary Estimate." In *The Ethnic Southerners,* pp. 88–115. Baton Rouge: Louisiana State University Press, 1976.

Twelve Southerners. *I'll Take My Stand: The South and the Agrarian Tradition.*
New York: Harper & Brothers, 1930.

"Two Southern Views." *Outlook* 69 (30 November 1901): 810–12.

U.S. Congress. *Hearings Before the Joint Committee on the Investigation of the Tennessee Valley Authority.* 75th Cong., 3d sess., 1938. Part 7.

Vance, Rupert B. "Rebels and Agrarians All: Studies in One-Party Politics." *Southern Review* 4 (Summer 1938): 26–44.

Villard, Oswald Garrison. "The Crumbling Color Line." *Harper's Magazine* 159
(July 1929): 156–67.

Wacker, R. Fred. "An American Dilemma: The Racial Theories of Robert E. Park
and Gunnar Myrdal." *Phylon* 37 (Summer 1976): 117–25.

Walton, H., Jr. "Another Force for Disfranchisement: Blacks and the Prohibitionists
in Tennessee." *Journal of Human Relations* 18 (First Quarter 1970): 728–38.

Waring, Thomas R. "The Southern Case Against Desegregation." *Harper's Magazine* 212 (January 1956): 39–45.

Waskow, Arthur. I. *From Race Riot to Sit-In, 1919 and the 1960s: A Study in the
Connections Between Conflict and Violence.* Garden City, N.Y.: Doubleday &
Co., 1966.

Watters, Pat. *The South and the Nation.* New York: Pantheon Books, 1969.

Weatherford, Willis D., and Johnson, Charles S. *Race Relations: Adjustment of
Whites and Negroes in the United States.* Boston: D. C. Heath and Co., 1934.

White, Walter. "Decline of Southern Liberals." *Negro Digest* 1 (January 1943):
43–46.

———. *A Man Called White: The Autobiography of Walter White.* New York: The
Viking Press, 1948; reprint ed., New York: Arno Press and *New York Times,*
1969.

———. *Rope and Faggot: A Biography of Judge Lynch.* New York: Alfred A. Knopf,
1929.

Williams, Roger M. *The Bonds: An American Family.* New York: Atheneum Publishers, 1971.

Williams, T. Harry. *Huey Long.* New York: Alfred A. Knopf, 1969.

Wilson, Edmund. "The Freight Car Case." *New Republic* 68 (26 August 1931):
38–43.

Woodward, C. Vann. "Hillbilly Realism." *Southern Review* 4 (Spring 1939): 676–81.

———. *Origins of the New South, 1877–1913.* Baton Rouge: Louisiana State University Press, 1951.

———. *The South in Search of a Philosophy.* Gainesville: University of Florida,
1938.

———. *The Strange Career of Jim Crow.* 3d rev. ed. New York: Oxford University
Press, 1974.

———. *Tom Watson: Agrarian Rebel.* New York: Macmillan Co., 1938.

———. "Why the Southern Renaissance?" *Virginia Quarterly Review* 51 (Spring
1975): 222–39.

Woody, R. H. "The Second Annual Meeting of the Southern Historical Association." *Journal of Southern History* 3 (February 1937): 83.

Workman, William D., Jr. *The Case for the South.* New York: Devin-Adair Co., 1960.

Wright, R. Charlton. "The Southern White Man and the Negro." *Virginia Quarterly Review* 9 (April 1933): 175–94.

Wyche, Billy H. "Southern Newspapers View Organized Labor in the New Deal Years." *South Atlantic Quarterly* 74 (Spring 1975): 178–96.

Young, P. B. "No Armistice in the Struggle for Social Justice." *Southern Frontier* 3 (February 1942): 1.

Young, Thomas Daniel. *Gentleman in a Dustcoat: A Biography of John Crowe Ransom.* Baton Rouge: Louisiana State University Press, 1976.

———. "A Prescription to Live By: Ransom and the Agrarian Debates." *Southern Review* 12 (July 1976): 608–21.

Zangrando, Robert L. *The NAACP Crusade Against Lynching, 1909–1950.* Philadelphia: Temple University Press, 1980.

Index

Abolitionists, 52, 180, 184, 187, 212;
  G. F. Milton on, 123–24, 129; G. W.
  Johnson on, 128–29
The Advancing South, 42
*The Age of Hate: Andrew Johnson and
  the Radicals*, 50–51
Agrarian debates, 60–62, 94
Agrarians. *See* Nashville Agrarians
Agricultural Adjustment Act, 134; cot-
  ton program, 135; liberal criticism of,
  137; and foreign policy, 138
Agriculture. *See* Tenancy system
Aiken, John Newton, 35
Alabama Policy Committee, 167, 168
Alexander, Will W., xv, 74, 84, 156,
  191; on southern liberal journalists,
  xiii; on lynching, 78; on reform, 94;
  and tenancy system, 135–37; lobbies
  for tenant farmers, 136–37; joins
  Resettlement Administration, 137;
  leaves Commission on Interracial Co-
  operation, 151; on black workers,
  157; on E. Talmadge's attack on colleges, 196; on Commission on Inter-
  racial Cooperation, 202–3
Amberson, William, 139
The American Credo, 23
*An American Dilemma: The Negro
  Problem and Modern Democracy*, 199
American Expeditionary Force, 18
American Federation of Labor, 157, 158
The American Mercury, 33
The American Scholar, 196
Ames, Jessie Daniel: on anti-lynching
  bill, 148; and Commission on Interracial Cooperation, 203; on black pro-
  test, 203; meets with G. B. Hancock,
  203; collaborates with V. Dabney,

204; on segregation, 204; on H. W.
  Odum, 206
Anderson, Sherwood, 60
Anderson, William D., 61
Anti-Catholicism, 45, 46, 47, 54, 55
Anti-lynching law, 31, 75, 76, 105, 216;
  G. F. Milton on, 100; Commission on
  Interracial Cooperation endorses,
  148. *See also* Lynching
Anti-Saloon League, 20, 43, 51, 99, 104
Arnall, Ellis Gibbs, 193
Ashmore, Harry S., 3–4, 223, 224,
  276 (n. 18)
Association of Southern Women for the
  Prevention of Lynching, 148, 203
Atlanta Constitution, 15, 193, 219
Atlanta Evening News: and Atlanta race
  riot, 25, 26
Atlanta race riot of 1906, 25–26

Baker, Ray Stannard, 25
Baker-Himel School, 14
Baltimore Evening Sun, 35, 218; G. W.
  Johnson and, 29; and southern liberal
  journalists, 33–34
Bankhead, John H., 137
Bankhead-Jones Farm Tenancy Bill,
  137, 140; and Southern Policy Com-
  mittee, 139
Barr, Stringfellow, 34, 65, 119; re-
  jected by Nashville Agrarians,
  58–59; challenges Agrarians, 60;
  debates J. C. Ransom, 61; on indus-
  trialism, 62; on tenancy system, 67;
  on lynching and rape, 82
Bartley, Numan, 223, 224
Beale, Howard K., 163
Bibb Manufacturing Company, 61

299

"Birth of a Nation," 8–10, 13, 234 (n. 15)

Black, Hugo, 172; and Ku Klux Klan, 169; W. White on, 265 (n. 54)

Black Codes, 30

Black Power, 226, 227

Black protest: and World War II, 197, 198

Black southern liberals, 95; and Commission on Interracial Cooperation, 24–25; on race relations, 91; southern liberal journalists appeal to, 201; and Durham Conference, 203–4; on segregation, 205; and southern liberalism, 208

Black voting, 44, 142–43; G. F. Milton on, 48; and Andrew Johnson, 53; southern liberal journalists on, 53–54; and Populism, 113; R. McGill on, 217

Black Workers and the New Unions, 158–59

Boaz, Franz, 85

Bond, Horace Mann, 204, 250 (n. 50)

Bowdoin College, 14, 35

Brotherhood of Sleeping Car Porters, 197

Bryan, William Jennings, 41, 43, 240 (n. 22)

Buell, Raymond Leslie, 137–38

Buffalo Evening News, 225

Butler, Benjamin, 6

Byrd, Harry F., 215

Calhoun, John C., 3, 7, 52

Camp, Lawrence, 166, 167

Cannon, Bishop James, 99–100

Carmack, Edward Ward, 17

Carter, Hodding, xiv, xv, 3, 6, 114, 222; on "Birth of a Nation," 9; education, 14; sees lynching victim, 26; plays at Ku Klux Klan, 26; on Ku Klux Klan, 27; at Bowdoin College, 35; into journalism, 36; on Prohibition, 106; on Huey Long, 108–10; on Reconstruction, 108–9, 263 (n. 30);

on New Deal, 109, 118, 119, 191–92; runs for office, 109–10; on war, 178, 182; on moralism, 189; awarded Nieman Fellowship, 191; works for *PM,* 191; in Egypt, 192; in Army, 192–93; morality and race relations, 193; on March on Washington Movement, 198; on southern liberalism, 215, 216; on cold war and civil rights, 217, 218; on Civil Rights movement, 226–27; death, 227; on FDR, 254 (n. 4); on poll tax, 260 (n. 29); on H. W. Odum, 260–61 (n. 37); on Hitler, 267 (n. 8)

Cash, W. J., xiv, 35; on "Birth of a Nation," 9; education, 15; on Atlanta race riot, 25; on 1928 election, 49; on Nashville Agrarians, 72, 245 (n. 39); on *Report on Economic Conditions of the South,* 166

Cayton, Horace R., 156–57, 158

Cell, John W., 12

Chambers, Lenoir, 35

Charlton, Louise O., 167

Chattanooga Evening Tribune, 189–90, 190–91

Chattanooga Free Press, 126, 189

Chattanooga News, 17, 40–41, 127, 189, 270 (n. 48); on A. E. Smith, 46–47; endorses H. Hoover, 49–50; on anti-lynching law, 75; on lynching, 76, 77, 79; and TVA election, 126

Chattanooga Times, 51, 125

Chivers, Walter R., 78

Citizen's and Taxpayer's League, 125, 127

The Citizens' Council, 223

Civil Rights movement, xv, xx, 225–28

Civil War, 6, 10, 13, 19, 175, 176, 180, 184, 211, 212, 216, 219, 222, 229; J. Daniels on, 7; V. Dabney on, 52, 131–32; Nashville Agrarians on, 68–69; G. F. Milton on, 93, 121–22, 124; and Rational Democracy, 127–28; and World War II, 187; and Civil Rights movement, 225

Civil War revisionist historiography,
122, 186–88
Clark, Emily, 34
Clay, Henry, 7
Cohn, David, 110
Cold war: and segregation, 217–18
Collapse of Cotton Tenancy, 137
Collins, Floyd, 15
Columbia Record, 90
Columbus Enquirer-Sun, 15, 28
Commission on Interracial Cooperation,
xiii, xv, 74, 75, 77, 78, 133, 135,
150, 159, 181, 202–3, 205, 211; ori-
gins, 24–25; on race relations, 79–
80; and black southern liberals, 91;
H. W. Odum's reorganization, 137,
151; endorses Bankhead-Jones Bill,
137; endorses anti-lynching bill, 148;
G. Myrdal on, 199
Committee of Industrial Organizations,
154, 158, 159, 167
Committee on Negroes in the Economic
Reconstruction, 135, 156
Commonwealth and Southern Corporation, 125
Communist party: in the South, 80–
81; and Southern Conference for Human Welfare, 170, 265–66 (n. 58);
and March on Washington Movement, 198
Cosmos Club, 191
Couch, W. T., 62, 112; and Southern
Conference for Human Welfare, 168;
and *What the Negro Wants*, 202
Council on Southern Regional Develop-
ment, 151, 168, 173, 174, 202
"Court-packing" bill, 155–56

Dabney, Richard Heath, 14, 18; on
black voting, 11; and Woodrow
Wilson, 16; on Prohibition, 17
Dabney, Thomas Smith Gregory, 5, 7
Dabney, Virginius (1835–94), 5
Dabney, Virginius, xiv, xv, xvi, xviii, 3,
5, 6, 44–45, 60, 72, 151, 168, 206,
217; education, 14; on W. Wilson, 16;

visits France, 18; commissioned to
write *Liberalism in the South*, 21; on
Atlanta race riot, 25; on J. T. Graves,
27; on G. W. Johnson, 28; and H. L.
Mencken, 33, 238 (n. 42); on *Baltimore Evening Sun*, 33–34; advised
by L. I. Jaffé, 35; writing *Liberalism
in the South*, 37; excludes G. F.
Milton, 51; on liberalism in southern history, 51–52; on black voting,
53–54, 143; on southern politics,
53–54, 113; on ecclesiastic power,
55; on Nashville Agrarians, 62,
71; on industrialization, 62; on
B. Mitchell, 63; on strikes, 64; on labor unions, 65; on tenancy system,
67, 136; on Old South, 69; on lynching and rape, 82; on race relations,
91; on Prohibition, 98–99, 99–100;
on Bishop James Cannon, 99–100,
252 (n. 8); on anti-lynching law, 105;
on Populism, 113; on leadership, 115,
257 (n. 45); on FDR, 117; on New
Deal, 119, 166–67; on Jefferson and
New Deal, 120; on Civil War, 131–
32; on Southern Policy Committee's
membership, 140–41; on poll tax,
142; on sit-down strikes, 154–55; on
"court-packing" bill, 155; on liberalism, 156; and Southern Conference
for Human Welfare, 169, 172; on
southern support for World War II,
175; on World War I, 176, 183; on
Nazism, 176–77; on Hitler, 177; on
pacifism, 179; on Munich crisis, 183;
on war, 183; on World War II, 184;
on moralism, 185; on E. Talmadge
and race issue, 193, 194, 196; on
black protest, 197, 198, 208, 209; on
black southern liberals, 201; on black
opinion, 202; collaborates with J. D.
Ames, 204; on Durham Conference, 205; and regional university for
blacks, 208, 211, 212; proposes end
to segregation on public transportation, 209–13; and Southern Regional

Council, 213, 219; awarded Pulitzer Prize, 215; on cold war, 218; on segregation, 219–20; defends segregation, 220–22; on interposition, 221; on desegregation, 224; retirement, 227–28; on Civil Rights movement, 227, 228–29; on Communist party, 248 (n. 20)

Daniels, Jonathan, xiv, xvi, 4, 7, 126, 168, 206, 213; education, 15; on Washington race riot, 25; travels in the South, 97; on Southern Policy Committee's membership, 140–41; on *Report on Economic Conditions of the South*, 166; on race issue, 172; on moralism, 185; on E. Talmadge and race issue, 193, 196; on liberalism and World War II, 194; on black protest, 203; on cold war and civil rights, 217; on southern liberalism, 217–18; on W. J. Bryan, 240 (n. 22); on Reconstruction, 264 (n. 31)

Darrow, Clarence, 41, 42

Davidson, Donald, 42, 55, 56, 58, 59, 60; and Agrarian debates, 62, 67–68; on strikes, 64; on Agrarianism, 68; on history, 69; on southern liberalism, 70–71; and Southern Policy Committee, 139; on SPC's membership, 140

Davis, John W., 40

Davis, Lambert, 60

Democracy: intellectuals on in 1920s, 22

Democratic party: in 1920s, 39–40

Depression, 55, 95, 116, 135, 145; southern liberal journalists on, 98

De Voto, Bernard, 187

Disfranchisement: in Virginia, 11

Dixiecrats, 216–17

Dothan Eagle, 16

Douglas, Stephen A., 51, 121, 127, 225; on slavery, 101

Dunning, William Archibald, 10, 13

Durham Conference, 204–5, 208, 209, 221

Dyer, Leonidas Carstarphen, 31, 75

Dykeman, Wilma, xv

Eagles, Charles, xvi, 213

Eighteenth Amendment. *See* Prohibition

Eisenhower, Dwight D., 223

Ellis, Ann Wells, 79

Embree, Edwin, 135, 136–37, 156

Episcopal High School, 14

Ethridge, Mark Foster, xiv, 35, 151, 168, 197, 202, 203, 204, 229; education, 14–15; on labor relations, 64, 244 (n. 26); on lynching, 77–78; on vertical segregation, 90; on segregation, 91; at Southern Conference for Human Welfare, 173; on southern support for World War II, 175; criticizes black protest, 198

The Eve of Conflict: Stephen A. Douglas and the Needless War, 100, 121, 129

Executive Order 8802, 197

Fair Employment Practices Commission, 105, 197, 198, 200

Farm Security Administration, 170

Faulkner, William, 4

Fifteenth Amendment. *See* Black voting; Reconstruction

The Fighting South, 26

Finkle, Lee A., 200, 201, 213

Folkways, 88; W. G. Sumner on, 86; and lynching, 87; and southern liberalism, 94; and regionalism, 147; and race relations, 149–50; and southern consensus, 163

Foreign Policy Association, 138

Foreman, Clark, 165

Fort, Tomlinson, Sr., 3, 7

Fort, Tomlinson, 5

Fourteenth Amendment. *See* Reconstruction

Freeport Doctrine, 103

Fugitive, 57

Fugitive Slave Act: G. W. Johnson on, 104–5

Fundamentalists, 21, 55; on evolution, 24, 41; on politics, 28

Gaines, Lloyd L., 172
Gaston, Paul M., xix
George, Walter F., 153, 165, 166, 167
Georgia Institute of Technology, 134
Gettysburg, 5, 7
Giddings, Franklin Henry, 86
Glass, Carter, 11
Graham, Frank Porter, 170, 217
Graham, Hugh Davis, 224
Grantham, Dewey W., 16, 31
Graves, John Temple, Sr.: and Atlanta race riot, 25
Graves, John Temple, xiv, 3, 6, 35, 151, 168; education, 15; on Washington race riot, 25; on Atlanta race riot, 25–26; defends father, 26, 27, 237 (n. 19); on Nashville Agrarians, 71–72; on anti-lynching law, 105, 148; on liberalism, 156; on FDR's "purge," 166; on New Deal, 167; on southern support for World War II, 175; on foreign policy, 179; on Munich crisis, 183; on G. F. Milton's *The Eve of Conflict*, 186; criticizes black protest, 198; on black southern liberals, 201; on segregation, 207; on V. Dabney, 208, 211; endorses Dixiecrats, 217; on W. Wilson, 239 (n. 6)
Greensboro Daily News, 15, 19, 35
Griffith, D. W., 8–10

Hall, Grover C., xiv, 51, 58, 238 (n. 44); education, 16; awarded Pulitzer prize, 28; as editor, 32; aids *Virginia Quarterly Review*, 34–35; and L. I. Jaffé, 35; on G. F. Milton, 37; on 1928 election, 37, 49; on A. E. Smith, 46; on race issue in 1928 election, 49
Hammond Daily Courier, 108
Hampton, Wade, 112
Hancock, Gordon Blaine, 209; on black

protest, 203; meets with J. D. Ames, 203; organizes Durham Conference, 203–4; on segregation, 204; chairs Richmond meeting, 205
Harlan County, Kentucky, 79
Harris, Joel Chandler, 32
Harris, Julian LaRose, xiv, 44, 58, 256 (n. 34); awarded Pulitzer Prize, 28; as editor, 32; and L. I. Jaffé, 35; on lynching, 77; and Southern Commission on the Study of Lynching, 78
Hayes, Roland, 74, 171
Hays, Brooks: joins Resettlement Administration, 137
"Herrenvolk democracy," 31
Hicks, John D.: on Populism, 113
Hill, Lister, 165
Hobson, Fred C., 33
Hooper, Ben W., 18
Hoover, Herbert, 18, 37, 46, 98, 115, 116, 118; carries five states in the South, 49
Hull, Cordell, 138, 179

Illinois State Historical Society, 104
I'll Take My Stand: The South and the Agrarian Tradition, 55, 56, 57, 74; on the South, 66
Institute for Research in Social Science, 28–29, 86, 144
Institute of Race Relations, Swarthmore College, 92–93, 123
Interim Southeastern Regional Advisory Committee, 151
International Labor Defense, 80, 81
Interposition, 220–21, 224

Jackson, Andrew, 50, 123
Jaffé, Louis I., xiv, 58, 177; education, 15; World War I, 19; awarded Pulitzer Prize, 28; on J. L. Harris' editorials, 32; contacts with other journalists, 35; on editorial writing, 35; on Solid South, 44–46; on Prohibitionists, 48; on 1928 election, 49; on *Liberalism*

in the South, 54; on Nashville Agrarians, 61; on industrialization, 63; on lynching, 76, 83

Jefferson, Thomas, 3, 17, 30, 37, 43, 112, 116, 120, 122–23, 228; V. Dabney on, 51–52; award named for by Southern Conference for Human Welfare, 169

Jim Crow system. *See* Segregation

Johnson, Andrew, 6, 17, 41; G. F. Milton on, 52–53

Johnson, Charles S., 86, 88–89, 135, 156, 160, 204, 206; Southern Commission on the Study of Lynching, 78; on vertical segregation, 90, 208; writes *Collapse of Cotton Tenancy*, 137; and Southern Policy Committee, 140; on race and class, 158–59; on race issue at Southern Conference on Human Welfare, 170; attends Atlanta meeting (1939), 173; at Durham Conference, 204; on slavery, 250 (n. 53)

Johnson, Gerald W., xiv, xv, 7–8, 21, 34, 51, 202; education, 15; on World War I, 18, 19, 183, 235 (n. 41); as leading southern critic in 1920s, 28–29; on South in 1920s, 29–30; on Reconstruction, 30, 111, 187–88, 226, 243 (n. 9); on race relations, 30; on southern journalism, 31–32, 36; and *Baltimore Evening Sun*, 34, 218; and L. I. Jaffé, 35; on G. F. Milton, 37; outlook in 1920s compared to G. F. Milton's, 39, 50–51; on Solid South, 44; on Prohibition, 48–49, 98–99, 104–5; on race issue in 1928 election, 49; on 1928 election, 49; on moralism, 51, 185–86; on Nashville Agrarians, 58–59, 62, 65–66, 71; on strikes, 64; on rural South, 67; on Old South, 69; on Depression, 72, 116, 117–18; on anti-lynching law, 75–76; on lynching, 76, 83, 84; on race prejudice, 84, 85; on Civil War, 102, 105, 128–29; on S. A. Douglas,

102; on Huey Long, 111–12; on FDR, 117, 254–55 (n. 6); on New Deal, 118, 121, 155–56; on Jefferson and New Deal, 120; on leadership, 128–29, 130–31; on tenancy system, 135–36, 259 (n. 21); on politics, 141; on regionalism, 147, 148; on C. V. Woodward's *Tom Watson*, 164; on FDR's "purge," 167; on war, 176, 178, 182; on Hitler, 177; on Nazism, 178; democracy compared to dictatorship, 180; on Munich crisis, 183; on Civil War and World War II, 187–88; on black protest, 197; on cold war, 218; death, 226; on Civil Rights movement, 226, 228; on W. Lippmann, 236 (n. 6); ambition, 237 (n. 27); on liberalism and segregation, 248–49 (n. 32); on poll tax, 260 (n. 29)

Johnson, Guy B., 251 (n. 61); speaks to Commission on Interracial Cooperation, 150; on *Gaines* decision, 172–73; defends Southern Regional Council, 207

Johnson, Herschel V., 5, 7

Jones, M. Ashby, 75, 95, 205

Jones, Marvin, 137

Journal of Social Forces, 29, 34, 86

Kennedy, John F., 227

Kilpatrick, James J.: and interposition, 220–21; on blacks, 221

King, Martin Luther, 215n

King, Richard H., 153, 262 (n. 2)

Kirby, Jack Temple, 13

Kirby, John B., 96

Knickerbocker, W. S., 61, 62

Know-Nothing party, 104

Knoxville Sentinel, 13

Ku Klux Klan, 6, 9, 10, 20, 21, 24, 37, 39, 43, 55, 72, 104; and southern liberals in the 1920s, 26–27; on politics, 28; as political issue, 1924, 40; and H. Black, 169

Labor unions, 153; B. Mitchell on, 63; in Birmingham, 157–58

Lanier, Lyle H., 70, 139

Leibowitz, Samuel S., 81

Lewis, John L., 158

Liberalism in the South, 21, 27, 28, 37, 65, 113; influence of 1928 election on, 51–52

Lincoln, Abraham, 8, 102, 103, 127, 188, 226

Lincoln-Douglas debates, 103

Lippmann, Walter, 22, 28; on journalists, 22; on H. L. Mencken, 23; G. W. Johnson on, 236 (n. 6)

Little Rock Arkansas Gazette, 3

Little Rock crisis, 223–24

Logan, Rayford, 202

Long, Huey Pierce, 97, 107–8, 114, 118, 121, 131, 132

Longworth, Alice Roosevelt, 32

Louisville Courier-Journal, 15

Lumpkin, Katherine DuPre, 169, 237 (n. 20)

Lynching, 21, 24, 28, 75, 76, 91, 112, 181; H. L. Mencken on, 23; in 1930, 78; and rural poverty, 83

Lynchings and What They Mean, 82, 83, 86

McAdoo, William Gibbs, 37, 45; runs for president, 38; southern support, 39; and Teapot Dome scandal, 39; and Ku Klux Klan, 40; on defeat in 1924, 40

McGill, Ralph, xiv, xv, xvi, 6, 8, 168, 206; on "Birth of a Nation," 9; education, 15; enters journalism, 15; on W. Wilson, 16–17; on H. L. Mencken, 33; observes ratification of Nineteenth Amendment, 38; on Nashville Agrarians, 58; on Prohibition, 105; studies Georgia agriculture, 133–34; awarded Rosenwald Fellowship, 134; travels in Scandinavia, 134; on anti-lynching law, 148; on T. E. Watson, 164; on FDR's

"purge," 166; on New Deal, 167; on Nazism, 182–83, 194; on dictatorship, 184; on World War II, 184; on moralism, 189; on E. Talmadge and race issue, 193–94, 196; backs E. G. Arnall, 193–94; on moralism and race relations, 194; on race relations, 200–201; on Durham Conference, 205; on Southern Regional Council, 207; on black voting, 217; criticizes Southern Conference for Human Welfare, 217; on cold war and civil rights, 219; on southern liberal reform, 219; on massive resistance, 223–24; on Civil Rights movement, 227; on Civil War, 227; on Viet Nam war, 227; death, 227; on poll tax, 260 (n. 29)

Macon Telegraph, 15, 77

Malone, Dudley Field, 41

March on Washington Movement, 197, 198, 213

Mason, Lucy Randolph, 169

Massive resistance, 221, 224

Matthews, Fred H., 86

Mays, Benjamin, 204, 234 (n. 15)

Memorials of a Southern Planter, 5

Mencken, H. L., 24, 28, 35, 60; as critic of American culture, 23; as critic of the South, 23–24; aids G. W. Johnson, 28; and southern liberal journalists, 32–33; advises Emily Clark, 34; on Scopes trial, 43

Mercer University, 15

Meredith, James, 227

Mertz, Paul E., 134, 165

Miller, Francis Pickens, 140, 143, 167, 173; organizes Southern Policy Committee, 138; on politics, 141; on Southern Conference for Human Welfare, 168; on Communist party, 265 (n. 58)

Miller, Kelly, 157

Milton, Abby Crawford, 38

Milton, George Fort, Sr., 13; on race relations, 11–12; on Prohibition, 17, 38; and Independent Democrats, 18;

and W. Wilson, 18; death, 40

Milton, George Fort, xiv, xv, 3, 4, 7,
17, 34, 37, 65, 87, 168; to Confederate Reunion, 5; education, 13–14; on
W. Wilson, 18; World War I, 18–19,
178; lobbies for woman suffrage, 38;
as W. G. McAdoo's publicity director,
38–39; outlook in 1920s compared
to G. W. Johnson's, 39; on Prohibition,
39, 46–47, 72, 98, 100–102; on
W. G. McAdoo, 40; on A. Johnson,
41, 50–51, 52–53; on father's heritage, 41; on Scopes trial, 41–42,
42–43; and H. L. Mencken, 43; on
W. J. Bryan, 43; compared to other
journalists, 43–44; on Solid South,
44–46; on H. Hoover, 50; on Nashville Agrarians, 59, 60, 62; and
Agrarian debates, 61; on industrialization, 62–63; on strikes, 64;
on reform, 66; chairs Southern Commission on the Study of Lynching,
78, 83; and southern liberalism,
78–80; on Scottsboro case, 80–81;
on Communist party in South, 81; on
race prejudice, 86; on slavery, 92–
93, 94, 252 (n. 16); on race relations,
92–93, 93–94, 181; on anti-lynching
law, 100, 105; on Stephen A. Douglas, 100, 102–3; on antebellum
period, 100–101; on Freeport Doctrine, 103–4; on southern politics,
112; on Rational Democracy,
115–16, 121–30, 143–44; on Depression, 116; on FDR, 117; on New
Deal, 118–19, 155, 167, 190; on
Jefferson and New Deal, 120; on Tennessee Valley Authority, 125–26; on
Civil War, 129; on leadership,
130–31; on tenancy system, 136,
139–40; on politics, 141; on poll tax,
142; on state rights, 148; on sit-
down strikes, 154; on liberalism,
156; on FDR's "purge," 166, 167; on
H. Black, 169; on race issue at
Southern Conference for Human Wel-

fare, 171–72, 190; on southern support for World War II, 175; on war,
176, 178, 180, 183; on Hitler, 177;
on pacifism, 179; on foreign policy,
179; on moralism, 184–86, 190; on
Civil War and World War II, 188;
loses *Chattanooga News*, 189; and
Chattanooga Evening Tribune, 189–
90; loses *Evening Tribune*, 190–91;
on Wendell Willkie, 190; on World
War II, 190; moves to Washington,
191; on E. Talmadge and race issue,
196; on civil rights, 225; on cold war,
225; on Reconstruction, 225–26;
death, 226

Milton, Sarah Fort, 4–5, 7, 233 (n. 5)

Mims, Edwin, 15, 55, 242 (n. 53); defends the South, 42; on Fugitive
poets, 57

The Mind of the South, 15, 163

Mitchell, Broadus, 157; on industrialization of South, 63–64; C. V. Woodward on, 161

Mitchell, George S., 158; on labor
unions in the South, 156–57; and
Southern Regional Council, 219; on
segregation, 220

Moderates, 222–25

Montague, Andrew J., 11

Montgomery Advertiser, 15, 28

Munich crisis, 183

Murphy, Edgar Gardner: on liberalism
and segregation, 248 (n. 32)

Myrdal, Gunnar: on southern liberalism, xv–xvi, 199–200; on R. E.
Park, 199–200; on moralism, 200; on
race relations, 200; and World War II,
200

Nashville Agrarians, 55, 83, 88, 112,
115, 134; on industrialism, 57–58;
on the South, 58; southern liberals'
response, 58–59; challenge S. Barr,
60; on tenancy system, 67; on southern history, 68–69; on progress, 70;
on race relations, 74, 246 (n. 42);

V. Dabney on, 132; and Southern
Policy Committee, 138–39; on
Bankhead-Jones Bill, 139; H. C.
Nixon on, 160
Nashville Banner, 15
Nathan, George Jean, 23
The Nation, 87
National Association for the Advance-
ment of Colored People, 75, 77, 211,
219; on lynching, 76–77; on lynching
and rape, 82; on segregation laws,
172; endorses March on Washington
Movement, 197
National Emergency Council. See *Re-
port on Economic Conditions of the
South*
National Industrial Recovery Act, 138,
154, 157
"Natural limits" thesis, 93, 252 (n. 16)
Nazism, 175–76, 188
Nazi-Soviet Nonaggression Pact, 184
Negroes. *See* Black southern liberals;
Black voting
New Deal, 56, 66, 97, 107, 115, 132,
134, 153, 167, 174, 180; on racial is-
sues, 96, 256 (n. 25); and tenancy
system, 134–37; and foreign policy,
138; H. W. Odum on, 145–46; and
labor organizing, 157; and Southern
Conference for Human Welfare, 169;
and cold war, 217
New South, xix, 65; Nashville Agrarians
on, 56; B. Mitchell on, 63; C. V.
Woodward on, 160–62
"New" southern liberalism, 153–54;
R. H. King on, 262 (n. 2)
Nichols, Roy F., 103
Nieman Fellowships, 191
Nineteenth Amendment. *See* Woman
suffrage
Nixon, Herman Clarence: on tenancy
system, 66; and Southern Policy
Committee, 139; on southern reform, 160; and Southern Conference
for Human Welfare, 168; on southern
economy, 245 (n. 37)

Norfolk Virginian-Pilot, 15, 19, 28,
35, 61
North Carolina Interracial Confer-
ence, 75
North Carolina Policy Committee, 168
North Georgia Review, 196
Nullification: South Carolina, 7

Odum, Howard W., xv, 28, 78, 86, 132,
133, 137, 153, 173, 202–3; and *Journal of Social Forces*, 34; on race relations, 75, 149–50; on folkways, 87;
on lynching, 87; on southern liberal
reform, 87; and "technicways," 88;
regionalism, 144–48, 150–51; to reorganize Commission on Interracial
Cooperation, 137, 151; on labor
unions, 159; and Southern Conference for Human Welfare, 168; attends Atlanta meeting (1939), 173;
on southern support for World War II,
175; on foreign policy, 179; organizes
Southern Regional Council, 205–6;
on J. D. Ames, 206; on segregation,
207–8
Old South, 187; V. Dabney on, 52;
Nashville Agrarians on, 56, 68–69;
southern liberal journalists on, 69–
70; R. E. Park on, 92; W. J. Cash
on, 163
Owens, Hamilton, 238 (n. 44); on *Baltimore Evening Sun*, 33–34
Owsley, Frank Lawrence, 139; on
Agrarianism, 68; on Civil War, 68–69

Park, Robert Ezra, 91, 156, 250 (n. 47);
on prejudice, 85; and B. T. Washing-
ton, 88; on race relations, 89–90;
G. Myrdal on, 199–200
Patrick, Luther, 167
Patterson, Malcolm, 17
Pepper, Claude, 165, 169, 217
Percy, William Alexander, 110
Phillips, Ulrich B., xviii
PM, 191
Poll tax, 97; southern liberals on, 141–

42; Southern Conference for Human Welfare on, 170

Poor whites, 136; H. L. Mencken on, 23; southern liberals on, 27–28, 31, 54, 67; and industrialization, 63; and lynching, 83–84; V. Dabney on, 132, 212; and poll tax, 142

Popular Sovereignty, 103

Populism: southern liberal journalists on, 112–13; C. V. Woodward on, 161–62; W. J. Cash on, 163

Progressive Era, xx, 4, 10, 11, 16, 43, 74; legacy in race relations, 12; compared to 1920s, 31; and race prejudice, 85

Prohibition, 17, 18, 24, 37, 38, 39, 43, 45, 47–48, 55, 72, 97, 104, 114, 117, 148, 203, 219; and Tennessee politics, 17–18; in 1928 election, 46–47; repeal, 98; and race relations, 100–7

Public Opinion, 22

Public Power League, 125–26

Pulitzer Prize, 3, 28, 76, 215

Purcell, Edward A., 22

Putnam, Carleton, 221

Rabinowitz, Howard N., 12

Race prejudice: and liberalism, 85, 248–49 (n. 32)

Race relations, xix; in city, 24–25; in Progressive Era, 86; R. E. Park on, 88–90; and Prohibition, 100–107; and regionalism, 149–50; G. Myrdal on, 200; Nashville Agrarians on, 246 (n. 42)

Race riots, 24–26

Racism, 10, 11, 85–86; as issue in 1928 election, 49; and G. F. Milton, 124; and economic factors, 135; and environmentalism, 136; C. V. Woodward on, 161–62; and Nazism, 181; and liberalism, 221–22, 248–49 (n. 32)

Radical Republicans. *See* Reconstruction

Raleigh News and Observer, 97

Ramsdell, Charles W., 93, 252 (n. 16)

Randolph, A. Phillip, 197, 198

Randolph, John, 50–51, 69–70

Ransom, John Crowe, 42, 55, 56, 58, 65; G. F. Milton on, 60; and Agrarian debates, 61; on tenancy system, 67; on progress, 70

Raper, Arthur F., 78, 82, 86

Rational Democracy, 121–30, 132, 146, 163–64; and leadership, 130–31; compared to Southern Policy Committee's Objectives, 143–44

Reconstruction, 6, 9, 13, 27, 31, 44, 48, 53, 104, 106, 110, 114, 128, 161, 174, 175, 178, 180, 188, 223, 229; southern liberal journalists on, 8, 53; Dunning school on, 10; G. W. Johnson on, 30; G. F. Milton on, 51, 53, 93–94, 128; C. V. Woodward on, 162; historians revise, 162–63; H. Carter on, 263 (n. 30); J. Daniels on, 264 (n. 31)

Redding, Saunders J., 206

"Red Summer" of 1919, 24, 25, 211

Regionalism, 132, 133, 144–48, 151–52; and race relations, 149–50; challenged by class division, 159–60; H. C. Nixon on, 160; and foreign policy, 179

Report on Economic Conditions of the South, 153, 165–66, 167, 170, 173

Resettlement Administration, 137, 151

The Reviewer, 34

Richmond News-Leader, 14

Richmond Times, 11

Richmond Times-Dispatch, 60

The Rise of Cotton Mills in the South, 63

Rockefeller Foundation, 135

Roosevelt, Eleanor, 169, 170

Roosevelt, Franklin D., 96, 97, 115, 131; and G. F. Milton's Rational Democracy, 122–25; on agriculture, 134; creates Resettlement Administration, 137; and "purge," 153, 165–68; and "court-packing" bill,

155; issues Executive Order 8802, 197; and black protest in World War II, 213; on race issues, 256 (n. 25)

Rosenwald Fellowships, 182, 257 (n. 3); awarded to R. McGill, 134

Rosenwald Fund, 135

Rowan, Carl, 222

Sancton, Thomas: criticizes southern liberals, 198–99

Schlesinger, Arthur, Jr., 187

Scopes, John Thomas, 41, 42

Scopes trial, 44, 55, 56, 57; southern liberals on, 41

Scottsboro case, 80–81; southern liberal journalists on, 248 (n. 19)

The Secession of the Southern States, 102

Segregation, xx, 4, 10, 12, 74, 75, 77, 91, 196; Commission on Interracial Cooperation on, 24; and Southern Commission on the Study of Lynching, 80; and sociologists, 86; and regionalism, 150; at Southern Conference for Human Welfare, 170; and "new" southern liberalism, 171; and Southern Regional Council, 207; and cold war, 218; and southern liberalism, 229–31

Sewanee Review, 11, 61

Singal, Daniel Joseph, xix, 34, 265–66 (n. 58)

Sit-down strikes, 154

Sklar, Robert, 9

Slavery, 52, 187; and southern liberalism, 52–53; Nashville Agrarians on, 69; R. E. Park on, 92; G. F. Milton on, 92–93; southern liberal journalists on, 93, 94; V. Dabney on, 132

Smedes, Susan Dabney, 5, 7

Smith, Alfred E., 36, 37, 39, 45, 46, 51, 56, 117

Smith, Ellison D., 165, 166

Smith, Lillian E.: on E. Talmadge and race issue, 196; criticizes southern

liberals, 199; criticizes Southern Regional Council, 207

Snelling, Paula: on E. Talmadge and race issue, 196

"Social equality," 91

Solid South, 36, 37, 49; C. V. Woodward on, 161; and Dixiecrats, 217

Sosna, Morton, xvi–xviii, 269–70 (n. 42)

Southern Commission on the Study of Lynching, 86, 94, 106; and Scottsboro case, 81; and southern liberalism, 81–82; report, 82; on ending lynching, 83; on poor whites, 84; on public opinion, 84

Southern Conference for Human Welfare, 153, 154, 167–71, 173, 181, 190; membership, 169; R. McGill criticizes, 217; and Communist party, 266 (n. 58)

A Southerner Discovers the South, 97

The Southern Frontier, 203, 206

Southern Historical Association, 62

Southern journalism: and racial conflict, xiii, 25; P. Watters on, 13

Southern liberalism, xv–xx; on Ku Klux Klan, 27; on moralism, 28; on poor whites, 31; on race relations, 31, 88, 91, 95; and Southern Commission on the Study of Lynching, 81–82; on reform, 94–95; on slavery, 95; and masses, 97–98; G. F. Milton's outlook, 124–25; on tenancy system, 134–37; on Bankhead-Jones Bill, 139; and "new" southern liberalism, 153; and C. V. Woodward's *Tom Watson,* 162; criticism of during World War II, 198–99; and segregation, 207; H. Carter on, 215; and racism, 221–22, 248–49 (n. 32)

Southern liberal journalists: on Reconstruction, 8, 53; education, 14–15; on war, 19, 176, 178, 186; on World War I, 19, 183; as critics of the South, 21; and the Commission on Interracial Cooperation, 25; on fun-

damentalism, 42; on Progressive
Era's legacy, 43–44; on Solid South,
44–46; defend A. E. Smith, 46–47,
48–49; on moralism, 51, 182–86; on
southern history, 53; on Nashville
Agrarians, 59, 72–73; on industrialization, 62–63, 68; on labor relations, 64, 154; on New South, 65; on
tenancy system, 67, 135–36; on Old
South, 69–70; on progress, 70; on
lynching, 76–77; on Scottsboro case,
81, 248 (n. 19); on poor whites, 83,
212; and prejudice, 85; on slavery,
93, 94; on race relations, 94, 172,
181, 196; on Depression, 98, 116;
on Prohibition, 99, 106; and majoritarianism, 107; on Huey Long,
110–11; on southern politics, 112;
on New Deal, 121, 167; on FDR,
130, 156; and foreign policy, 138,
179; on politics, 141–44; on poll tax,
141–42; on black voting, 142–43;
and regionalism, 145–48; on anti-
lynching law, 148; on state rights,
148–49; on sit-down strikes, 154–
55; on "court-packing" bill, 155–56;
on liberalism, 156; on southern poverty, 159; on C. V. Woodward's *Tom
Watson*, 162; on leadership, 163–64;
on *Report on Economic Conditions of
the South*, 166; on FDR's "purge,"
166; on Southern Conference for Human Welfare, 168–69; and race issue
at SCHW, 171–72; on Hitler, 177; on
pacifism, 179; democracy compared
to dictatorship, 180–81; on black
protest, 197–98, 200–201, 213–14;
on H. S. Truman's civil rights legislation, 216; on Dixiecrats, 217; and
cold war, 217–18; on *Brown* decision, 220; as moderates, 222–25; on
massive resistance, 223; and segregation, 229–31; and Unionism,
230–31; on "business progressivism," 240–41 (n. 23)

Southern Newspaper Publishers Association, xiii–xiv
Southern Policy Committee, 133, 151–
52, 165, 173; endorses Bankhead-
Jones Bill, 137; origins, 138; and
foreign policy, 138; and Nashville
Agrarians, 138–39; membership,
140–41; and southern politics, 140–
44; on poll tax, 142; and Southern
Conference for Human Welfare, 168
Southern Regional Council, 208, 210,
213, 216, 221; origins, 202–6; on
segregation, 207, 219
Southern Regions of the United States,
145–47, 149, 165; H. C. Nixon
on, 160
Southern Tenant Farmers' Union, 135
Soviet Union, 184, 188, 217
Spanish Civil War, 182
Stars and Stripes, 192
State rights, 216; and Prohibition,
47–48, 99; G. F. Milton on, 51, 242
(n. 47); and Civil War, 52; southern
liberal journalists on, 148–49
Steel Workers Organizing Committee,
158
Stevens, Thaddeus, 225
Stevenson, Adlai E., 222–23
Stokely, James, xv
Stoney, George C., 170, 171
The Story of Don Miff, 5, 234 (n. 7)
Sumner, William Graham, 86, 94; and
folkways, 87; on slavery, 93
Supreme Court, 48, 105, 219; *Dred
Scott* decision, 103; "court-packing"
bill, 153; H. Black appointed, 169;
Gaines decision, 172, 208; *Brown*
decision, 216, 220, 223; on desegre-
gation, 220

Talmadge, Eugene, 164, 210; and race
issue, 193–94, 196
Tate, Allen, 56, 64, 139; on E. Mims,
57; on Agrarianism, 68; on southern
liberalism, 70–71

Teapot Dome, 39

Tenancy system, 133, 142; Nashville Agrarians on, 66–67; and New Deal, 134–37; Committee on Negroes in the Economic Reconstruction on, 135–37; G. W. Johnson on, 259 (n. 21)

Tennessee Electric Power Company, 125–26, 127, 189

Tennessee Valley Authority, 125–26, 189; Odum seeks affiliation, 174

Textile mills: B. Mitchell on, 63; strikes, 64; C. V. Woodward on, 161

Thomas, Norman, 117

Thomas Jefferson Award of SCHW, 169

Tillman, Benjamin, 112

Tindall, George B., 18, 21, 42, 66, 140, 240 (n. 22)

Trinity College, 15

Truman, Harry S, 216, 217

Tugwell, Rexford, 137

Twelve Southerners. *See* Nashville Agrarians

Unionism, 7, 122, 127, 185, 209, 212, 216, 219, 222; and southern liberal journalists, 8, 230–31; and Andrew Johnson, 52–53

United Automobile Workers, 154

United Mine Workers, 158; and race issue, 157–58

United States Steel Corporation, 154, 158

University of Chicago, 88

University of Mississippi, 15, 227

University of North Carolina, 15, 28

University of North Carolina Press, 21, 62, 202

University of Tennessee, 14

University of Virginia, 14

Urban League, 197

Vance, Rupert B., 162

Vanderbilt University, 15, 56

Vertical segregation, 95, 173, 174, 196, 199–200, 205, 207–8, 213–14, 216, 218–19, 222, 230; R. E. Park's diagram, 90; and southern liberalism, 90–92; and regionalism, 150; C. S. Johnson revises, 159; and "new" southern liberalism, 170; and *Gaines* decision, 172; Dabney advocates, 221

Viet Nam War, 227

Villard, Oswald Garrison, 77

The Virginia Quarterly Review, 34–35, 44, 60, 71, 111, 228

Volstead Act, 101, 104

Wade, John Donald, 25

Wagner-Costigan Anti-Lynching Bill, 148

Wake Forest College, 15

Warren, Robert Penn, 139; on race relations, 246 (n. 42)

Washington, Booker T., 157; and R. E. Park, 88

Washington Times, 14

The Wasted Land, 147

Watson, Thomas E., 132, 160; C. V. Woodward on, 162; G. W. Johnson on, 164; R. McGill on, 164

Watters, Pat: on southern journalism, 13

What the Negro Wants, 202

Wheeler, Wayne, 51

White, Walter: on lynching, 82; criticizes southern liberals, 198; on H. Black, 265 (n. 54)

White Citizens' Council, 222

Williams, Aubrey, 169

Willkie, Wendell, 190, 270 (n. 48)

Wilson, Edmund, 80–81

Wilson, James Southall, 34

Wilson, Woodrow, 4, 9, 16, 18, 43; H. L. Mencken on, 23; W. G. McAdoo and, 38

Woman suffrage, 38

Woodward, C. Vann, 16; on southern reform, 160; on New South, 160–62; on leadership, 164; on segregation,

253 (n. 24), 276 (n. 18)

World War I, 43, 122; in the South, 18; intellectuals' disillusionment, 19, 22; and Nazism, 177–78

World War II, xvi, 183–84; southern support for, 175; and black protest, 197–98

Wright, Charlton, 90

Young, P. B., 204, 212